39765339
v3

Encyclopedia of Family Life

Encyclopedia of Family Life

Volume 3
Filial responsibility – Men's roles

Editor

Carl L. Bankston III
University of Southwestern Louisiana

Project Editor

R. Kent Rasmussen

SALEM PRESS, INC.
Pasadena, California   Hackensack, New Jersey

Managing Editor: Christina J. Moose
Project Editor: R. Kent Rasmussen
Manuscript Editor: Robert Michaels
Development Editor: Wendy Sacket
Research Supervisor: Jeffry Jensen
Acquisitions Editor: Mark Rehn
Photograph Editor: Karrie Hyatt
Production Editor: Joyce I. Buchea
Design and Layout: James Hutson
Indexer: Robert Michaels

Frontispiece: James L. Shaffer

Library of Congress Cataloging-in-Publication Data

Encyclopedia of Family Life / editor, Carl L. Bankston III; project editor, R. Kent Rasmussen.
   p. ; cm.
Includes bibliographical references (p.   ) and index.
ISBN 0-89356-940-2 (set)
ISBN 0-89356-943-7 (vol. 3)
   1. Family—North America—Encyclopedias. 2. Domestic relations—North America—Encyclopedias. 3. Family services—North America—Encyclopedias. I. Bankston, Carl L. (Carl Leon), 1952-   . II. Rasmussen, R. Kent.
HQ534.E53 1999
306.85'097'03—dc21   98-42491
                                                         CIP

First Printing

PRINTED IN THE UNITED STATES OF AMERICA

Contents

Encyclopedia of Family Life

Filial responsibility

RELEVANT ISSUES: Aging; Parenting and family relationships

SIGNIFICANCE: With the advent of modern medicine, people live longer, posing the question of who is responsible for parents' physical, emotional, and financial needs when traditional roles are reversed and parents become children

Filial responsibility is the responsibility of children to their parents. As advances in medicine since the early years of the twentieth century have made it possible for humans to live longer, healthier

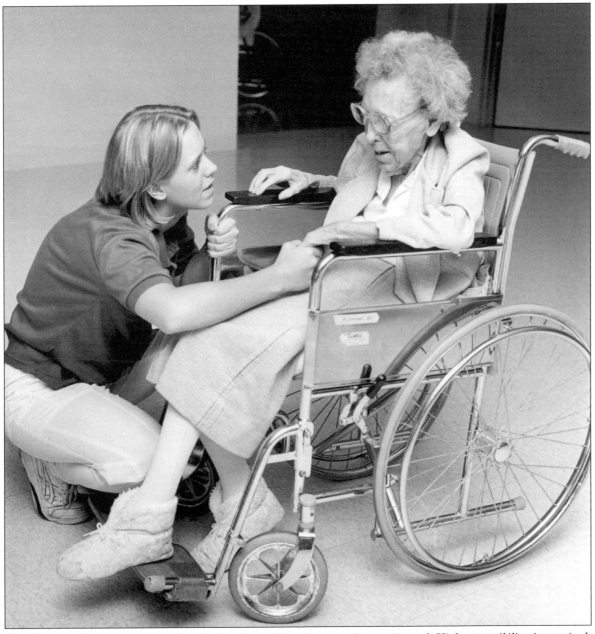

Growing numbers of aging people with health problems have made questions of filial responsibility increasingly urgent. (James L. Shaffer)

lives, a social problem has arisen. Persons who approached fifty years of age during the 1990's likely have two living parents. These parents, who are often seventy years old or older, may already be under custodial care. If they do not already receive custodial care, they certainly may require it as they age.

For society the question arises as to how this care is to be provided and by whom. Historically, filial responsibility traditionally devolved upon women who raised their families, worked in the home, and cared for aging parents who were part of the household or lived nearby. However, in the late twentieth century multigenerational households became increasingly rare. Young adults in the fast-growing economies of developing nations moved away from rural areas to larger population centers, leaving their aging parents behind to fend for themselves. Twentieth century women joined the workforce in increasing numbers, leaving no one at home to care for elderly parents.

As members of the baby-boom generation, persons born between 1946 and 1964, approached middle age in the late twentieth century, elderly care replaced child care as the primary concern of families, both monetarily and practically. Caring for aging parents is not new. However, combining elderly care, child care, and careers outside the home has created a new level of responsibility for adults, especially for women, in their middle years. In the late 1990's demographic studies showed that individuals in the workforce were more likely to have living parents than they were to have dependent children. In the United States these same demographic trends began to indicate that "gray panthers" outnumbered "young lions."

In other parts of the world, care of the elderly has been legislated. Chinese law, for example, requires that adult children support their parents. If the children are dead, their children are required to care for their grandparents. Failure to comply can result in prison sentences. Similar legal statutes exist in Morocco, Tunisia, Japan, and Singapore. However, in the Republic of Georgia, parents who do not fulfill their parental duties can be legally denied the financial support of their adult children. In the late twentieth century, with the human life span increasing, adult children found it necessary to develop plans for elderly care that acknowledge the wisdom and value of their aging parents while providing for their parents' possible need for long-term care. —*Barbara C. Stanley*

See also Aging and elderly care; Ancestor worship; Extended families; Family caregiving; Life expectancy.

Filipino Americans

RELEVANT ISSUES: Race and ethnicity; Religious beliefs and practices; Parenting and family relationships

SIGNIFICANCE: People of Filipino ancestry frequently have distinctive values and customs regarding family, and there are large Filipino populations in the United States and Canada

By 1990 there were more than 1.4 million people identifying themselves as Filipinos in the United States and an estimated 127,000 in Canada. Both countries experienced a continuous flow of immigrants from the Philippines from the 1970's through the 1990's. About 40,000 entered the United States and about 6,500 entered Canada each year. Although Filipinos lived in all parts of the United States in that period, Southern California and Hawaii were home to large, concentrated Filipino communities. About 740,000 members of this group lived in California and another 170,000 lived in Hawaii. More than half of all Canadian Filipinos lived in Ontario, primarily in Toronto. The large numbers of Filipinos, the continuing flow of new arrivals, and the existence of large ethnic communities all helped to maintain distinctive Filipino American family customs.

In general, Filipino American families who live in areas where there are few other people from the Philippines retain few distinctive family characteristics. In the large Filipino concentrations, such as Los Angeles, continual contact among Filipinos has helped members maintain cultural continuity.

Cultural Values and Family Relations. Four widely recognized key cultural values guide Filipino family relations and family customs. These are *utang na loob* (moral debt), *hiya* (shame), *amor proprio* (self-esteem), and *pakikisama* (getting along with others). Children, from the Filipino perspective, owe an eternal debt to their parents, who gave them life. Children are therefore expected to show obedience and respect to parents and grandparents.

Filipino Americans celebrate a traditional holiday. (James L. Shaffer)

The cultural value *hiya* dictates that individuals feel ashamed when they fail to behave according to expected social roles, which are often thought of in terms of family relations even when they involve people who are not actually family members. Younger people are expected to show respect for their elders at all times. When children greet an older person, such as a grandparent, they show respect by taking the elder's hand and bowing slightly to touch the back of the hand with the forehead.

Older brothers and sisters are not to be treated as equals but are addressed as *kuya* ("big brother") and *ate* ("big sister"). Moreover, older friends are often called *kuya* or *ate*. Children call unrelated adults *tita* ("aunt") or *tito* ("uncle"). People who do not seem to recognize or care about these types of social relations may be referred to as *walang hiya* ("shameless"), a term that expresses very strong disapproval.

Even when people violate social expectations, others will be reluctant to criticize them openly

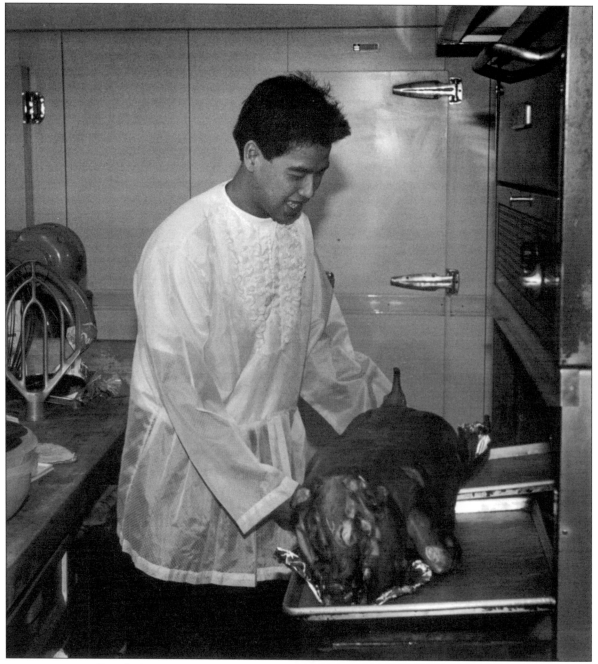

Lavish feasts are a traditional part of Filipino weddings. (James L. Shaffer)

out of fear of offending their sense of *amor proprio*. Criticisms must be indirect, and they depend on individuals' own sense of shame. *Pakikisama*, or getting along with others, dictates that people avoid direct confrontation. In terms of the family, it also means that individuals should always place the interests of the family and the maintenance of relations within the family first and consider their own interests and desires as secondary.

In respect to these customs and values, life in North America has often led to tension within Filipino families. Children raised in the United

States, for example, sometimes feel that it is humiliating to place the hands of elders against their foreheads. Adults, in turn, feel frustrated if children refuse to follow accepted customs, and they sometimes see their children as rude or even *walang hiya*. Young people exposed to American ideas of individualism also find it difficult to place the interests of the family before their own, which parents may find disturbing.

Baptism and Sponsors. Godparents or sponsors are virtual members of Filipino families, a cultural practice known as *compadrazgo*. When children are due to be baptized, mothers and fathers ask a number of men and women to stand as sponsors or godparents for their children. Two of the sponsors are recognized by the Church as children's godparents, but Filipinos rarely distinguish between these two primary sponsors and the other secondary sponsors; all are referred to as the children's *ninongs*, if they are men, and *ninangs*, if they are women. Sponsors are regarded as being close to additional parents, and they are expected to help the children in any way they can. They give the children presents on birthdays and other major occasions and they play key roles in baptisms, religious confirmation, and wedding ceremonies.

Since sponsors have an obligation to help children, people in the Philippines often seek out powerful or influential persons to play this role. In the United States and Canada, however, it is much more common for close friends to act as sponsors, creating formal, customary ties among people who refer to each other as *compadre* or *copare* and *comadre* or *comare* (literally "co-father" and "co-mother"). Friends, even if they are not actually sponsors of one another's children, often shorten these terms and address each other simply as *pare* or *mare*.

Wedding Customs. Since the majority of Filipino Americans are Roman Catholics, the Roman Catholic Church is usually central to wedding ceremonies. Even when Filipinos marry in civil ceremonies, they almost always get married again in the Church. In the Philippines, grooms' families traditionally pay all wedding expenses. Some Filipino families native to the United States or Canada have adopted the North American custom in which brides' families pay wedding expenses, but most either continue to follow Filipino ways or compromise and share costs.

Weddings in the Philippines, especially in the countryside, are often lavish events in which families spend far beyond their means providing food and entertainment for large numbers of guests. Filipino Americans rarely go to these extremes, however, and most restrict their guest lists to friends and relatives. Still, food remains an important part of wedding ceremonies, and guests at Filipino American marriages can expect to find a large array of Filipino dishes.

Wedding rites among Filipino Americans often retain many Spanish Roman Catholic customs not seen in other North American Roman Catholic weddings. During weddings in which couples adhere strictly to Filipino traditions, bridegrooms give brides silver coins, known as *aras*, which symbolize wives' control of household finances. This type of traditional wedding includes the bride's and groom's sponsors as well as the maid of honor and the best man. One set of sponsors holds the veil, one holds a rope, and one holds a candle. Brides wear gowns that are very similar to those worn in other American weddings, but instead of tuxedos grooms and the best man may wear the *barong tagalog*, the formal Filipino shirt.

—*Carl L. Bankston III*

BIBLIOGRAPHY

Almirol, Edwin B. *Ethnic Identity and Social Negotiation: A Study of a Filipino Community in California.* New York: AMS Press, 1985.

Bandon, Alexandra. *Filipino Americans.* New York: New Discovery Books, 1993.

Espiritu, Yen Le. *Filipino American Lives.* Philadelphia: Temple University Press, 1995.

Hollnsteiner, Mary Racelis, with Maria Elena B. Chiong, Anicia A. Paglinauan, and Nora S. Villanueva. *Society, Culture, and the Filipino: Introductory Readings in Sociology and Anthropology.* Quezon City, Philippines: Institute of Philippine Culture, 1975.

Kim, Hyung-Chan. *The Filipinos in America, 1898-1974.* Dobbs Ferry, N.Y.: Oceana Publications, 1976.

Mangiafico, Luciano. *Contemporary American Immigrants: Patterns of Filipino, Korean, and Chinese Settlement in the United States.* New York: Praeger, 1988.

Menez, Herminia Quimpo. *Folklore Communication Among Filipinos in California.* New York: Arno Press, 1980.

Ng, Franklin, ed. *Asian American Encyclopedia.* 6 vols. New York: Marshall Cavendish, 1995.

Root, Maria P. P. *Filipino Americans: Transformation and Identity.* Thousand Oaks, Calif.: Sage Publications, 1997.

See also Chinese Americans; Compadrazgo; Japanese Americans; Korean Americans; Latinos; Mail-order brides; Pacific Islanders; Patriarchs; Rites of passage; Roman Catholics; Southeast Asian Americans; Vietnamese Americans; War brides; Weddings.

Film depictions of families

RELEVANT ISSUES: Divorce; Economics and work; Marriage and dating; Parenting and family relationships

SIGNIFICANCE: The depiction of families in cinema reflects the social, moral, and political upheavals of the United States in the twentieth century

From the beginning of American cinema, the family as an institution received scant consideration from Hollywood in its efforts to develop a profitable means of reaching a mass audience. As areas of popular appeal became more verifiable and standardization of virtually every aspect of film production became economically necessary, Hollywood inevitably sought successful story formulas and techniques and, when they were found, pursued them.

Families in Early Silent Films. Although the nuclear family, consisting of one father, one mother and their children, was represented in the earliest Westerns and slapstick comedies, the family unit formed a mere backdrop to what was more important: action. Filmmaker D. W. Griffith moved the family to a position of importance by interjecting ideological and political themes into emotionally charged family situations. *Birth of a Nation* (1915), which depicts the Civil War and its aftermath through the conflicts of two families, one northern and one southern, dramatizes disturbing racial fears and a deep suspicion of radical change within the emotional context of the family. In this film, as in those that were produced into the late 1920's, remarkable expressiveness in the depiction of family crises is achieved by combining music (*melos*) with drama in melodramatic expositions of the emotional and moral dilemmas of the characters. In *Seventh Heaven* (1927), a man and woman seek to overcome the anonymity and heartlessness of the city, mired in despair and cynicism, and create a refuge, or "seventh heaven," in their apartment in Paris. The home is an idealized space that is established and protected against the outside world, specifically from forces that are produced by an increasingly impersonal and hostile mass urban society. *Sunrise* (1927) concerns a rural family threatened by a city woman who seduces the husband. The marriage of the husband and wife is later renewed in the city, as the film captures the ambivalence toward the American shift from the country to the city.

Depression-Era Family Images. In the 1930's audiences preferred to view optimistic films about human beings who triumph over oppressive political and social chicanery. Many films continue to present the family as a sanctuary from external repression—the family itself representing the moral center of such films' universe and the morality of characters being assessed through their demonstrations of self-sacrifice for the good of the family. To Depression-era audiences with their difficult socioeconomic circumstances, the most immediate sense of family was communicated through its economic status. In *Imitation of Life* (1934) the home is closely associated with the family's pancake business. The succession of family moves— from the house to the back of the store and finally to a lavish town house—reinforces the family's commitment to its business. The loss of an elderly couple's home in *Make Way for Tomorrow* (1937) signals the end of their marriage. The nuclear family's moral position is opposed in some instances by the desires of women, especially regarding motherhood. In *Stella Dallas* (1937) Stella, unable to overcome her coarse background and seeking to ensure her daughter's marriage to a society man, gives her up to her former husband and his new, refined wife. Although the film details Stella's enormous self-sacrifice, it anticipates films of the following decade, in which women's desires seem to undermine family stability.

Reflections of Social Upheaval. The image of the American family as it evolved through the 1940's is one that presents many affirmative views of marriage and family as well as of society at large. *A Tree Grows in Brooklyn* (1945) connects family, education, and the quality of future life in the case of Francie, who is forced to consider sacrificing her desire for education in order to help support her fatherless family. *I Remember Mama* (1948) is a nostalgic tribute to the mother of a Norwegian family living in San Francisco during the early 1900's. Yet, even in apparently optimistic films such as *Meet Me in St. Louis* (1944) and *Father of the*

Set in St. Louis at the time of its 1904 world fair, Meet Me in St. Louis *reflected an unabashedly optimistic view of American families.* (Museum of Modern Art, Film Stills Archive)

Bride (1950), which trace the courtship and engagement of a naïve heroine, the nightmare episodes suggest deep-seated anxieties about family and community stability. *The Best Years of Our Lives* (1946), which represents a large chunk of American society in the depiction of three returning veterans who begin to readjust to the modern postwar ambience, appears to reflect gradual erosion of cultural confidence in the nuclear family.

Postwar American discontent with the changing roles of women in wartime as well as dissatisfaction with the suffocating middle-class lifestyle is perhaps most graphically displayed in *Mildred Pierce* (1946), which examines the collapse of the social and moral order brought about by Mildred's assumption of the place of her father.

Family Melodrama. In the 1950's the traditional image of marriage, family, and home underwent more critical reflection. More women entering the workforce along with increased mobility, suburbanization, and educational opportunities produced a "generation gap," which stressed the alienation of family members because of the inability of the family to fulfill individual needs. In cinema, the family moved from merely enhancing external conflict to actually causing it. In *A Place in the Sun* (1951), family influences develop a pattern of displaying desire and repression. The frustration of George Eastman is reflected in his desperate attempts to reach an amoral place, free from familial morals and social restraints.

The family melodrama, noted for its artificial

Spencer Tracy walks Elizabeth Taylor down the wedding aisle in Father of the Bride. (Museum of Modern Art, Film Stills Archive)

Although it was heavily toned down from the novel on which it was based, the 1957 film Peyton Place *shocked American audiences with its negative portrayal of middle-class families.* (Museum of Modern Art, Film Stills Archive)

framework and stylistic excess, appears to comment sharply upon the American small town, whose nuclear and extended families are distorted into a world in which human virtues have calcified into repressive conditions or have disappeared altogether. *Written on the Wind* (1957) articulates the disparate and complex problems of the wealthy Hadley family, only appearing to arrive at a solution while suggesting that the conflicts are actually unresolvable. Other films, such as *Cat on a Hot Tin Roof* (1958), reflect a metaphoric search for an

ideal husband, lover, or father who will stabilize the family and integrate it into the larger community. In *Giant* (1956), *The Long Hot Summer* (1958), *From the Terrace* (1960), and *Home from the Hill* (1960) the conflict centers on a contradictory view of marriage in which marriage either liberates one from the family or perpetuates the family. In *Picnic* (1955) the lovers escape from the repressive community but fall into the same traps that ensnared their parents. In middle-class families, however, the conflict involved in passing the father role from one generation to the next does not evolve from family wealth or a decadent aristocratic view of life. Thus, fathers' anxieties and sons' insecurities provide clear criticisms of society's expectation of male adulthood. James Dean's portrayal of the tormented son in both *East of Eden* (1954) and *Rebel Without a Cause* (1955) seeks to pose an alternative to the hypocritical older generation and anticipates the counterculture movement of the 1960's. Other films indict the social pressures that have victimized the well-meaning patriarch.

The scramble to compete with television led most studios to produce mostly adult entertainment. Making films for children was limited to Walt Disney studios, which expanded from solely producing cartoons in 1928 to producing action films such as *Treasure Island* in 1950. From there Disney became the undisputed king of family entertainment. Mastering the formula for certain profits, Disney has continued into the 1990's with animated successes such as *Beauty and the Beast* (1991) and *The Lion King* (1994).

Films of the Counterculture Movement. From the social upheavals of the 1960's a counterculture movement arose in which American youth pressed their grievances against their elders. *Bonnie and Clyde* (1967) argues for perspectives contrary to those of the established order and contrasts traditional family loyalties and responsibilities to the bonds of the Barrow family gang. The alternative family, though doomed, seems to underscore the ineffectuality of the traditional family.

The generational shift in values forged an even more radical message in *Easy Rider* (1969), whose soundtrack sustained a psychedelic cross-country motorcycle trip that attempted to legitimatize motorcycles and drugs as suitable subjects for America's youth and to promote the psychological relevance of rock music. In the film, the two motorcycle "cowboys" reject hypocrisy in their lives and attempt to reinvent traditional values.

Marriage as an institution received its share of criticism. The ineffectuality of traditional values in marriage and family are depicted notably in *Who's Afraid of Virginia Woolf?* (1966), in which a couple plays games to combat the sterility of their marriage, and in *The Graduate* (1967), which dissects a suffocating family environment. Despite Benjamin's seduction by Mrs. Robinson, a friend of his parents, and his eventual rescue of her daughter

Elaine from a marriage prescribed by her parents, the film actually provides no suggestion that the marriage of Benjamin and Elaine will fare any differently from that of their parents.

In the 1970's the emphasis upon individual self-realization at the expense of the family as an institution continued to be reflected in film. In *Five Easy Pieces* (1970), also a road film, the road represents noncommitment and freedom from the family and its values. The ultimate celebration of the extended "family" in *Woodstock* (1970), a three-hour documentary film of the three-day rock celebration of love and peace in August, 1969, was necessarily reevaluated with the release of *Gimme Shelter* (1970), a documentary of the Rolling Stones' concert at Altamont, California, during which a young man was killed by members of the Hell's Angels gang, who had been hired as security.

Depictions of Family Corruption. *The Godfather* (1972), an epic of a crime family whose activities are related to U.S. history and its social context, seems to allegorically arraign the cynicism and corruption of the seventies. Heroic and imbued with strength of character, the Corleone men conform to their own strict code of tradition, patronage, and honor. The film does much toward assimilating the values of the counterculture into the mainstream, and through its emphasis on the historical and social function of the Corleone family it suggests a coming-of-age. This film was followed in 1973 by *American Graffiti*, a deceptively happy film about adolescence that resists the disillusion and despair of adulthood. Compressing complex, myriad events into the last night of summer, *American Graffiti* depicts archetypal characters who glimpse the fate life has in store for them as they edge nearer to adulthood and family responsibility. If the loss of innocence, however, is inevitable, as it appears in *American Graffiti*, perhaps it could be exorcized. In *The Exorcist* (1973), a terrifyingly extreme example of teen rebellion, adolescent Regan wreaks havoc on her mother and the adult world but is cured with no memory of her ordeal.

The theme of corruption within the family reverberates into the upper classes in *Chinatown* (1974), in which a private detective investigates a conspiracy to divert the flow of Southern California's water and uncovers its mastermind, Noah

Cross, who "owns" the police, and Noah's daughter whom he has incestuously abused and who remains in control of the daughter of their union. The film emphasizes the detective's ineffectuality and his own victimization in the face of overwhelming cynicism and corruption.

Films of Family Intrusion. The idea that the family must be secured against external threat appears in many films of this period. The intrusion upon domesticity in *Jaws* (1975) assumes the form of a shark, which forces Brody to prove himself and allows him to return to home and family only after he has undergone a rite of passage. In the era of the Vietnam War and Watergate, the film responds to political and social shocks emanating from a natural and instinctive force that has no rational motivation. When the family is threatened in *Poltergeist* (1982) by the living dead, the mother endures an ordeal to preserve the family union. The remake of *Cape Fear* (1991) graphically depicts a family's struggle against a vengeful, brutal psychopath, through which the family is renewed. Other films depicting obstacles to domestic fulfillment depend on role reversals. *Country* (1984) chronicles a wife's labors to keep the family farm against a callous government and an insensitive husband. The husband in *Kramer vs. Kramer* (1979) proves his strength by caring for his son after a divorce, and in *Ordinary People* (1980) the wife is the main source of disharmony within the family.

The Shining (1980) provides the fullest examination of the family and explicitly comments on the madness of the patriarchal domestic unit while also describing the process by which the patriarch, undone by fears and obsessions of powerlessness, destroys his own family. Other horror films register the cultural shocks of families with missing fathers. *The Lost Boys* (1987) depicts Michael, who lives with his divorced mother and his eccentric grandfather and falls in with a group of vampires. While the mother in *Fright Night* (1985) is ineffectual to the point of nonexistence, the adult world in general is pointedly oblivious to the plight of the protagonist.

Despite the success of films that describe the alienation and blankness of American culture in the 1970's and 1980's, other films attempt to escape to a less troubled pre-Vietnam War, pre-Watergate world of relative innocence. The impulse toward nostalgia in the 1980's is clearly manifested in *Back to the Future* (1985) and *Peggy Sue Got Married* (1986), both presenting an idealized, utopian past dominated by wholesome family values. During the more conservative 1990's, Hollywood, inspired by the success of *Home Alone* (1990), churned out more "family friendly" films that return to more traditional arrangements. Although depictions of the past in modern film appeal to many viewers, it is through viewing the films of the past that a clearer sense of the present is achieved. Evolving depictions of the family in film record for posterity the social, moral, and political upheavals of the United States in the twentieth century.

—*Mary Hurd*

BIBLIOGRAPHY

Belton, John. *American Cinema/American Culture.* New York: McGraw-Hill, 1994. Presents film history from the 1890's through the 1990's as a cultural history that focuses on topics and issues, as opposed to a chronology of events.

Biskind, Peter. *Seeing Is Believing: How Hollywood Taught Us to Stop Worrying and Love the Fifties.* New York: Pantheon Books, 1983. Discusses Hollywood films of the Cold War years, roughly from 1948 to 1960, in terms of characteristic themes, subjects, and plots and excavates "hidden" messages buried within.

Cagin, Seth, and Philip Dray. *Born to Be Wild: Hollywood and the Sixties Generation.* Boca Raton, Fla.: Coyote, 1994. Originally published as *Hollywood Films of the Seventies* (New York: Harper and Row, 1984), this book follows the films of "Political Hollywood," charting the values of the counterculture and their persistent influence on the mainstream.

Elsaesser, Thomas. "Tales of Sound and Fury: Observations on the Family Melodrama." *Monogram* 4 (1973). Explicates and evaluates the role of melodrama in film.

Schatz, Thomas. *Hollywood Genres.* New York: Random House, 1981. Analyzes Hollywood cinema in terms of dominant Hollywood genres, with a focus on family melodrama.

See also Baby-boom generation; Entertainment; Film ratings; Literature and families; Nuclear family; Pornography; Television depictions of families; Women's roles.

Film ratings

RELEVANT ISSUE: Art and the media

SIGNIFICANCE: The U.S. film industry, self-regulated for many years, adopted a voluntary film ratings system in 1968 that was designed primarily to provide parents with cautionary advance information on the content of films

Cinema, from its beginnings in the late nineteenth century, has been an international industry subject to some form of censorship or regulation—either governmental, self-imposed, or voluntary. Government regulation focused on special political, social, or religious ideas in some authoritarian countries. In democratic countries, it was imposed most often during wartime. When industry self-regulation was allowed, it ensured that films adhered to the mores of the national culture, especially those affecting family life. In many countries, governmental and self-imposed regulations usually intertwined and reinforced each other, but in America the practice of self-regulation evolved into voluntary regulations under the leadership of the Motion Picture Association of America (MPAA).

Historical Background. From its beginning, because of its enormous popularity, American cinema had to confront laws and regulations involving censorship and film content. Films are believed by many to have the power to modify individual beliefs and feelings, particularly when it comes to the family.

Part of the problem with imposing regulations involves whether cinema is an art form guaranteed freedom of expression and protected by the First Amendment of the U.S. Constitution, or whether the film industry simply is a business like any other and subject to legal regulations. The problem stems from a difference in interpretation of the First and Fourteenth Amendments. The First Amendment categorically states, "Congress shall make no law . . . abridging the freedom of speech, or the press." The U.S. Supreme Court has stated, however, that the Fourteenth Amendment gives local governments some powers regarding these rights and freedoms. Specifically, states and cities can prevent exposure of children to books and cinema. It is this clash of interpretation between the states and the federal government that lies at the heart of the censorship problem.

In 1907, Chicago was the first city to form a film censorship board, followed two years later by New York. By 1922, more than thirty states had passed, or were debating, legislation concerning statutory censorship. In the early 1920's, Hollywood scandals shocked the nation for months. The lives and immoral behavior of many film stars were constantly sensationalized by a press eager to feed juicy bits of scandal to the public. During the early 1920's, the harassment of screen luminaries reached its highest intensity.

Hollywood fought back and formed the Motion Picture Producers and Distributors of America (MPPDA) in 1922 under the guidance of Will H. Hays, former U.S. postmaster. The organization, known simply as the "Hays Office," had as its objective policing and governing the film industry without outside interference. Hays's political appeal was formidable, and he stopped all attempts at state censorship. In 1930, the MPPDA established the Motion Picture Production Code, a self-regulatory attempt at censorship.

MPPDA Production Code. From its inception in 1922, the MPPDA, the trade association of the American film industry, attempted to create a positive public image so that families would continue attending films. Hays, concerned that reform might do to movies what it did to alcohol, adopted a soft approach using self-censorship rather than penalties. In the 1920's, Hays established a self-regulating purity code that prohibited on-screen profanity, licentious behavior, suggestive or explicit nudity, illegal drug traffic, sexual perversion, white slavery, miscegenation, venereal disease, actual childbirth scenes, children's sex organs, ridicule of the clergy, and deliberate insult to individual countries (quickly forgotten during World War II) or people of a particular race or creed. Known as the Hays Production Code, its aim was to eliminate vulgarity and suggestiveness, which were to be replaced by good taste on such subjects as the American flag, brutality, criminal sympathy, rape, and the institution of marriage, to name a handful of topics.

Hays authorized revision of the code in 1930, with clauses added regarding obscenity, vulgarity, liquor, and adultery to help codify stricter guidelines that went into effect on July 1, 1934. He created the Production Code Administration

(PCA) to regulate it and appointed a well-known Roman Catholic layman, Joseph I. Breen, to run it. The PCA was able to acquire almost total dictatorial powers within the film industry because studios belonging to the MPPDA needed a certificate of approval signed by Breen.

The dictates of PCA regulation were in effect for some twenty years, until the mid-1950's, when they became basically unenforceable. Following World War II, films began to reflect important social issues, and pictures in the United States and abroad began to challenge in court and in the public

One of the first films released without an industry seal of approval, 1953's The Moon Is Blue *openly ridiculed virginity and so successfully flouted conventional notions of morality that it helped to bring down the Hays Code.* (Museum of Modern Art, Film Stills Archive)

forum the concept of a PCA seal. Eventually, sweeping political, social, and economic changes, along with several U.S. Supreme Court decisions regarding censorship, obscenity, and the constitutional status of cinema, led the MPAA (the MPPDA had changed its name to the Motion Picture Association of America in the mid-1940's) to a self-regulating, voluntary rating system in 1968.

The MPAA, the Rating System, and Its Purpose. The movement away from self-censorship to a voluntary film rating system came about when Jack Valenti became president of the MPAA in 1966. Valenti inherited a situation in which filmmakers were making frank, more open pictures, and were paying little heed to self-restraint. He soon realized that the old Production Code system was dated and censorious, and that parents were at a loss to determine which pictures were suitable for their children.

Valenti's first major step was to abolish the old Hays Production Code. On November 1, 1966, he instituted a new voluntary rating system for the film industry. Over the next twenty years, the ratings system was modified and expanded from four to five categories: G (General Audiences), all ages admitted; PG (Parental Guidance Suggested),

By the late 1990's the importance of film ratings was such that many theaters listed them in their advertisements and marquees. (James L. Shaffer)

with some material possibly not suitable for children; PG-13 (Parents Strongly Cautioned), with some material possibly inappropriate for children under thirteen; R (Restricted), for which children under seventeen require an accompanying parent or adult guardian; and NC-17, with no one seventeen years old or younger admitted. Valenti said his purpose in switching to a voluntary rating system was to offer advance information based on the amount of violence, sex, or "adult" language in a film so parents could choose for their children.

The MPAA film ratings apply only to films shown in the United States. Other countries use their own rating systems. In Great Britain, for example, the British Board of Censors uses only three categories. In Canada, almost all the provinces have their own film classification boards that issue ratings. In Ontario and Quebec, for example, a four-category approach is used, whereas Vancouver, British Columbia, employs a six-category rating.

How Films Are Rated. The MPAA employs a full-time Rating Board based in Los Angeles. The Rating Board views approximately 350 submitted films each year, and each of the board's eight to thirteen members must view it from a parental perspective. The members fill out rating forms, and ratings are based on the majority of votes. There are no special qualifications for board membership, except the members must have a shared parenthood experience, must possess an intelligent maturity, and most of all, must have the capacity to put themselves in the role of most American parents so they can view a film and apply a rating that most parents would find suitable and helpful.

No studio, producer, or distributor is required to submit a film. If they choose not to submit their films, however, they cannot use one of the MPAA federally registered certification ratings. They also have the right to question a rating, reedit a film to obtain a different rating, or appeal the rating decision to a ratings appeals board comprising between fourteen and eighteen members. This appeals board serves as the final arbiter; its decision cannot be appealed.

Since the 1920's, controversy has always surrounded the Production Code and later censorship and rating systems, but overall the system has worked because the MPAA has a worldwide market research department. Every year, the MPAA hires the Princeton Opinion Research Corporation to conduct a scientific poll on ratings. The findings of these annual reports are consistently favorable. The MPAA makes it clear that its ratings do not judge quality or appraise the creativity or artistic value of a film.   —*Terry Theodore*

BIBLIOGRAPHY

Brodie, John. "Sex! Controversy! PR!" *Variety* (August 29, 1994).

Geir, Thom. "How Film Ratings Work." *U.S. News & World Report* (September 9, 1996).

Medved, Michael. *Hollywood vs. America.* New York: HarperCollins, 1992.

Sandler, Adam. "H'Wood: 'R' Kind of Town." *Variety* (September 12, 1994).

Valenti, Jack. *The Voluntary Movie Rating System.* Washington, D.C.: Motion Picture Association of America, 1996.

See also Entertainment; Film depictions of families; Television rating systems.

Focus on the Family

DATE: Founded in 1977

RELEVANT ISSUES: Art and the media; Marriage and dating; Parenting and family relationships; Religious beliefs and practices

SIGNIFICANCE: A Christian organization, Focus on the Family reaches an international audience through radio broadcasts and more than fifty ministries that provide information on issues related to the family

Focus on the Family was established by James C. Dobson in 1977. Reared in a Christian home, Dobson received his Ph.D. in child development from the University of Southern California (USC). Prior to founding Focus on the Family, he taught pediatrics at the USC College of Medicine and was an attending staff member of the Children's Hospital in Los Angeles in the Child Development and Medical Genetics division. He sought to integrate his skills as a psychologist and his religious beliefs to influence children and families. Perceiving what he believed to be a continued disintegration of the family, Dobson resigned from his positions and formed Focus on the Family.

The organization began with a twenty-five-minute weekly broadcast on a few dozen radio stations. Focus on the Family developed into an international organization with more than fifty ministries employing approximately 1,200 employees. The original weekly program became a daily broadcast aired on four thousand radio stations worldwide. This program and ten other Focus on the Family broadcasts are heard in more than seventy countries. The organization's activities include eleven periodicals sent to 2.9 million people a month; seminars; a newspaper column; and educational services, including the Institute for Family Studies, Focus on the Family Publishing, a counseling enrichment program, the National Day of Prayer, films, and videos. In addition, the organization responds to as many as 55,000 letters a week, offers professional counseling and referrals to a network of 1,500 therapists, and addresses public policy and cultural issues.

Focus on the Family's mission statement, published in *Focus on the Family: Who We Are and What We Stand For* (1997), emphasizes why the organization exists: "Focus on the Family's primary reason for existence is to cooperate with the Holy Spirit in disseminating the Gospel of Jesus Christ to as many people as possible, and, specifically, to accomplish that objective by helping to preserve traditional values and the institution of the family." The organization reflects in all its ministries the belief that God ordained and blessed the institution of the family, and it sees its values and techniques to build stronger families as drawn from the Bible and from Judeo-Christian ethics. As founder and president of Focus on the Family, Dobson attempts to carry out the mission of the organization by teaching men, women, and children about home and family life through biblical traditions.

—*Sue Bailey*

See also Family values; Religion.

Foodways

RELEVANT ISSUES: Parenting and family relationships; Sociology

SIGNIFICANCE: If romantic love might be described as the ethereal flame that often ultimately results in the desire to found families, food is the more prosaic substance that can cement new families into cohesive units; foodways describes how families consume

The very beginning of families is associated in the popular imagination with foodways: Newly married couples are sprinkled with rice, symbolic of fertility and abundance. There is often an elaborate wedding feast, relived through memories, wedding photographs, or home videotape recordings. Wives, once pregnant, have a cultural license to demand foods, no matter how seemingly bizarre, that will satisfy them and make them comfortable with their condition. After the birth of a child, the first concern of new mothers is to provide nourishment, be it mother's milk, cow's or goat's milk, or a scientifically concocted substitute that will get their new babies off to a good nutritional start.

Social Indicators. As families grow and mature, foodways are a telling indicator of their social health. Parents may develop patterns in the preparation and consumption of food that take on the aura of tradition. The extended family—grandparents, in-laws, and other relatives—may also participate in these food-related endeavors. Family reunions almost always center around the foods that have become familiar and cherished over time. Fathers may pride themselves on their backyard grilling techniques. Mothers may have prized recipes they share or particular dishes they prepare for special occasions. The children may learn to cook simple dishes or contribute their fishing catch to the family larder. The preparation and sharing of food may very well be the quintessential family activity, because it is nearly universal and lends itself to both custom and variation. The intimacy of family life is supportive of the communal sharing that is a typical family activity.

Ethnic Heritage. The foodways of Americans are of particular interest in the study of the relationship between family and food, because even the overarching symbols of America—whether cornucopia or melting pot—might be construed as food-related, while the abundance of American foodstuffs has been a key element in the image of America as the promised land for many immigrants. The foodways of many of the ethnic groups that have settled in the United States and Canada have been among their most enduring cultural markers, which linger on in the familial settings of immigrant groups even after many of them have adopted the food customs of mainstream society and abandoned their native tongue. The former

One of the first concerns of new mothers is to provide their babies with proper nutrition. (James L. Shaffer)

Greater reliance on fast-food restaurants has been one of the most dramatic changes in modern eating habits. (James L. Shaffer)

difficulties of life in the "old country" are forgotten and gradually distilled into a nostalgia over the special dishes of the season.

Influence of the Discovery of the Americas. World food sources received a great boost in variety and taste with the "Columbian exchange," which was the result of the discovery and settling of the New World at the end of the fifteenth century. Tomatoes, potatoes, pumpkins, and corn are only a few of the foods that were discovered by the early European explorers of the Americas. However, the first colonists of the United States nearly starved during their initial few winters, and new food products discovered in America were sometimes viewed with both suspicion and aversion. Families of the early settlers subsisted in the main on diets made up of cornbread, molasses, salt pork, and the game and fish that were in abundance. It was only over time that improvements in food transportation, preservation, and refrigeration, animal and plant breeding, and nutritional knowledge made it possible for families to enjoy foods that were varied, free of contaminants, and tasty.

The diverse ethnic makeup of the United States and Canada has gradually resulted in national cuisines that include dishes created by cooks of many nationalities. It would be difficult to characterize the common food customs of the United States because of the great ethnic and social diversity of successive waves of immigration. One may say that the foodways of North America are in many respects the mirror of society. These foodways change over time as society changes—and not always for the better. Citizens and residents of the United States may not be aware that North Americans did not always enjoy the relative abundance of food that has come to characterize the late twentieth century. Early North American settlers were indebted to the Native American peoples for their assistance in providing the settlers with sufficient foods so that they could survive their first winters. Idealized portraits of family food customs characterize only the more fortunate families in the twentieth century and may be in imminent danger of becoming a thing of the past.

Modern Influences. Family meals, which serve not only a nutritional but also a socializing function, have been supplanted in the late twentieth century by food habits abetted by the increasing use of processed foods, a greater reliance on fast-

food chains, and a decline in joint family meals because of family members' conflicting schedules and dual-income households. Among the less appealing features of family life in the late twentieth century has been an increasing deterioration of the distinctiveness and inventiveness of food preparation and customs among the middle and laboring classes. In place of distinctive foods there has arisen a marked increase in the use of foodstuffs mass-produced and mass-marketed as commodities. Because of the increasing prevalence of one-parent and working-mother families, it is often difficult for parents to find the time to prepare family meals, which causes families to rely increasingly on packaged meals. The more intensive social life of many families outside the home has also contributed to the breakdown of family mealtimes, during which family members eat and converse together.

The increasing economic disparity between the wealthy few and the less affluent majority during the final two decades of the twentieth century has had an adverse impact on families' food habits. In order to make ends meet, parents might find that they must obtain further education or additional jobs, thus allowing them less time for the relaxation of family get-togethers. On the other hand, social legislation enacted during the post-World War II era ameliorated to some degree the food situation of lower-income groups by making food stamps available, although poor people's access to food stamps was severely restricted because of welfare reform in the late 1990's.

New Cultures. Many fast-food restaurants have targeted the family as the primary market for their products. Suburban locations, simple menus, and even play areas designed to appeal to young children are a prominent feature of MacDonald's and other fast-food chains, which not only characterize the American landscape but have also become worldwide outposts of American culture.

The very concept of the family has also undergone change since the middle years of the twentieth century, as a variety of new definitions of the family have been brought about by social transformations based on ideology and religion. Interestingly, foodways sometimes insert themselves into these changes. For example, one of the primary attractions of a number of twentieth century "cult" religions and communal-style living arrangements

Efforts of school cafeterias to provide nutritionally balanced meals tend to lose out to the eating habits that pupils learn elsewhere. (Hazel Hankin)

has been the willingness of their adherents to share food and meal customs with initiates. The women's movement has also had an impact on family foodways. Women who pursue careers outside the home are often either too preoccupied or too tired to engage in major culinary activities on a daily basis. The food industry caters to this socioeconomic category by touting the advantages of convenience foods and eating out, sometimes to the disadvantage of family life.

Other social issues have been responsible for focusing popular concern on the family and its food supply. The public outcry over the dangers of the ever-increasing use of pesticides, for example, has been a major factor in the movement to return to a simpler lifestyle and to consume organic foods. In many cases this has also stimulated a resumption of family life centered around foods that are believed to be healthful and nutritious. Another trend that has contributed in a positive way to food quality has been the greater interest in ethnic and gourmet cooking, which has characterized the upper middle class in the second half of the twentieth century.   —*Gloria Fulton*

BIBLIOGRAPHY

Brown, Linda Keller, and Kay Mussell, eds. *Ethnic and Regional Foodways in the United States: The Performance of Group Identity.* Knoxville: University of Tennessee Press, 1984.

Camporesi, Piero. *The Magic Harvest: Food, Folklore and Society.* Cambridge, Eng.: Polity Press, 1993.

Fieldhouse, Paul. *Food and Nutrition: Customs and Culture.* London: Croom Helm, 1986.

Goody, Jack. *Cooking, Cuisine and Class: A Study in Comparative Sociology.* Cambridge, Eng.: Cambridge University Press, 1982.

Hooker, Richard J. *Food and Drink in America: A History.* Indianapolis: Bobbs-Merrill, 1981.

Levenstein, Harvey A. *Paradox of Plenty: A Social History of Eating in Modern America.* New York: Oxford University Press, 1993.

McIntosh, Elaine N. *American Food Habits in Historical Perspective.* Westport, Conn.: Praeger Publishers, 1995.

Visser, Margaret. *Much Depends on Dinner: The Extraordinary History and Mythology, Allure and Obsessions, Perils and Taboos, of an Ordinary Meal.* New York: Grove Press, 1986.

See also Cultural influences; Eating habits of children; Holidays; Mealtaking; Supplemental Nutrition Program for Women, Infants, and Children.

Foster homes

RELEVANT ISSUES: Economics and work; Parenting and family relationships; Sociology

SIGNIFICANCE: Two-thirds of children apprehended by child welfare agencies because of neglect or abuse are cared for in foster homes; thus, foster families are an important component of child-welfare services

In the late eighteenth century, increased urbanization, industrialization, and immigration to North America combined to produce children who lived in the streets of cities. Initially, this phenomenon of children roving the streets was seen as the result of the lack of work; however, it was quickly pathologized and interpreted as the result of an inadequate family environment. Inadequate families were seen as creating "maladjusted" children in need of protection.

Expanding social control of families was legitimized by the evolving knowledge of the developing professions of medical doctors and social workers. In the eighteenth and nineteenth centuries, "maladjusted" children were placed in institutions such as poorhouses. American reformers,

however, were interested in developing alternative care for children. One such alternative was to place these children with families.

Development of Foster Care. The first types of foster homes were not caring families but instead often used foster children as cheap domestic or farm labor. Over time, social workers set standards for proper care of children in foster homes. In the late twentieth century the main intent of a foster family was to function as a substitute family for the foster child to help the child heal and pursue healthy life goals.

To become an approved foster family, all family members must go through a rigorous screening process. The eligible candidate family has to file an application, provide letters of reference, and agree to the release of information from government departments, professional practitioners, and various agencies to the child welfare agency. A criminal record check is carried out on all family members 18 years of age and older. All adult members of the candidate foster family are interviewed to assess their willingness to be a part of the foster family. A home study is undertaken that includes looking at the motivation to foster, the physical home requirements, the personal characteristics of the potential foster family members, and the expected impact of fostering on the family's biological children. Once a family has been accepted as a foster family and a child has been placed with the family, a social worker carries out frequent follow-ups to monitor the well-being of the foster child and help with difficulties the foster family may encounter.

The entire family plays an important role in foster care, even though the majority of caring typically is carried out by foster mothers. When a family becomes a foster family, all immediate family members, and sometimes extended family members, are affected. Foster families are forced, every time a foster child enters the family, to renegotiate many of the normally taken-for-granted aspects of family life. This process bears similarities to the struggles of blended families.

Foster Family Dynamics. Some foster families care for foster children on a long-term basis, others on a shorter-term basis. Foster children often are placed for a six-month period with a family. Foster families and foster children have little time to get to know each other because the often reluctant foster child typically is brought into the foster family by a social worker, at very short notice, with little background information.

Most foster mothers describe an initial "honeymoon" period in which the foster child does not exhibit any social or emotional problems. When the foster child starts to feel more comfortable in the family, however, he or she often begins to exhibit more social and behavioral problems. One of the most important conditions for a successful foster home placement is a balanced level of expectations between the foster family and foster child. If these expectations are incongruent, the chance that the foster placement will break down increases.

One of the most important expectations of foster mothers is the belief that with the right amount of love, care, and patience they will be able to help the child. Many foster mothers realize after some time, however, that many foster children are severely traumatized and need more than the love, care, and patience they can provide. The children need extensive professional counseling for multiple problems. As a result, many foster mothers want more training and learn how to develop skills to deal with difficult foster children.

Another development in foster care is examining how to keep children from developing multiple social and behavioral problems. Several child welfare agencies are examining the merits of the policy of keeping a child in the biological family for as long as possible, even if the family is dysfunctional. There is a movement developing that feels that when biological parents do not demonstrate appropriate parenting skills and neglect or abuse a child, the child should be removed relatively soon and placed in foster care to minimize the negative effects of prolonged exposure to an abusive family. This development ultimately would result in fewer children entering foster care with multiple social and behavioral problems.

The Future of Foster Care. The major issue facing foster home care services is the unattractive responsibility of caring for a severely traumatized child with little or no financial compensation. In some child welfare jurisdictions, foster parents' labor is strictly voluntary. Women are the primary caregivers in foster care, and as more women, particularly women with school-aged children, enter the workforce, they are less attracted to fostering.

Furthermore, for women who want to engage in home care, it is much more attractive to get involved in home day care, which is better paying and does not carry the stress of around-the-clock responsibility for children.

Another type of foster care, elder foster care, is threatening to compete with child foster care for the services of foster families. The majority of children in foster care are preteens and teenagers, a difficult group of children to care for. Elder foster care is based on the notion that some elderly people are not able to live on their own but do not need the intensive care of a nursing home. These people can be cared for by foster families, for a fee, if their own families cannot provide care. For some women, elder care is a more attractive alternative than caring for a troubled teenager. The supply of foster families willing to take in teenagers may decrease as elderly foster care increases.

Increased professionalization of foster care services has developed in North America to combat these problems. Professional foster parents are expected to undergo more training and develop more skills in how to deal with troubled preteens and teenagers. In return, foster parents will be able to reach different levels of care status when they satisfy certain criteria. The more training and the higher the level of care, the more financial compensation they can expect.

Professionalization has not yet taken place in all jurisdictions. Foster care is not federally organized; therefore, every jurisdiction may have different standards and criteria for fostering. All jurisdictions, however, face the same problems. If no solutions are found, child foster care as an option for the care of children with unsuitable homes is in danger of elimination.   —*Baukje Miedema*

BIBLIOGRAPHY

Berridge, David, and Hedy Cleaver. *Foster Home Breakdown.* New York: Blackwell, 1987.

Donzelot, Jacques. *The Policing of Families.* New York: Random House, 1979.

Kendrick, Martin. *Nobody's Children.* Toronto: Macmillan, 1990.

Kulp, Jodee. *Families at Risk.* Minneapolis: Better Endings, New Beginnings, 1993.

McKenzie, Brad. *Current Perspectives on Foster Family Care for Children and Youth.* Toronto: Wall & Emerson, 1994.

Maluccio, Anthony N., Edith Fein, and Kathleen A. Olmstead. *Permanency Planning for Children.* New York: Tavistock, 1986.

Mansfield, Danielle F. W. *Goodbye, Baby Venus.* Boston: University Press of America, 1993.

See also Adoption issues; *Alsager v. District Court*; Blended families; Child Welfare League of America (CWLA); Family caregiving; Guardianship; Homeless families; *In loco parentis*; Orphans; Social workers; Substitute caregivers; Volunteerism.

Freudian psychology

RELEVANT ISSUES: Children and child development; Health and medicine; Parenting and family relationships

SIGNIFICANCE: The most significant impact of Freudian psychology is that of focusing parental and professional attention on the subtle emotional messages parents give children and on the quality of the mutual attachments between them

Sigmund Freud (1856-1939) was a Viennese physician and the founder of psychoanalysis, a method of treating emotionally disturbed patients. His method explored patients' dreams, fantasies, and spontaneous behavior as cues to bring back painful forgotten memories. These "unconscious" memories seemed to be the source of patients' problems. Freud's significance for the family stems from his discovery that so many troubling memories involved conflicting emotions concerning family relationships in patients' early childhood.

Freudian Views of the Family and Sexuality. Freud wrote prolifically over a forty-year period, frequently clarifying and modifying his earlier views. The Freudian psychologists that followed him frequently added their own emphases. Nevertheless, one theme persists throughout Freudian writings. Crucial to the formation of personality are the relationships of early childhood, including the emotions, affections, passions, hates, loves, and jealousies based upon these relationships.

Freud first directed his attention to the sexual passions. In infancy, the "oral stage," the sexual passions are expressed orally, as it is the mouth with which infants most react to their first love, their mothers. Later, in toddlerhood, the "anal stage," the anal area becomes the focus of concern; the frustrations and challenges of controlling the anal musculature are central to the child-caretaker relationship.

In three-year-olds, genital sensations become more important. At this age the relationship between male children and their mothers increases in emotional intensity, with a distinctly erotic tinge. Jealousy and guilty love become directed at those, such as fathers, who rival male children in competing for the attentions of their first love, their mothers. For males, Freud termed this dilemma the "Oedipus complex," after the mythical Greek king Oedipus, who killed his father and married his mother. For females, Freud called the corresponding stage the "Electra complex," after the mythological figure Elektra, who helped slay her mother. The key to resolving these conflicts was "identification," or the fantasy incorporation of the adequacies, mannerisms, and ideals of the same-sex parent. Trauma or excessive frustration at some point could arrest development. Loving and adequate parents were important throughout childhood.

Freud's Concept of Aggression. In later writings Freud broadened his motivational discussions beyond the sexual and gave more attention to mechanisms of control. Aggression is also important as it, like sex, can seldom be expressed in its rawest and most impulsive forms. Like the sexual, aggression's more primitive forms are best expressed in indirect, displaced, circuitous, and less destructive ways. Impulses, sexual and aggressive, in their most primitive forms compose collectively the "id." The ideals one acquires (the superego) from identification with admired parents offer sets of built-in controls. Thus every child becomes selectively involved with some of the goals and ideals of their culture, sometimes with irrational intensity. More rational controls are those of the "ego," or the conscious self. The ego can adjust ideals and impulses to the real situation in a way that is consistent with a person's self-picture. Adequate, controlling parents, themselves emotionally attached to important social values, are equally as important to the process of developing inner controls as loving parents are to developing an ego that survives infantile conflicts.

One of the most important ways in which Freud influenced the family was through his impact on the post-Freudian psychoanalysts who elaborated upon Freudian themes. One group, called "object-relations" theorists, emphasized the nature and quality of the emotional bonding between infant children and caretaking adults as prototypic of later close relationships. A second group, the "ego psychoanalysts," emphasized the motivation of the conscious self to develop its own potential, "to be all one can be." Erik Erikson hypothesized that this ego development continues with a new intensity in the role experimentation of adolescence. To ego psychoanalysts family conflicts could result as much from motives that have to do with the pressures of releasing one's natural talents, contrary perhaps to parental expectations, as from repressed sex or aggression.

Rise of Freudian Influence. Freud introduced his theory to the New World in a speech in 1909,

Many plays by Eugene O'Neill dealt with stresses within families. (Nobel Foundation)

and within a decade some European psychoanalysts had begun to practice in the United States. At first, the theory had more impact upon the elite patients of these therapists than upon typical family life. Writers such as James Joyce, D. H. Lawrence, and Eugene O'Neill incorporated Freudian themes into their works. Yet, popular views of Freud remained highly inaccurate. A common misconception was that Freud advocated unrestrained sexual expression as a cure for human anxiety. One effect of lifting repression began to occur in the 1920's: Slowly families were becoming freer in discussing sexual matters.

The high point of Freudian influence upon American culture occurred in the years 1945 to 1970. A large number of the psychoanalysts who had fled Nazi Germany migrated to the United States. The "talking therapy" of Freud had proved useful in treating war-related battle fatigue. Psychoanalytically-based psychiatry was a sought-after medical specialty. Popularizers of Freud included film producers and newspaper columnists. Many psychiatrists, such as the esteemed Karl Menninger, seemed limitless in their optimism about the potential benefits of psychoanalysis, extending the range of analytically treatable conditions to include schizophrenia, psychopathy, and even crime.

No influence upon the American family was greater during the era from 1945 to 1975 than pediatrician Benjamin Spock. Spock's influence was based upon a book which sold some twenty million copies annually: *The Common Sense Book of Baby and Child Care.* Much of Spock's common sense was right out of Freud. In contrast to the advice of earlier learning psychologists that children could develop good habits by rigid adherence to schedules, Spock encouraged little restraint in parents' expressions of love for their infants: Holding, rocking, and touching infants and singing to them were all natural and good. Spock cautioned against unnecessary pressure or harshness in weaning and toilet training. He dealt with childhood sexual interest as natural and normal, although he cautioned against parental immodesty, which could intensify the erotic pressures of the Oedipal period. Spock was also in favor of setting limits, although he, like Freud, felt that parental example was the most effective of all instiller of values.

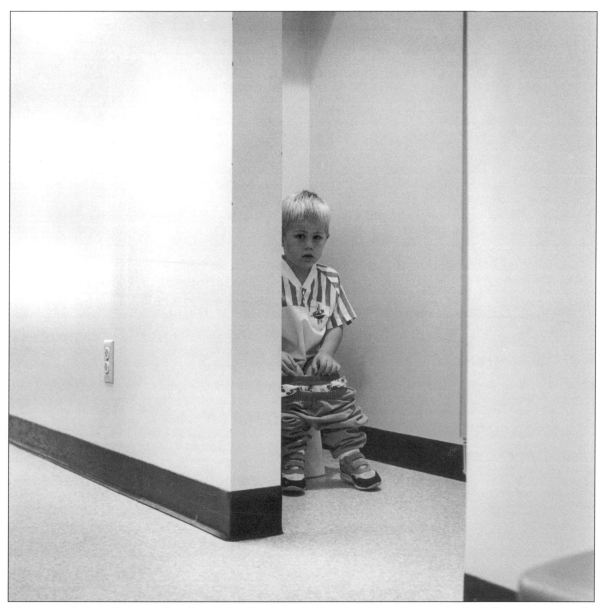

Modern psychological research has found that Freudian theories about the influence of toilet training on personality development were overstated. (James L. Shaffer)

Criticism, Crisis, and New Affirmations. So exuberant was the post-war enthusiasm for psychoanalysis that disappointment seemed almost inevitable. The disappointment that occurred was, however, exaggerated by a confluence of forces. Psychoanalysis as therapy often failed to change unwanted behavior. The talking therapy seemed to result in little benefit for such conditions as schizophrenia or in treating the poor and unedu-

cated. Competing treatments such as antipsychotic drugs for schizophrenia proved embarrassingly effective.

Newer and more careful research did not always support Freudian hypotheses concerning parent-child relations. Different styles of toilet training and weaning did not seem to effect the types of consistent differences in personality characteristics predicted by Freud. Neither fathers of homosexuals appeared colder nor the mothers of incipient schizophrenics more ambivalent than other parents. It appeared that Freudians underestimated the effects of such biologically rooted variables as heredity and temperament. Regardless of parental attitudes and practices, at least some children were shown to remain shy and timid, while others were venturesome risk takers from birth.

A final influence that poses some problems for the Freudian model is the temper of the times. Freudian psychology seemed most clear in its prescriptions for families, such as the ideal family of the 1950's, which included fathers as breadwinners and mothers as homemakers. Freud conceived of a controlling male "father" figure as essential to identity formation in both males and females.

Modern life departs radically from this model with surprisingly mild consequences. The many modern women who derive an important part of their identity from careers would be seen by Freud as neurotics, probably compensating for earlier losses. Survey evidence suggests that such women are at least as happy as housewife controls. In 1993, 43 percent of all children experienced a home without both biological parents, a condition Freud would have considered pathogenic. The problem with Freud's theory is that most of these children (two-thirds by some estimates) survive broken homes without devastating emotional scars.

Perhaps the modeling function, like the caretaking function, is not closely linked to specific characters in the biologically determined family romance described by Freud. Parenting involves love and control, but the sexual division of labor may be arbitrarily assigned to these functions.

Freud and the Test of Time. With all the caveats made necessary by newer scholarship and experience, a core of Freud's propositions have endured the test of time. Loved children, even in atypical households, are more likely to thrive than unloved ones. The quality of the relationship between caretakers and children is important. The most significant feelings and values may be communicated in ways that cannot be put into words. Feelings, including sexual and aggressive feelings, can be more effectively channeled if they are acknowledged. Patterns established in childhood are re-

peated in adult life. The child is father to the man. Freud's ideas endure because they contain a residue of essential truth. —*Thomas E. DeWolfe*

BIBLIOGRAPHY

Burnham, John C. *Paths into American Culture: Psychology, Medicine, and Morals.* Philadelphia: Temple University Press, 1988.

Gay, Peter. *Freud: A Life for Our Time.* New York: W. W. Norton, 1988.

Hale, Nathan G. *The Rise and Crisis of Psychoanalysis in the United States: Freud and the Americans, 1917-1985.* New York: Oxford University Press, 1995.

Hall, C. S. *A Primer of Freudian Psychology.* New York: Mentor, 1954.

Miller, P. H. *Theories of Developmental Psychology.* New York: W. H. Freeman, 1993.

Torrey, E. Fuller. *Freudian Fraud.* New York: HarperCollins, 1992.

See also Allport, Gordon; Bonding and attachment; Electra and Oedipus complexes; Erikson, Erik H.; Father-daughter relationships; Father-son relationships; Love; Mental health; Toilet training.

Friend networks

RELEVANT ISSUES: Aging; Parenting and family relationships; Sociology

SIGNIFICANCE: Friendships are voluntary and important relations, functioning largely in the social and emotional realm and varying systematically by gender and life circumstances

People are embedded in networks of friends who provide social support, surrounding and safeguarding people as they negotiate life's challenges. Scientific study of these important social relationships over the life span, however, is relatively recent. Sociologists are only beginning to learn about the range and function of friendship, and even how people define the term.

Friends and Family. The distinction between friends and family appears to be blurring, primarily because of changes in the social norms governing kinship and the rethinking of the concept of the family. It is not uncommon to hear a close friend being described as a brother or sister or a sibling or parent being called a friend. Individuals also report "fictive kin," so-called aunts, uncles, and others with no blood ties who are considered

Changing perceptions of family have worked to blur distinctions between family members and friends. (James L. Shaffer)

members of the family. African Americans in particular make frequent reference to fictive kin. Gay men and lesbians also create "families of choice" from their friends as substitutes for, and often in the absence of, support from families as more traditionally defined.

Generally and formally, however, kinship is seen as an ascribed or obligatory relationship and friendship as an achieved or voluntary relationship. It may be that kin address needs of a more generative and instrumental nature, whereas friends address needs of a more social and emotional nature. Correspondingly, researchers generally agree that friendship has a positive effect on the morale and life satisfaction of older adults,

free of some of the role-specific obligations and issues associated with kin relations.

Friendships over the Life Course. The proportions of and contact with friends vary in systematic fashion over the family life course. Friends serve variously as complements and substitutes for kin relationships. For example, in adolescence, the peer group increases dramatically in importance, with a concomitant emotional distancing from the family of origin and kin relations. Friendship numbers and contact maintain these high levels in early adulthood, then decrease with marriage and the responsibilities of parenthood. After the emptying of the family nest in mid-life, friendships may increase again, followed by a decrease in old age.

Gender plays a significant role in the development of friend networks. (James L. Shaffer)

In later life, it is believed that family again assumes a more prominent position, in part because of the death and relocation of friends as well as the potential need for care (under the relatively strict purview of kin).

The Role of Gender. Gender plays a significant moderating role in the nomination of and interaction with friends. Paul Wright, among others, has written that women interact with their friends in a face-to-face manner, with an emotional and personalized focus, whereas men interact with their friends in a side-by-side orientation, often organized around some external activity.

Along similar lines of thought, women and men have been described in these contexts as role generalists and role specialists, respectively representing a more holistic or specific focus. Perhaps these differences underlie the greater number of friends reported by men in a variety of recent studies. Women and men also differ in what they give, receive, and appreciate in their friendships. Women rate dimensions of care and concern more highly in their friendships than do men, who rate shared activities and common values more highly.

The gender composition of the friendship dyad affects these patterns. Same-sex friendships tend to intensify the above characteristics. It has been suggested that the traditional male sex role produces barriers to emotional intimacy in men. Moreover, a common finding in the friendship literature is "homosociality," or the propensity of individuals to identify as friends a greater proportion of members of their own sex (as well as of their own ethnicity, race/culture, and age, among other characteristics). Little is known about cross-sex friendships, although there has been some indication that when women and men interact in friendship, the differences between them appear to be lessened. Furthermore, cross-sex friendships evidence somewhat higher reciprocity and greater self-disclosure on the part of men.

Perhaps not surprisingly, women's friendships and same-sex friendships tend to be of longer duration. As duration increases, so does the similarity between women and men in their friendships. Disability and advanced old age also increases the similarity between women's and men's friendships.

Circumstances of Life. The events, conditions, and circumstances of life often lead to changes in the membership of friendship networks, as noted in reference to the family life course. Marriage and other exclusive intimate relationships combine the friendship networks of couples, and members of couples that separate often find that they lose some of their friends. The death of a spouse, which is more common among women than among men, returns people to single status. Women who are bereft of their spouses are reported to cultivate "societies of widows" or supportive friendship groups of women. Parenthood also introduces changes in the composition of and interaction with friendship networks, as couples with children organize their activities around those of their children.

Many of the events marking such changes, including widowhood, occur with disproportionate frequency in the later years. Retirement, for example, may signal the erosion of work-based friendship networks for men. Because men's friendships tend to be instrumental, retirement from a job may leave a man with little in common with his friends from work. Relocation may either enhance friendship contact, as individuals move to be nearer to their friends, or restrict contact, as individuals move to be nearer to kin. Age-segregated and age-integrated housing options also affect opportunities for friendship development and maintenance.

It should be noted that frequent contact is not a prerequisite for friendship, and new friends may be added to an individual's social network throughout the life course. Common sources of friendship development, at many stages of the life course, include the neighborhood or home setting, community and social organizations including religious groups, academic and vacation activities, and even other friends who introduce their friends to one another.

Friendship Conceptualization. The many aforementioned contexts of friendships give some ideas about the meaning of the term. Friendships function largely in the affective arena, involving sharing of personal thoughts and feelings; expressions of intimacy, affection, and appreciation; and the bolstering of support and self-concept perhaps made possible by a sense of trust, loyalty, and commitment. A second broad function of friendship reflects its communal or shared nature. Friends engage in activities of mutual interest and often

Peer-group pressures increase dramatically as children move into their adolescent years. (Mary LaSalle)

assist each other in both instrumental and affective tasks, possibly drawing on their common similar experience. A third function reflects the fact that friends are sources of fun, recreation, and sociability.

There is surprisingly little evidence of variation in these functions of friendship over the course of life. Perhaps the function and perception of friends are established in early life and maintained over time. There are minor exceptions to this pattern, however. Older people tend to view friends in more specific and individual terms than do younger persons, who correspondingly adopt a more general or relational interpretation of the term "friend."

There is some evidence of racial and cultural or ethnic differences in friendship conceptualization, particularly among older persons. For example, among Canadian seniors, those of British ancestry identified a greater number of friends than did French Canadians. Furthermore, the French lived closer to their friends and had more frequent contact than did seniors in other ethnic groups. First Nation or native seniors identified vastly greater number of friends than did nonnatives. These results suggest that differing definitions may underlie these differing numbers of friends.

Friendships play a significant role in the lives of individuals and in the functioning of society. Understanding the friendships of individuals provides a window onto the understanding of individuals themselves. —*Brian de Vries*

BIBLIOGRAPHY

Adams, R. G., and R. Blieszner. *Older Adult Friendships: Structure and Process.* Newbury Park, Calif.: Sage Publications, 1989.

Blieszner, R., and R. G. Adams. *Adult Friendship.* Newbury Park, Calif.: Sage Publications, 1992.

De Vries, Brian. "The Understanding of Friendship: An Adult Life Course Perspective." In *Handbook of Emotion, Aging, and the Life Course,* edited by C. Malatesta-Magai and S. McFadden. New York: Academic Press, 1996.

Gilligan, Carol. *In a Different Voice: Psychology Theory and Women's Development.* Cambridge, Mass.: Harvard University Press, 1982.

Kahn, R. L., and T. C. Antonucci. "Convoys over the Life Course: Attachments, Roles and Social Supports." In *Life-span Development and Behavior,* edited by P. B. Baltes and O. G. Brim. New York: Academic Press, 1980.

Matthews, S. H. *Friendships Through the Life Course.* Newbury Park, Calif.: Sage Publications, 1986.

Miller, S. *Men and Friendship.* San Leandro, Calif.: Gateway Books, 1983.

Rubin, L. B. *Just Friends: The Role of Friendship in Our Lives.* New York: Harper & Row, 1985.

Wright, Paul H. "Men's Friendships, Women's Friendships and the Alleged Inferiority of the Latter." *Sex Roles* 8 (1982).

See also Couples; Extended families; Family life cycle; Gay and lesbian families; Men's roles; Retirement; Women's roles.

Full nest

RELEVANT ISSUES: Demographics; Parenting and family relationships

SIGNIFICANCE: Co-residence of parents and adult children increased during the 1980's and 1990's

The phrase "full nest" refers to parental homes that include adult children who have not left home or who have returned. Demographic figures show that during the 1990's approximately one in four young adults ages eighteen to thirty-four resided in parental homes. In the past, young adults were more likely to leave home to get married than to achieve independence. Young adults are likely to leave home to become independent if they live in stepparent or single-parent families or if they live under crowded conditions.

Full nests are more indicative of adult children's needs and situations than of parents' circumstances. Economic factors, such as unemployment, underemployment, or a lack of affordable housing, make it difficult for young adults to embark on independent living. Young married couples must often temporarily reside with parents until they can afford their own residences. Adult children who have left home return for a variety of reasons, including separation and divorce, low wages, job loss, and their wish to save money to establish an independent existence after completing college. The negative effects of the full nest are influenced by children's marital and parental status. Support for grandchildren as well as adult children exerts pressure on parental resources. Parents whose adult children return home as a result of divorce report more negative effects than parents of never-married children. Residence-sharing agreements between parents and adult children, stipulating adult children's financial contributions to the household, laundry and cooking tasks, acceptable noise levels, and grandchildren discipline, is recommended to prevent conflicts and enhance family interaction. Residence-sharing agreements may be temporarily beneficial, but most parents want their adult children to establish or reestablish their independence.

—*Marie Saracino*

See also Empty nest syndrome; Parenting.

Funerals

RELEVANT ISSUES: Race and ethnicity; Religious beliefs and practices; Sociology

SIGNIFICANCE: Concepts and practices regarding death continue to change with changing times

During colonial times in North America, death was not denied. Common belief acknowledged the existence of an omnipotent, concerned God and individual immortality. Life was viewed as a symbolic pilgrimage through the wilderness of the present world to the ultimate home. Death was a beginning rather than an end.

Funerals in Colonial Times. The majority of the population in the colonial era lived in small communities, in which mutual dependency and primary relationships flourished. The deaths of individuals were community losses. The community assisted bereaved families. Women family members washed and laid out bodies in the home, which was often the location of funerals. Male family members and friends constructed coffins. Bodies lay in people's rarely used rooms, which were often called dead rooms. A pall of fringed black cloth was draped over coffins. When women died in childbirth, a white sheet was substituted for the black pall. Mirrors in the house were covered from the time of death until the funeral. A death watch was held by family and close friends. Following funerals, men carried the coffins to burial sites, to be laid in graves they had dug. Women remained at the homes in which funerals had taken place.

Funerals served a social function in which large numbers of people, including children, partici-

pated. Gifts were made to the living as an announcement of death. Burials were followed by funeral feasts. Funeral cakes, sometimes emblazoned with the initials of the deceased, were served by the English and the Dutch. Funerals became costly extravagances. Death was heralded by the tolling of church bells. Funeral inviters, wearing black with long streamers on their hats, notified relatives and friends of the deceased about the impending funeral and requested their presence. Social propriety deemed that no one attend funerals uninvited.

Funerals in the Nineteenth Century. Attitudes toward death changed in the nineteenth century. Previously viewed as harsh reality, death came to be seen as a muted, beautiful event with the deceased part of the life of the living. The importance of corpses was shown symbolically by the luxuriousness of burial containers and by elegant, elaborate, death-related rituals and paraphernalia. By 1850 undertakers offered a selection of caskets from company catalogs. A variety of styles, materials, and colors were available. Caskets became objects of beauty and were lined with colorful fabrics. Floral backgrounds and small bouquets on tables by the caskets completed the scene.

Beautification of death furthered the trend of allowing the dead a greater role in life. The death bed became the center of the death ritual. It was considered important that family and intimate friends be present during a dying person's final moments. Everyone acknowledged the impending event, and it was viewed as a privilege to be witness to it. It was hoped that the dying person would utter statements of submission to God's will. Death was viewed as a release and an escape from the sadness of the world.

Draping covered the doors of houses in which deaths occurred. The rooms in which the deceased lay or the entire downstairs areas of their houses were draped in black or deep shades of gray. Dark veils hung in doorways. Black was the appropriate color for the bereaved, functionaries, shrouds, hearses and their plumes, casket palls, and horses. Shrouding folds were incorporated into widows' dress. Mourning bonnets included waist length streamers and widows' veils. Mourning wear indicated persons' degree of kinship with the deceased and defined periods of mourning. By the late nineteenth century, white was accept-

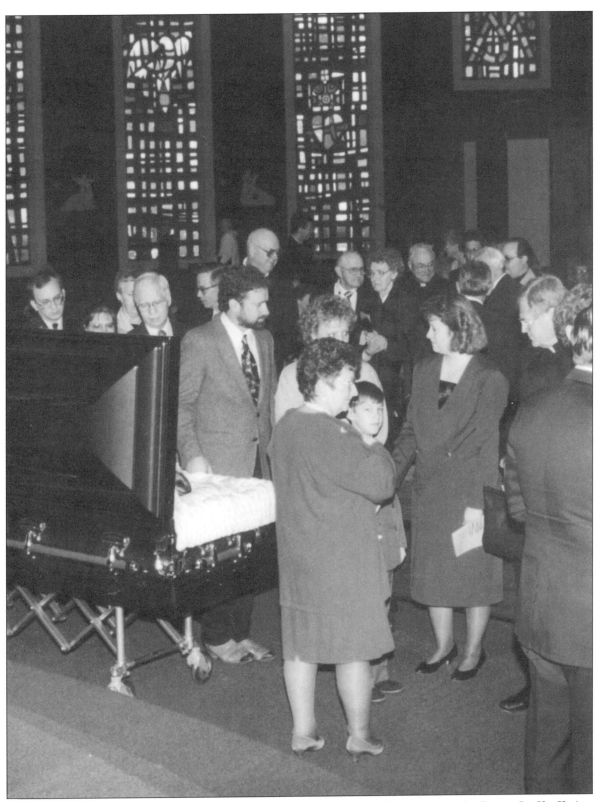

Open-casket funerals are modern American manifestations of the beautification of death. (James L. Shaffer)

Funerals have traditionally been important occasions for bringing together family members. (James L. Shaffer)

able for summer mourning. Mourners were prohibited from participating in social or recreational activities for six months. Rules of mourning extended to correspondence and calling cards. Etiquette necessitated that persons inquire about all the details surrounding individuals' deaths.

Until the 1840's burials occurred in crowded churchyards or charnel houses. Remains were often moved as cities grew. Addressing public health concerns, "rural" cemeteries were located in secluded areas. Based on the idea of cemeteries for the living rather than for the deceased, landscape gardening techniques were employed. Relatives and friends gathered in pastoral settings to remember the departed.

Funerals in the Twentieth Century. The twentieth century witnessed changes in perception of the relationship between death and dying. Death has become a taboo subject and an alien event. The visible presence of death has declined. Death is for the elderly.

During the twentieth century funeral directing, a product of urban development, evolved from vocations that occasionally provided services for funerals. Funeral homes moved from store fronts to large residences to elegant, stylish buildings that provide all necessary services. The funeral industry standardized funeral ritual in the United States. A general form of the funeral in the late twentieth century included rapid removal of bodies to funeral homes, embalming, viewing, and disposal by burial. New techniques in embalming have given rise to an Americanized form of wakes, which focus on displaying corpses in attractive settings. The context of wakes is predominately social. Almost all funerals include a type of religious service. Burials, which immediate family members may attend briefly, are usually a less important phase of the funeral ritual.

Differing Religious Practices. Within Judaism all rites honor the dead and comfort mourners. Jewish law decrees that Orthodox Jews be buried in consecrated ground within twenty-four hours of death. The bodies of the deceased are readied by holy societies and draped with linen garments. The closed-casket funeral services are held at synagogues or Jewish funeral homes. The cutting of garments or black ribbon begins funeral services, which include a reading of psalms and eulogies. At the cemetery each family member places earth on the casket. Beginning with the funeral service, shivah, or the period of mourning, lasts seven days and terminates with final family prayers and a symbolic walk. On the first anniversary of deaths, families gather at synagogues and dedicate the headstones at deceased persons' graves.

Roman Catholics nearing death receive the ritual anointing of the sick by a priest. Dying persons are greeted by priests who recite litanies or read from the scriptures. Oil is blessed with a prayer of thanksgiving. Dying persons' foreheads and hands are anointed. Prayers, Communion, and a final blessing complete the ceremony. The funeral ritual begins with vigils or wakes. Family and friends assemble for the Rosary. Caskets are taken to churches for the Mass of the Christian Burial, which begins when priests sprinkle caskets with Holy Water. Homilies recounting persons' lives, Communion, prayers, comments by family members, and a blessing with incense are included in the Mass. Processions travel to consecrated Roman Catholic cemeteries for the Rite of Committal, during which prayers and songs are offered.

Death and Funerals Among Different Cultures. The African American community generally perceives death as a celebration of life marking the end of a person's journey on Earth. Church funerals are an essential feature of church membership. Local church customs are followed. Vocal music by soloists and choirs are prominent in funeral services. Burials are highly emotional for mourners. Flowers, essential for grief, give visual comfort. Food and drink are provided by relatives or church members following burial services. Funer-

als are occasions for families to gather together.

Native American peoples have differing beliefs and customs regarding death and funerals. At death, which is sacred to the Dakota people, afterlife begins. The soul journeys south to the Ghost Road, which leads to the spirit land where deceased humans and animals reside. When the Dakota believe that death is near, people gather their valuables and other goods to give to family members and close friends. Impending deaths are acknowledged and proper appreciation is shown. Family and friends unite when persons die. Appropriate grief is shown through tearing clothes, cutting hair, scratching or cutting forearms or face, or wearing black.

First-generation Mexican Americans mourn more strictly than subsequent generations. These mourners adopt a restricted lifestyle that may last two years. Women wear black, pray daily, and are initially emotional. Subsequent generations of Mexican Americans, whose mourning period is shorter than that of first-generation Mexican Americans, use professional funeral services. Dress is not restricted, but prayer continues to be of importance. Funeral rites follow Roman Catholic ritual. Novenas are said for nine days following a person's death. Candles are lit for the deceased in churches. Death is an important time for assembling families.

Among Japanese Americans, go-betweens may represent families in dealings with Japanese funeral directors, the arbiters of proper funerals. Funeral services, which involve wakes, are often held in the evening for families and the community. Families attend the cremation of corpses or graveside services, which are often held at family plots. Ceremonies follow Buddhist or Christian traditions. *Koden*, a gift of money in small envelopes with donors' names, is customary at funerals. Gifts are given by bereaved families to guests attending funerals.

Funeral services in Italian American culture follow Roman Catholic ritual. The color and shape of floral arrangements have traditional significance. Funeral processions travel by the homes or workplaces of the deceased. Dating from the time of the horse-drawn carriage, gifts of money have been given to assist bereaved families. Funerals are a time for families to gather together.

—*Mary Pat Balkus*

BIBLIOGRAPHY

Barley, Nigel. *Dancing on the Grave.* London: John Murray, 1995.

Crissman, James K. *Death and Dying in Central Appalachia.* Urbana: University of Illinois Press, 1994.

Jackson, Charles O., ed. *Passing: The Vision of Death in America.* Westport, Conn.: Greenwood Press, 1977.

Jones, Constance. *R. I. P.: The Complete Book of Death and Dying.* New York: HarperCollins, 1997.

Metcalf, Peter, and Richard Huntington. *Celebrations of Death.* Cambridge, England: Cambridge University Press, 1961.

See also African Americans; Ancestor worship; Death; Family gatherings and reunions; Grief counseling; Japanese Americans; Jews; Native Americans; Roman Catholics; Widowhood.

Gangs

RELEVANT ISSUES: Children and child development; Parenting and family relationships

SIGNIFICANCE: For many urban and suburban youths, gangs, as a perceived safe harbor of recognition, acceptance, and economic viability, become a surrogate or substitute family

The existence of urban gangs is not a new phenomenon in the United States; however, the number of them has increased annually since World War II. In the 1980's and 1990's individual gangs not only increased in number, but also changed to include members often as young as eight years old, to admit groups composed of young women, to allow multiracial affiliation, to participate in more violent and drug-related activities, and to leave inner cities for the suburbs and smaller cities.

Defining a Gang. Although statistics are frequently inaccurate because not all groups are identified and because regions have no standardized definition of the term "gang," a 1994 U.S. Justice Department study of various major metropolitan regions reported the existence of 1,000 organized gangs with approximately 50,000 members in the 1970's and 5,000 gangs with 250,000 members in the 1980's. Added to their growing proportions, the proclivity among gangs for violence was revealed, as gang-related homicides increased by more than 250 percent from 1979 to 1990.

Although a variety of definitions exist, essentially, a gang includes three or more persons, bonded together by race, national origin, culture, or territory, who associate on a continual basis to commit criminal acts. Gang membership is tenuous and changes often; thus, the most successful gangs are those in a constant state of recruitment and those with a sufficient economic base, normally gained through drug trafficking.

Why Youths Join Gangs. Although the media's depiction of the gang member as an abused youth from a broken home in a disadvantaged neighborhood illustrates the profile of many young people involved in gang activity, it is not true across the board. Gang membership is not bound by age, sex, race, academic achievement, or economic status. What most gang members appear to have in common is that they come from biological family units that are either too restrictive or too loosely structured, which, consequently, results in youth's inevitably low sense of self-esteem. Thus, gangs become a source of identity and, more important, function as surrogate families and support units for their members.

Gangs deliver unqualified acceptance as effectively as they peddle drugs, and for many youths in the inner cities this total sense of identity may be the first they have ever encountered, since their own biological families may have deserted, ignored, or disowned them. Self-appointed, usually authoritarian gang leaders initiate almost all newcomers into membership, because having greater numbers increases their power base and personal prestige. To youths raised in the inner cities, where role models are often pimps, drug dealers, and racketeers because they have money and "respect," gang leaders and recruiters offer mystery, glamour, excitement, and economic rewards not found in menial jobs. Additionally, gangs offer a "home," drugs to use and sell, and weapons, often considered the mark of manhood.

Gangs Offer "Family Values." Much more tempting, however, are the intangibles dangled by gang recruiters. Gangs offer support and protection, a sense of belonging, a clear sense of association, structure, a valued role, and status. Thus, the message of gang affiliation speaks to basic human needs. Teenagers ache to belong, to be supported in their aspirations, and to be cared about, ingredients that are so imperative to their makeup that some are even willing to die for them. Consequently, gangs function as surrogate families for youths. As gang members, youths share a common collective identity, a common name, common symbols and signs, common turf, and a common language, much as a traditional family would. Aside

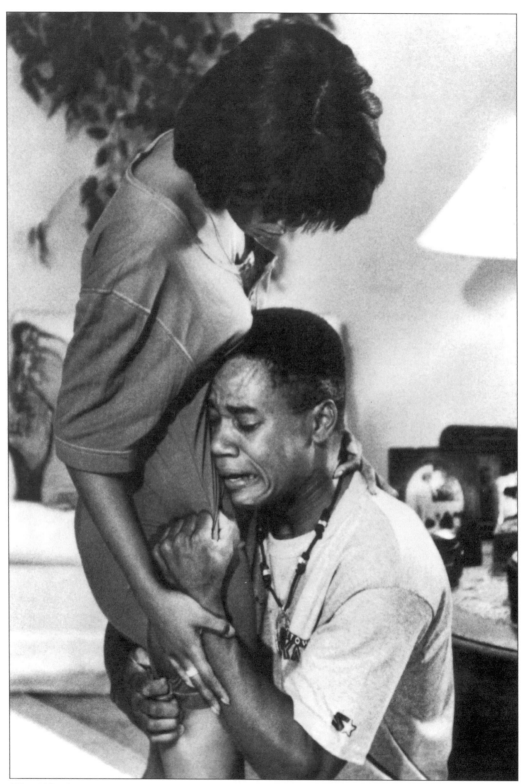

The 1991 film Boyz 'N the Hood *was a realistic exploration of family and gang problems in Los Angeles's rough South Central district.* (Museum of Modern Art, Film Stills Archive)

U.S. States with the Most Youth Gangs in 1997

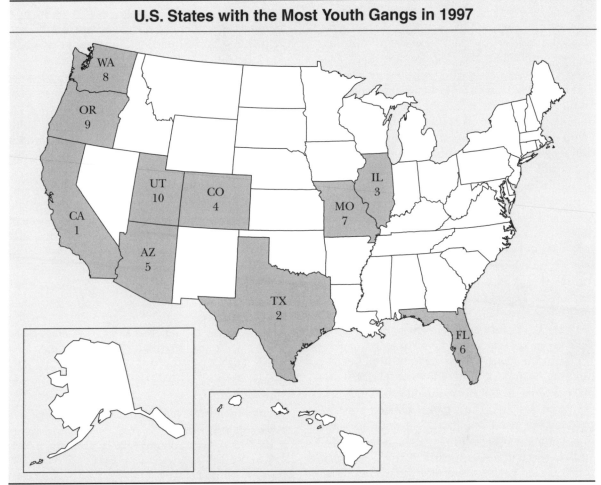

Source: Christian Science Monitor (July 7, 1997)
Note: Numbers indicate overall rankings.

from school, church, and family, peer groups are the most important vehicle for shaping values. Moreover, when peer groups and "family" are integrated, it is doubly effective in clarifying who the members are and what their roles in society are to be. As members of gang families, youths feel assured of support and respect however twisted such a lifestyle may seem.

Often gang membership is a family tradition, and recruiting becomes a ritualized custom. Some 80 percent of recruitment is informal through family members, usually cousins or older brothers whom the young desire to emulate. In addition, inducted gang members who become parents may dress their babies in gang colors and teach their toddlers gang signs and vocabulary.

For some, the myth of the United States as the great melting pot has given way to a perception of divergent groups held together by a weakened system of loosely defined laws. Thus, gang affiliation becomes a reaction to its membership's concept of social reality.

In this mode of thought, violence becomes legitimate and is viewed as a means of upward social mobility, of earning a reputation, and of "being somebody." Gang members often view middle-class values as a plot, created to permit discrimination against them. They tend to reject the well-intentioned advances of their middle-class teachers and social workers who advocate responsibility, ambition, and postponement of immediate gratification in the interests of long-term goals.

Other members are lured by gang life because of a loss of community standing. Many transplanted ethnic groups may have been important in the communities they left and are now thrust toward ignominy in the ghettos of the inner cities. The family name, which used to mean something in the old country, is no longer of any consequence. Thus, youths seek identity through gang membership, and the trend becomes cyclical: Society rejects the parent, the parent rejects the child, and the child rejects society. Additionally, those striving to "make it" in a new environment are frequently preoccupied with their work or careers, and both biological parents are often employed, thus leaving their children bored, unsupervised, and with enough time on their hands to seek out neighborhood gangs. Another factor affecting this group, an economic one, becomes part of the appeal of gangs. As children observe their parents working hard and having nothing to show for it, the lure of quick riches through drug deals for gangs is an immediate attraction.

Life in the Gang. Gangs are substitute families for their members, although these families may make extensive and unreasonable demands and are often abusive. Thus, gangs replace not only parental but also disciplinary figures in the traditional family. Consequently, goals, identified roles, and responsibilities are clearly defined. Violence, romanticized by television and the movies, is accepted and required behavior and the only real authority in the inner city for gang members.

Gang affiliation is marked by stages. Stage one is that of youths who hang around gangs and long to be members. Stage two is that of persons who by family tradition or prowess are destined to become members. Stage three is that of affiliates or "gang bangers," active members in groups. Stage four is that of hard-core members, who live only for the gang and are noted as "down for the hood."

Initiation into gangs is marked by rituals, much as rites of passage might be marked by biological families. Even the term used to describe the actions of novice gang members, "courting the gang," connotes a type of ritualistic behavior. Initiations, which can be anything from simple fights to drive-by shootings or murders, offer symbolic evidence of potential members' manhood. Once initiates become members, they are permitted to wear the gangs' colors and accepted attire, usually oversized to create "sagging." Additionally, new members are encouraged to "mark their territory" by painting graffiti images of the gangs' symbols and language.

Qualities revered by gangs include physical prowess, bravery, smartness or the ability to con, shrewdness, repartee, risk-taking behavior, freedom from constraints, and independence. Thus, most behavior is emotion-motivated, but without having learned appropriate feeling responses, this behavior is often impulsive and egocentric. Although limited responsibility is required for belonging, the accepted fantasy among gang members is that they are leaders of men, protectors of young children, and deterrents to racial and ethnic prejudices. Unfortunately, there is often a gap between their aspirations and their ability to achieve them.

—*Joyce Duncan*

BIBLIOGRAPHY

Arnold, David O., ed. *The Sociology of Subcultures.* Berkeley, Calif.: Glendessary Press, 1970.

Bloch, Herbert Aaron. *The Gang: A Study in Adolescent Behavior.* Westport, Conn.: Greenwood Press, 1976.

Cummings, Scott, and Daniel Monti. *Gangs: The Origins and Impact of Contemporary Youth Gangs in the United States.* Albany: State University of New York Press, 1993.

Decker, Scott. *Life in the Gang: Family, Friends and Violence.* New York: Cambridge University Press, 1996.

Yablonsky, Lewis. *The Violent Gang.* Baltimore: Penguin Books, 1972.

See also Abandonment of the family; Domestic violence; Dysfunctional families; Extended families; Juvenile delinquency; Prison inmates; Rites of passage.

Gay and lesbian families

RELEVANT ISSUES: Children and child development; Parenting and family relationships; Sociology

SIGNIFICANCE: While no connection has been found between parents' sexual orientation and negative consequences for their children, children are harmed by the homophobic practice of removing them from the home of their gay or lesbian parents solely because of the parents' sexual orientation

The nuclear family is one of many different family forms found in the United States and Canada. Single-parent, two-parent, and repartnered families, both heterosexual and homosexual, reflect the permeable kinship structure of the North American family. Family structure or composition is but one of many factors related to children's well-being. The emotional and financial health of families has been found to have greater influence on children's self-esteem than family structure alone.

Best Interests of the Child. The question of what constitutes the "best interests of the child" is a primary concern expressed in custody and adoption litigation. The concept of "best interests" re-

The right to be parents has been the subject of a long legal struggle among members of the gay and lesbian community. (James L. Shaffer)

fers to both the physical and emotional well-being of children. Often courts have assumed that healthy parent-child relationships are precluded by homophobic societal attitudes. Homophobia is defined as an irrational fear of homosexuals that is exhibited covertly and overtly in verbal and physical aggression toward or avoidance of lesbian women and gay men. Homophobia also operates when courts fear that children raised by homosexuals may become homosexual themselves. Assumptions made in courtrooms about the difficulties children will likely experience if they are raised by lesbian mothers or gay fathers are not based on what is known about such children.

Frequent concerns about gay and lesbian parenting focus on three main areas: children's gender identity, gender roles, and sexual orientation. Gender identity refers to one's self-concept as being female or male. Gender roles refer to socially prescribed behaviors and attitudes considered appropriate for females and males in a given culture. Sexual orientation refers to a person's emotional or sexual attraction toward others. When people are sexually attracted to both men and women, their orientation is called "bisexual." When attracted to the opposite sex, people are described as having a "heterosexual" orientation. When females are attracted to females (and are thus lesbians) and men are attracted to men (and are thus gay), they are said to have a "homosexual" orientation. Gender identity, gender roles, and sexual orientation must be considered separately when describing human behavior. When children do not exhibit prescribed behavioral gender roles, they can still have a clearly defined gender identity. Likewise, sexual orientation does not determine gender roles.

Children of lesbian mothers are as certain about

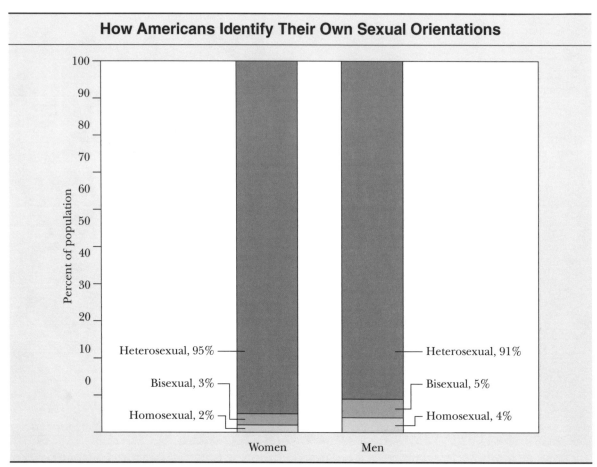

How Americans Identify Their Own Sexual Orientations

Percent of population

Women — Heterosexual, 95% — Bisexual, 3% — Homosexual, 2%

Men — Heterosexual, 91% — Bisexual, 5% — Homosexual, 4%

Source: *The Janus Report* (1993)

their gender identity as children of heterosexual mothers. No evidence of gender identity disorder has been linked to children growing up in lesbian households. In terms of gender roles, boys and girls in both heterosexual and homosexual families express preferences for gender specific toys in equal degrees. In regard to sexual orientation, the proportion of daughters who identify as lesbians is generally equal in heterosexual and homosexual families, while 90 percent of adult sons of gay fathers identify as heterosexuals, reflecting the one-in-ten estimate for the general population. No causal connection has been found between parents' sexual orientation and negative consequences for their children. What does cause harm to children is the homophobic practice of removing them from the home of their parents solely because of the parents' sexual orientation.

Parent-Child Relationships. Two primary influences on children's social-emotional development are the type of attachment formed between infants and caregivers and the parenting style of caregivers. Attachment theory points to the quality of interaction between caregivers and children during infancy that can foster secure or insecure attachment or bonding. When primary attachment figures are responsive to children's vocalizations and distress signals, children are said to form an internal representation of the self and environment as trustworthy and good.

Research on parenting style has consistently pointed to authoritative parenting as a positive influence on self-concept formation in children. Authoritative parents combine firm control with warmth and acceptance of children. Authoritarian parents are overly controlling and lacking in warmth, while permissive parents are either indulgent (showing great warmth while exerting little control) or neglectful (showing little warmth while exerting little control). Adolescents from authoritative families have the lowest levels of emotional distress and the highest levels of social-emotional adjustment as compared to adolescents

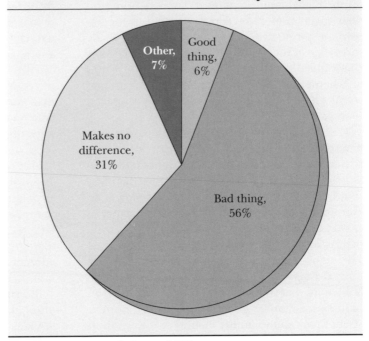

Women's Attitudes Toward Gay Adoption

Other, 7%
Good thing, 6%
Makes no difference, 31%
Bad thing, 56%

Source: The Pew Research Center (1998)
Note: A cross-section of women were asked if the trend of more gays and lesbians adopting children was a good thing or a bad thing for society.

from permissive or authoritarian families. Neglectful parenting is associated with the most negative outcomes for psychological well-being in children, regardless of parental sexual orientation.

In a 1995 study that compared children conceived by donor insemination and raised by lesbian couples with a control group of children from heterosexual dual-parent families, cognitive functioning and behavioral adjustment of the children in both groups was the same. Likewise, a 1997 study in the United Kingdom found that children raised in lesbian two-parent and single-parent families from infancy on showed that mothers' lesbian sexual orientation had no negative impact on the quality of parenting or their children's social-emotional health.

Children growing up in lesbian and gay families have frequently experienced their parents' divorce. In trying to deduce specific effects of lesbian and gay parental figures on children, it is essential to distinguish between outcomes for children growing up in nontraditional families, such as divorced families, from those of specifically gay and lesbian families. Children growing up in single-parent families differ depending on their social context or support system, prior discordant parental relationships leading up to divorce, age at time of divorce, and gender. The key factor in children's well-being after divorce relates to whether or not divorce diminishes parental conflict and improves childrens' relationship with each parent.

The literature on stepfamilies concludes that heterosexual stepmother families generally experience more problematic stepparent-child relationships than heterosexual stepfather families. Children brought up in lesbian households, however, frequently view a mother's female partner as an additional family member rather than as a competitor of an absent father. In addition, in their 1997 book *Growing Up in a Lesbian Family: Effects on Child Development*, Fiona Tasker and Susan Golombok found that young adults brought up in lesbian postdivorce families generally were more positive about their family identity than were young adults brought up in heterosexual postdivorce families. A key component of young adults' acceptance of their family identity is the presence of open and positive attitudes toward gay issues on the part of their lesbian mothers.

Extended Family and Friendship Networks. In contrast to more traditional perspectives, research suggests that children brought up by gay and lesbian parents benefit from their own experience of diversity in that they may be more open toward and appreciative of differences in a modern multicultural society. Generally, younger children in lesbian-mother households do not encounter more teasing or bullying than children from heterosexual single-parent or stepfamily backgrounds. Young people in gay and lesbian families, however, have reported peer group teasing about their own sexuality during early adolescence, before they have established a clear sexual orientation with their peers.

Sexual orientation may be viewed in three ways: desire for someone of the same gender, sexual contact with a partner of the same gender, and identification as a lesbian, gay, or bisexual person. Children brought up in lesbian families were found to be no more likely than children from heterosexual families to be attracted to persons of the same gender. Nevertheless, Tasker and Golom-

bok found that significantly more young people from lesbian-mother families than from heterosexual families reported having experienced a sexual relationship with someone of the same gender. Young adults from lesbian households were more open to same-sex attraction and were more likely to act on their feelings toward a same-sex partner than were young adults from heterosexual families. Young adults from lesbian-mother families were no more likely than young adults from heterosexual families to seek professional mental health care, and they reported rates of anxiety or depression that were equal to those of the general population. Social factors may account more for the willingness of persons raised in lesbian-mother families to experience same-gender relationships than for the actual experience of same-gender attraction or the development of a bisexual or homosexual identity.

Research is needed to compare children born into lesbian and gay families or adopted by single lesbians or gay men with children born into seemingly heterosexual families that experience divorce and subsequent primary parental relationships with a same sex partner. The key point is that negative outcomes solely based on parental sexual orientation cannot be assumed for children brought up in lesbian and gay families.

Homophobia and Mentally Healthy Families. When forming gay or lesbian families, homosexuals must frequently exercise greater awareness and intentionality than heterosexuals who form families, which is both expected and "normal." In her article "Sexual Identity and the Discontents of Difference" in *Ethnic and Cultural Diversity Among Lesbians and Gay Men*, Carla Trujillo describes the "triple consciousness" of gay and lesbian identity formation and subsequent decision making. First, lesbians and gays must contend on a daily basis with how society views homosexuals. Second, gays and lesbians must distinguish between society's reflected appraisals of them and how they actually see themselves. Third, and perhaps most challenging, is the necessity of resolving the cognitive dissonance between how gays and lesbians see themselves in response to societal messages. These three levels interact and are continually present as gays and lesbians seek their "true inner selves." The dividends in character formation and empathy resulting from this "inner work" can include a greater appreciation of difference as well as a more conscious form of parenting. Often, such families also reach out to one another so that an extended family network is constructed involving deeply felt loyalty and comfort.

The most pernicious effects of homophobia deny the status of "normal human beings" to those who deviate from prescribed sex roles. This fluidity of identity, when seen as a positive thing, can provide children and adults the freedom to acknowledge a wider range of potentials and life paths than traditionally presented. Of course any description of gay and lesbian families must be situated in a particular cultural, ethnic, racial, and social-class context. While individuals have a wide range of public and private identities, gay and lesbian families by definition are to some extent political, public entities. The healthy identity of the gay and lesbian family requires clear self-knowledge by each family member and, ideally, provides optimal freedom for individual expression and affirmation of others.   —*Carol A. Radich*

BIBLIOGRAPHY

Brophy, J. "New Families, Judicial Decision-making, and Children's Welfare." *Canadian Journal of Women and the Law* 5 (1992).

D'Augelli, A. R., and C. J. Patterson, eds. *Lesbian, Gay, and Bisexual Identities over the Lifespan: Psychological Perspectives.* New York: Oxford University Press, 1995.

Elkind, David. "School and Family in the Postmodern World." In *Child Growth and Development (1997-1998)*, edited by Ellen N. Junn and Chris J. Boyztzis. 4th ed. Guildford, Conn.: Dushkin/McGraw-Hill, 1997.

Greene, Beverly, ed. *Ethnic and Cultural Diversity Among Lesbians and Gay Men.* Vol. 3 in *Psychological Perspectives on Lesbian and Gay Issues.* Thousand Oaks, Calif.: Sage Publications, 1997.

Martin, A. *The Lesbian and Gay Parenting Handbook.* New York: HarperCollins, 1993.

Tasker, Fiona, and Susan Golombok. *Growing Up in a Lesbian Family: Effects on Child Development.* New York: Guilford Press, 1997.

See also Alternative family types; Cohabitation; Couples; Domestic partners; Family values; Marriage laws; Single-parent families.

Gender inequality

RELEVANT ISSUES: Children and child development; Parenting and family relationships

SIGNIFICANCE: Even as more and more women work outside the home, gender roles and gender socialization consolidate women's unequal status in the family

The family is often described as the most basic unit of society, with significant economic, religious and cultural implications. In the latter half of the twentieth century many of the presuppositions about what constitutes a family were called into question, resulting in passionate debates about the values and characteristics of the American family. One area that garnered significant attention was the relationship between males and females in the family—among both adults and children. In particular, many women called into question their traditional roles as mothers and wives, which tied them to domestic labor and child rearing. Concerns were also raised as to the impact of subtle gender cues within the family on the development of girls and boys and how these might promote further inequality.

Family Evolution in the Twentieth Century. Although it may not have always matched with reality, the popular definition of a middle-class family in the 1950's had clear contours. The family was a heterosexual unit consisting of a husband who was considered the "head" of the household and a wife who was its "heart." Fathers worked outside the home and provided for their families financially. Mothers managed the domestic chores, including cooking, cleaning, and child raising. Fathers oversaw the finances and disciplined the children, while mothers provided emotional support. There was a well-defined division of labor and hierarchy in the family. In addition, fathers were the role models for boys and mothers the role models for girls. Gender was a key determinant in the social reproduction of family roles. This caricature, spurred by television as it came of age in the 1950's and supported by mainstream religions and culture, became a lasting ideal for the North American family.

In the 1960's increasing numbers of women began to question the inequality of opportunity and rewards created by the division of labor in the

From an early age children are trained to think in terms of separate male and female domains. (James L. Shaffer)

middle-class family. The notion that a "man's home is his castle" left women wondering why their equally hard work did not result in equal standing in the family. Women became openly frustrated that their options in life were few and restrictive. In *The Feminine Mystique* (1963), Betty Friedan expressed the feelings of many women when she questioned the promise of fulfillment to be found in housework.

As women's options increased, the social norms of the male-dominated households of the previous generation remained. While women won legal rights, they were expected, because of prevailing social norms, to put their husbands and families before their careers. The formation of the National Organization for Women (NOW) in the mid-1960's, which was led by Friedan, was symbolic of the mood of many women. NOW was born of the frustration over the choice women faced between motherhood and their careers.

In the 1970's, family life came under increasing scrutiny. Topics that threatened the sacred status of the traditional family were opened up for debate. In 1972 *Ms.* magazine was launched as the first real alternative to a genre of women's magazines centered on domestic life that dated back to the turn of the century. Women's magazines had historically focused on women's role in the family; they had included articles on how to cook, how to raise children, and how to please husbands, while avoiding politics. Advertising campaigns for appliances and cleaning products exploited women's

Now largely relics of the past, "men only" signs were always more common than their "women only" counterparts. (James L. Shaffer)

domestic status. *Ms.* openly questioned traditional female roles in the family and society and adopted the feminist rallying cry: "The personal is political." In 1977 Marilyn French authored *The Women's Room*, a national best-seller that chronicled the frustrations of a wife and mother in what would have been considered at the time to be an ideal family. Covering the period when the women's movement came of age between the 1950's and 1970's, *The Women's Room* resonated with so many women's experiences of family life that it became a classic of feminist literature.

Marriage Contract. While some feminists have sharply criticized traditional marriage as an unfair work contract, others have sought to alter the terms of the relationship. While membership in poor families has always required that both husbands and wives work, in traditional middle-class families only men worked outside the home. This created an unequal economic situation in that men performed paid labor while women performed unpaid domestic labor. The psychological result of this arrangement was that men were deemed to control the money that they had earned while women had to ask for compensation or even seek allowances from their husbands. The flow of money in traditional single-income families only served to further perpetuate the asymmetrical power relationship between husbands and wives. In addition, many legal and commercial activities presumed that men held the family purse strings. Some merchants required a husband's consent for major purchases. Nineteenth century laws allowed men to revoke their wives' purchases if they deemed them frivolous. This economic paternalism lingered long after the laws formalizing it fell by the wayside, so that women continued to have difficulty in acting as autonomous economic actors such as in the acquisition of credit.

Children and Gender. Much research has been done on the impact of gender in the development of children. It is known that gender involves much learned behavior. Without overt training, children by the age of two can identify the gender of human images—a powerful indicator of the significance of gender in North American society. From the moment children are born and wrapped in pink or blue blankets, many overt and subtle social cues exist that help mold male and female behavior. While establishing strong gender differentia-

tion does not necessarily entail inequality, it can lead to gender biases. For example, if young girls play only with dolls, if the predominant images they see are of women as mothers, and if they are told that they will grow up to be wives and mothers, the socialization they must overcome is great. Fathers and mothers also act as significant family role models in helping to create possible life and career choices for their daughters and sons. The clear differentiation of children by gender activities has allowed commercial advertising to carefully target the toy market and has helped to socialize boys and girls so that girls do not identify with many career tracks. Throughout the latter half of the twentieth century educators and the media have become more sensitive to gender images and presented women as capable of flourishing in a variety of careers.

Divorce. The inequalities of marriage do not end when couples divorce. Divorce represents a vexing issue for the women's movement. Most feminists through the 1970's fought to liberalize divorce laws as a means to get women out of abusive relationships. However, the financial impact of divorce was often felt hardest by women, because women in traditional families had little work experience outside the home and were often responsible for raising their children. Public transfer payments in the form of welfare and Aid to Families with Dependent Children (AFDC) were sharply cut in the 1980's and 1990's, while private transfer payments in the form of child support by divorced fathers was too often withheld or minimal, giving rise to the term "deadbeat dads." However, research evidence has indicated that the economic misfortune of divorced women may be short-lived and that in the long term many divorced women fair well financially and emotionally.

—*Maurice Hamington*

BIBLIOGRAPHY

Beneria, Lourdes, and Catharine R. Stimpson. *Women, Households, and the Economy.* New Brunswick, N.J.: Rutgers University Press, 1987.

Coontz, Stephanie. *The Way We Never Were: American Families and the Nostalgia Trap.* New York: Basic Books, 1992.

DeVault, Marjorie L. *Feeding the Family: The Social Organization of Caring as Gendered Work.* Chicago: University of Chicago Press, 1991.

Dornbusch, Sanford M., and Myra H. Strober. *Feminism, Children, and the New Families.* New York: Guilford Press, 1988.

Ehrensaft, Diane. *Parenting Together: Men and Women Sharing the Care of Their Children.* Urbana: University of Illinois Press, 1990.

French, Marilyn. *The Women's Room.* New York: Ballantine Books, 1977.

Friedan, Betty. *The Feminine Mystique.* New York: W. W. Norton, 1963.

Thorne, Barrie, with Marilyn Yalom. *Rethinking the Family: Some Feminist Questions.* Boston: Northeastern University Press, 1992.

See also Cult of True Womanhood; Dual-earner families; Equalitarian families; Equality of children; Family economics; Feminization of poverty; Gender longevity; Men's roles; Son preference; Women's roles.

Gender longevity

RELEVANT ISSUES: Aging; Demographics; Health and medicine; Parenting and family relationships

SIGNIFICANCE: Because the life expectancy of females is about seven years longer than that of males in North America, gender longevity increases the likelihood of widowhood and influences many other aspects of family life

Because of their longer life expectancy, more than 50 percent of North American women sixty-five years of age and older are widowed, whereas the rate is only 13.6 percent for men in the same age group. Men typically die before their wives do. U.S. and Canadian census data indicate that men tend to marry women who are, on average, four years younger than they are. This increases the likelihood that women will be left as widows. Women more than sixty years old far outnumber men, and widows are the single largest group in the older American population.

Life Expectancy and Gender Roles. The United States and Canada are aging societies. The U.S. National Center for Health Statistics reported that in 1996 life expectancy reached a record high of 76.1 years in the United States and 79 years in Canada. This compares to 80 years in Japan, 64 in the Russian Federation, and 54 in Haiti. In most industrialized societies there are almost as many elderly people as younger adults and children, meaning that the proportion of elderly people in the population is increasing. The implications of this fact cannot be understated. Aging as a social phenomenon will receive increasing attention in coming years. Increased longevity alters the social structure. Because women's life expectancy has increased more rapidly than that of men, there were 150 women for every 100 men sixty-five years of age and older in 1996 and more than 250 women for every 100 men eighty-five years of age and older.

One implication is that there will be more older people living in more varied family, community, and institutional settings than was previously the case. Kinship structures will become more complex as more households contain such combinations as father with son, child with great-grandparent, sister with sister-in-law, or former husband with former wife.

Health, Gender, and Longevity. If male and female employment and family roles become more similar and women experience the stresses and risks that are thought to cause earlier death in men, the gap between the life expectancies of the sexes may narrow. Research on sex differences in the causes of death has indicated that women may be less vulnerable to death for genetic reasons, but this has been difficult to prove scientifically. Health trends among males and females in North America have indicated that the lifestyles of men and women have become more similar; in particular, women's lives have become more like men's. This change has unfortunate implications for women's health and longevity. For example, during the mid-1990's women smoked almost as much as men. While smoking among men had declined by almost half, the rate for women had remained constant. Among older smokers, men have been twice as likely to quit as women. Thus, it is no surprise that lung cancer has almost equaled breast cancer as a leading cause of death for women.

Smoking has been only one indicator of the greater stresses women encountered during the mid-1990's. Many studies of adult women in the labor force showed that in addition to bearing the same or greater stress at work (due to lower wages and slower advancement), women were still doing more work around the home and taking on more of the burdens of child rearing than were the men in their lives. The role conflict created by the responsibilities of home and job has affected both women and men, but women have continued to feel the stress of this role conflict more heavily. Although there have been some improvements, the situation has remained unbalanced and more stressful for women. In general, women have taken on occupational roles in addition to their homemaker roles in most households, while men have retained their traditional occupational roles, while accepting few additional responsibilities at home. Only broader sharing of parental and household responsibilities can benefit the whole family. Extensive evidence has indicated that role sharing enriches most family relationships.

Gender and Age Stratification. Age is a factor of social inequality when persons of different ages are treated differently or channeled into statuses and roles that carry differing degrees of prestige and power. All human societies are stratified by age and gender. As individual persons advance through their lives, age and gender roles interact in patterning their behavior and consciousness. "Act your age," "be a man," and "she's a real lady" are examples of familiar expressions that let persons know whether their behavior conforms to the

Recognition that breast cancer is a leading cause of death among women has led to increasing public demands to find cures. (Ben Klaffke)

The greater longevity of women has meant that many more women than men become widowed. (James L. Shaffer)

role expectations associated with their sex and age. People often discover that certain roles are not open to them because of their age or sex. They may be forbidden to drive a car or serve their country in war, and they may be forced to retire from their jobs. All societies differentiate among their members on the basis of gender and age. Men and women of different ages are accorded differing amounts of income, power, or prestige,

and these patterns contribute to the society's system of stratification. For example, a man who has gained the position of chief executive officer of a big company firm will have money, power, and great prestige. When he retires, he may still have great wealth, but he will lose the prestige associated with his position. Should he die and leave all his wealth to his wife, his widow will have the wealth and the prestige that comes with it, but she will have little power unless the fortune is so large that she can become a philanthropist whom others petition for gifts.

After their working years are over, men tend to suffer a greater decline in social status than women, because they have derived much of their personal identity from their occupational roles. Although retirement generally presents men with more difficult social and emotional adjustments than women, most studies of the effects of retirement and loss of occupational roles show that all but a small minority of people adjust to retirement with few lasting negative effects. As the elderly enter their last years, however, the number of men decreases rapidly. Widows often must live in old-age communities and nursing homes that have few men. Thus, in old age the issues of gender and age stratification converge: The problems of older persons are largely the problems of older women. For example, more than 40 percent of all women age sixty-five and over live alone. For many of them the darker side of aging is loneliness and the fear that failing health will lead to increased dependence on others. Modern societies need to develop social policies directed toward relieving the burdens of the very old, especially those who are alone and cannot call upon family members for support or resources.   —*Robert D. Bryant*

BIBLIOGRAPHY

Bleier, Ruth. *Science and Gender: A Critique of Biology and Its Theories on Women.* New York: Pergamon Press, 1984.

Brotman, H. B. *Every Ninth American.* Washington, D.C.: U.S. Government Printing Office, 1982.

Epstein, Cynthia Fuchs. *Deceptive Distinctions: Sex, Gender, and the Social Order.* New Haven, Conn.: Yale University Press, 1989.

Goffman, Erving. *Gender Advertisements.* Cambridge, Mass.: Harvard University Press, 1979.

Myerhoff, Barbara. *Number Our Days.* New York: Simon & Schuster, 1978.

Riley, Matilda W. "Age Strata in Social Systems." In *Handbook of Aging and the Social Sciences*, edited by R. Binstock and E. Shanas. 2d ed. New York: Van Nostrand Reinhold, 1985.

See also Ageism; Aging and elderly care; Empty nest syndrome; Family caregiving; Family life cycle; Gender inequality; Life expectancy; Marriage squeeze; Midlife crises; Nursing and convalescent homes; Retirement communities; Widowhood; Women's roles.

Genealogy

RELEVANT ISSUES: Kinship and genealogy; Parenting and family relationships

SIGNIFICANCE: Searching for ancestors and learning more about family members through tracing blood lines has always been a fundamental way of understanding family life

Genealogy is one of the most popular ways of understanding family life. Family members have a natural curiosity about their ancestors and about the longevity of their families. They take pride in learning about their families' achievements and struggles, and they are sometimes surprised to find that they are related to famous people or to others who have been successful. Genealogy is the search for roots—an idea popularized by author Alex Haley, when his book *Roots* (1976) and the television series based on it stimulated Americans to think about their place in history and the role their families have played in their neighborhoods, communities, and country.

Since antiquity family lines, or genealogy, have been transmitted through the generation of oral testimony and the written record. The Bible, for example, not only has many passages of genealogy, but families also have used their Bibles to record their lines of descent. Greeks and Romans attributed their ancestry to the gods and sometimes to animals such as bears and wolves. Genealogy has been important in establishing family claims to property. In countries such as England, genealogy has determined social class and position.

Genealogy helps to ground families, to give them a sense of where they came from and where they might be going. Genealogy is inclusive. Because it traces bloodlines, it is important to find out about every family member, even if the genealogical search begins with interest in just one family member. Genealogy provides a sense of continuity with the past, or it can be used to establish connections for families that want to know more about themselves. Everyone, every family, has stories to tell, adventures to be relived. Each generation treasures memories of a family's journey through life; but each generation also forgets. Searching for roots helps preserve and even expand families' stories. While individuals find out about their families, they also discover aspects of themselves.

Libraries often have local history and genealogy sections in which amateur historians can begin their research. Books and articles about the subject of genealogy are abundant, and persons with very little research training often become experts about searching public records for evidence of their families' past. Historians, biographers, and other researchers often hire genealogists to investigate the history of families, and certain organizations—most notably the Church of Jesus Christ of Latter-day Saints (Mormons)—not only have genealogical records but also publish guides for individuals seeking to discover more about their ancestry.

Where Genealogists Begin. There is no one beginning to genealogical study. There are probably as many reasons for studying genealogy as there are genealogists. For example, there may be a death in the family, and one or more family members may wish to put together some kind of remembrance of the deceased. Stories about the departed person may be collected through conversations, informal interviews (sometimes tape recorded), and note taking. The genealogist may wonder if all the anecdotes about a family member are true or whether they tell the whole story of the person's life. When this stage is reached, the genealogist may begin to ask questions that make the study of genealogy a more formal and rigorous matter. The genealogist wants to know when and where certain events happened, who else was present, or who else in the family might have information about the event or the person. Sooner or later, beginning genealogists will look for a way of verifying stories and events and of learning more about them.

Before beginning a search for records outside the home, many genealogists advocate making a statement or list of family facts, beginning with the current generation. This account contains information such as dates of birth, marriage, divorce, military service, death—and almost any significant event in a family's life. Family occupations, places of residence, and membership in organizations are also recorded. Next to each piece of data

about the family is the source of the information: a father, mother, uncle, family friend, or neighbor. Sources are fully identified by first, middle, and last names. If sources can remember how they came by family information, the genealogist can add this information to the account. It is important to realize that genealogists not only record what they know but also establish their own records for future generations, so that interested family members may carry on or fill in aspects of the genealogical account that are incomplete. Keeping a meticulous, ongoing journal of a genealogical investigation not only ensures that no vital information is forgotten or lost but also clarifies for the genealogist exactly those areas in which further genealogical investigation is needed.

If there is enough data, a file for each family member can be established, working from the present generation backward. It is crucial that genealogists have some idea how far into the past they wish to go. In part, deciding this is based on what genealogists want to know and what family stories they may wish to reconstruct. For example, many Americans want to know how their families came to the United States and how their families struck roots. Such a genealogical story might take researchers one, two, or three generations back in time. Going beyond three generations is likely to take considerable time and perseverance, since researchers must then go well beyond families' living memory.

The Search for Records. Most families—even if they do not have members interested in genealogy—have records that would aid a genealogical investigation. The most common records in a family's possession are birth certificates, death certificates, passports, voter registration cards, property deeds, tax returns, various kinds of legal papers, letters, and maybe even diaries or journals. These items give full names, dates, and addresses that aid genealogists in assembling a chronology of a person's or a family's history.

Other family possessions can easily be overlooked because they are not thought of as records. A family Bible may record significant events in family history. A family's books may have dates or other comments in the margins that help to date or place the whereabouts of family members. Family photographs may have dates and other explanatory information on them. Even old bills and

Photographs and original documents are important parts of a family's genealogical record. (Arkent Archive)

"archive." Even a postcard with a postmark on it may date an important event or journey.

A trip to the library yields a collection of books on how to find records of family life. If a family has an immigrant background, there may well be passenger ship records that can be checked. If a family had a business, there may be records in a county courthouse. Many how-to genealogy books provide addresses and phone numbers of government offices that can assist in the search for family records.

Genealogical research can be time-consuming and sometimes frustrating, but genealogical researchers have an advantage over other kinds of researchers. If genealogists are researching the life of family members, it is easier to obtain vital records because the genealogists are family members. In other words, many kinds of records are open only to family members. It is thus important for genealogists to have at hand proof of their relationship to the research subject.

Various ethnic groups also have organizations that can assist genealogists, so that Polish families, for example, can enlist the aid of their church, which may have records of christenings as well as newsletters and other materials that contain information about family members. Parish records in Poland can also be accessed to trace a family's origins in the "old country." For Poles and other groups, the Mormon Church has microfilmed records that are deposited in Family History Centers throughout the country. Not to be overlooked are foreign consulates and embassies, which can sometimes direct callers to sources of information in the foreign countries from which their families emigrated. The Swedish Information Service, for example, publishes a newsletter and accepts queries.

The National Archives in Washington, D.C., has census records that may help genealogists to track

receipts may have dates and addresses that help to recapture where a family has lived and worked.

Families do not always realize that records may also be stored in old trunks and other containers long forgotten but still accessible in cabinets, attics, basements, and barns. Sometimes, just talking to relatives produces reminiscences and vital information about the location of family records. Most families have an archive—a treasury of their history—but they do not think they have one because it is not located in one place and no one would think to call the evidence of a family's life an down family members. Internet research has made it possible to have access to research libraries all over the world, and many reference desks at these libraries respond to e-mail inquiries. It is also possible to do an independent Internet genealogical investigation. Sometimes such an investigation is as simple as typing in a name, which may turn up the results of genealogical investigations that include the genealogist's family. Of course, the more common the family name, the less likely it is that such a search will be specific enough to result in obtaining data about an individual family or family member.

New York City, where many immigrants first landed, is especially rich in records. The main branch of the New York Public Library has a section devoted to genealogical searches, and the library can also be accessed on the Internet. For most genealogical purposes, however, a visit to the library is necessary to read microfilm rolls that contain census reports, marriage records, and other documents. A Mormon Family History Center may be the closest record depository for the novice genealogist.

Making a Record: The Role of Oral History. Some genealogists find that the easiest way to begin keeping records of family history is to talk with family members—individually or in groups, depending on what seems most practical and comfortable for genealogists and family members. Taking notes and recording conversations are usually essential. Notes often take the form of follow-up questions while the tape recorder frees the genealogist/interviewer from having to summarize or report on conversations. Experienced genealogists know that no detail is too trivial. Family members may say they know nothing, but once they begin to reminisce, details from long ago suddenly surface. Experienced genealogists also know that they must be patient—that family members may at first be reluctant and even embarrassed to talk. However, once they are primed with a few questions or the genealogists relay information to them that they have discovered about the family, then more family members begin to open up, realizing that they are part of an exciting effort to reclaim or to strengthen family identity. If they come to feel part of the genealogical process, they often go out of their way to contribute new material and leads for additional research.

Many books about oral history provide helpful tips about how to interview people. These books often advise persons not to begin oral histories until genealogists have compiled a full account of what they already know about their families. Such written reports help genealogists to focus on what is to be asked in oral interviews. Once the oral interview process begins, genealogists let family members know that they will be kept informed and that the information they gather will be shared at regular intervals. Sharing information may also be the occasion for reinterviewing family members, for as genealogists master their material, it is likely that additional questions will arise.

Oral historians suggest that beginning interviews with open-ended questions is best. Formulations such as "What do you remember about . . .?" give interviewees time to answer the question in an informal and relaxed manner. Very gradually questions can become more specific as genealogists probe more deeply into family issues or personalities. Some interviewers like to write out all their questions in advance; others prefer a more spontaneous approach and jot down broad categories of questions or topics. The order of questions also helps to elicit maximum information. Some interviewers begin with simple questions about facts, trying to nail down dates and places, names and relationships.

Oral history is more like an art than a science. This means that interviewers must be sensitive to what family members want to say, making sure not to rush interviewees or to interrupt them. It is inevitable in all interviews that there will be digressions, when—from the interviewer's point of view—the conversation gets off track. In most cases, genealogists advise that it is best to allow interviewees to digress. At a pause in the conversation it is always possible to redirect the conversation back to the genealogist's areas of concern.

Oral historians recommend that before and after interviews, interviewers should ask about written records. Often interviewees can supply additional documents after their memory has been stimulated. Documents may be not only written records but also family photo albums and other souvenirs (for example, a trophy, a badge, an award).

Although tape recorders have become very common in oral history interviews, genealogists suggest that interviewers ask for permission to re-

Photo albums are an important part of many family genealogical records. (Hazel Hankin)

cord interviews. Most people recognize the tape recorder as a way to keep an accurate record, but they may feel more comfortable being recorded in a quiet and perhaps private place. Sometimes, genealogists have found it helpful to joke with family members to ease their self-consciousness or wariness about interview sessions. Note taking while recording also takes the interviewee's mind off the tape recorder and gives a nervous interviewer the opportunity to focus his or her eyes on a notepad. Taking notes is also helpful during moments of awkward silence, when genealogists or interviewees are at a loss for words.

Oral historians find that if rapport is established, the results of oral interviews can be very fruitful. Sometimes playing back tapes or transcribing them stimulates genealogists to ask new questions or to embark on new areas of investigation. Writing up reactions to interviews may also energize genealogists and open up new areas of family history. It can be very time-consuming to type up complete transcripts of interviews. Genealogists sometimes call on family members for help. If that option is not available, genealogists may index their tapes: Instead of writing out word for word what was said during interviews, they use tape recorders with counters and make brief summaries of important information. Such an index might look like this:

009 Uncle Bill remembers when the family moved to the old neighborhood in (he thinks) 1952.
123 He says the family moved here in 1972.

Increasingly, genealogists conduct e-mail interviews, and with relatives scattered over many states or even countries electronic forms of communication provide relatively inexpensive ways of conducting research. Of course, the old-fashioned way—writing letters and making telephone calls—adds a personal touch that may bind families closer together in their search for their roots.

Creating a Family Tree. Making a chart or tree of a family can be an end in itself or the first step in writing a family history. The tree may also help to identify gaps in research and areas that family members may eventually be able to fill in. Many families have what is called a "progenitor"—for example, a grandfather or great-grandfather who established the family in its country of residence. The tree would begin with him (in most cases it is

a male, although it is important not to overlook instances in which a woman or a group of men and women are families' progenitors). Dates of birth, marriage, and death are specified. If the progenitor was previously married, this fact would also be recorded.

The tree begins with facts, although eventually it can branch out to include more colorful details and stories, capsule biographies, excerpts from oral histories, and even photographs. What the tree looks like depends, in part, on the family's history—the number of ancestors and progenitors, for example. Many books on genealogy include samples of genealogical charts, as do biographies of famous people. Some trees look like maps; others take on a geometrical shape, with each member occupying a separate box.

The Adoptee as Genealogist. The adopted child who becomes a genealogist develops a set of special skills. Certainly tact and sensitivity are uppermost. Books that deal with adoptees in search of their birth families advocate that special attention be paid to the adoptive parents, who may have reservations about—or even resist—adoptees' efforts to find their birth parents. Adoptive parents often regard children's adoption as a rebirth and feel rejected when their adopted children seek out their birth parents. Birth parents may also be reluctant to acknowledge their children, for they may not welcome revisiting their past, which may involve dealing with painful memories. In other cases, birth parents and adoptive parents have acknowledged their children's need to know about their ancestry.

Adoption law changed in the late twentieth century as records were sealed and adopted children received new birth certificates. However, these procedures have been challenged as more and more adopted children have researched their ancestry. There is, in fact, an open adoption movement that has helped adopted children investigate their family history, but many states and government agencies remain reluctant to release such information. Experts in foster care and adoption recommend that adoptees read the stories of persons who have found their birth parents and experienced varying reactions to their reunions with their birth families.

Understanding a Kin Group and Family. It is essential to realize that each race or ethnic group

Family genealogical records help keep alive the histories of families, such as that of these Italian immigrants at Ellis Island in 1905. (AP/Wide World Photos)

may have customs and ways of remembering family history that are unique to them. Genealogists, in other words, study not only the history of their families but also the history of the ethnic groups, neighborhoods, and communities to which they belong. A sound knowledge of immigrant history—for example, an awareness of how Poles, Italians, or the Irish came to the United States—is essential to genealogists who belong to these groups. Why families settled in certain cities, regions, and localities may have to do with employment patterns among ethnic groups and races. A family history, in other words, may very well reflect larger histories, which in turn help to explain why a family worked in and moved to a certain area. Similarly, religious factors help to explain why families organized themselves around churches, synagogues, and mosques. Social clubs and societies often arise out of religious affiliations.

Different Presentations of the Genealogical Record. There are many ways to write the history of a family. A genealogist may collect and edit interviews with family members. Interviews might be edited as autobiographies that include photographs and documents. Still another approach is to maintain a journal or diary: a dated, ongoing record of a genealogist's research, which may include collections of records and testimony from family members. Journals may take the form of highly organized scrapbooks, arranged by year or by individual entries on family members. Whatever the organization of such a book, it can become an aid to further research if it is indexed, so that family members reading it can quickly find data on family names, places, jobs, and other information. Such books could well contain a section on family gossip. Some of this material may be unsubstantiated rumor or speculation. If it is labeled as such, it may stimulate other family members to confirm or refute family lore. Similarly, a section could be organized around hot topics or issues in a family's history. Conflicting versions of events or personalities can be recorded in such a section.

What is most important is that genealogists determine their purpose. Do they wish to collect information, to interpret it, to suggest further avenues of research? Do they wish to assemble a corroborated history or a more casual, informal family album of reminiscence? With the development of video cameras, there is also the possibility of making a genealogical project into a kind of documentary film. Important family sites can be filmed; Super 8 films can be transferred to videotape and edited. Genealogy then becomes a collective enterprise, perhaps directed by family members who have conducted genealogical research.

Fiction writers have always drawn on their families for stories, and it may be that genealogical research can be presented as a nonfiction story as well. In short, genealogists may become historians, autobiographers, fiction writers, biographers, interviewers, photographers, and filmmakers. Each approach presents another facet of family history and another way to tell a trace of a family's genealogy and history.

—*Carl Rollyson*

BIBLIOGRAPHY

Allen, Desmond Walls, and Carolyn Earle Billingsley. *Beginner's Guide to Genealogical Research.* Bountiful, Utah: American Genealogical Lending Library, 1991. Comprehensive introduction to genealogy including chapters on family sources, organizing family records, using libraries and archives, census records, courthouse research, military records, and ethnic genealogy.

Davis, Cullom, Kathryn Back, and Kay Maclean. *From Tape to Type.* Chicago: Library Association, 1977. Contains chapters on collecting oral history, interviewing, transcribing, and editing, as well as a glossary and bibliography. Several illustrations show how to organize interviews, cross reference, and take notes.

Dollarhide, William. *Managing a Genealogical Project.* Baltimore: Genealogical Publishing Company, 1988. Contains a list of sample forms (relationship chart, family data sheet, research log, ancestor table, research journal, correspondence log), types of genealogical projects, a glossary of genealogical relationships, and reference tips, such as basic rules of note taking.

Ehrlich, Henry. *A Time to Search.* New York: Paddington Press, 1977. Chapters on searching adoption records, individual stories of adoptees, reunions with birth parents, and interviews with adoptive parents.

Handlin, Oscar. *The Uprooted.* Boston: Little, Brown, 1951. Classic of immigration history, with chapters on peasant origins, the crossing, new work in the New World, religious life, different generations of immigrants and their children, immigrant alienation from American life, restrictions on immigration, and the promise that the United States has held for generations of immigrants.

Hey, David. *The Oxford Guide to Family History*. New York: Oxford University Press, 1993. Guide to constructing a family tree, with an account of how families have functioned in history, chapters on researching court and municipal records and church registers, and the origins of family names.

Polking, Kirk. *Writing Family Histories and Memoirs*. Cincinnati: Writer's Press, 1995. Chapters on how to begin writing a family history, getting help from others, learning how to write dialogue, ideas for topics, becoming the family historian, tips on interviewing, different methods of organization, format and writing style, and where to find information in libraries, courthouses, and electronic search services.

Terkel, Studs. *Hard Times: Oral History of the Great Depression in America*. New York: Pantheon, 1970. A popular oral historian, Terkel provides a good model of how to shape and organize oral history interviews.

See also Adoption issues; Ancestor worship; Bilateral descent; Birth order; Extended families; Family: concept and history; Family History Library; Family trees; Haley, Alex; Lineage.

Generation X

RELEVANT ISSUES: Demographics; Sociology
SIGNIFICANCE: "Generation X" is a term used to refer to the generation of individuals born after the so-called baby boom

The term "Generation X" was originally made famous in Great Britain during the early 1960's. It was used to describe a generation of alienated and apparently violent youth, particularly gangs known as "mods" and "rockers." The concept gained renewed popularity in the early 1990's after the 1991 publication of the novel *Generation X: Tales for an Accelerated Culture* by Canadian author Douglas Coupland. This novel described the ennui, quiet tribulations, and diminished hopes of people in their twenties. In the months following the book's publication, the phrase was taken up by the North American media and quickly entered everyday discourse.

Although "Generation X" is said to refer to those individuals who were born after the baby boom (roughly corresponding to the period between 1946 and 1964), it is sometimes difficult to know precisely who is included or excluded. At times, the concept seems to refer only to people born in the mid- to late 1960's and at other times to those born after 1960. The term "Generation Y" is sometimes used to describe people born in the 1970's.

In his novel, Coupland characterizes a member of Generation X, or more popularly, a "Gen X'er," as anybody who works for somebody wearing a ponytail (in other words, a baby boomer). The implication is that Gen X'ers have not had the same economic or career opportunities as did baby boomers. The novel also coined the term "McJob" to refer to the types of thankless, minimum-wage jobs in which many of Coupland's generation found themselves trapped.

According to Coupland and others, Gen X'ers also tended to be raised in broken homes. As depicted in Cameron Crowe's 1993 film *Singles*, Gen X'ers themselves have problems maintaining long-term relationships. The implication is that members of this generation are unlikely to have large or stable families. The lives of Gen X'ers have been shaped by their exposure to television and the mass media. The tone of much Generation X culture is ironic yet surprisingly gleeful, as exemplified in films such as *Slacker* (1992) and *Clerks* (1995), in which characters engage in seemingly pointless and interminable debates about the meaning of Madonna and *Star Wars*.

Many observers have been critical of the concept of Generation X, including those whom the term is supposed to identify. Some complain that those who identify with the concept indulge in self-pity. The critics argue that most Gen X'ers come from fairly privileged middle- and upper-middle-class families and that compared to any other generation in North American history (with the exception of the baby boomers), Gen X'ers are relatively affluent. Such critics also argue that if Gen X'ers could see themselves in a global context, they would realize that they are still part of the richest 10 percent of the world's population.

Mostly children of "baby boomers," so-called Gen X'ers are members of the first generation born after 1960. (James L. Shaffer)

The 1992 film Slacker *depicts the ethos of Generation X.* (Museum of Modern Art, Film Stills Archive)

Some spokespeople for and representative figures of Generation X include film directors Richard Linklater and Quentin Tarentino, actors Ethan Hawke and Winona Ryder, and rock stars Courtney Love (from Hole) and James Hetfield (from Metallica).

—*Kegan Doyle*

See also Baby-boom generation; Baby boomers; Echo effect; Generational relationships.

Generational relationships

RELEVANT ISSUES: Aging; Children and child development; Parenting and family relationships

SIGNIFICANCE: Providing the context for continuity and change, different generations within families have long been the subject of philosophers and sociologists and raise issues of caregiving and interfamilial abuse

The concept "generation" represents a unique integration of historical and biographical time and events. Generational status and identification affect not only family relations but public policy as well, as the modern debate over "generational equity" in social security and medical care illustrates. Continuity and change are central themes in a sociological understanding of generations.

Generations: Continuity and Change. Interest in the "generation gap" did not originate in the social movements of the 1960's. The ancient Greek philosopher Aristotle wrote of generational differences in his *Rhetoric*, saying that "The young are brave but intemperate, the old temperate but cowardly. To put it generally, all the valuable qualities that youth and age divide between them are united in the prime of life." For Aristotle the prime years were between thirty and fifty.

David Hume explored the relationship between biological and political continuity. He considered the political consequences of the life cycle of human generations. To do so, he asked what would happen if the human cycle were altered to mimic the butterfly or caterpillar. Each generation would disappear to be followed by a new one made up of individuals who emerge simultaneously. In this situation, he suggested, each generation would reinvent a form of government suitable to its needs. Thus, a central function of human generations is to ensure continuity in political and social institutions.

The widest generational gap experienced by most people is that separating grandparents and grandchildren. (James L. Shaffer)

Emphasizing the role of generations in changing these institutions, Auguste Comte linked generational succession to social progress. He attributed the pace of progress to the human life span and the thirty-year period between generations, suggesting that if the average life span were shortened or lengthened, the pace of progress would also change. For Comte, the older generation operates to slow the pace of progress. The longer they are present, the slower the progress.

Other scholars went beyond the biological dimension to the social. That is, they saw that age groups are united and influenced by the "spirit of the age," or Zeitgeist. Thus, Martin Heidegger wrote of "the inescapable fate of living in and with one's generation" as a way of understanding the confluence of individual and generational destinies.

In his 1927 essay "The Problem of Generations" Karl Mannheim saw generations as "conditioned within the process of life itself." Mannheim thus emphasized the transition of cultural heritage from generation to generation as the logical consequence of the human life cycle. He wrote,

> It is a matter for historical and sociological research to discover at what stage in its development, and under what conditions, a class becomes class-conscious and similarly, when individual members of a generation become conscious of their common situation and make this consciousness the basis of their group solidarity. Why have generations become so conscious of their unity today?

By "today," Mannheim was referring to 1927. For Mannheim, belonging to a generation involved two components: "chronological simultaneity" and shared "historicocultural space."

From a sociological viewpoint generations provide the context for both change and continuity. These dynamics are also present in family life. Parents struggle to convey cherished values to their children even as children chafe to reform social and political institutions. Late life brings changes in the resources and abilities of the elderly. Yet it is the continuity of intergenerational affection and commitment that enables family members to care for dependent elders.

Adolescence. Perhaps the most enduring view of adolescence is a 1904 text published by the psychologist G. Stanley Hall, who viewed adoles-

cence as a time of "storm and stress." For Hall, adolescence was a life stage somewhere between "savagery and civilization," with the adolescent struggling to reconcile primitive impulses with civilizing restraints.

Psychoanalytic perspectives on adolescence echo this view. Anna Freud suggested not only that disruptive and rebellious behavior is common in adolescence, but also that the absence of such behavior indicates developmental problems. According to Anna Freud,

> We all know individual children who as late as the ages of 14, 15, or 16 show no such outer evidence of inner unrest. They remain . . . "good" children, wrapped up in their family relationships, considerate sons of their mothers, submissive to their fathers, in accord with the atmosphere, ideas, and ideals of the childhood background. Convenient as this may be, it signifies a delay of normal development and is, as such, a sign to be taken seriously.

Perhaps as a result of these and related writings many parents expect to encounter rebellion and stress during their children's adolescence. Yet most large-scale studies suggest that they will be pleasantly surprised. Most adolescents experience neither turbulence nor rebellion. Instead, large studies of adolescents in the United States, Great Britain, and other countries suggest that a minority (possibly 20 percent) of adolescents manifest behavior problems or psychopathology.

Nonetheless, as a transition period between childhood and adulthood adolescence presents unique challenges for young people and their families. Decisions made and actions taken during this period can have lifelong repercussions. Young people face the challenge of coming to terms with sexuality and intimacy. They must position themselves for effective participation in the labor market. A significant minority of adolescents experience such despair that they take their own lives. Still others may become pregnant or contract human immunodeficiency virus (HIV) and acquired immunodeficiency syndrome (AIDS). It is not surprising that parents (and their children) approach adolescence with trepidation.

Historians date the emergence of adolescent subcultures in the United States to the establishment of militias, in which young men shared a common experience that was dictated not by class

In contrast to popular perceptions, most adolescents do not go through a period of rebelliousness. (Dick Hemingway)

or culture but by age. Indeed, this seems to be the hallmark of generational identification. The Vietnam War protest movement was led by young men subject to military conscription (the draft). Dictated by a nation's history and an individual's age, these events vividly illustrate the role of a generation in social progress.

Late-Life Generational Relations. As the U.S. population ages, more families face the challenge of maintaining healthy relations between generations of adults. Rather than being an extension of parent-child dynamics, these late-life relationships are distinguished by their parity. Individuals come to them with comparable resources, authority, and power. This intergenerational parity is partly attributable to the declining economic importance of agriculture. Prior to the Industrial Revolution land ownership determined family income. Control of the family farm afforded the older genera-

tion authority and power over the young. Because few people survived to old age, three-generation households were not common. Yet, a higher proportion of the elderly lived with their children than is the case in the late twentieth century.

Despite a modern tendency to romanticize intergenerational households, coresidence across generations was neither voluntary nor entirely free of conflict. Modern intergenerational residence patterns have been characterized by "intimacy at a distance." While adults seldom share households with their parents, they have frequent, voluntary contacts by telephone and through personal visits. These contacts reflect and contribute to stronger emotional bonds between the generations.

Caregiving. The average American woman can expect to spend more years caring for aging parents than raising children. Meeting the physical

Increasing longevity has allowed many grandparents greater opportunities to involve themselves in the lives of the younger generations. (James L. Shaffer)

needs of an older adult can impair personal-emotional bonds between the generations. Caregivers often experience resentment and guilt while providing intimate assistance to a loved parent. Dependent elders, on the other hand, may be embarrassed and demoralized by their frailty and need. In a three-generation family, the younger generation can feel (and be) neglected by parents who are overwhelmed with elder care.

Caregiving can destroy family relationships, leading to divorce and alienation. Conversely, the experience of caring for a loved one can strengthen relationships. Although modern research is inconclusive, popular wisdom and practitioners in the field suggest that the health of spousal and intergenerational relations before the caring for elderly parents commences is important to the success of caregiving. If parent-child relationships have been characterized by tension or abuse, late life caregiving will probably be unsuccessful. Even in the context of strong and healthy relationships caregiving can jeopardize family life. Family meetings, often facilitated by professionals, have proven helpful. Caregivers themselves often benefit from support groups that provide advice, sharing, and information.

Grandparents. As people live longer, they experience grandparenthood longer and have more opportunities to contribute to and influence their families. By the late twentieth century there were more than fifty-eight million grandparents in the United States ranging in age from 30 to 110. Nearly half were under the age of 60. Grandparents fill a variety of functions. They transmit the family heritage, provide role models for their grandchildren, serve as nurturers, devote time to listening to their grandchildren and engaging in unstructured activities, mediate conflicts, act as buffers between parents and children, and support and care for grandchildren whose parents are in crisis. The important contribution of grandparents to the healthy development of children has just begun to be understood.

Grandparents participate in their grandchildren's lives even when the parents are divorced. In the United States and Canada growing numbers of grandparents have pursued legal remedies to secure their rights to visit their grandchildren. Grandparents rights associations have been organized in both countries to address this issue. Par-

ents seeking divorce can ensure that grandparents' visitation rights will be respected by stipulating them in divorce agreements. Some states have enacted legislation to ensure such visitation rights.

Divorce, illness, death, and substance addiction may result in grandparents assuming custody of their grandchildren. In the United States an estimated 3.4 million children live with their grandparents. In at least a third of these homes grandparents are the primary caregivers. An estimated 44 percent of grandparents spend one hundred or more hours per year caring for their grandchildren. Among African Americans the proportion of grandparents providing custodial care is roughly three times that among whites. Custodial grandparents often face significant challenges. Access to financial assistance, health-care coverage, social services, and even education may depend on whether grandparents have legal custody of their grandchildren. Yet, securing legal custody of their grandchildren can be brutally painful if the parents are alive, requiring the grandparents to demonstrate that their own children are unfit to serve as parents. Grandchildren in such relations often have behavioral and emotional difficulties stemming from trauma or neglect. Few custodial grandparents have a peer group to provide support and empathy. The American Association of Retired Persons (AARP) has established a Grandparent Information Center that serves as a clearinghouse for information and coordinates volunteer support groups.

Generational Conflict and Family Violence. The intimacy and importance of nuclear families place tremendous pressure on generational relations. The proliferation of "how to" books for parents has disempowered some parents, persuading them that their role is so difficult that help from

---

A Month for Closing the Generation Gap

Parenting Without Pressure has designated October National Communicate with Your Kid Month. The purpose of this annual event is to improve communication between parents and their teenage children in order to improve adolescent-parent relationships generally.

social workers, guidance counselors, and others is essential. Recent years have also seen the proliferation of "how to" books for adult children of aging parents, ample testimony to widespread interest in enhancing such relationships. The emerging focus on how to achieve optimal intergenerational relations has gone hand in hand with the growing awareness of the pathological dimension of such relations. Family violence, manifested as abuse of dependent and vulnerable members, is most often intergenerational.

There are many parallels between child and elder abuse. Reports of both have increased. Both occur more often in families that are isolated from the broader community than in those that are not. Both are more common among families under stress, as from unemployment or caregiving, than among those that do not suffer such stress. Both are characterized by the presence of vulnerable and dependent victims. However, there are also important differences between child and elder abuse. In the case of child abuse the state can assume custody of children under the principle of *parens patriae,* despite objections from parents and children themselves. There is no similar principle when the victim is a legally competent adult. Professionals who work with abused elders rely on victim's willingness to report incidents and pursue legal remedies. Older parents are reluctant to admit that their children are abusive. Thus, cases of elder abuse, even when detected, often arise in circumstances that preclude effective intervention.

Generational Equity. Concern over the generational equity of social-security systems is growing in the United States and Canada. In the United States an organization known as Americans for Generational Equity, or AGE, argues that the modern structure of the social-security system favors older generations at the expense of the young. This argument is based on the notion that individuals identify more closely with their age peers (their "generation") than with their families. Opponents of AGE's critique argue that benefits to older generations also enhance the quality of life experienced by their children, freeing family resources that might otherwise be devoted to the needs of the elderly. This debate will affect public policy related to health care and retirement in coming decades.   —*Amanda Smith Barusch*

BIBLIOGRAPHY

Deats, S. M., and L. Tallent, eds. *The Aching Hearth: Family Violence in Life and Literature.* New York: Insight Books, 1991. Examines literary perspectives on family violence.

Garbarino, J. *Adolescence: An Ecological Perspective.* Columbus: Charles E. Merrill, 1985. Major textbook examining historical and theoretical views of adolescence, individual development, and family dynamics that was developed to help students, parents, and professionals understand adolescent development in a broad social context.

Haber, Carole. *Beyond Sixty-Five: The Dilemma of Old Age in America's Past.* New York: Cambridge University Press, 1983. Careful examination of the status of the elderly in colonial and postcolonial America that effectively counters the "myth of a golden age" when the elderly were universally respected and revered. Also examines the changing role of elders as life expectancy extended the period when adults were not raising dependent children.

Longman, Phillip. *Born to Pay: The New Politics of Aging in America.* Boston: Houghton Mifflin, 1987. Written while the author was receiving financial support from Americans for Generational Equity (AGE), this book presents the AGE argument in a compelling and well-documented form.

Mace, N. L., and P. V. Rabins. *The Thirty-six-Hour Day: A Family Guide to Caring for Persons with Alzheimer's Disease, Related Dementing Illnesses, and Memory Loss in Later Life.* Baltimore: Johns Hopkins University Press, 1981. Popular classic that addresses the many difficulties encountered by family members who care for a victim of Alzheimer's disease and offers practical advice about emotional and interpersonal dynamics that seriously complicate the family life of caregivers.

Pfeifer, S. K., and M. B. Sussman, eds. *Families: Intergenerational and Generational Connections.* New York: Haworth Press, 1991. Collection of theoretical essays by major social scientists that addresses a tremendous range of topics including caregiving, marriage, family ethical dilemmas, ancestor worship, transfer of resources, mothers, fathers, and grandparents.

Wolff, K. H., ed. *From Karl Mannheim.* 2d expanded ed. New Brunswick, N.J.: Transaction, 1993. Collection of essays that includes "The Problem of Generations" as well as an introduction placing Mannheim's thoughts in historical and cultural context.

See also Aging and elderly care; Baby boomers; Battered child syndrome; Elder abuse; Family caregiving; Family trees; Favoritism; Generation X.

Genetic counseling

RELEVANT ISSUES: Children and child development; Health and medicine

SIGNIFICANCE: Families at risk of bearing children with genetic disease may undergo counseling in order to help them consider pregnancy- and birth-related options

Genetic counseling involves the application of the laws of inheritance to family history in order to determine the approximate risk of genetic disease. Counseling generally involves two possible issues: Either a family member of one or both parents has been diagnosed with a genetic disease or the parents have had one child with a genetic disease and wish to determine the risk associated with having another child. Counselors discuss these issues with parents, assessing the possible risk of genetic disease faced by future children. Parents are then able to better consider options such as birth control, sterilization, or abortion. If parents do not consider these options as viable, counselors may offer suggestions as to the management of possible illnesses.

Austrian botanist Gregor Mendel, whose discoveries in genetics during the 1850's and 1860's laid the basis for modern inheritance (Archive Photos)

Parents most commonly inquire about the possibility that their future children may be born with Down syndrome, which is associated with an extra copy (trisomy) of chromosome 21. The most important factor in assessing the risk of having a child with Down syndrome is the age of the prospective mother. By investigating family history and a prospective mother's age, a counselor can assess the risk of her having such a child. A pregnant woman can be diagnosed for Down syndrome (and other genetic diseases associated with chromosomal abnormalities) through prenatal chromosome analysis following amniocentesis or chorionic villus sampling. Advances in genetic analysis have made it possible for doctors to screen patients for many congenital diseases by observing patterns of deoxyribonucleic acid (DNA) in fetuses.

The calculation of risk is simplest when genetic traits follow the regular inheritance laws discovered by the nineteenth century geneticist Gregor Mendel. Counselors first develop a chart, or pedigree, that illustrates blood relationships among extended family members and indicates which members have a particular disease. Most such disease traits are either dominant or recessive. Dominant traits are always expressed. For example, the neurological disease Huntington's chorea is associated with a dominant gene. If a parent carries the gene, the child will have a 50 percent chance of acquiring the trait and the disease from the parent. Cystic fibrosis is associated with a recessive gene; the child can develop the disease only if two recessive genes are present. If both parents are carriers of the disease, as determined from the pedigree, the child will have a 25 percent chance of acquiring two recessive genes according to Mendalian laws.

The purpose of genetic counseling is not to make parents' decisions for them. Prenatal counseling can only determine the odds that children will acquire certain diseases. Parents must decide for themselves whether to carry such children to term. If a fetus has already been diagnosed with a particular disorder, counselors may provide aid and advice on possible effects to the family and the prognosis of the illness. Counselors can also inform parents of agencies that may help them to deal with the problem. —*Richard Adler*

See also Birth defects; Eugenics; Genetic disorders; Heredity.

Genetic disorders

RELEVANT ISSUE: Health and medicine
SIGNIFICANCE: Genetic disorders represent inherited forms of disease which, subject to the laws of inheritance, often recur within families

Genetic disorders represent germline (sperm or egg) mutations present within all cells of the body. Because they are inherited, such disorders may recur within each generation of the family. In this manner they differ from birth defects, which generally result from spontaneous mutations or genetic errors affecting only individuals. While birth defects also represent congenital defects, they are usually not passed on to offspring.

Molecular Basis of Genetic Disorders. The molecular basis for genetic disorders is found within genes that make up the chromosomes, the deoxyribonucleic acid (DNA) protein complexes containing the hereditable determinants of organisms. When expressed, each gene encodes a protein. The proteins that are encoded in turn determine the function of the cells, tissues, and ultimately organisms themselves. Any gene defect, therefore, has the potential for a significant impact on the health of organisms. If the defect is found within the germ, the cell's defect will be passed on to any offspring. In this manner, genetic disorders may run in families.

Different forms of the same gene are called alleles. For example, the gene that determines type A blood is the same gene as that which determines type O blood, but the gene for type A and type O blood are different alleles. The form or allele of a gene is called its genotype; the physical manifestation or visible effect of the gene product is called the phenotype.

Forty-six chromosomes are found in normal human cells. They encode a total of some 100,000 different genes. Forty-four of the chromosomes do not determine the sex of individuals and are called autosomes. Two chromosomes, the X and Y chromosomes, determine the sex of individuals. Cells of females contain two X chromosomes while those of males contain one X and one Y chromosome. The chromosomes are found in twenty-three pairs, with one member of each pair inherited from each parent This means that except for those genes on the X or Y chromosome (in males), all genes are found in pairs. If an allele determines the phenotype, even if present in only one copy, it is considered dominant. If the same allele must be present on both members of the chromosomal pair to determine the phenotype, it is considered recessive.

Most (but not all) genetic disorders are the result of recessive alleles. As a result, however, such disorders often recur within families and occur only in those individuals who inherit the defective allele from both parents. The parent with one normal (dominant) allele is considered a carrier, and usually suffers no phenotypic effect as a result. If each parent is a carrier, the child has a one in four chance of inheriting the disorder.

Genetic Disorders Within Populations. Certain forms of recessive alleles often run in families and even within certain ethnic populations. For exam-

Down syndrome is associated with possession of an extra chromosome. (James L. Shaffer)

This Texas woman and her husband did not know they carried the recessive gene associated with sickle-cell anemia until their fourth child (pictured) was born with the disease. (AP/Wide World Photos)

ple, the recessive allele which is associated with sickle-cell anemia is prevalent in a high proportion (more than 10 percent) of individuals of African or Mediterranean ancestry. The BRCA1 allele, associated with certain forms of inheritable breast cancer, is normally found in only a small proportion of women in the United States and Canada (less than one in eight hundred). Among Jewish women of Eastern European (Ashkenazi) ancestry in these countries, however, the BRCA1 allele is present in approximately 1 percent of the population.

It is unclear why such deleterious genes would be so highly prevalent. In part, this may be the result of intermarriage within given ethnic populations. In addition, under certain circumstances, the presence of a single copy of a recessive allele may provide a selective advantage to individuals. For example, a single copy of the sickle-cell gene provides resistance to malaria. There is some evidence that the presence of a single gene associated with Tay-Sachs disease may produce some resistance to tuberculosis. Under these circumstances, the gene associated with a genetic disorder may benefit individuals. Such individuals are more likely to survive and pass on the gene to descendants.

Determination of Genetic Disorders. If couples suspect that they may be at risk of genetic disorders, they often seek the advice of genetic counselors. Generally, such couples already have had a child with such a disorder, or they have family members who suffer from an inherited disease. By developing a pedigree, a chart that provides a family history of such disorders, counselors are able to advise families as to the risk or likelihood of their own children inheriting a defective allele.

Some disorders are the result of a single gene. If the disorder is considered autosomal dominant, children who inherit the defective allele will develop the disorder. If the trait is autosomal recessive, children will develop the disorder only if two defective alleles are inherited. If either parent does not carry the allele, children may become carriers, but they will not suffer from the disorder. If the allele is found on the X chromosome, it is considered sex-linked. Such disorders are almost always found in males, since they possess only a single X chromosome. In part, the purpose of the Human Genome Project, an internationally coor-

dinated effort initiated in 1990 that maps all genes on human chromosomes, is to pinpoint the sites of those genes associated with genetic disorders.

With advances in prenatal testing, it is often possible to determine the presence of many disorders in developing fetuses. Genetic disorders diagnosed before birth often create a unique quandary for the families in question. This is especially painful when the defective allele is dominant and no treatment for the disease is available. For example, if a potential parent is known (or suspected) to carry a gene for the fatal illness Huntington's chorea, the chances of passing it (and the disease) on to a child is one chance in two. Prenatal testing, which can determine whether the child has inherited the gene, is now available. If the fetus is found to have inherited the gene, the parents must decide whether the mother should carry the pregnancy to term, knowing the child will probably succumb to the disorder.

Screening of Genetic Disorders. Genetic screening involves the determination of whether a particular genotype is present in individuals, putting them at risk of contracting a genetic disorder. The results of such screening can help determine whether persons' own health is at risk or whether their offspring may be at risk.

If presymptomatic screening confirms the presence of an allele associated with a genetic disorder, early medical intervention may sometimes improve the prognosis of the disorder. In some cases the symptoms of the disorder may be preventable. For example phenylketonuria, a disorder in which the amino acid phenylalanine cannot be metabolized, can be controlled with special diets low in that amino acid.

Genetic screening is often used to determine whether healthy individuals may have genes that pose a threat to their offspring (carrier screening). For example, the gene for Tay-Sachs disease is especially common among Ashkenazi Jews. Widespread use of genetic screening has resulted in a significant reduction in the number of children born with the disorder. Similar forms of screening for sickle-cell anemia and the thalassemias, both common among persons of African or Mediterranean ancestry, have lowered the incidence of newborns with these disorders.

Such screening is not without risk. As noted above, an ethical dilemma may result from diagnosis of a disorder with a poor prognosis. In addition, family members may suddenly discover that they are at particular risk. With the advances in technology that allow for screening comes the potential for understanding and potential treatment of an increasing number of disorders.

—*Richard Adler*

BIBLIOGRAPHY

Bishop, Jerry. *Genome.* New York: Simon & Schuster, 1990.

Bosk, Charles. *All God's Mistakes: Genetic Counseling in a Pediatric Hospital.* Chicago: University of Chicago Press, 1992.

Davies, K. E. *Human Genetic Disease Analysis: A Practical Approach.* New York: IRL Press, 1993.

Gilbert, Patricia. *The A-Z Reference Book of Syndromes and Inherited Disorders.* San Diego: Singular Publishing Group, 1996.

Gormley, Myra. *Family Diseases: Are You at Risk?* Baltimore: Genealogical Publishing, 1989.

Hendin, David, and Joan Marks. *The Genetic Connection: How to Protect Your Family Against Hereditary Diseases.* New York: William Morrow, 1978.

Sorenson, James. *Social Aspects of Applied Human Genetics.* New York: Russell Sage Foundation, 1971.

See also Attention-deficit hyperactivity disorder (ADHD); Birth defects; Disabilities; Eugenics; Genetic counseling; Heredity; Human Genome Project; Learning disorders.

Gessell, Arnold L.

BORN: June 21, 1880, Alma, Wis.
DIED: May 29, 1961, New Haven, Conn.
AREA OF ACHIEVEMENT: Children and child development
SIGNIFICANCE: Gessell studied child behavior, developing scales for measuring such behavior at different ages and helping to devise the development quotient for children

A pediatric psychologist with a Ph.D. and M.D. from Yale University, Arnold Gessell was heavily influenced by the work of G. Stanley Hall. After teaching at Los Angeles Normal School, he moved to Yale as professor of education. He remained there for the rest of his career. In 1911 he founded the Yale Clinic for Child Development (later known as the Gessell Institute) and served as its director until the end of his career in 1948. He and his collaborator L. B. Ames were the first to use photographic techniques and one-way mirrors in research, and their method was documented in *The Mental Growth of the Pre-school Child* (1925). Gessell's scales of measurement of child behavior at key ages, divided into categories measuring motor, adaptive, linguistic, and personal-social growth, helped in the calculation of children's development quotient (DQ), once considered a predictor of intellectual ability. *Infant and Child in the Culture of Today* (1942), coauthored with Frances Ilg, demonstrated a physiological approach in which cultural or learning factors had little significance. Despite its deficiency as a theory of developmental behavior, this book greatly influenced child-rearing practices in the 1940's and 1950's, principally because it was descriptive, nonabstract, and useful in normative studies of developing children.

—*Keith Garebian*

See also Bonding and attachment; Child rearing; Childhood history; Hall, G. Stanley; Heredity; Mental health; Puberty and adolescence.

Godparents

RELEVANT ISSUES: Children and child development; Parenting and family relationships; Religious beliefs and practices
SIGNIFICANCE: Godparents, in both secular and religious contexts, are persons specially designated by parents to act as mentors for their children

The concept of the godparent originated with the Christian practice of assigning children religious mentors at the time of baptism. Baptism, or christening, marks children's entry into the faith and signals the formal beginning of their relationship with the Christian God. Roman Catholics and other Christians believe that baptism removes the stain of Original Sin.

The guiding principle of Christian family concepts is that a community of faith surrounds children as they grow toward maturity. Godparents help parents, siblings, and other extended family members to teach children religious ways and practices and to present by example the notion of Christian belief. Godparents assist parents with

Godparents are usually assigned as religious mentors when children are christened. (James L. Shaffer)

the moral and spiritual education of children, a commitment that is considered to be lifelong.

In the late twentieth century the role of godparents expanded into more secular spheres by Roman Catholics and other Christians, humanists, and many nonreligious individuals. Parents seeking to enlarge the community of support for their offspring enlist one or two other adults to perform a special role in their children's upbringing. By designating one or two godparents, they essentially muster additional support for the daunting task of rearing children to maturity. This may take the form of moral and spiritual support or entail more concrete material assistance, such as providing child care, giving gifts, and engaging in entertainment and cultural events. Although godparents do not make formal religious vows, they are committed to the welfare of their godchildren.

Roman Catholic Baptism, Godparents, and Naming. The Roman Catholic religion holds that people enter life as sinners, marked by the stain of Original Sin inherited from Adam and Eve, who, according to the Old Testament, were banished from Paradise—the Garden of Eden—when they ate the forbidden fruit. Newborn children inherit this primordial sin despite their personal innocence. Baptism is the spiritual mechanism by which the stain of Original Sin can be removed. This allows individuals to receive God's grace and be welcomed into the Christian family.

Baptism is a Sacrament, or a visible sign of receiving grace. In the early Christian Church it was most commonly adults who were received into the new religion and baptized. The tradition of infant and child baptism did not become well established until after the fourth century C.E. In order to initiate adults, the Roman Catholic Church appointed sponsors who helped guide and prepare initiates into the rites and dogma of the Church. The role of sponsors for new adult converts developed over time into the present concept of the godparent.

According to the views of Roman Catholics, children and adults cannot enter the community of believers without being baptized. Roman Catholic doctrine teaches that if infants or children should die before being baptized, they cannot unite with God in heaven and enjoy everlasting life in the presence of God. For this reason, infant baptism is important to Roman Catholics. If baptism erases all stain of Original Sin from persons' souls, baptism after the age of reason (deemed to be seven years of age) removes all sins and the accompanying requirement of atonement for sins. Roman Catholic dogma holds that individuals who die immediately after baptism go to heaven without having to spend any time in purgatory expiating past wrongs.

Although children may have one godparent of each gender, Church protocol requires only one godparent. Godparents undertake an explicit spiritual role as children's religious mentors. Roman Catholics use the term "sponsor" to indicate a religious mentor for an adult candidate for baptism. The role sponsors play is different from that of godparents, for sponsors actively help instruct candidates, or catechumen, in the doctrines of Roman Catholicism.

At the time of baptism, godparents pledge to be responsible for the spiritual welfare of infants and agree to set a Christian example for their godchildren. In their lives and behavior, godparents are expected to demonstrate an outward commitment to righteousness and goodness that children can emulate. The Roman Catholic Church stipulates that godparents must be adults who actively practice the Roman Catholic religion, go to church regularly, and receive the Sacraments. Godparents must have received the Sacraments of baptism, Holy Communion, and confirmation and be comfortable with the moral teachings of the Church.

Some godparents take on a major role in the lives of their godchildren on a regular, consistent, almost daily basis, always "being there" for the children. Other godparents may restrict their presence to major events such as graduations, birthdays, and holidays, offering little more to sustain the lives of their godchildren.

Roman Catholic tradition requires that parents choose saints' names for their children, although there is flexibility in the choice of names. To evoke particular saints is to seek out their intervention as guiding influences and protectors. The Church calendar designates a feast day for each saint. Many Roman Catholics inherit at least one of their given names by being born on a particular saint's day. Parents may admire the traits of eponymous saints and confer their names on their children in the hope that the saints' example will inform their children's lives.

Godparents in Other Christian Sects. Christening is the term often employed to describe Christian, non-Roman Catholic baptisms. Most Christian sects follow the practice of infant baptism and the designation of godparents found in the Roman Catholic Church. The Episcopalian Church in the United States and the Anglican Church in Canada and Great Britain follow a similar practice in the baptism of infants. Lutheran, Presbyterian, and Methodist congregations also follow the practice of infant baptism. In Canada, the United Church performs infant baptisms for its members.

Legal Status of Godparents. It is commonly believed that godparents are designated as children's legal guardians, but the religious ceremony of designating godparents carries no legal weight. Parents may designate any adults, godparents or not, as potential guardians for their children. In the United States and Canada the determination of legal custody is made by the courts, not the parents, although parents may indicate their preferences and express their will. Conversely, persons designated as legal guardians may refuse to act as legal guardians or caregivers. The courts follow the best interests of children in assigning child custody to permanent guardians.

Secular Godparents. Many Christian sects mark the birth of children with the event of baptism. In modern North American society, where the culture rests on a plurality of beliefs about religious and spiritual matters, it has become increasingly popular for parents to designate godparents who play no explicit spiritual role. In the social formation of their children, parents wish to enlist the help of adults they admire. Sociologically, this makes sense, because the kinship circle in the postmodern period has shrunk in most cases to the immediate family, which may be fragmented by divorce, separation, or death.

Parents often choose friends or relatives to play a special role in their children's lives. They endeavor to enrich their children's lives by creating a future relationship between them and their godparents. Parents may choose close friends for this role as a way of honoring them. They may choose persons who are childless and who may be able to offer their children a commitment in terms of time and resources. Mothers and fathers may seek a friend who could serve as a mentor in one particular area, such as a feminist exemplar for their young daughter or son or an accomplished artist or athlete whom they wish their children to emulate.

By exposing their children to the personalities of godparents over the sustained period of their childhood development, parents hope to solidify in their children the admired characteristics of godparents. They may admire godparents' sense of humor and intelligence, their social, political, or religious commitment, their enthusiastic outlook, or their good-natured temperament. Regular, personal interaction with chosen mentors will give their children another frame of reference upon which to model their behavior and conduct and a different reflection of the self from that which their parents provide. It will broaden and enrich the children's lives.

Whether godparents play a formal religious role or more of a social, personal one, they are chosen by parents to have a special, positive influence on the lives and destiny of their children. At best, godparents offer their resources and character to expand children's experiences and give them a fuller understanding of what it means to be human.
                                          —*Patricia Bishop*

BIBLIOGRAPHY

Hill, John W. B. *Thinking About Baptism.* Toronto: Anglican Book Centre, 1991.

Lewinski, Ron. *Guide for Sponsors.* Chicago: Liturgy Training Publications, 1993.

McBrien, Richard P. *Inside Catholicism: Rituals and Symbols Revealed.* Edited by Barbara Roether. San Francisco, Calif.: Collins Publishers, 1995.

MacDonald, John F. *The Sacraments in the Christian Life.* Slough, England: St. Paul Publications, 1983.

Martos, Joseph. *Doors to the Sacred: A Historical Introduction to Sacraments in the Catholic Church.* Garden City, N.Y.: Doubleday, 1981.

Stoutzenberger, Joseph. *Celebrating Sacraments.* Rev. ed. Winona, Minn.: St. Mary's Press, 1993.

Worgul, George S. *From Magic to Metaphor: A Validation of Christian Sacraments.* New York: Paulist Press, 1980.

See also Baptismal rites; Compadrazgo; Cultural influences; Extended families; Father figures; Names; Religion; Roman Catholics.

Gomez v. Perez

DATE: Decided on June 17, 1973

RELEVANT ISSUES: Law; Parenting and family relationships

SIGNIFICANCE: This U.S. Supreme Court decision ruled that states may not deprive illegitimate children of important benefits that are generally accorded to other children

This case originated when a Texas man named Francisco Perez refused to provide support for his illegitimate child, Zoraida Gomez. When the child's natural mother sued Perez, the state courts ruled that a biological father had no legal obligation to make payments for an illegitimate child. The decision was based on both the statutes and common law in the state of Texas. The case was then appealed to the U.S. Supreme Court, whose justices declared that the relevant state's law was unconstitutional because it violated the Equal Protection Clause of the Fourteenth Amendment.

In a *per curiam* opinion, the Court ruled that states were prohibited from invidiously discriminating against illegitimate children by depriving them of essential benefits that were generally available to other children. The Court noted that fathers were required to support all legitimate children even when they did not maintain custody and that it was "illogical and unjust" not to extend the same benefits to those children whose biological parents were not married. Expanding upon earlier precedents, the case of *Gomez v. Perez* acknowledged that if states recognized judicially enforceable rights for children generally, the U.S. Constitution mandated that equal rights must be extended to the children of unmarried parents.

—*Thomas T. Lewis*

See also Child support; Children born out of wedlock; Equality of children; Unwed fathers.

Grandparents

RELEVANT ISSUES: Aging; Parenting and family relationships

SIGNIFICANCE: Of all people older than sixty-five years of age, more than nine out of ten are grandparents, persons who fulfill a great variety of roles within their family relationships and in maintaining family continuity

Rapid changes in society, in health and social mobility, and in the styles of family life increase the complexity of family networks. Grandparents and other family members continually adapt and adjust their activities and attitudes to include changes in the role expectations of grandparents, grandchildren, and the middle (parental) generation. Whenever a child is born, a new grandparent is born and a three-generation family is formed. The grandparent-grandchild bond is second only in emotional importance to the parent-child bond. Grandparents contribute to building family strengths and giving families a sense of "rootedness."

Importance of Grandparents. Research indicates that grandparenthood is a very active aspect of family life, not only for young children but for young adults as well. The stereotyped picture of a grandmother sitting alone in a rocking chair is not an accurate reflection of the status of grandparenthood. Grandparents are often not very old nor are they lonely and isolated. The majority live in close proximity to at least one grandchild. Most young adults have at least one grandparent and many have multiple grandparents in varied combinations.

It is not uncommon for people in their thirties to become grandparents. On the other hand, it is also not uncommon for people to become grandparents for the first time when they are in their sixties. A dramatic awareness of the "emergence of grandparenthood" occurred when the much publicized baby-boom generation entered the realm of grandparenthood.

The interests and lifestyles of family life contribute to an ever-increasing diversity of patterns of grandparent roles and relationships. Yet, with diversity comes an increasing uncertainty felt by grandparents and other family members regarding role expectations. Questions have arisen as to the place of grandparents, the meaning of grandparenthood, the reciprocal role of grandchildren, and the expectations of grandchildren in their relationships with their grandparents.

For a variety of reasons, including high levels of mobility and the frequency of divorce and remarriage, grandparents and families are often uncertain about what grandparents' expected roles should be. Parents' roles are more established or institutionalized than grandparents' roles. Most families, however, have a distinctive and emotional expectation about the importance of grandparents in their families.

The widespread sentiment of the role and place of grandparents extends across the United States, as is reflected in an act of the U.S. Congress, which declared 1995 the "Year of the Grandparent." In its declaration, Congress highlighted the importance of grandparents as follows:

> Whereas grandparents bring a tremendous amount of love and power for good into the lives of their grandchildren;
> Whereas grandparents, in partnership with parents, help deepen every child's roots and strengthen every child's wings so that every child may soar into adulthood with a glad heart and a confident spirit;
> Whereas grandparents are a strong and important voice in support of the happiness and well-being of children;
> Whereas grandparents often serve as the primary caregivers for their grandchildren, providing a stable and supportive home environment;
> Whereas grandparents should be acknowledged for the important role they play within families, and for the many and varied contributions they make to enhance and further the value of the family and family traditions;
> Whereas public awareness of and appreciation for the contributions of grandparents should be strengthened;
> Whereas grandparents should be encouraged to continue as a vital force in the shaping of American families today and into the future;
> Whereas the Nation acknowledges the contributions of grandparents by celebrating National Grandparents Day each September; and
> Whereas there should be a year-long national celebration of grandparents and grandparenting:
> Now, therefore, be it
> *Resolved by the Senate and House of Representatives of the United States of America in Congress assembled,* That 1995 is designated the "Year of the Grandparent" . . .

Grandparent Roles. Research on grandparent-grandchild relationships has identified several categories underlying these relationships. Grandparents provide grandchildren with love and companionship, highlighted by the sharing experience between them and the time they spend together having fun and pursuing their mutual

A Special Day for Grandparents

A presidential proclamation issued in 1979 designated the first Sunday in September following Labor Day to be National Grandparents Day. The purpose of the annual event is to honor grandparents by publicly calling attention to the strength, information, and guidance that older persons can offer.

interests. Grandparents lend their grandchildren emotional support, often providing them with comfort, understanding, counseling, nurturance, and a sympathetic and empathetic ear. Grandparents serve as role models. Some grandchildren look up to their grandparents as examples, seek their advice, and are influenced in their values and behaviors by the expectations and advice of their grandparents.

Grandparents represent continuity, because their age and family position make them family historians. Although some families express greater interest in their family heritage than others, it is to grandparents that families look for explaining traditions and rituals. Grandparents and grandchildren exchange gifts. Some grandparents have greater resources or interest than other grandparents in providing gifts for their grandchildren and other family members. Grandparents offer guidance and discipline. Families differ in the extent to which parents desire the input of grandparents in child rearing. Some seek grandparents' assistance and advice while others prefer that grandparents maintain a hands-off policy in the disciplining of their children. In some families, grandparents play an active role in providing primary child care, because parents are absent or because of their difficult work schedules.

Grandparent roles and family relationships vary at different stages in the family life cycle, depending on whether children are very young, in their teenage years, or adults. Many other social and cultural factors influence the contributions that grandparents and grandchildren make to the lives of one another, including the ages and number of grandparents per grandchild, the ages and number of grandchildren per grandparent, the health of grandparents, grandparents' financial

Birthday celebrations can be important occasions for bringing grandparents closer to their grandchildren. (Hazel Hankin)

status, and religious or ethical perspectives. The role of the middle (or parental generation), their resources, and the stresses they experience are significant factors in the way in which the grandparent role develops.

In addition to grandparents' expected roles, grandchildren are usually expected to play specific roles in relationship to their grandparents. Grandchildren should offer their grandparents love and affection and take time to visit them. Grandchildren have a responsibility to tend to their grandparents' needs and are a part of their grandparent's sense of the future.

Quality of Grandparent-Grandchild Relationship. For grandparent-grandchild relationships to be successful grandchildren should experience a feeling of closeness with their grandparents. They should feel that their grandparents know them and understand their feelings, hopes, and activities, while knowing their grandparents' feelings, hopes, and activities. Moreover, grandparents should exercise a positive influence in the lives of their grandchildren, and grandchildren should experience their relationships with their grandparents as authentic friendships, not as associations maintained by parents as intermediaries.

The increasing distances separating members of extended families have required grandparents to communicate with their grandchildren less directly. (James L. Shaffer)

Several factors contribute to the quality of grandparent-grandchild relationships. Grandchildren generally feel a closer intimacy with grandmothers; granddaughters are often more expressive of emotive closeness with grandparents than are grandsons. Only or first-born children often indicate that they feel a more special bond with their grandparents than do their siblings and sense that their grandparents know them better. The quality of the grandparent-grandchild relationship is stronger among children whose parents actively encourage frequent contacts with grandparents than among children whose parents show less interest. Grandchildren from stepfamilies often feel a somewhat closer and more direct relationship with their grandparents than do grandchildren in single-parent families. Such family situations seem to create a greater opportunity for grandparents to maintain supportive relationships with their grandchildren.

How near grandparents and grandchildren live to one another is another factor influencing the quality of their relationships. Grandchildren living closer to grandparents usually feel emotionally closer to them than grandchildren who do not live so near to them, and they feel that their grandparents know them better. Frequency of contact is another important factor in the quality of grandparent-grandchild relationships. Although frequency of contact is often associated with proximity, some grandchildren live near grandparents with whom they have little contact, whereas other grandchildren may live some distance from their grandparents and have frequent contact with them through letter writing or on the telephone.

One of the most distinctive influences contributing to the quality of the grandparent-grandchild relationship is the frequency of their "one-on-one" contact, during which they spend time alone together or are involved in activities that primarily involve just them (even if only by mail or other form of remote contact). Such one-on-one contact contrasts with broad family reunions or other kinds of family gatherings and activities in which large numbers of people are present.

Shared Activities of Grandparents and Grandchildren. Activities are the means by which grandparents and grandchildren make and maintain contact. They are the vehicle for the expression of affection and the context in which they get to know one another. They are the avenues of influence and service. Some activities are unstructured. Grandchildren or grandparents may visit one another or they may stay together for a time. In such cases, their activities follow the natural course of the day's activities, tasks, or recreational opportunities. On other occasions, they share special events and activities, including family gatherings, family outings, and the celebration of holidays.

In contrast to such activities, grandparents and grandchildren also come together for specially designated purposes. The attendance of grandparents at grandchildren's cultural events or performances is a familiar sight in most communities and is fondly remembered by grandparents and grandchildren alike. In another type of shared activity, grandchildren visit grandparents' homes and assist them in various tasks, such as cutting thistles on the farm, baking cookies, or going shopping. Grandchildren often attribute their interest in hobbies or their ability to perform their careers to the attitudes they formed while "helping" their grandparents.

Engaging in outdoor, crafts, and community activities are more characteristic of activities that grandchildren share with their grandfathers. Caring for family members' health and visiting neighbors and friends are more characteristic of activities that grandchildren share with their grandmothers. Grandparents' and grandchildren's ages usually influence the types of activities they share. Older grandparents more frequently read books and tell stories with their grandchildren, while younger grandparents more often shop, eat, and take vacations together with their grandchildren. Not surprisingly, grandparents and grandchildren living some distance from one another frequently share news by writing letters and communicating via electronic mail.

Multicultural Influences in Grandparenting. Race and ethnicity play an important role in grandparents' degree of involvement in family life. Research suggests that African Americans, Asian Americans, Italian Americans, and Latinos are more likely to be involved in the lives of their grandchildren than are other groups. The apparent greater involvement of ethnic grandparents may be the result of the greater extended kin networks within these groups. Studies involving grandfathers in African American and white fami-

Cookies are traditional icons for warm feelings that children have for their grandparents. (James L. Shaffer)

lies have found that the grandfather role is more central in the lives of African American and white men than in the lives of other groups.

African American families seem to exchange services with one another. For example, grandparents care for grandchildren and grandchildren care for grandparents.

A high level of grandparent support has been found among Native Americans. One study found that 26 percent of Native American elderly persons cared for at least one grandchild and that about 67 percent of older Native Americans live within five miles of their kin, with whom they engage in various mutual support activities. Grandparents often ask their children to allow their grandchildren to live with them for a time, so that the grandparents can teach the grandchildren about the Native American way of life.

Family Form and Grandparenting. Grandparents seem to take on even greater importance in single-parent and stepparent families than in dual-parent families. They frequently act as a stabilizing force for their children and grandchildren when families are divorcing and reforming as single-parent families or stepfamilies. Nearly 30 percent of all families with children are single-parent families and 63 percent of African American families are headed by single parents. Nearly 90 percent of single-parent families are headed by women. More than one million children each year experience their parents' divorce.

Children in single-parent families report greater closeness and active involvement with their grandparents than children from intact families. Children in stepfamilies are even closer to their grandparents. A possible explanation for the close grandparent-grandchild relationship in some stepfamilies is that the sojourn of grandchildren through the processes of family separation, single-parent families, and stepfamily life renders grandparents an enduring anchor in a shifting and unstable world. The effects of divorce are different for custodial grandparents (parents of custodial parents) than for noncustodial grandparents. The most common situation in the event of divorce is that maternal grandparent relationships are maintained or enhanced while paternal ones diminish. While in some stepfamily situations the grandparent-grandchild bond becomes exceedingly strong, in others grandparents are unable to maintain contact with their grandchildren. All fifty states in the United States statutorily provide an avenue by which grandparents can petition the courts for visitation rights over parent's objections or other obstacles.

Stepfamilies have created stepgrandparents, who are often confused about their grandparenting roles. Unlike grandparents, stepgrandparents have no biological ties to stepgrandchildren and have spent less time with them.

Grandparents as Child Rearers

In 1997 *Christian Science Monitor* columnist Marilyn Gardner reported on three late-twentieth century social trends that have worked to involve many grandparents—especially grandmothers—more directly in raising their own grandchildren. These include:

- The increasing employment of mothers in the workplace, which has left responsibility for day-to-day care of their children in the hands of their own parents.

- Rising rates of divorce and out-of-wedlock births have caused many young parents to return to their own parents' homes, inevitably drawing grandparents into taking on child-rearing responsibilities.

- Rising rates of drug and legal problems among young parents have left many children directly under the care of their grandparents.

Source: Christian Science Monitor (May 8, 1997).

Grandparents Who Parent Their Grandchildren. It is estimated that more than seven million grandparents raise grandchildren. Social problems, such as drug use and alcoholism, joblessness, street crime, homelessness, incarceration, deaths, acquired immunodeficiency syndrome (AIDS), abuse and neglect, parental immaturity, and poverty are some reasons why grandparents raise their grandchildren. As a group, these grandparents are burdened in several ways. The majority of them have less than a high-school education and low incomes. Twelve percent of African American children are raised by their grandparents compared with 6 percent of Hispanic children and 3.6 percent of white children. Grandmothers form the majority of grandparents raising grandchildren in the urban African American community. Despite negative emotions and various problems that may arise, caregiving grandparents feel useful and also derive satisfaction from the knowledge that they are rescuing their grandchildren.

—*Gregory E. Kennedy*

BIBLIOGRAPHY

Bengtson, Vern L., and Joan F. Robertson, eds. *Grandparenthood.* Beverly Hills, Calif.: Sage Publications, 1985. Brings together applied and scholarly articles representing varied perspectives on the character and status of grandparenthood.

Cherlin, Andrew, and Frank Furstenberg. *The New American Grandparent: A Place in the Family, a Life Apart.* New York: Basic Books, 1986. Considers identity questions for grandparents, their relationships to their children and grandchildren, and their changing roles in the family.

Kennedy, Gregory E., and C. E. Kennedy. "Grandparents: A Special Resource for Children in Stepfamilies." *Journal of Divorce and Remarriage* 19 (Fall-Winter, 1993). Presents descriptive insight into the distinctive characteristics of grandparent-grandchild relationships in different family forms.

Kornhaber, Arthur. *Contemporary Grandparenting.* Thousand Oaks, Calif.: Sage Publications, 1996. Synthesizes the modern knowledge about grandparenting and discusses grandparents' role in families and society.

Minkler, M., and K. M. Poe. *Grandmothers as Caregivers.* Newbury Park, Calif.: Sage Publications, 1993. Provides background information on the caregiving role of grandparents and on their relationships with their grandchildren.

Sanders, Gregory F., and Debra W. Trygstad. "Stepgrandparents and Grandparents: The View from Young Adults." *Family Relations* 38 (January, 1989). Presents an in-depth consideration of the step-grandparent experience.

Tron, Lillian E. "Grandparents: The Family Watchdogs." In *Family Relationships in Older Life*, edited by Timothy H. Brubacker. Beverly Hills, Calif.: Sage Publications, 1983. Discusses grandparent responses in times of family stress and transition.

See also Child rearing; Extended families; Family albums and records; Family gatherings and reunions; Favoritism; Generational relationships; Holidays; In-laws; Visitation rights.

Gray, John

BORN: 1951, Houston, Tex.

AREAS OF ACHIEVEMENT: Art and the media; Sociology

SIGNIFICANCE: In exploring practical communication between the sexes, Gray has asserted that different socialization patterns linked to different sex roles can interfere with communication, aggravating issues of conflict instead of resolving them

John Gray, author of Men Are from Mars, Women Are from Venus. *(Frank Capri/SAGA/Archive Photos)*

John Gray is the author of popular psychology self-help books and a seminar leader and lecturer. He obtained a bachelor's degree and master of arts degree in Eastern philosophy from Maharishi International University in Fairfield, Iowa, and a Ph.D. from Columbia Pacific University in San Rafael, California.

His first book was *What You Feel, You Can Heal* (1984), based on a form of therapeutic letter writing, which lead to a seminar program. He became a lecturer specializing in male-female relations and achieved some commercial success with the books *What Your Mother Couldn't Tell You and Your Father Didn't Know* (1994) and *Men, Women, and Relationships: Making Peace with the Opposite Sex* (1993). He became best known for his 1992 book *Men Are from Mars, Women Are from Venus*. This book caught the public fancy and was followed by *Mars and Venus in Love* (1996), *Mars and Venus Together Forever* (1996), *Mars and Venus in the Bedroom* (1997), and *Mars and Venus on a Date* (1997). The basic concept of the series is that through conditioning, if not innate differences, men and women think, feel, perceive, react, and love differently. According to Gray, men tend to be rational problem solvers, often with a brusque style, while women are intuitive and attuned to emotions; these differences thus hamper communication and create misunderstandings.

—*William L. Reinshagen*

See also Bonding and attachment; Couples; Marriage; Marriage counseling; Open marriage.

Grief counseling

Relevant issues: Aging; Divorce; Parenting and family relationships

Significance: Grief counseling helps individuals and families work through their normal grief reactions following a loss

Grief is a normal, natural, and necessary set of reactions following the death of a loved one, divorce, loss of health or a job, retirement, or any other significant loss. Grief affects every aspect of health—namely, emotional, physical, psychological, intellectual, social, and spiritual health. Although it is possible to recover from grief on one's own, grief counseling is especially appropriate following the death of a loved one. Such a loss can unbalance a family's status quo and cause serious disruptions of life patterns. According to J. William Worden's *Grief Counseling and Grief Therapy* (1991), "counseling involves helping facilitate uncomplicated, or normal, grief to a healthy completion of the tasks of grieving within a reasonable time frame." Worden identifies four grieving tasks: accepting the reality of the death, experiencing the pain, adjusting to the changed environment, and restoring emotional energy for reinvesting in life.

Many factors influence how and how long families grieve, including the age of the deceased and the survivors, the cause of death, and the degree of attachment. It is also true that adults, children, and adolescents grieve and express their pain differently. Grief counseling addressed to both individuals and the family as a whole can hasten the accomplishment of the grieving tasks by encouraging family members not only to respect each other's feelings but also to communicate and interact in a positive manner.

Modern Western culture, especially in the United States in the late twentieth century, has become a death-denying society, according to Elisabeth Kübler-Ross, the author of *On Death and Dying* (1969). Because most people die in hospitals rather than at home, children and adults tend to consider death an abnormal phenomenon rather than a natural part of the life cycle. Unfamiliarity with death in turn has led to a reluctance among friends and relatives to talk to the bereaved about their loss. Sometimes, in an effort to console, well-meaning persons offer such comments as "It's God's will" or "Be thankful for the years you had together." Statements like these can be hurtful to bereaved persons, whose normal grief reactions of denial, anger, sadness, or guilt, do not allow for a detached perspective.

Counseling can enable the bereaved to talk about their loss and express feelings in the presence of professional facilitators. Talking about the loss to a good listener, one who is nonjudgmental and who focuses on feelings with an unconditional positive regard, can help persons work through grief more confidently. Family members are encouraged to share their feelings with each other, respect the fact that they may feel differently, and explore for themselves the rationality of their feelings.

Elisabeth Kübler-Ross, the author of On Death and Dying. *(AP/Wide World Photos)*

Grief counseling can help individual survivors and families accept the reality of their loss, work through the pain, and restore their emotional energy. In addition, counseling can help bereaved families construct an accurate memorialization of the deceased and thereby reach a successful resolution.
—*Janice Bacino Bodet*

See also Death; Divorce; Family therapy; Funerals; Suicide; Support groups; Widowhood.

Group marriage

RELEVANT ISSUES: Marriage and dating; Parenting and family relationships

SIGNIFICANCE: Group marriage is an agreement that links three or more people in a projection of a common future marked by cohabitation, emotional interdependence, economic sharing, and sexual access to persons in addition to one's spouse or prime lover

In theory, group marriage has the unique advantage of providing sexual variety for both men and women within a stable marital configuration. Group marriage differs from communal living. Communes, or places that house between five and more than one hundred persons of all ages, have a high turnover rate. Commune residents are not limited to any specific marital status. They must share money, possessions, time, and space. Property is owned jointly and goods are distributed equally under the direction of a central figure. In group marriage, members usually pool a portion of their incomes to meet household expenses and decide on small asset purchases informally. Members reach consensual decisions for the purchase or distribution of major assets. Their home is usually owned by one legally married couple.

Each group works out its own details of sexual access—when, how often, and where. Most groups have a fixed rotation schedule. Most group members report that they engage in sex more often and enjoy it more. Groups in which sexual jealousy is disruptive tend to break up, while groups in which sexual jealousy is not rampant are more likely to survive.

Studies by Larry and Joan Constantine show that children of group marriages tend toward a high degree of independence and require minimal guidance. They accept responsibility more than they avoid it. Typically, such children think of themselves as having an inner nuclear family within an outer family. Researchers state that what affects child development most is the nature and quality of parents' interactions with them and with each other rather than the structure of the family.

There is no reliable estimate of the number of

group marriages in the United States, because they are not legal. The Constantines reported the existence of about eighty group marriages in the United States in 1973. In a study of thirty-one such marriages, they found that model participants were in their early thirties and already married to one spouse. The largest reported group was composed of six adults. Researchers suggest that the group offers greater economic and emotional security, because it is cheaper for persons to live as a group than in couples, and quarrels do not leave persons emotionally isolated. The potential for emotional growth and for getting feedback is greater among group marriages than among couples. Differences of opinion may be resolved by feedback from the group.

In the 1990's members of group marriages were able to communicate with one another in discussion groups on the Internet via the Group Marriage Alliance Web Page and were able to subscribe to *Loving More Magazine.*   —*Marian Wynne Haber*

See also Communal living; Couples; Household; Marriage; Monogamy; Open marriage; Polygyny; Sexuality and sexual taboos.

Guardianship

RELEVANT ISSUES: Law; Parenting and family relationships

SIGNIFICANCE: Legally appointed guardians care for children and others deemed unable to provide for their own needs, fulfilling some of the functions of the family

A guardian is a person or entity who has legal responsibility for the care and management of another person. This care usually is exercised for minor children or adults who have been declared in court to be incapable of acting for themselves, primarily those who are deemed mentally or physically incompetent to handle their own affairs. Typically, a guardian takes care of an individual's personal needs, including shelter, education, and medical care. A guardian may not have physical custody but has virtually the same legal powers and responsibilities as a parent.

Duties of Guardians. As early as the nineteenth century, courts held that the tuition and custody of an orphan could be committed to one person and the care and management of the orphan's estate to another person. Such guardians were expected to take into their possession, for the use of their child wards, the profits of all lands, heritable property, goods, and chattels (including slaves). The guardian was required to manage properly any funds received on behalf of the child and to protect all property and assets belonging to the child.

The orphan's court of 1841 stipulated that all guardians should render annual accounts of their activities. Clerks would issue *ex officio* summons to those guardians who failed to render such accounts. The rights and duties of guardians required that they be responsible for providing for the basic and special needs of minor wards, including food, clothing, shelter, consent and requirement for medical care, and enrollment and maintenance of appropriate education. Guardians were expected to notify the court in writing whenever their wards' addresses changed, and they had to obtain permission from the court to move wards to a residence in another state or country.

Modern guardians may take legal action to obtain child support for their minor wards and explore eligibility for Aid to Families with Dependent Children (AFDC), Social Security benefits, Veterans Administration benefits, Indian child benefits, and other public or private funds. A guardian has the authority to consent to a ward's application for a driver's license, and such guardians are held liable if the child is involved in property damage or accidents involving a motor vehicle. The court may set other conditions on the guardianship and order additional duties and responsibilities.

Historical Context. The concept of guardianship developed in early English law was closely modeled on principles recognized in earlier Roman law. Under Roman law, mentally impaired persons were deemed incapable of engaging in any activity recognized by the law, regardless of whether a guardian had been appointed. These mentally impaired individuals could not make purchases even though they had money of their own, and they could not receive or convey title to property, act as witnesses, enter into contracts, or be married. If such actions occurred while an individual was deemed mentally competent, these actions were deemed valid even if the individual was under the care of a guardian. Similar principles have been applied to children, on the basis that their mental faculties are not well enough developed for them to be allowed or expected to take on adult responsibilities and rights.

English law was more concerned with the protection of property than with the care and safety of mentally impaired individuals. In the thirteenth century, the royal benevolence to protect both the person and the property of individuals deemed to be "natural fools" was tempered by the Crown's right to receive and retain profits generated by these subjects' property. In the time of Lord Coke, guardians were appointed by the Lord Chancellor following a jury trial. The pervading principle in guardianship proceedings revolved around the king's (or state's) role as protector rather than titleholder. From this benevolent protection was born the doctrine of *parens patriae*, or the Crown as ultimate parent of all citizens. This legal doctrine was enunciated in the early Chancery decision of *Eyre v. Shaftsbury* in 1722.

Historically, guardianship was promoted as a legal mechanism that offered mentally impaired individuals the chance to take the risks of life, exercising individual rights without suffering severe consequences. In the twentieth century, particularly during the 1960's, guardianship was attacked as an overintrusive legal invasion of individual rights. Guardianship is no longer universally viewed as the cure for family and social dilemmas involving mentally impaired and incompetent family members.

Family Life and Guardian Relationships. Guardianship planning for children and adults is a growing concern for all families. By the year 2000, an estimated 80,000 children will be involved in family experiences that call for guardianship planning.

Adults who are raising children without legal authorization from the courts may experience problems when parental authority from a parent or court is required. Some communities and institutions, however, are accommodating of guardians who are raising other people's children. The state of California has created a form that gives permission to an individual who is not a child's parent to enroll a child in school and make medical decisions on his or her behalf without court authorization under some circumstances.

Guardianship is subject to change as a family's lifestyle changes. Such arrangements may be terminated if the guardian, the child, a parent, or another interested party petitions the court to end the guardianship. The person seeking to terminate the guardianship must prove to the court that such guardianship is no longer necessary for the protection of the minor or adult ward. Some individuals believe that guardianship results in a deprivation of personal rights and civil liberties because a judicial determination must be made that the individual ward has acquired or regained competence. Until such time, the guardian may continue to make economic, legal, and personal choices that affect the ward's well-being.

Guardians need not be related to their wards. The courts may decide to appoint a guardian when there is no parent or relative who is able or available to meet the needs of an individual because of death, incapacity, abandonment, military obligation, or other reason.

A guardian also may provide financial management of a ward's assets, although sometimes a second person known as a conservator, or guardian of the estate, is appointed for this purpose. Guardianship establishes a legal relationship between a ward and an adult guardian, but it does not sever the legal relationship between the biological parents and a child ward. If they are still living, the biological parents are legally required to provide financial support for their child. In practice, however, such financial support often becomes the guardian's responsibility. Any funds received by guardians must be used for their wards' benefit. Depending on the amount of money involved, the guardian may be required to file periodic reports with the court showing how much money was received and how it was spent. If a biological parent dies without a will, the child has certain automatic inheritance rights.

Modern Guardianship. As a general rule, guardianships are not granted for children unless parents give their voluntary consent, have abandoned their child, or have been found to be unfit to have custody of their child by a judge. Permanent guardianship procedures stipulate that any individual may file a petition for permanent guardianship. The petition of guardianship should include the name, sex, residence, and date and place of birth of the child or adult ward. In addition, the petition should provide the facts and circumstances supporting the need for permanent guardianship. The name and address of the prospective guardian and a statement that the prospective guardian agrees to accept the duties and responsibilities of guardianship also should be included in the petition.

A court investigator will likely interview the person filing for guardianship, the child, and the child's parents if they are alive and available. Based on these interviews, the investigator makes a recommendation to the judge. The judge then reviews the case for guardianship and decides whether to appoint the person as guardian. This decision usually is rendered after a hearing is held. The court must find that the appointment is in the best interest of the child or adult ward. A last will and testament also may be used to name a guardian for a child.

Guardianship of a child ceases when the child reaches legal age, when he or she dies, when the assets designated to support the child are exhausted (if the guardianship was established solely to administer finances), or when a judge determines that a guardian is no longer necessary. Guardians may step down from their roles with permission from the court, or guardianship may be transferred if the court deems that the performance of the original guardian is not in the best interests of the child or adult ward.

—*Deborah Bass Artis*

BIBLIOGRAPHY

Allen, R. C., E. Z. Ferster, and H. Weihofen. *Mental Impairment and Legal Incompetency.* Englewood Cliffs, N.J.: Prentice-Hall, 1968.

Johns, A. Frank. *Guardianship from 1978 to 1988 in View of Restructure.* Greensboro, N.C.: North Carolina Bar Association, 1988.

Levine, Carol, and Gary Stein. *Orphans of the HIV Epidemic: Unmet Needs in Six U.S. Cities.* New York: The Orphan Project, 1994.

See also Child abandonment; Child custody; Child rearing; Children's rights; Family law; Foster homes; *In loco parentis*; Juvenile courts; Wills and bequests.

Habitat for Humanity International (HFHI)

DATE: Founded in 1968
RELEVANT ISSUES: Economics and work; Sociology
SIGNIFICANCE: Habitat for Humanity International collaborates with families living in substandard housing to make it possible for them to own their own homes

Eliminating poverty housing is the goal of Habitat for Humanity International (HFHI). The organization is a nonprofit ecumenical Christian foundation that provides simple, decent, affordable housing for less fortunate families. Volunteers of all ages from every walk of life and economic level work with Habitat families to build, repair, or renovate homes. According to biblical principles, these homes are provided with no-interest, no-profit mortgages to selected families.

The Family Selection Committee for local affiliates screens applicants. The selected families are required to put in what is called "sweat equity"— that is, between 300 and 500 hours of work on

A Habitat for Humanity home under construction. (James L. Shaffer)

their homes or the homes of other Habitat families. A small down payment is also required. Low monthly mortgage payments are usually less that the family would have to pay for rent. The cost of Habitat homes built in the 1990's ranged from an average of $2,300 in overseas projects to an average of $38,000 in North American projects. Costs of homes differ according to location and costs of labor, land, and materials.

The idea for this ecumenical Christian ministry began in 1968 with Clarence Jordan and Millard Fuller, who started what they called the Fund for Humanity. In 1973, the organization widened its scope, tackling international problems with a community project in Zaire. In 1976, the organization changed its name to Habitat for Humanity International. During its first four years, Habitat for Humanity expanded to sixteen projects in North America, Africa, and Central America. In 1997 Habitat for Humanity International had about 1,400 affiliates in the United States and 299 in 54 countries outside the United States. As of 1997 Habitat for Humanity had built 60,000 houses and set itself the goal of building 100,000 by the year 2000. Former U.S. president Jimmy Carter, often called the most famous Habitat volunteer, has helped with building houses every year since 1984 in various cities across the United States (Jimmy Carter Work Projects).   —*Eril Barnett Hughes*

See also Home ownership; Homeless families; Volunteerism.

Haley, Alex

BORN: August 11, 1921, Ithaca, N.Y.
DIED: February 10, 1992, Seattle, Wash.
AREAS OF ACHIEVEMENT: Art and the media; Kinship and genealogy
SIGNIFICANCE: Haley generated significant interest in family history through the publication of his book *Roots*

Alex Haley spent most of his early life in Henning, Tennessee, and other Southern communities, and he was greatly influenced by the stories his maternal grandmother recounted about their family traditions, which had been passed on from one generation to the next. Haley served in the U.S. Coast Guard from 1939 to 1959, and he spent much of his time writing in order to reduce boredom on

long voyages. He assisted African American revolutionary Malcolm X in writing *The Autobiography of Malcolm X*, which was published in 1965.

In 1965 Haley turned his interests to studying his family history. In 1972 he established the Kinte Foundation to store records that aid in tracing African American genealogy. Based on his grandmother's stories of their family and twelve years of his own research, he completed *Roots: The Saga of an American Family* in 1976. This history begins with his ancestor Kunta Kinte in Gambia in 1767 and follows seven generations of Haley's family in America, dramatically portraying their struggles as slaves and later as free people. In 1977 Haley received a special Pulitzer Prize for *Roots*. An eight-part television series was made from *Roots* and broadcast in 1977. It became one of the most popular shows in American television history, attracting about 130 million viewers.   —*Alvin K. Benson*

See also African Americans; Family gatherings and reunions; Family trees; Genealogy; Lineage; Literature and families; Myths and storytelling; Slavery.

Hall, G. Stanley

BORN: February 1, 1844, Ashfield, Mass.
DIED: April 24, 1924, Worcester, Mass.
AREAS OF ACHIEVEMENT: Children and child development; Education
SIGNIFICANCE: As one of the pioneers of American psychology, Hall founded the first American psychological journal and was the first president of the American Psychological Association

G. Stanley Hall had an amazingly varied career. With great bursts of energy, he studied, lectured, and wrote about a wide range of topics related to psychology and education. After studying for the ministry he switched to philosophy, in part because his ideas seemed too liberal. He studied philosophy and physiology in Germany, and in 1878 he became the first American to have a Ph.D. in psychology. In the 1800's he founded the first American psychology laboratory at The Johns Hopkins University and became the first president of the brand new Clark University in Worcester, Massachusetts. The theory of evolution influenced Hall's psychology, which he called genetic psychology, the name he gave to the second of several

Alex Haley with various editions of his books. (Archive Photos/Jim Britt)

journals he founded. After popularizing child study and the questionnaire method of collecting data, he moved on to study adolescence. His huge two-volume work entitled *Adolescence: Its Psychology and Its Relation to Physiology, Anthropology, Sociology, Sex, Crime, Religion and Education* was published in 1904. At the age of seventy-eight he published a book on the psychology of old age. Hall is credited with making Americans aware of psychoanalysis by bringing the Austrian psychoanalyst Sigmund Freud and the Swiss psychologist Carl Jung to Clark University in 1909 to discuss their works with American psychologists. — *George A. Morgan*

See also Aging and elderly care; Childhood history; Educating children; Freudian psychology; Generational relationships; Gessell, Arnold L.; Mead, George H.; Motherhood; Puberty and adolescence; Sexuality and sexual taboos.

Head Start

DATE: Launched in July, 1965
RELEVANT ISSUES: Children and child development; Education; Law; Parenting and family relationships; Race and ethnicity
SIGNIFICANCE: The Head Start program promotes the intellectual, physical, and social development of preschool children living in poverty

Established under the Economic Opportunity Act of 1964, Title II, and approved on August 20, 1964, Head Start was launched in July, 1965, as part of President Lyndon B. Johnson's "Great Society" programs known as the War on Poverty. The program seeks to disrupt the cycle of poverty by helping impoverished and disadvantaged preschool-age children to acquire education and skills necessary for success in primary school and beyond. In the mid-1990's, the program served about 750,000 children. A total of nearly fourteen million children had been served since 1965.

Broadly, Head Start is charged with promoting the physical, cognitive, social, and emotional growth of young children in poor families. The program accomplishes these goals through community-based preschool classes, health screenings, provision of nutritious meals, social service referrals, family support, and other services. It is a comprehensive program for early childhood development.

Program Administration and Goals. Head Start involves federal, state, and local governments, as well as private community organizations and parents. The program is primarily funded by the federal government, which allocated about $3.5 billion annually in the mid-1990's. Communities typically contribute cash and services that account for about 20 percent of the total operating costs. The national program is administered by the Administration for Children, Youth and Families of the U.S. Department of Health and Human Services. The actual services are provided by more than two thousand local organizations, which must meet certain performance standards set and enforced by the federal government. Sometimes these local service providers are schools, but more often they are community groups (including home-based service providers).

Head Start is an overwhelmingly popular program, receiving bipartisan support for more than three decades. This kind of support is rather unique among the Great Society social welfare programs, most of which eventually came under attack by conservatives as wasteful, inefficient, misguided, or fraud-ridden. Part of the program's attractiveness is its emphasis on attacking the root causes of poverty, as opposed to merely treating its symptoms. Numerous studies have confirmed that the greatest impact on attacking poverty's roots is made in children's earliest years. By focusing on three- to five-year-olds, Head Start is thought to efficiently target resources. The program received a major boost in funding and other resources on its twenty-fifth anniversary in 1990, when the U.S. Congress passed by an almost unanimous vote the Head Start Expansion and Improvement Act.

Following this logic, an Early Head Start program was added in 1994 to help children from birth to three years old. Due to the nature of this population, Early Head Start is more focused on nutrition, neonatal care, home visits, and child care than the programs aimed at preschool children. Nevertheless, the basic philosophy of Head Start, which seeks to address the needs of the "whole child" and to uphold the role of parents, remains a bulwark of Early Head Start.

While Head Start is aimed at children in poverty, it serves children from a variety of ethnic and community backgrounds. In the late 1990's about a third of the children enrolled in Head Start were

Head Start was designed to give children living in poverty a better chance to succeed in their educations. (AP/Wide World Photos)

white, about a third were African American, and about a quarter were Hispanic. The remainder were of Asian American, Native American, and other backgrounds. Since 1972 Head Start has embraced disabled children; in the late 1990's about 12 percent of Head Start children were disabled. Head Start services are offered in both urban and rural areas.

Role of Families and Communities. When Head Start was launched in 1965, it was explicitly charged with working closely with the parents of poor children and with the communities in which they live. These mandates seem to have contributed to the program's longevity and success.

Head Start programs are available to children in families that live beneath the federal poverty line (about $14,500 for a family of four in the mid-1990's). It is assumed that such families are hard pressed to provide for the nutritional needs of their children, that the parents (or single parents) might be in need of child-care services in order to work or increase their education, that these parents might be poorly equipped to provide the critical learning and social skills their children will need in school, and that the very condition of poverty can create other obstacles that handicap children's learning potential.

Although Head Start is best known for its focus

Head Start participants in Texas. (Diane C. Lyell)

on early childhood education, local Head Start programs administer services in four other component areas: health, social services, nutrition, and parent involvement. This last component area is regarded as especially critical to the overall success of the program. Leaders of Head Start repeatedly emphasize that parents remain the primary caregivers and educators of their children and that the family is the principal influence on a child's development. Rather than supplanting the family, therefore, Head Start seeks to integrate parents into the planning and administration of their local programs. Parents assist in developing curricula, volunteering or working as aides in classrooms, hiring staff, and evaluating program services. In addition, every local Head Start program has a policy council that oversees the running of the program; at least half of the members of each policy council are parents of enrolled children.

Local Head Start programs also work to connect poor families with their communities. This effort has been characterized as a partnership of parents, government, and society, in which all the resources of the community are brought together to provide for the care, development, and growth of society's youngest members. Local Head Start service providers are afforded a large degree of autonomy in order to ensure a high level of community involvement. Local autonomy also allows programs to be tailored to the particular needs of different communities and promotes experimentation with service provision. The program has thus been seen as a vehicle not just for the development of individuals but also for social change.

The goal of connecting families with the larger community is also evident in the Migrant Programs branch of Head Start. Migrant Head Start targets children whose families move into communities only for a portion of the year, usually in pursuit of agricultural work. Local Migrant Head Start services might be provided for only a few weeks out of the year and frequently last most of the working day. Besides providing education and child care (often in a bilingual environment), the program attempts to link migrant families with the broader range of health, social, and other services available in the community. As of the mid-1990's Migrant Head Start programs served about 34,000 children in thirty-eight states.

Developments in the late 1990's, including the increasing incidence of single-parent households and new requirements that parents receiving public assistance undergo training and secure employment, further taxed the ability of poor families to adequately provide for their children. In addition, crime, violence, and drugs increasingly threatened the lives of poor children. Efforts were being made at the federal and community levels to address these new challenges through additional modifications to Head Start programs, regulations, and funding. Despite the success of Head Start, many worried that the family as an institution was losing ground among the country's poor.

—*Steve D. Boilard*

BIBLIOGRAPHY

Advisory Committee on Head Start Quality and Expansion. *Creating a Twenty-first Century Head Start.* Washington, D.C.: U.S. Department of Health and Human Services, 1993.

Ames, Lynda J. *Women Reformed, Women Empowered: Poor Mothers and the Endangered Promise of Head Start.* Philadelphia: Temple University Press, 1997.

Clark, Joan C. *Behavior of Preschoolers and Their Teachers: Little Children Draw Big Circles.* Springfield, Ill.: C. C. Thomas, 1991.

Phillips, Deborah, and Natasha J. Cabrera, eds. *Beyond the Blueprint: Directions for Research for Head Start's Families.* Washington, D.C.: National Academy Press, 1996.

Washington, Valora, and Ura Jean Oyemade. *Project Head Start: Models and Strategies for the Twenty-first Century.* New York: Garland, 1995.

————. *Project Head Start: Past, Present, and Future Trends in the Context of Family Needs.* New York: Garland, 1987.

Zigler, Edward, and Susan Muenchow. *Head Start: The Inside Story of America's Most Successful Educational Experiment.* New York: Basic Books, 1992.

Zigler, Edward, and Sally J. Styfco. *Head Start and Beyond.* New Haven, Conn.: Yale University Press, 1993.

See also Children's Defense Fund (CDF); Children's rights; Culture of poverty theory; Day care; Edelman, Marian Wright; Educating children; Schools.

Health of children

RELEVANT ISSUES: Children and child development; Health and medicine

SIGNIFICANCE: At each stage of development, children experience different health needs and have different abilities to be actively involved in good health practices

The healthy growth and development of children are influenced by genetic and environmental elements. Yet, genetic and environmental elements can also contribute to unhealthy growth and development, as can be seen by infant mortality rates and the incidence of preventable diseases and abnormal development.

Health and Infant Mortality. Infant mortality in the United States has been declining, but it is still higher than in many other countries, including Japan, the Scandinavian countries, Great Britain, and Canada. In the United States there are nearly twice as many infant deaths among African Americans as among whites. Infant deaths among Hispanics approximately equal those among whites. Individual states vary greatly in their infant mortality rates. Teenage pregnancies and out-of-wedlock births are believed to be important factors in infant mortality, primarily because of associated risk factors such as poverty, substance abuse, or low levels of education. Preventable diseases such as tuberculosis and measles can contribute to infant mortality, but their effect can be decreased through access to primary health care. The same relationship exists for abnormal development, as seen in birth defects.

The causes of health problems or deaths in infants and older children are related to factors in society at large. These range from poor maternal

Families in the pediatric emergency waiting room of a New York public hospital. (Hazel Hankin)

Many families that cannot afford regular health care depend on the emergency rooms of public hospitals to look after the health of their children. (Hazel Hankin)

health during pregnancy, to the decline in immunizations for some preventable diseases, to the presence and the use of health-threatening substances in the environment, to the lack of availability and use of health care, to the lack of family support resulting in accidents or death. Knowledge of these factors can affect the ability of parents and caregivers to provide an environment for infants and children that promotes healthy growth and development.

Prenatal Health. Sound prenatal health is an important factor in the development of healthy infants and children. The total dependence of unborn children on their mothers for nourishment and healthy development emphasizes the importance of a thoughtful approach to pregnancy at any age. Unplanned or unrecognized pregnancies can affect the health of infants and children if expectant mothers engage in activities that may prevent normal healthy development. Pregnancy in teenagers can create special problems, because growing mothers will compete with their fetuses for nutrients such as calcium, phosphorus, and iron. In addition, teenagers with low body weight are in danger of having infants with low birth weight, which is one of the leading causes of infant mortality. The thoughtful approach to pregnancy requires that mothers stop and think about what they are doing to themselves and how their behavior will affect their unborn children.

For example, foods and medicines ingested by mothers will be passed on to their unborn babies. Some substances pass quickly to fetuses while others pass on to them slowly. Still others concentrate in unborn children. The wrong drug or medicine during the first twelve weeks of pregnancy, when most birth defects are caused, could damage babies' development. Medical professionals generally agree that the use of drugs, alcohol, tobacco, and caffeine during pregnancy may have a harmful effect on fetuses, but they disagree on how much is too much. Expectant mothers can discuss these matters with health care providers to determine the appropriate approach to each individual pregnancy.

If women take drugs during pregnancy, either prescription or illicit drugs, their children can be born with drug dependencies or birth defects. Prenatal exposure to drugs such as cocaine and heroin has been associated with retarded growth, drug withdrawal, abnormal behavior, and drug dependency in infants. Prematurity and low birth weight have also been associated with drug exposure during pregnancy. Alcohol consumed during pregnancy is associated with fetal alcohol syndrome (FAS), which is characterized by a pattern of physical and mental defects. These include growth deficiencies, heart defects, and malformed facial features. Mental retardation is also associated with this syndrome. Fetal alcohol syndrome is considered to be an acute health problem, because it is associated with increased alcohol consumption in adolescents, who have a relatively high birth rate.

Smoking tobacco during pregnancy can cause nicotine and carbon monoxide to decrease the flow of blood and oxygen to unborn children. Infants of mothers who smoke may be born prematurely, have low birth weights, and be more susceptible to respiratory infections after birth. Caffeine in coffee, tea, chocolate, and soft drinks acts as a stimulant, but it builds up in concentrated amounts in the placenta. The effects of this are not completely known, but studies on animals have linked caffeine to bone deformities and the development of cleft palate.

Spina bifida is another condition that may be caused by unfavorable environmental patterns. This birth defect of the lower spinal cord develops shortly after conception and results in muscle paralysis, spine and limb deformities, and bowel and bladder problems. Spina bifida is believed to be caused by a combination of genetic and environmental factors, but the American Medical Association has noted that the children of women who use hot tubs are almost three times more likely to have this defect than the children of women who do not. Women who intend to become pregnant are thus encouraged to restrict their use of hot tubs and saunas.

Preventable Disease Control. One of the major factors in the health of infants and children is access to immunizations. A vaccine, a substance made of dead or weakened bacteria or virus cells, is given either by injection (shot) or orally so that infants' and children's bodies may build defenses against preventable diseases. Immunizations cause the body to produce antibodies that fight against particular diseases and continue to protect against future exposures. Infants must be vaccinated against mumps, measles, polio, German measles, diphtheria, pertussis (whooping cough), tetanus, chicken pox, and Hib disease (associated with bacterial meningitis). In addition to protecting infants and children against specific diseases, immunizations help to ensure that they will not suffer from the side effects of these diseases, which can include hearing loss and damage to the nervous system or heart.

Older children may require booster shots for some diseases. The American Academy of Pediatrics has worked with the U.S. Centers for Disease Control (CDC) to establish a schedule for immunization of infants and children. Children's primary health care givers should be consulted on the appropriate schedule of immunizations. Regardless of the particular immunization schedule, it is important that children be immunized in order to prevent disease outbreak before they begin kindergarten at ages four to six and when they are in middle or junior high school at ages eleven to twelve. Primary health care givers should also be consulted about the possibility of adverse reactions to vaccines. The chance of adverse reactions is slight, but in some instances mild fever or soreness may be experienced. When compared with the greater danger posed by the diseases against which vaccines guard, such reactions are minor.

In addition to immunizations before starting school, children should be tested for tuberculosis. There has been a resurgence of tuberculosis in the United States, causing serious concern in childcare or educational settings. This disease can cause lymph node infection, pulmonary complications, and possibly a form of meningitis. Because early symptoms resemble those associated with the common cold, tuberculosis has the potential to spread to other children or adults working with children.

Exposure to Health-Threatening Substances. Many substances in the environment can pose a

Immunization and the Action of Vaccines

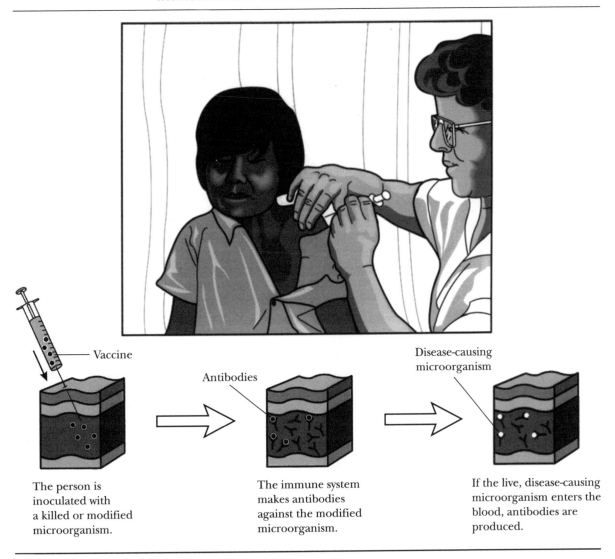

Vaccine

Antibodies

Disease-causing microorganism

The person is inoculated with a killed or modified microorganism.

The immune system makes antibodies against the modified microorganism.

If the live, disease-causing microorganism enters the blood, antibodies are produced.

threat to the health of infants and children. Because of their less developed immune systems and small body size, children have lower resistance to toxic substances and may be at greater health risk than adults. Exposure can take different forms, such as inhalation of secondhand smoke or dust, absorption of chemicals that come in contact with the skin, or ingestion of solids or liquids. Secondhand smoke from cigarettes, pipes, or cigars can be released into the air from two sources. Mainstream smoke is first inhaled into a smoker's mouth and nasal passages before being exhaled. Sidestream smoke is more dangerous for nonsmokers, because it goes directly into the air from burning tobacco. It has higher concentrations of harmful compounds such as benzene and formaldehyde than mainstream smoke and has carbon monoxide levels that may be two to fifteen times higher than in mainstream smoke.

Studies have shown that secondhand smoke is detrimental to infants and children. Smoking by pregnant women may cause premature babies to be susceptible to respiratory distress syndrome. Babies of parents who smoke have a higher rate of lung diseases, such as bronchitis and pneumonia, in their first two years of life than babies of nonsmoking parents. Studies have also shown that babies of smokers may have problems with speech, intelligence, and attention span. Children ages five to nine years old have shown impaired lung function from secondhand smoke. Asthma attacks can be triggered by secondhand smoke. It is apparent that smokeless environments will give infants and children the best possible opportunity for healthy growth and development.

Infants and children are also at risk of exposure to toxic chemicals that may be used in households. Cleaning agents and insecticides may be absorbed through the skin if infants and children are accidentally exposed to them. The potential for absorption through the skin may be higher with those substances that contain organic solvents to maintain the chemicals' liquid form or to boost cleaning power. Acute exposure to toxic chemicals may have less severe results, such as nausea, dizziness, or fever, but chronic exposure could lead to the development of multiple chemical sensitivities or life-threatening diseases such as cancer. It is important to keep toxic chemicals out of the reach of children as well as to limit children's exposure

to them. The use of more natural cleaning products and insecticides may help reduce the possible development of long-term health problems.

Environmental Hazards. As infants and children develop, so does their tendency to put objects and substances into their mouths. Those objects that are small enough can pose a health threat if they are swallowed or lodged in the esophagus or lungs. Other substances that can be swallowed may pose a long-term health threat because of their chemical effects on the body. This is especially the case with lead, which may be present in paint and water pipes in older homes as well as in the soil in and around homes. Lead, whether swallowed or inhaled through dust, can build up in the blood and cause long-term effects such as learning disabilities, decreased growth, hyperactivity, impaired learning, and possibly brain damage. These effects can be reduced by medical treatment if lead poisoning is diagnosed early enough. Parents should have their children tested for lead poisoning if their homes contain paint that is more than thirty years old. Other ways to reduce the likelihood of lead exposure include keeping toys and pacifiers clean and preventing children from chewing on painted surfaces such as window sills, cribs, or playpens. Finally, parents should remember that good eating habits can help reduce the effects of lead; a diet with the appropriate amounts of iron and calcium will decrease the ability of the body to absorb lead.

Use of Alternative Health Care. The increasing cost of health care in the United States has placed it out of the reach of many infants and children. For parents who have no access to health insurance, the need to locate less expensive forms of medical care has become increasingly important. Alternative remedies to Western medical treatments are available, but many health care providers do not consider these as replacements for prescription drugs and surgery. However, more health care providers have begun to recognize that dietary changes supplemented by vitamins and herbs can alter the course of diseases. Some health care givers recognize that Western medical treatment can be combined with alternative treatments to support children's health. Parents working together with such health care givers may be able to provide children with less expensive but effective health care.

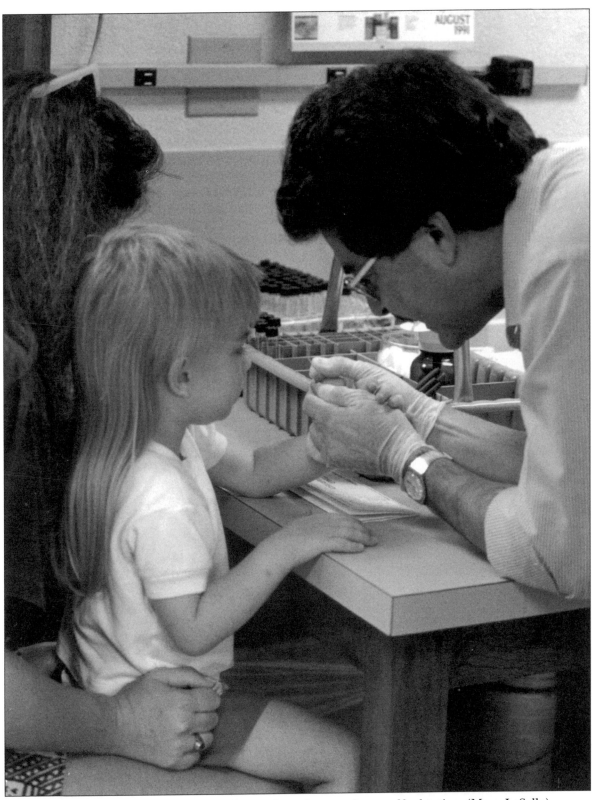

Regular health care of children involves such routine procedures as blood testing. (Mary LaSalle)

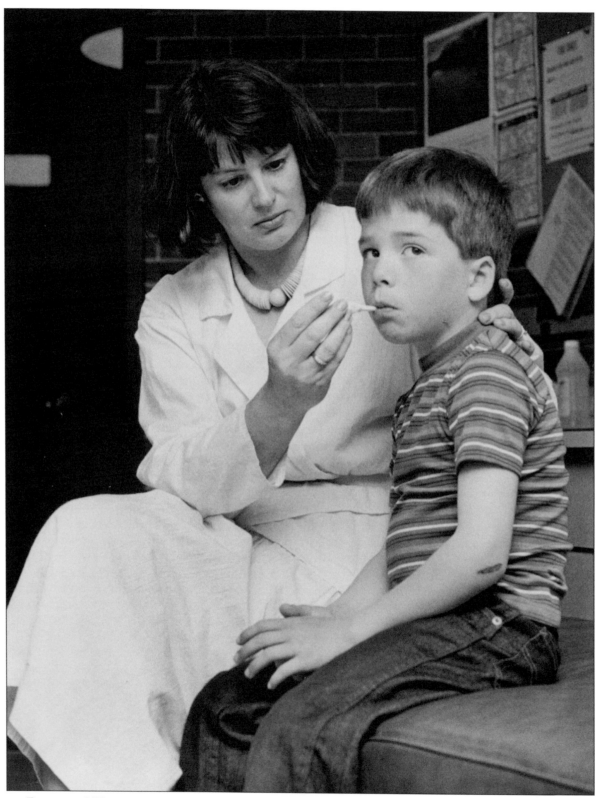

For many children, even routine procedures such as temperature-taking cause anxiety. (James L. Shaffer)

Parents and caregivers should ask two questions when considering the health of children. First, is there something in the environment that should be removed in order to promote the health of children? Second, if children become ill, what should be done to help them recuperate? By taking inventory of the elements in the environment, parents and caregivers can make better decisions that will affect the long-term health of children. They must remember that a small investment in time or thought can prevent a very large financial investment in medical care that may be required as a result of no, or poor, decisions about children's health.   —*Cherilyn Nelson*

BIBLIOGRAPHY

Behrman, Richard E., ed. *Nelson Textbook of Pediatrics.* 14th ed. Philadelphia: W. B. Saunders, 1992. Standard pediatrics textbook that is written to be understood by nonspecialists and covers both common and uncommon causes of infectious disease in children.

Edelstein, Sari F. *The Healthy Young Child.* Minneapolis/St. Paul: West Publishing Company, 1995. Discusses infants from birth to one year old, toddlers and preschoolers from one to five years old, and elementary-age children from six to eight years old in terms of growth, development, physical activity, nutrition, safety, hygiene, and modern health issues.

Gravelle, Karen. *Understanding Birth Defects.* New York: Franklin Watts, 1990. Discusses the nature of birth defects, how to prevent them, and what to do for children who have them.

Reuben, Carolyn. *The Healthy Baby Book: A Parent's Guide to Preventing Birth Defects and Other Long-Term Medical Problems Before, During, and After Pregnancy.* New York: Jeremy P. Tarcher/Perigee, 1992. Straightforward guidebook on children's health written for parents.

Spock, Benjamin, and Michael B. Rothenberg. *Dr. Spock's Baby and Child Care.* New York: Simon & Schuster, 1985. Updated version of Spock's classic advice to parents on all aspects of child rearing and common childhood health problems.

Trahms, Christine M., and Peggy L. Pipes, eds. *Nutrition in Infancy and Childhood.* 6th ed. New York: McGraw-Hill, 1997. Comprehensive overview, written for both professionals and nonprofessionals, of the nutritional needs of both healthy and sick children from infancy through adolescence, the development of food habits, and the prevention of chronic diseases through dietary intervention.

Wicks-Nelson, Rita, and Allen C. Israel. *Behavior Disorders of Childhood.* Englewood Cliffs, N.J.: Prentice Hall, 1991. Standard textbook on the mental health problems of children.

See also Alcoholism and drug abuse; Attention-deficit hyperactivity disorder (ADHD); Behavior disorders; Birth defects; Child abuse; Child care; Child safety; Disabilities; Health problems; Pediatric AIDS; Sudden infant death syndrome (SIDS).

Health problems

RELEVANT ISSUE: Health and medicine

SIGNIFICANCE: Because any problem affecting a member of the family system affects the entire system, the health problems of one family member affect the entire group

To understand how health problems affect families, it is helpful to consider the family as a system. That is, a family forms a social unit; each member has a relationship with every other member, in addition to having relationships outside the family. The family system is important in teaching its members about what it means to be a mother, father, sister, brother, wife, husband, child, friend, pupil, worker. Among many other things, the family teaches values and attitudes about health and illness. Furthermore, the family provides for the physical, emotional, and spiritual needs of its members.

How Health Problems Challenge Families. As an example of how a simple health problem can affect an entire family system, consider a child with a fever. The child's day-care center does not allow the child to attend if he or she has a fever. Thus, someone must stay at home with the child unless a baby-sitter can be found. The parents must decide who will stay at home, and an argument ensues. The mother stays home but loses a day's pay because she has used up all her sick days. This means that the family cannot pay all of its monthly bills. Financial stress causes more arguments between the parents. The child begins to develop behavior problems because of family stress. The entire system is at risk.

The health care delivery system in the United States tends to focus on individuals with health problems, without consideration of the effects of individuals' illnesses on the family system. However, to a greater or lesser extent the health problems of one member challenge the coping abilities of the entire system. Furthermore, evidence suggests that families have a powerful effect on the health or illness of its individual members. Some researchers believe that family interactions actually cause persons to be either healthy or ill.

The family influences the health of its individual members on at least three different levels. First, the family is important in the lifestyle choices its members make. Smoking, consuming alcohol or other drugs, and eating particular foods are examples of lifestyle choices that influence the possible development of serious illnesses such as heart disease and cancer. Second, the family influences how its members perceive symptoms that could signal illness, whether or not they seek medical care, what types of health care providers

they consult, and how quickly they seek care. Studies have shown that many mothers play an extremely powerful role in this area. They often determine whether family members are well enough to attend school or day care and make initial contact with health care professionals, particularly for themselves and their children. Finally, families determine how well their members follow prescribed treatments recommended by health care providers.

When persons have health problems, the effect on the family system varies according to many factors. These include how serious the illness is. A child's ear infection is not as serious as cancer. The stability and strength of the family and the stressors on the family are also important. A child's ear infection is more stressful in a family in which the parents are out of work or other children are already ill. How the family responds to illness plays a role, as does its resources. For example, illnesses are less of a challenge to families that have adequate health insurance. The charac-

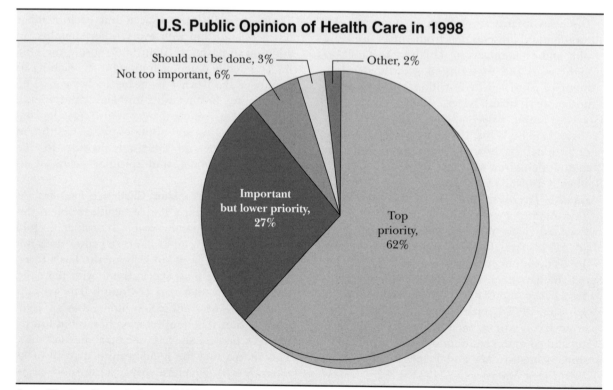

U.S. Public Opinion of Health Care in 1998

Should not be done, 3%
Not too important, 6%
Other, 2%
Important but lower priority, 27%
Top priority, 62%

Source: The Pew Research Center (1998)

Note: In early 1998 the Pew Research Center conducted a nationwide survey in which 1,200 adults were asked how high a priority reforming national health care should be for the federal government during the coming year. This chart summarizes responses.

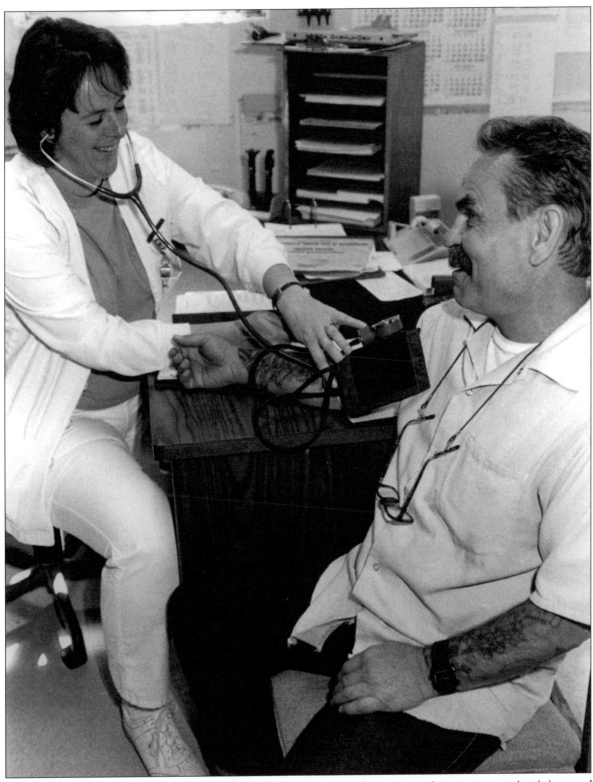

As people grow older, regular checkups and physical examinations become more important to maintaining good health. (Ben Klaffke)

Regular exercise is another important component of health maintenance. (James L. Shaffer)

teristics of illnesses is another factor: Families are usually less challenged by brief illnesses than by chronic illnesses. Some illnesses, such as acquired immunodeficiency syndrome (AIDS) or alcoholism, may be perceived as shameful, cutting off families from necessary resources due to embarrassment or guilt. Family responses also depend on members' beliefs about illness and health, which are heavily influenced by families' ethnic, cultural, and religious backgrounds. For example, some ethnic groups regard health and illness as a matter of fate that remain uninfluenced by human intervention. Such groups would be unlikely to engage in preventive health behavior.

Adaptive and Maladaptive Families. Many researchers have examined the characteristics of families who respond in a healthy or adaptive way to its members' health problems and families for whom illness results in less healthy responses, such as divorce or substance abuse. Families who have a sense of control over life, who stick together, who are flexible, and who value family time appear better able to meet the challenges of illness. Good communication is essential, as are good problem-solving and decision-making skills. Less adaptive families suffer from anxiety and are less clear about family members' roles. They also suffer from many other stressors and hardships. Support groups, in which other families can show them how to communicate better and work together in a more productive fashion, may help such families.

Genetic Disorders and Chronic Illnesses. Families have particular difficulty coping with genetic disorders. If persons know they are carriers of a genetic disease, they must decide whether or not to have children. If a genetic disorder becomes apparent after the birth of a child or in later life, the parents may feel guilty about having passed the problem along to the child. They may become anxious about their other children or question whether they should have additional children. Genetic counseling is available for people at high risk of genetic disorders.

Chronic illnesses pose their own challenges. Such illnesses involve many uncertainties. Asthma, for example, may be controllable most of the time, but it may suddenly become a life-threatening crisis. Dealing with the possibility of crisis in addition to dealing with actual crises creates additional stress. In addition, chronic illnesses challenge every aspect of the family system. If wage earners have chronic health problems, not only might other family members be required to seek work, but the illness itself may strain family finances. Because of high deductibles, copayments, and uncovered medical expenses, even families with health insurance may be overburdened by family members with chronic illnesses. In addition, families' income may drop considerably if wage earners cannot work regularly.

Sometimes children must assume adult roles at very young ages. If a parent is preoccupied with the care of a chronically ill spouse, children may have to assume responsibility for the care of the home or yard, for shopping, or for taking care of younger siblings. How families interact with school and community also changes. If illness befalls a family, it may no longer have time to participate in its usual social activities. Families sometimes become socially isolated or fail to make use of available professional resources. This may be due to their feelings of guilt or embarrassment because family members are ill. Mental illness, for example, is stigmatized by many. Sometimes social isolation is due to others' fears and misconceptions about illness. For example, many people shun cancer patients, fearing that the disease may be contagious.

Addictions and Terminal Illness. Addiction is another serious health problem for families. Smoking is problematic because of the large number of health conditions associated with chronic use. Smokers are more vulnerable to chronic or terminal diseases such as chronic bronchitis, emphysema, lung cancer, and heart disease. Babies exposed to cigarette smoke in the womb are more likely to be small and have problems associated with low birth weight. Furthermore, some evidence ties smoking to an increased risk of sudden infant death syndrome (SIDS). Children in homes in which someone smokes are more prone to ear infections. Not only must families deal with the impact of diseases related to smoking, but smokers might experience guilt or blame for others' health problems.

The effect of alcoholism or drug use on the family has been well studied. Intergenerational problems with alcoholism and other addictions are not unusual. The risk that persons may become alcoholic is about four times greater if they have alcoholic parents. Some theorists believe that eating disorders are also common in families with addictions. Because of the differences in socialization between boys and girls, researchers think that it may be more common for boys to become addicted to alcohol or other drugs and for girls to suffer from eating disorders. Families with addictions tend to live in a constant state of crisis because of the unpredictable behavior of addicts. Because addicts are regarded by some as moral failures or as persons who lack willpower, families with addictions tend to hide their problems. Some children may act out the stresses within the system, however, leading them to be truant from school, use drugs, or become pregnant. Others may respond by becoming overachievers. The entire family must receive help to recover from this serious problem. Such family support groups as Al-Anon and Alateen have achieved some success in helping the families of addicts.

The death of a family member is possibly the greatest stressor the family system experiences. Deaths in families became even more stressful in late twentieth century America; medical advances have meant that the death of a child is no longer a common experience. Diseases formerly fatal can often be cured. Technology leads persons to expect miracles. Furthermore, terminal illness, death, and funeral rites have been removed from the home, so that many families are not accustomed to death as part of their life experience. Like all other health problems, death requires major shifts and puts enormous strains on the family system.

Help for Families. Many health professionals have become more aware of the need to examine the effects of illness on the entire family system. Nursing and mental health professionals, in par-

Methods of Cancer Treatment

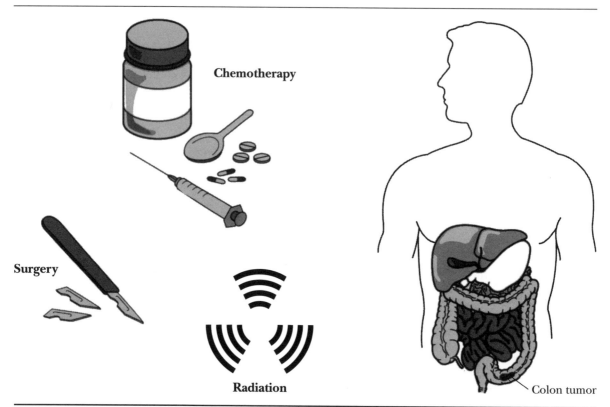

Chemotherapy

Surgery

Radiation

Colon tumor

The presence of a malignant tumor requires some form of treatment or a combination of treatments, usually beginning with its surgical removal and followed by radiation therapy and/or chemotherapy (the use of anticancer drugs).

ticular, are trained to deal with families challenged by health problems. Many families have found support from groups established particularly to help them deal with health problems. Some of these are sponsored by local health care facilities, others by national organizations, and still others by concerned volunteers. Many self-help books dealing with health problems and families are available. Increasingly, support groups and information on illness and the family are available through the Internet. Churches and other religious organizations have also traditionally supported families with health problems.

—*Rebecca Lovell Scott*

BIBLIOGRAPHY

Berger, Diane. *We Heard the Angels of Madness: How One Family Dealt with Manic Depression.* New York: William Morrow, 1992. Chronicle of a family's experience in dealing with the problem of a family member' manic-depressive illness.

Bordow, J. *The Ultimate Loss: Coping with the Death of a Child.* New York: Beaufort Books, 1982. The death of a child is a major crisis for the family. This book offers vignettes and commentary about coping with this loss.

Danielson, C. B., et al. *Families, Health, and Illness: Perspectives on Coping and Intervention.* St. Louis: Mosby, 1993. Written to help health professionals understand the role of families in health and illness, this book includes chapters on the theories of family function and dysfunction and case studies illustrating the responses of hypothetical families to various illnesses.

Donnelly, K. F. *Recovering from the Loss of a Loved One to AIDS.* New York: St. Martin's Press, 1994. One of a series of books by this author on recovery from catastrophic events, this work deals with individual and family responses to a death due to AIDS.

Kalb, R. C., and L. C. Scheinberg. *Multiple Sclerosis and the Family.* New York: Demos Publications, 1992. A slim volume by experts in various fields, this book discusses how multiple sclerosis affects the family system, covering its effects on parenting, how to deal with physicians, financial and legal implications, fertility, sexuality, and advocacy.

Lefley, H. P, and D. L. Johnson. *Families as Allies in Treatment of the Mentally Ill: New Directions for Men-tal Health Professionals.* Washington, D.C.: American Psychiatric Press, 1990. Although written for mental health professionals, this book is readable and possibly helpful to families dealing with mental illness.

Mace, N. L., and P. V. Rabins. *The Thirty-Six-Hour Day: A Family Guide to Caring for Persons with Alzheimer's Disease, Related Dementing Illnesses and Memory Loss in Later Life.* Rev. ed. Baltimore: Johns Hopkins University Press, 1991. Guide for persons with family members who have debilitating memory-loss illnesses.

Sanders, C. M. *How to Survive the Loss of a Child.* Rocklin, Calif.: Prima Publishing, 1992. Written by a psychologist specializing in bereavement, this book tells the story of the effect on her own family of the death of a teenager.

Strong, M. *Mainstay.* Boston: Little, Brown, 1988. Personal account of the author's struggles to cope with the changes brought about in her family by the unexpected chronic illness of her husband. Also a guide for the healthy spouse of a chronically ill person.

Virag, I. *We're All in This Together.* New York: Newsday, 1995. Essays and stories about families facing breast cancer.

See also Abortion; Acquired immunodeficiency syndrome (AIDS); Alcoholism and drug abuse; Alzheimer's disease; Americans with Disabilities Act (ADA); Attention-deficit hyperactivity disorder (ADHD); Disabilities; Eating disorders; Euthanasia; Fertility and infertility; Health of children; Mental health; Pregnancy; Support groups.

Heredity

RELEVANT ISSUES: Health and medicine; Kinship and genealogy

SIGNIFICANCE: Advances in genetic science have increased public understanding of heredity and presented families with more choices and dilemmas than ever before in human history

Heredity is the transmission of physical traits, behavioral tendencies, strengths, and weaknesses from parents to children via parental genes. All traits can be influenced by factors other than genes, such as prenatal nutrition, nutrition during infancy, learning, exposure to toxic substances, transmission of disease organisms from parents to children, and the physical properties of children's early environment such as heat, light, physical contact, feeding, and stimulation. Such environmental factors that can cause children to resemble their parents are sometimes called ecological inheritance.

To complicate the picture, most scientists believe that nearly every trait is a combined product of genes, ecological inheritance, and unique environmental factors. It is therefore not possible to ask whether a characteristic is caused by genes or by the environment. Rather, it is more useful to understand the process by which genes and environmental factors interact to influence a person's characteristics, because that knowledge can show how to intervene to prevent diseases and improve the quality of life.

Historical Perspective. Although the cellular reality of genes was not discovered until 1953, philosophers and scientists in the Western world have always wielded a great deal of influence with their strong beliefs about heredity. The ancient Greeks believed that fathers' sperm contained preformed children. The contribution of mothers to their children's development was limited to providing a womb in which children grow. This belief was not inspired by any scientific examination of reproduction; rather, it reflected a cultural system in which children belonged solely to fathers.

Throughout the early history of the Western world, it was also believed that the initial, inherited characteristics of children—nature—could not be changed by life circumstances—nurture. Like the belief that children inherited their traits solely from their fathers, the idea of unchangeability can be seen as reflecting the cultural systems of early European societies. In these systems power, privilege, and wealth were held by a few families, and most people lived in poverty and lacked political and human rights. The belief that nature made some people unchangeably better than others supported a system in which most people did not share in the wealth or power of their societies.

These two beliefs, that inheritance was primarily patrilineal and that nature was unchanging and more powerful than nurture, continued to influence public policy and scientific research well into the twentieth century. For example, the symptoms of fetal alcohol syndrome (FAS) were documented by scholars in ancient Rome and many times throughout subsequent European history. It was also noted that children with FAS often had alcoholic parents. However, it was believed that children with FAS had inherited their fathers' "bad blood." The persistent belief in the overriding power of inheritance kept the primary cause of FAS, the mother's consumption of alcohol during pregnancy, from being discovered until the late twentieth century.

Genes. Genes are made up of strands of deoxyribonucleic acid (DNA) and arranged in pairs, called chromosomes. One half of children's total chromosomes comes from their fathers, while the other half comes from their mothers. The chromosomes inherited by children are not exact copies of those from either of their parents. First, children inherit only half a strand of chromosomes from each parent. Second, by a process called recombination some of each parent's genes are rearranged or "scrambled" during the formation of egg and sperm cells. Third, the chromosomes in sperm and egg are made by copying parents' recombined genes. This copying process is not perfect, and mutations, gene breakage, or extra chromosomes can sneak into the process. Finally, children's gender is determined by which half of the father's DNA is inherited. All egg cells have X chromosomes, while some sperm have X and some Y chromosomes. If children receive two X chromosomes, they will be females; if they receive one X and one Y chromosome, they will be males.

Genes contribute to the development and functioning of the body by regulating the production of protein. Each gene provides a molecular sequence that acts as a code or blueprint for making a particular protein. Protein, in turn, provides the structure for every cell in the body. Not all genes are active all the time; some scientists estimate that less than 10 percent of the total amount of DNA is ever activated in a person's lifetime. Genes can also switch on and off in response to the activity of other genes, hormones, or the passage of time.

Some traits are primarily a result of the action of one gene. Dominant traits are those which only require one gene from one parent in order to be expressed—that is, to become part of a person's body. Recessive traits are those which require one gene from each parent in order to be expressed. For example, brown eyes are a dominant trait. If children inherit the gene for brown eyes from one parent and the gene for blue eyes from the other, their eyes will be brown. Blue eyes are a recessive trait; children must inherit a gene for blue eyes from both parents in order to be blue-eyed. Because brown-eyed parents can carry the genes for blue eyes, it is possible for two brown-eyed people to have blue-eyed children. Many inherited diseases are either dominant or recessive one-gene traits.

Most traits are rarely the result of single genes. Rather, genes work together with other genes and with environmental cues to build the body. For example, in developing embryos, particular genes on the outer embryo layers are activated to build proteins used in skin and neural tissue because of cues from the inner embryo layers and from the placenta. If these same cells are transplanted to an inner embryo layer, different genes will be activated and protein for muscles, skeleton, or internal organs will be produced.

The fact that genes can be switched on and off explains why persons can have genes for a disease, such as a particular type of cancer, or unregulated cell growth, and never actually develop the disease. Factors in person's internal and external environment must work together with other body processes before genes are turned on. This means that genetic characteristics are not always fixed and unchangeable, as was once believed. In addition, if other, competing genes are also activated, persons may not develop significant diseases. The presence of competing genetic and environmental factors may explain why some persons with a hereditary disease such as cystic fibrosis are severely affected by the disease while others have only mild symptoms. The same genetic problem is present in both cases, but the competing factors are different.

Inheritance and Heritability. Two related concepts that are often confused with heredity are inheritance and heritability. Inheritance refers to everything that is passed from parents to children—that is, both ecological inheritance and genetic heredity. Heritability is a statistical expression that refers to inheritance. The proportion of individual differences in a trait that can be accounted for by inheritance is the trait's heritability. For example, the heritability of differences in human height is 0.50. This means that half of the differences among the heights of members of a population are due to inherited factors, including, but not limited to, their genes. Members of one group of people who have suffered from poor nutrition during childhood may reach adult heights of 3 to 5 feet, whereas members of another group of people who have been well nourished may reach heights of 5 to 7 feet. Because the heritability of height in both groups is 0.50, about half of the differences among people within the shorter group are due to inheritance, as are half of the differences among people in the taller group. The differences between the two groups, however, is not inherited. In fact, 5-foot-tall persons in the shorter group may have exactly the same genes as the 7-foot-tall persons in the taller group. Heritability can only be calculated for groups of people who are all exposed to similar environmental conditions.

The concept of heritability is sometimes difficult to distinguish from heredity, and the two are often confused. It is helpful to remember that a trait with a high heritability statistic is not necessarily hereditary for several reasons. First, the number of individual differences influences the size of the heritability statistic. Lung capacity, which is strongly influenced by environmental factors such as smoking, nutrition, and exercise, has a higher heritability than the number of fingers on the human hand, which is almost completely controlled by genes. The reason for this surprising result is that lung capacity varies tremendously among individuals, whereas the number of fingers almost never varies.

How Hereditary Traits Are Studied. It is important to understand the difference between inheritance, heritability, and heredity, because most studies of heredity in human beings are actually studies of persons' entire inheritance, their genes, and some portion of their environment. There are three research methods for studying human heredity: family studies, adoption studies, and twin studies. In family studies, researchers look for patterns of certain diseases or traits in families over several generations. Because this type of study includes families' genes and family environment, the fact that a trait occurs more frequently in some families than in others does not necessarily mean that their genes are responsible. If researchers find some patterns that correspond with known

Studies of identical twins have made major contributions to research in genetics. (James L. Shaffer)

genetic laws, however, then genes are probably responsible. For example, the blood disease hemophilia is known to be genetic, because it is passed from mothers to sons; girls carry the gene, but they rarely contract the disease. This type of trait is called an X-linked trait, because the gene is carried on the X chromosome.

In adoption studies, parents are compared to their children who have been adopted and reared by different families. The similarities between biological parents and adopted children are due to genes or prenatal environmental factors shared by parents and children, such as nutrition. In twin studies, identical twins (those who have developed from the same egg and are genetically identical) and fraternal twins (those who have developed from different eggs and are genetically no more similar than siblings) are compared to each other to determine how they differ in particular traits. If identical twins are more similar in particular traits than are fraternal twins, the heritability statistic will be high and the traits may be strongly influenced by genes. However, even in such cases genes may not be the sole influencing factor, because identical twins also experience more similar environments than do fraternal twins. Studies of identical twins who have been adopted by different families and reared separately control for this problem, although nongenetic inheritance such as prenatal exposure to diseases cannot be ruled out.

Human heredity has been studied indirectly for two reasons. First, it is very difficult to study the action of genes themselves; the means to do so only became widely available to scientists in the early 1990's. Second, people cannot be subjected to the same research procedures as animals. It is possible to study heredity in animals by using selective breeding. That is, each generation of breeding partners is carefully selected to encourage some traits and diminish others. For example, laboratory mice can be bred for size, speed of learning, or susceptibility to particular diseases. Although selective breeding involves both inheritance and heredity in each generation, it is assumed that changes in traits that accumulate over many generations are probably the result of genes.

Advances in the Understanding of Genes. By the early 1990's more precise methods for studying genes at the molecular level had been developed. In the early 1980's scientists had begun to map, or

discover, the function of every gene in human DNA. The specific genes responsible for many hereditary diseases, such as some types of cancer, Huntington's chorea, and Tay-Sachs disease, were discovered in this process. The mapping of genes fostered the development of blood tests to determine if persons had inherited them. In addition, the genetic mechanism regulating cell growth and death had been uncovered. This will foster the development of treatments for cancer and for some diseases of aging that are caused by excessive cell death, such as Alzheimer's disease. Finally, scientists have learned how to clone several large animals by transferring DNA from adult animals directly into egg cells. Human cloning had become theoretically possible by the late 1990's, although it has been banned in the United States and Canada for ethical reasons.

Family Risk and Responsibility. Many traits have a high heritability and are probably influenced strongly by genes. These include physical traits and diseases such as cancer, heart disease, and high blood pressure. Behavioral traits such as shyness, conservatism, intelligence, vulnerability to alcoholism, schizophrenia, and depression may have a genetic component as well. Even if specific genes for these traits are not found, the fact that so many illnesses run in families makes it important for persons to know their families' health history.

The hereditary diseases for which genetic tests have been developed pose many dilemmas for families. The fact that persons possess disease genes does not necessarily mean that they will develop the corresponding diseases. Persons may worry more about developing disease symptoms if they test positive for genetically influenced diseases than if they abstain from testing altogether. Relatives who have not been tested may not want to know that genetic diseases run in their families, but persons who have been tested may feel that it is their responsibility to inform them. Financial considerations may intrude as well, because some insurance companies may declare that positive genetic test results constitute "preexisting conditions," prompting them to deny people coverage when they develop the diseases.

Parents may also pass diseases on to their children, making family planning an agonizing decision. Many prenatal genetic tests are available for diseases that are fatal to children, posing the ethical dilemma of whether or not women should continue their pregnancies if the children they bring into the world will live short, painful, and hopeless lives. Terminating pregnancies contradicts many parents' religious beliefs, making it sometimes difficult for them to determine what is in the best interests of their children.

Given these ethical dilemmas, many people prefer not to be tested, and most medical professionals will not perform genetic tests in the absence of family counseling. Scientific advances in genetics may well have outstripped the social changes needed to deal with them. The human costs and benefits of genetic discovery are routinely considered when new research is planned.

—*Kathleen M. Zanolli*

BIBLIOGRAPHY

Bishop, Jerry, and Michael Waldholtz. *Genome: The Story of the Most Astonishing Scientific Adventure of Our Time.* New York: Simon & Schuster, 1990. Describes the history of the Human Genome Project and tells the story of many families affected by hereditary diseases.

Harris, Jacqueline. *Hereditary Diseases.* New York: Henry Holt, 1993. The basic information about heredity, genes, and diseases is presented in simple language and illustrations.

Jackson, John. *Genetics and You.* Totowa, N.J.: Humana Press, 1996. An easy-to-follow discussion of the personal and family implications of heredity, genetic testing, and family planning.

Pierce, Benjamin. *The Family Genetic Sourcebook.* New York: John Wiley & Sons, 1990. Details the mechanisms of heredity and disease, making recommendations for families on genetic testing, counseling, and interpreting family history.

President's Commission for the Study of Ethical Problems in Medicine and Biomedical and Behavioral Research. *Screening and Counseling for Genetic Conditions.* Washington, D.C.: U.S. Government Printing Office, 1983. Gives the facts of many genetic diseases and details the rights of people undergoing genetic testing and the responsibilities of health professionals.

Thompson, Larry. *Correcting the Code.* New York: Simon & Schuster, 1994. Describes the development of genetic medicine and the possibility of cures for a variety of problems in which genes play a role.

Wingerson, Lois. *Mapping Our Genes: The Genome Project and the Future of Medicine.* New York: Penguin Books, 1991. Discusses the implications of gene testing and the possibilities of curing genetic diseases.

See also Behavior disorders; Birth control; Birth defects; Eugenics; Genetic counseling; Genetic disorders; Human Genome Project; Twins.

Hinduism

RELEVANT ISSUES: Marriage and dating; Parenting and family relationships; Religious beliefs and practices

SIGNIFICANCE: A thousand years before the common era the Vedas, or the "books of knowledge" and other Sanskrit texts, lay the foundation of Hindu beliefs, upon which the Indian family, caste, and social roles are based

Basically a polytheistic belief system, early Hinduism was practiced by worshiping primarily male devas associated with the natural phenomena of the sky, fire, and wind. Although no one creator god was defined, the many gods were viewed as simply expressions of one power. This monotheistic notion is mythologized in the creation hymn of Prajapati, "the Lord of Beings," who was born of the sacrificial fire. From this first cosmic act, all of the universe came into being. The hymn describes that from the primordial giant's mouth came the Brahmins, or the priests and scholars; from its arms came the Kshatriyas, or the warriors and rulers; from its thighs came the Vaisyas, or the merchants and traders; and from its feet came the Sudras, or the laborers. Clearly stated in the myth is that each social group was of equal importance; each class was essential for the stability of society. This fundamental belief gave divine sanction to the four great classes of Hindu society, known as the caste system; the belief in dharma, or "duty"; and the doctrine of karma and rebirth.

The Caste System and Duty. The caste system stratifies a society into segregated, hierarchal units. Each social group is united, closed, and hereditary, being held together by birth, common occupations, common customs in marriage, common traditions in religion, common social patterns, common food practices, and common

Indian American women at the entrance to a Hindu temple in New York City. (Hazel Hankin)

Hindus in New York City's Queens borough celebrate the Festival of Ganesh, the son of Shiva. (Hazel Hankin)

names. Caste, often referred to as jati, is an endogamous social group, and all members are therefore expected to marry within their caste.

A right or meritorious action is determined by the dictates of dharma. The concept of dharma refers to individuals' duty according to their social class and also their stage in life. Individuals bear responsibility to both society and to themselves. Just as society is divided into four classes, individuals' lives are divided into four stages, or ashramas. The first stage is as students of the Hindu scriptures studying at the feet of gurus, or teachers. The second stage, the householder stage, requires that students return home, marry, and maintain a family, raising sons for future necessity. The third stage is that of forest dwellers, who mentally withdraw and detach from material pleasures by meditating on spiritual development. In the fourth stage, the sannyasins or ascetics break all ties with the temporary world both mentally and physically by wandering the earth with no attachments to the past. Even in the urbanized and industrial world, all Indians are expected to follow this path.

The concept of karma refers to both actions and intended results. It is assumed that all actions bring results; individuals' present situation is the result of actions performed in the past, and one's present actions determine one's future situation. Only by right actions according to duty may individuals be liberated from the cycle of rebirth. Individuals, then, have control over their life experiences and future births.

Codifying the laws of social and religious behaviors, the volumes of religious texts, Dharmasastra or "code of behavior," interpret the Hindu scriptures in the context of modern society. At the beginning of the common era, the most influential work, the laws of Manu, marked the origin of what is viewed as Hindu law: the social obligations and duties of individuals at each stage of life and in the various castes; the appropriate social conduct of women and men, wives and husbands, and daughters and sons; the formulas of religious rituals; the issues of purity and pollution; information on birth, death, marriage, and punishment; and other details of daily Hindu life.

Joint Family as a Social Net. In the Hindu religious system, family is the fundamental basis of society. Every Indian is believed to be born with a sacred duty to the family. Nothing is more important than the well-being and unity of the family and maintenance of its traditions and honor. A joint or extended family is characterized by strong tradition and pride. It is a group of people who live as one household, partake of food cooked from a common kitchen, hold property in common, share income, participate in common family worship and rituals, and guarantee the continuation of traditional family values. Primarily patriarchal and patrilineal, the joint family elevates the father to the head of the household; his younger brothers and wives and children live with their sons and wives and children under one roof, sharing the household finances and property. Males have authority over females, and the elders have authority over the younger members of the family. The extended family is a microcosm of the society, and all members are essential contributors to the whole family, seeing themselves as mutually dependent on and supportive of other members for the good of the family and ultimately of society.

Importance of Male Children. As prescribed in the most important ashrama, the householder stage, marriage is a religious duty as well as a lifelong commitment. Among Hindus, marriage is viewed as the union of two families rather than two individuals. Marriages are usually arranged by elders, parents, and matchmakers to ensure religious and caste endogamy, occupational compatibility, and cultural and moral harmony.

Having children is considered a blessing. Families hope for the birth of a son and rejoice when the first male is born. A male heir is seen as a religious and economic necessity for families. A son guarantees continuation of the generations, protection of the family, financial security, and performance of the last rites after the father's death, ensuring safe departure from the illusory world. A special mutual dependence exists between fathers and sons. Sons obey their fathers, giving unwavering respect and providing complete support to them when they are alive as well as after they die. Fathers, in return, give their sons a good education, the best marriage arrangement, and inheritance of property. Although fathers are the ultimate authority, good mothers are in charge of the young children, building a strong bond with their daughters and sons.

Undesirability of Daughters. Whereas male children provide salvation, spiritual benefits, continuation of generations, and assurance of social dignity, female children do not hold such an honorable position in Hindu society. Daughters play no ceremonial part at parents' funerals, they have marginal status in the household, and they function as temporary members of the family. Their maintenance, education, dowry, and future widowhood place a large financial burden on families, whose primary duty is to find husbands for their daughters. At the time of Manu, to ensure financial security for daughters when they separated from their natal families, material goods of jewelry, cash, clothes, and household items were given to them as stridhana, or their own property. By the 1850's stridhana was replaced with the custom of dowry, a reward to grooms and their families. In modern times, daughters' families commonly amass wealth in the form of cash, gold, and modern luxuries, such as cars and refrigerators, to be given to boys' families in the hope of increasing their daughters' status and chances for lifelong economic security.

The marriage bond is sacred particularly for wives. The power of wives lies in their religious duty toward their husbands and the continuation of their family lines by begetting sons. Built into the social structure is the notion of the faithful wife, or pativrata, a husband's true partner who helps him in every possible way to achieve his goals in life. After marriage, wives are obedient to their husbands, revering them as gods. Husbands and wives are bound to each other until death, and their oneness is believed to continue on into the other world. Divorce, then, is an unacceptable practice in India.

The Subordinate Role of Wives. Societal norms pressure wives not to remarry after their husbands' deaths. Widowhood is an unfortunate situation for Indian women. Until the nineteenth century, Hindu scriptural instructions specified the proper conduct of widows. Widows were blamed for their husbands' deaths; they had no rights to property and were perceived as inauspicious and impure. Unless their sons protected them, they had no place to go and were expected to spend the rest of their lives mourning the deaths of their husbands. Self-immolation on their husbands' funeral pyres, known as suttee, was the ultimate sacrifice of "real" or "true women" to show their undying devotion to their husbands. Fear of poverty, austerity, and social ostracism placed enormous pressure on widows to go through with the ceremony. Although it was abolished in 1829, the practice of suttee is considered honorable; women in the past who practiced suttee are exalted as saints, and some Hindus visit sacrificial sites as part of pilgrimages.

Hinduism is a way of life for Indians. It teaches that the individual, society, and the cosmos are interdependent. The necessity to maintain order is based on the belief in a stratified society, commitment to dharma, and selfless actions. Even though the twentieth century has brought a few changes to the religious system, Hindus celebrate the family and emphasize the importance of family harmony and unity. The individual is subordinate to the family structure. These values are powerful images in the ancient writings and teachings of the Ramayana and Mahabharata and have spread in Indian communities worldwide in song, dance, art, and drama as well as among the elders who are living models of duty and sacrifice.

—*Tamara M. Valentine*

BIBLIOGRAPHY

Baker, Sophie. *Caste: At Home in Hindu India.* London: Jonathan Cape, 1990.

Doniger, Wendy, and Brian K. Smith, trans. *The Laws of Manu.* New York: Penguin Books, 1991.

Lannoy, Richard. *The Speaking Tree: A Study of Indian Culture and Society.* New York: Oxford University Press, 1971.

Mandelbaum, David. *Society in India.* 2 vols. Berkeley: University of California Press, 1970.

Mukhopadhyay, Carol Chapnick. *Women, Education, and Family Structure in India.* Boulder, Colo.: Westview Press, 1994.

Ross, Aileen. *The Hindu Family in Its Urban Setting.* Toronto: University of Toronto Press, 1961.

Uberoi, Patricia, and T. N. Madan, eds. *Family, Kinship, and Marriage in India.* New York: Oxford University Press, 1993.

See also Arranged marriages; Dowry; East Indians and Pakistanis; Endogamy; Extended families; Family: concept and history; Gender inequality; Religion; Teen marriages.

Hochschild, Arlie Russell

BORN: January 15, 1940, Boston, Mass.

AREAS OF ACHIEVEMENT: Economics and work; Sociology

SIGNIFICANCE: Hochschild researched the "second shift," the time that persons spend performing housework after performing paid labor outside the home

Arlie Hochschild, professor of sociology at the University of California, Berkeley, coauthored with Anne Machung *The Second Shift: Working Parents and the Revolution at Home* (1989), which explored parents' attitudes about how they use their time each day before and after work. She confirmed what previous research had shown: Women spend more time than men on child care and household tasks. She concluded that most persons feel they do all they can to balance the needs of family life and work and careers. As a result, she called for the restructuring of the workplace and society to better accommodate the needs of families, especially those with young children.

In order to determine how persons apportion their time, Hochschild studied employees at every career level of a large midwestern corporation and their family members in *The Time Bind* (1997). She observed that although the company offered family-friendly work policies, workers chose not to take advantage of them. She concluded that for most workers, work was more important than family, speculating that this is a result of society's devaluation of the family. *—Joann Driggers*

See also Dual-earner families; Feminist sociology; Second shift; Women's roles; Work.

Holidays

RELEVANT ISSUES: Marriage and dating; Race and ethnicity; Religious beliefs and practices

SIGNIFICANCE: In industrialized modern societies typified by a modified nuclear family, the celebration of holidays and family traditions, whose origins often reach back centuries, is an important time for interchange and extended family contacts

The celebrations that unite families along generational lines focus on the histories of either the families themselves, singular persons, or the folk images of peoples or ethnic groups. Family celebrations include rites of passage and coming-of-age celebrations. Holidays based on singular persons generally bridge the gap between individual families and others as they celebrate a shared inheritance, such as the birthdays of presidents. Finally, the celebrations of peoples, nations, or ethnicities include family traditions and broader folk traditions, such as Christmas. Family traditions have three main components—food, festivals, and fraternizing. Holidays include customs within individual families or groups, calendar customs that are often work or school holidays, and folk festivals, such as St. Patrick's Day.

Family Celebrations. Family holidays center on personal milestones within family groups. Births are initially acknowledged with baby showers given by relatives for expectant parents. Once babies are born, birth announcements proclaim the new family additions, while ceremonial initiation rites range from brisses, or circumcision of newborn Jewish males, to infant baptisms in Roman Catholic and some Protestant households. In contrast, the Native American tradition of the Cherokee postpones children's big celebration, the naming ceremony, until toddlers are three years old.

The excitement of birth is celebrated anew with yearly birthday parties, when children are showered with gifts from family and friends. The first people to celebrate the birthdays of children, or the *Kinderfest*, were the Germans, who placed presents on children's breakfast seats the morning of their birthdays. Hispanic children celebrate with gifts and piñatas. For many girls coming-of-age parties are given. In Latino cultures they are called the quinceañera, or fifteenth birthday party, and in other groups sweet sixteen parties. Not all celebrations take the form of parties, however. Hindu children take flowers to temples and pray for a special blessing, while Chinese children simply add one year to the Chinese New Year in February while awaiting the transition to adulthood, which happens at the age of thirty.

Within family groups secular and religious signposts exist, such as first Communion rites for Roman Catholic children at the age of seven; confirmations, or maturity celebrations for Roman Catholic and Protestant children when they reach their early teens; and Bas or Bar Mitzvahs for Jewish girls and boys, respectively. Japanese Americans reserve one day a year for the Girls, or Dolls, Festival on March 3 and the Boys Festival on May 5, which is honored with carp-shaped kites and mock samurai battles. Celebrated for more than one thousand years, these celebrations pay homage to tradition and instill in children respect for traditional roles.

Weddings and Anniversaries. All cultures solemnize marriage as a turning point, because it signi-

Annual Family Holidays and Special Events

January	National Yours, Mine and Ours Month	
February	World Marriage Day	Second Sunday of month
February 14	Valentine's Day	
February 14	Read to Your Child Day	
March	National Talk with Your Teen About Sex Month	
April	National Family Reading Week	Last week of month
April 10	Siblings Day	
May	Universal Family Week	Second full week of month
May	National Family Week	Week following first Sunday of month
May	National Pet Week	Week following first Sunday of month
May	National Childcare Awareness Week	Second week of month
May	Unmothers Day	First Sunday of month
May	Mother's Day	Second Sunday of month
May 15	United Nations International Day of Families	
May 18	Visit your Relatives Day	
May-June	National Family Month	Mother's Day through Father's Day
June 14	Family History Day	
June	Father's Day	Third Sunday of month
June	National Family Day	First Saturday of month
June	Children's Sunday	Second Sunday of month
July	National Purposeful Parenting Month	
July	Twin-o-Rama	
August	Twins Day	First Saturday of month
August	Family Day	Second Sunday of month
August	Middle Children's Day	Second Saturday of month
August	American Family Day	First Sunday of month
September	National Housekeepers Week	Second full week of month
September	National Grandparents Day	First Sunday after Labor Day
September	National Pet Memorial Day	Second Sunday of month
September	Adult Day Care Center Week	Third week of month
October	Communicate with Your Kid Month	
October	National Family Sexuality Education Month	
October	Universal Children's Week	First week of month
October	National Infertility Awareness Week	Third week of month
October	Mother-in-Law Day	Fourth Sunday of month
November	National Adoption Week	Thanksgiving week
November	National Family Caregivers Week	Last week of month
December	National Stress-Free Family Holidays	

Source: *Chase's 1998 Calendar of Events.* Chicago: Contemporary Books, 1997.

fies the beginning of a new family group. In some cultures this simply means that families add on additional rooms and become more inclusive, as in the traditional matrilineal society of the Hidatsu tribe of Native Americans. More often marriage signifies a breaking away of young people to form their own households. Secular and religious celebrations that may seem bittersweet to parents and exciting to newlyweds include bridal showers, bachelor and bachelorette parties, rehearsal dinners, and wedding themselves. Weddings are governed by many rules of etiquette. These include who pays for them and what participants are supposed to wear. At wedding receptions fathers traditionally dance with their daughters and mothers with their sons. Brides often wear elaborate Victorian-style gowns of white and carry sentimental family talismans—"something old, something new, something borrowed, and something blue." For example, brides carry as bridal handkerchiefs the baptismal caps they wore as infants. Every year, the significance of weddings is remembered at anniversary celebrations at which traditional and modern gifts are given, ranging from paper or clocks on the first anniversary to diamonds on the sixtieth.

The one celebration not always anticipated is the celebration of family members' deaths. Traditions include religious or secular ceremonies at funeral homes. Some ethnic traditions define the types of caskets in which the deceased are to be buried and their dates of interment, while others leave these decisions to families themselves. In Irish American families the funeral is followed by a wake, which includes eating and drinking. In Jewish families the Kaddish, a prayer solemnizing the event, is repeated yearly at deceased persons' graves.

Family traditions, depending on ethnicity, include both secular and religious elements. As most religions involve ceremonial meals, most families prepare and eat them. Foods are prepared with the participation of many family members. For Scandinavian families one such traditional food is a potato pancake called lefse. German families bake Kuchen, a rich stuffed pastry dish, while Jewish families serve potato pancakes, or latkes, with applesauce. The English celebrate with plum pudding and the Irish with carrot pudding. Polish Americans eat kielbasa sausage and Serbian immigrants make kifle, the Belgrade cookie. The recipes for such foods migrated across the oceans in the memories of immigrants, enabling them to celebrate holidays and build an edible bridge to their family's ancestry.

Some calendar customs celebrate the family. On the second Sunday in May, children in the United States honor their mothers. Mother's Day was conceived in 1907 and originally focused on a church service, but later it was marked by giving mothers gifts and serving them breakfast in bed. The ritualistic remembrance of mothers harks back to rural England, when people made offerings to their mother churches during Lent. In Canada a mid-Lenten Sunday called Mothering Day is dedicated to remembering people's churches or parents. Similar to Mother's Day, Father's Day is dedicated to fathers. It is celebrated on the third Sunday in June.

National Holidays. The United States and Canada have special calendar customs to remember significant persons in their histories. These holidays generally commemorate either national or folk heroes. Those honored stand out as folk images or represent the spirit of the people. In the United States civil rights leader Martin Luther King, Jr.'s birthday is celebrated on January 15, while the birthdays of presidents George Washington and Abraham Lincoln are celebrated on Presidents' Day in February. In Canada Queen Victoria's birthday is celebrated in May. Farther south, a Mexican holiday, Cinco de Mayo, is celebrated with gusto in Los Angeles. On May 5 this three-day fiesta of mariachis and dancing commemorates the victory of the Mexican guerrilla army supporting Benito Juarez over better-equipped French forces. October 12, a national holiday remembering Christopher Columbus's discovery of the New World in 1492, has led to cultural clashes, because his arrival preempted the native cultures of the Americas.

While such figures are saints of a civil religion, other celebrated figures include Christian saints. On March 17 the Irish celebrate St. Patrick's Day, on November 30 the Scots celebrate St. Andrew's Eve, on March 1 the Welsh celebrate St. David's Day, and on June 13 the Italians celebrate St. Anthony's Day. Sicilians celebrate St. Joseph's Day on March 19 while Spanish and Puerto Ricans celebrate St. James Day of the Fiesta of Santiago. These

After children decorate eggs for Easter they enjoy hunting for them on Easter morning. (Cindy Beres)

celebrations marking various ethnic groups' national festivals are typified by music, literature, and patriotic fervor. St. Patrick's Day has been adopted by the dominant culture and is celebrated with buttons, gags, and parades. St. Joseph's Day is a religious holiday celebrated by those who await the swallows at the mission of San Juan Capistrano in California. For families, these observances are a time to get together and celebrate their ethnic and religious heritage.

Yearly Folk Celebrations. Another group of calendar customs are national folk celebrations. These holidays or holy days are a form of secularized religion, insofar as they are celebrated in one way or another by the majority of the nation and assume universal meaning stretching back into folk history. The first such holiday each year is New Year's Day. New Year's Day begins with New Year's Eve and renditions of "Auld Lang Syne." Many people observe New Year's Day by watching the Rose Parade in Pasadena, California, where families camp out to view the parade and then cheer their favorite football teams onto victory in the various bowl games.

A month later, on February 14, people celebrate Valentine's Day, during which children and lovers exchange valentine cards. The elaborate valentines of lace and ribbons date to the Victorian period. Although the original purpose of this holiday was to honor Christian martyrs, it eventually became a holiday idealizing romantic love.

Spring Celebrations—Christian, Jewish, and Muslim. In the Christian world the Easter season actually begins with the forty-day period of Lent.

The Tuesday before Ash Wednesday is Shrove Tuesday, a day of feasting and, in New Orleans, of parades, dancing, and mumming. Easter, which became a part of the Christian calendar in 325 C.E., celebrates the passion and resurrection of Jesus Christ. The underlying pagan spring or fertility rites have been perpetuated in Easter through flowers and eggs brought by the Easter Bunny. The Easter season is second only to Christmas as an important holiday for family gatherings and a reaffirmation of family values. Just before

Easter families dye eggs in preparation for Sunday morning egg hunts, while traditional foods such as hot cross buns are prepared. Many families buy new Easter outfits for their children. After attending church services on Easter morning, families picnic and share in traditional family meals.

Like Easter, the Jewish celebration of Passover (Pesach) is a time of family togetherness. Centered on Jewish history, Passover commemorates the flight of the Jews from ancient Egypt. A traditional meal, or seder, is prepared that is reminis-

In North American society May Day is a holiday that probably means more to children than to most adults. (Cindy Beres)

cent of that hurried event. At this meal unleavened bread, known as matzo, and bitter herbs are served. People of all ages participate in the Passover celebration, but children are a special focus, as they play games with nuts, such as heads or tails (*Shpitz tzi Kopp*). Families also attend services at synagogues.

Muslim homes also focus on the family and reinforce their religious beliefs during spring celebrations. Ramadan, a time of reflection, is a month of fasting from mid-January to mid-February. The meal at the end of the day, including special foods such as iftar (dates), becomes a time of sharing. However, the big celebration during Ramadan is Eid-ul-Fitr, the Festival of Fast-Breaking, a joyous occasion during which people give special gifts to charity, wear traditional attire, pray communally, and visit friends and relatives. Following the end of Ramadan the next Islamic event focuses on the Hajj, or pilgrimage to Mecca. The day after the Day of Arafat in mid-April is the Festival of Sacrifice, or Eid-ul-Adha, which emphasizes giving to charity, attending prayer services, wearing new clothes, visiting relatives, and giving gifts to children.

April Fools Day, a day for silly jokes and riddles that school children adore, and May Day, an ancient fertility holiday, follow the period of spring holidays and regenerative celebrations. In Roman Catholic schools May Day celebrates Mary, the mother of Jesus, with a pageant and the crowning of a May Queen. Other festivals are of a secular nature, including Earth Day and Arbor Day. Earth Day is a particular favorite of children, who recycle and encourage their parents to do the same. People plant trees to mark Arbor Day, which traces its history to the Grange movement of the 1870's and honors farmers and the earth. For Christians, May also marks the end of the Easter season with Pentecost (Whitsunday) and the Ascension, whereby families attend church services and young people are often confirmed. For Jews, the spring celebrations end with Shavuot, a traditional feast including dairy foods that commemorates the end of the forty years in the desert after the Jews' flight from Egypt.

Summer Holidays. The first holiday of summer is Memorial Day, or Decoration Day, at the end of May. It remembers the dead and those who died in the service of their country. In rural America summer traditionally was the time to clean graveyards and tend cemeteries. Buddhists celebrate Obon, the feast of the Dead. Bracketed by Memorial Day in May and Labor Day in September, summer is the period of family vacations, barbecues, beach parties, and trips to the park. Longer days and fewer school hours allow families to play together and visit distant relatives. In the United States the centerpiece of the season is the Fourth of July, or Independence Day, and in Canada it is Canada Day on July 1, which celebrates the birth of the Dominion of Canada. African Americans in Louisiana and Texas celebrate Juneteenth on June 19, a holiday marking the day General Gordon Granger spread the news of the Thirteenth Amendment on June 19, 1865, emancipating the slaves. Juneteenth is a day of family picnics, parades, and traditional baseball games marking the injustice of slavery and the accomplishments of African Americans since slavery was abolished. As on the Fourth of July, families celebrate Juneteenth by spending time outdoors, watching fireworks displays, and shooting off rockets and firecrackers in towns across the United States. Labor Day, on the first Monday in September, has traditionally been the last family barbecue of the year and a day to shop for new school clothes. While Labor Day marks the time when many college students move to their new homes in dormitories across America, it signifies for their younger siblings a time of new teachers and classrooms. The family orientation of Labor Day has usurped its original purpose as a trade-union holiday.

Autumn Festivities. At the onset of autumn many groups celebrate the end of the harvest and the beginning of cooler weather. Several major Jewish holidays are celebrated in early autumn, including Rosh Hashanah, the Jewish New Year and the beginning of the High Holiday season. The blowing of the ram's horn, or shofar, signifies the power of Jehovah. Traditional foods abound, such as challah, or egg bread, apples symbolizing sweetness and health, carrots symbolizing prosperity, fish symbolizing fertility, and honey symbolizing sweetness. Ten days later families move from this happy celebration to Yom Kippur, or the day of atonement, followed by the harvest festival of sukkoth, a day of thanks and a fertility holiday.

Several autumn holidays are enjoyed by children and families alike. For Hindu children the

The Halloween trick-or-treating tradition diminished in popularity during the 1990's because of growing public concern over safety. (James L. Shaffer)

celebration starts in late October or early November with Dewali, the festival of lights, which marks the beginning of the Hindu New Year—the day Rama (a manifestation of Vishnu) vanquished the demon Ravana. Presents are exchanged, accounts settled, games played, and traditional foods such as sabji kofta (vegetable balls), dahl (lentils), and puri (puffed bread) savored.

Jack-o'-lanterns are a favorite symbol of the cal-

endar holiday Halloween, celebrated on October 31. Originally a Gaelic holiday marking summer's end, it was adapted as English Plough Day when ploughmen begged for gifts and threatened harm to those who did not comply. For the Christian world it became All Soul's Day in the eighth century, the night before All Saints' Day. Some aspects of these holidays still linger in Halloween, although children focus on wearing costumes and

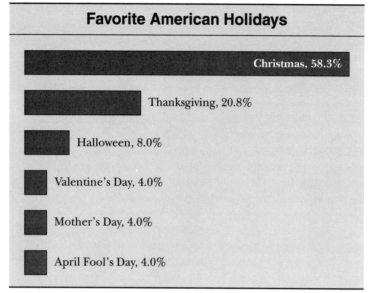

Favorite American Holidays

Christmas, 58.3%

Thanksgiving, 20.8%

Halloween, 8.0%

Valentine's Day, 4.0%

Mother's Day, 4.0%

April Fool's Day, 4.0%

Source: Parentsroom website (1997)

Note: In late 1997 Parentsroom conducted an informal poll among visitors to its website. These people—most of whom visit the site because of their interest in parenting—were asked to name their favorite holiday. This chart summarizes the responses. Percentages are rounded to the nearest 0.1%.

"trick or treating." In some areas children go from door to door requesting treats, usually candy, although in urban areas private parties with dunking for apples, games, and trick or treating in indoor malls has replaced the door-to-door experience.

On November 11 Canada celebrates Remembrance Day and the United States observes Veterans' Day, both of which mark the "eleventh hour of the eleventh day of the eleventh month," when the guns fell silent at the end of World War I. These holidays, honoring all the veterans of the armed services who have fought for their countries, are celebrated by flying flags at half-mast and by graveside ceremonies remembering the deceased.

The largest fall holiday and one that draws families together across the United States and Canada is Thanksgiving, which is celebrated on the second Monday of October in Canada and the fourth Thursday of November in the United States. For both countries, which were settled by England, Thanksgiving is an adaptation of Lammas, or Loaf Mass, a holiday in the Middle Ages during which farmers gave thanks for their crops. The American festival originated in 1621 after the Pilgrim colo-

nists' first harvest and is celebrated by eating traditional foods such as pumpkin pie and turkey. Abraham Lincoln declared Thanksgiving Day a national holiday during the Civil War. Some cultural groups have other ways of giving thanks. Central European immigrants honor "Good King Wenceslas" on September 23, while the Chinese celebrate the autumn moon with moon cakes—a symbol of the gentle, quiet moon of autumn, a female element of the *yin.* Thanksgiving Day evolved into a secular holiday, symbolized by the Macy's Thanksgiving Day Parade in New York City, which kicks off the Christmas season in the United States and brings families together to view huge balloons hovering over the parade.

Christmas Traditions and Winter Holidays. A number of winter holidays take place at year's end. The Jewish holiday of Hanukkah, an eight day festival, usually falls in December and remembers the rebellion of the Maccabees in the second century B.C.E. A menorah of nine candles, eight of which are lit on eight successive days, symbolizes the oil in the temple that should have lasted one day, but burned for eight. The holiday is a fun-filled one in which children play with dreidels, or four-sided toys spun like tops, and receive gifts.

On December 12 many Latinos celebrate the feast day of their patron saint, Our Lady of Guadalupe. A birthday party with dancing and singing and church services round out the celebration in the American Southwest. In Swedish families the eldest daughter bakes Santa Lucia buns for her family on December 13 and, wearing a wreath of candles in her hair, delivers family members breakfast in bed. In Latino families the tradition of honoring the Christ child is acted out with a door to door procession (*posada*) from December 16 to the 23, while Hispanic children commemorate the journey of Mary and Joseph to Bethlehem and their search for an inn. For seven nights the neighbors turn the children away, but on the eighth night they are welcomed with feasting and games.

On Christmas, the holiday commemorating the birth of Christ in Bethlehem, families erect crèches to remember the Christmas story, attend church services, decorate evergreen trees, perform nativity plays, gather to sing carols, and share large holiday meals. Christmas is primarily a birthday party for Jesus, but it has another secular quality, which has grown steadily over the years. Christmas Day is on December 25 because the Romans chose to "baptize" the Saturnalia feast of Kalends and the birthday of Mithras. While druids added mistletoe to the event, the English exchanged Christmas cards, and Father Christmas somehow mingled with the Dutch *Sinterklaas* to become the jolly red-dressed gift giver of the American Christmas. In most families gifts are opened on either Christmas Eve or Christmas morning, before or after church services. In Canada the first weekday after Christmas is Boxing Day, a day for exchanging gift-wrapped boxes with employees and friends. Family celebrations differ by region. In Chicago families meet for lunch by the tall Christmas tree at Marshall Fields department store, while in Washington, D.C., families watch the national tree being lit on the Capitol grounds. In New York some families ice skate at Rockefeller Plaza while others watch the ballet "The Nutcracker." Still others light up their houses and boats in gaudy displays of bright, twinkling lights. For several days after Christmas African American families celebrate Kwanza, the feast of the first fruits, by exchanging gifts, lighting candles, and participating in special family activities. Lasting from December 26 to the New Year, Kwanza began in 1966 to honor the heritage of African Americans and affirm their commitment to their families and communities. Finally, with New Years' Eve, the old year draws to a close and a New Year is welcomed.

Buddhists recall the baby Buddha on his birthday on April 8. Vietnamese enjoy their New Year on Tet Nguyen-Dan, during which families get together and feast. On Tet, Vietnamese cleanse the old, placate the household spirit of Tet, and put family affairs in order. The Chinese New Year is another period of feasting on the first new moon of the sign of Aquarius. This holiday is the most important one in the Chinese calendar, during which families feast and remember their ancestors. The climax of the holiday is the Golden Dragon parade, with firecrackers and much frivolity. Sweetened candies and bright red fruits symbolizing luck intermingle with the enjoyment of the thousand-layer sweet cake representing longevity.

Most holidays and traditions are grounded in either ethnic/religious beliefs or reinforce the folk image of a people. The types of holiday activities in which people engage and the kinds of food they eat make it possible to trace the heritage of many holidays back centuries. In general, such festivals are ways to unite families and friends and remember the histories of families, persons, or peoples.　　　　—*Michaela Crawford Reaves*

BIBLIOGRAPHY

The Book of Holidays Around the World. New York: E. P. Dutton, 1986. A comprehensive and thorough discussion of holiday traditions and their significance on a global scale, with a particularly easy-to-follow and calendar-style format.

Chambers, Wicke, and Spring Asher. *The Celebration Book of Great American Traditions.* New York: Harper & Row, 1983. Focuses on customs for events such as weddings, anniversaries, and family holidays, detailing dress, styles, and variations for an array of traditions and family practices.

Cohen, Hennig, and Tristam Potter Coffin, eds. *The Folklore of American Holidays.* Detroit: Gale Research, 1987. This work, emphasizing aspects of folklore in holidays and traditions, compiles data on most major holidays of the United States with extensive background information, citations from popular publications, games, stories, songs, and recipes.

Gordon, Michael, ed. *The American Family in Social-Historical Perspective.* New York: St. Martin's Press, 1984. Includes numerous essays on the different faces of the family in America and explores from an academic viewpoint immigrant and native-born families and the interaction of authority and tradition within the context of the broader dominant culture.

Takaki, Ronald. *A Different Mirror: A History of Multicultural America.* New York: Little, Brown, 1994. Highly readable and entertaining scholarly work focusing on the experiences of various ethnic groups within the United States since the seventeenth century, including the traditions and experiences of such groups as Native, Asian,

African, Irish, and Jewish Americans. Primarily a cultural history, the book nevertheless presents a comprehensive view of family life within a variety of cultural contexts.

Wilson, John F. *Public Religion in American Culture.* Philadelphia: Temple University Press, 1979. Outlines and examines the development of a folk image in the United States from inaugural speeches to celebratory events and argues that civic piety exists and is maintained by a sequence of holidays/holy days. Particularly interesting is the contention that a public religion, not a civil religion, exists.

See also African Americans; Chinese Americans; Divorce; Family gatherings and reunions; Foodways; Hinduism; In-laws; Japanese Americans; Jews; Muslims; Recreation; Roman Catholics.

Home ownership

RELEVANT ISSUES: Economics and work; Parenting and family relationships

SIGNIFICANCE: Purchasing a home, which can provide financial and emotional security for family members, is the largest and most important investment that most families make during their lifetimes

Owning a home is a vital component of the American and Canadian dream. For most, it is a firmly held life expectation that is as realistic as expecting to find a marriage partner, receive a solid education, and obtain employment. Housing represents more than just shelter. As the most immediate aspect of the community living experience, housing shapes people's lives. As Sir Winston Churchill said: "We shape our buildings, and afterwards our buildings shape us."

Need for Housing. At a basic level, some form of housing is required to protect families from the hazards of the natural environment. Housing is needed to provide privacy in which family relationships can develop. Homes in which families live also influence the kinds of neighbors, schools, stores, and recreation available. Housing reflects status in the eyes of the community, serves as a storehouse of memories, incorporates important societal values, and contributes to family wealth. At the same time, housing is a frequent object for the expression of families' drive for improvement.

Home ownership has been favored over renting since the founding of the United States and Canada. A major attraction which drew settlers to the North American continent was the opportunity to own a home. This possibility remains a strong attraction to immigrants in the late twentieth century. Home ownership is considered crucial for family security, stability, and prosperity. It is a basic value shared by families regardless of age, income, ethnicity, or geographical location. The value of owning a home, not only for families but for society as a whole, was simply stated by Abraham Lincoln: "The strength of a nation lies in the homes of its people."

Types of Ownership. Three types of home ownership exist. Families can elect to buy a home with fee simple ownership. This gives families the greatest number of rights to use and hold property. Fee simple ownership is the most common way in which families in Canada and the United States own their homes; it awards them the right to use the sky above, ground below, and property itself in a manner deemed most appropriate. Families' rights are only restricted to the extent that they infringe on those of neighbors.

A second alternative is condominium ownership. With this type of ownership, families purchase individual housing units within a complex, have title to the units, and become members of a condominium association. The association owns the land on which the housing unit is located, as well as any common areas, such as a clubhouses, that are used by all households belonging to the association. Membership in the condominium association entitles families to help make decisions regarding how the association manages the condominium complex.

Cooperative ownership is a third form of home ownership. This involves becoming a stockholder or member of a cooperative—a corporation that owns a piece of land and the housing units that are built on it. As members of the corporation, families have the right to exclusively occupy one of the dwellings owned by the corporation. Families participate in the cooperative as tenant-stockholders and have voting rights to determine corporation management.

All three forms of home ownership can be applied to any housing structural style. Preference surveys and actual housing selections indicate that most families opt for fee simple ownership of detached single-family houses. A single-family house that does not share walls with any other house, is occupied only by family members, and has its own yard is the most popular and predominant form of housing in the United States and Canada. While most detached single-family houses are built on site using conventional construction techniques, some are manufactured in factories and then placed on owners' property. Manufactured homes have emerged as an affordable type of housing. Multifamily housing units are common in urban communities because of land constraints. Apartments, duplexes, and townhouses can be purchased through condominium or cooperative ownership arrangements.

Trends in Home Ownership. At the beginning of the twentieth century less than one-half of Canadians and Americans owned their homes.

Home ownership rates declined from 1900 to 1920 because of poor economic conditions and then increased during the more prosperous 1920's. A steep drop in home ownership occurred during the Great Depression. In 1940 the United States recorded the lowest rate of home ownership—44 percent—in the twentieth century.

After World War II there was a surge in home ownership that continued until 1980. Because of a strong economy, favorable tax laws, and enhanced financing opportunities, the rate of home ownership reached 60 percent within two decades after World War II. Federal income tax laws made interest on mortgage and property tax payments tax deductible, encouraging many families to purchase homes. The introduction of amortized, long-term mortgages, often in the form of Veterans, Federal Housing, and Farmers Home Administration loans, gave many Americans the opportu-

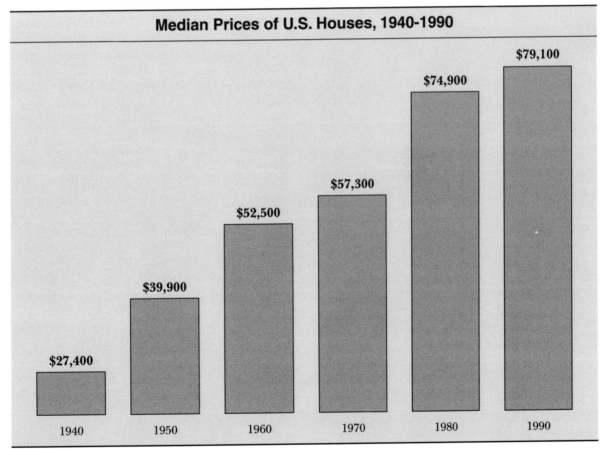

Median Prices of U.S. Houses, 1940-1990

$79,100 — 1990
$74,900 — 1980
$57,300 — 1970
$52,500 — 1960
$39,900 — 1950
$27,400 — 1940

Source: *Christian Science Monitor* (June 24, 1997)
Note: All figures are in adjusted 1990 dollars.

nity to buy a home. Similar incentives were offered in Canada in addition to large-scale construction supported by government programs.

There was a slight drop in the home ownership rate during the 1980's that caused considerable alarm, but the rate began to increase again during the 1990's, during which slightly less than two-thirds of Americans and Canadians owned their own homes. At the same time, surveys revealed that nine out of ten people preferred home ownership. Research also indicated that families made considerable sacrifices in order to purchase a home, such as renting inexpensive apartments and taking on a second job to save money for a down payment. Expanding home ownership remains a societal goal. U.S. president Bill Clinton announced an initiative in 1996 to raise the nation's home ownership rate by two percentage points by the year 2000. Canada's prime minister Jean Chrétien supported innovative mortgage options in 1997 to make it easier for families to match incomes and financing arrangements.

Home ownership rates vary among states in the United States. In the 1990's West Virginia had the highest rate at 74 percent and New York the lowest at 52 percent. Home ownership rates also differ among Canada's provinces. Newfoundland had the highest rate at 79 percent in the 1990's while Quebec had the lowest at 56 percent. For both countries home ownership tends to be more prevalent in less urbanized areas.

Advantages of Home Ownership. Because each family is unique, the advantages of home ownership vary according to a family's situation, values, income, and needs. The basic guideline is that home ownership should be considered as a means to accomplish family goals. A major advantage of home ownership is that it acts as a forced savings plan, since payments on mortgage principal are retained as equity. In 1996 American families had more than four trillion dollars in home equity, comprising more than one-half of their total net worth. Given proper maintenance, home ownership can be a good long-term investment as the value of homes appreciates over time. In Canada the net worth of families who purchased a home in 1965 was $198,000 higher in 1995 than families who rented during that same time. Property taxes, interest payments, and some initial purchase fees can be deducted from taxable income. Because

inflation causes prices and incomes to rise, mortgage payments become cheaper in real dollars as the years go by. As equity accumulates it then becomes easier for families to step up to a second, larger home.

Home ownership often enhances a family's sense of control over its members' lives and environment. Home owners take on greater responsibilities for their homes, neighborhoods, and communities. Another important advantage is that home owners can customize their homes to suit their needs and tastes. Home ownership also results in a greater sense of personal well-being and positively influences children's lives. Finally, a sense of personal accomplishment and prestige develops from being able to purchase a home.

Home ownership is not for all families. The alternative is renting, a form of dwelling possession in which families act as tenants and receive the exclusive right to use a property, such as an apartment, in exchange for payment of a specified amount of money. Financial considerations are often the major barrier to buying a home. The monthly mortgage payment is generally higher than rent payments. Whereas renters have minimal maintenance costs, owners must cover regular maintenance costs and undertake periodic repairs. Home owners also do not have as much mobility as renters.

Family Life Cycle and Home Ownership. For young single people, renting is typically a better choice than owning, as mobility and the need to limit housing expenses may be high. For those individuals who do not marry, condominium or cooperative ownership may be the best decision. When couples first form, mobility often remains high, so that renting may still be preferred. It is when families expand that home ownership becomes crucial. Owning a detached single-family house is usually preferred, because it allows families to adapt or add space to meet changing needs. Space needs are considerable during this phase, especially the need for bedrooms, bathrooms, and indoor and outdoor play areas for children. Extra pressure is placed on living areas. Single-parent families have essentially the same home ownership needs as dual-parent families.

When children leave home, they usually take with them only the essentials, leaving other possessions behind with their parents. When people en-

The moment a family enters a new home is always special. (Diane C. Lyell)

ter the empty nest stage, ownership of a single-family detached house is still common. Space requirements diminish, but housing pressures may continue because of visits from children and grandchildren. Children may even return home for extended time periods, perhaps with their own families, if they undergo a divorce or experience financial setbacks. Space for an elderly parent may also be needed.

During active retirement, housing costs can diminish after the mortgage has been paid off. In the 1990's almost 60 percent of individuals fifty-five years and older owned their homes outright. Home ownership comprised more than one-half of their net worth. Some couples change over to condominium ownership or choose to rent during active retirement, but most persons remain in a single-family detached home owned in fee simple. Finally, when persons enter restricted retirement, they may find it necessary to move to a smaller house, rent an apartment, live with a child, or move into a facility for the elderly.

Home Buying Process. Purchasing a home first involves determining needs and wants, with all family members participating. Some considerations are location and neighborhood safety, schools, interior spaces, yard size, and energy efficiency. Newspaper advertisements, real estate shopper guides, and real estate agents are all sources of information. Determining how much the family can afford for housing is important. In attempting to approve a home buyer for the type and amount of mortgage wanted, lenders evaluate ability and willingness to repay a loan. Credit and employment history, total family income, and planned use of the property in question are all considerations. A rule of thumb is that a family can spend 30 percent of its monthly income on housing.

Because home buyers can seldom pay cash to purchase a house given the high costs involved, obtaining financing is crucial. With a mortgage, buyers convey some of their property rights to a lender as security on a loan. Mortgages can be obtained through commercial banks, savings institutions, and mortgage bankers. The two most common types of mortgages are fixed and adjustable-rate mortgages. Fixed rate mortgages are fully amortized, with principal and interest paid off at the end of a fixed period of time, typically thirty years. Adjustable-rate mortgages are generally fifteen to thirty year mortgages, with the interest rate adjusted periodically to reflect changes in economic conditions. The primary advantage of adjustable-rate mortgages is that they initially have a lower interest rate. The annual percentage rate charged, the amount of down payment required, the terms of the mortgage, and the closing costs are four criteria used to assess mortgages.

Once a home and financing have been determined, families negotiate the purchase price and enter into a contract. During this negotiation process, a home inspection report is obtained that details the quality and condition of the property. A property appraisal of the home's worth and an indoor air quality test might also be performed. Closing is the final step in which the down payment, typically ranging from 3 to 20 percent of the sale price, is paid. At this point buyers also review and sign loan documents, pay closing costs, and receive title to the property.

As housing costs and environmental concerns about the resources required for housing have increased during the 1990's, there has been exploration of alternative forms of home ownership and types of structures. Small homes under 1,250 square feet, condominium ownership of factory-produced housing, cooperative ownership of patio homes placed on small lots, and homes built of recycled and natural materials have become more common than they were previously. Innovations that allow a greater number of families in the United States and Canada to become home owners are a natural outgrowth of families' desire to join the ranks of home owners.

—*Kenneth R. Tremblay, Jr.*

BIBLIOGRAPHY

Brunette, William Kent. *The Mortgage Handbook.* New York: Plume, 1997. Provides information on selecting and comparing mortgages, determining how much families can spend on housing, and understanding the mortgage approval process.

Irwin, Robert. *Tips and Traps When Buying a Home.* New York: McGraw-Hill, 1997. Reviews the procedure for purchasing a home, focusing on helpful strategies to make the best possible choices, beginning with identifying needs and wants and ending with moving into a home.

Lennon, Robin. *Home Design from the Inside Out.* New York: Penguin Books, 1997. Considers how to create a home to meet family needs from a holistic interior design perspective, including suggestions regarding indoor air quality and use of natural materials.

Marcus, Clare Cooper. *House as a Mirror of Self.* Berkeley, Calif.: Conari Press, 1995. Employs an environmental psychology perspective to express the impact that homes have on the psyches of family members and how families select and decorate homes to reflect who they are.

Santucci, Robert M., Brooke C. Studdard, and Peter Werwath. *Home Improvement, Renovation, and Repair.* New York: John Wiley & Sons, 1995. Outlines valuable ideas and techniques to maintain homes in prime condition for changing family needs and future resale.

Thomsett, Michael C. *How to Buy a House, Condo, or Co-op.* Yonkers, N.Y.: Consumer Reports Books, 1996. Organizes the home buying process with consideration given to condominium and cooperative ownership as well as to purchasing a manufactured home.

Tremblay, Kenneth R., Jr., and Lawrence Von Bamford. *Small House Designs.* Pownal, Vt.: Storey Publishing, 1997. Illustrates small homes from Canada and the United States, with discussions on environmentally conscious and affordable housing.

See also Communities; Family demographics; Family economics; Family life cycle; Home sharing; Homeless families; Retirement communities; Tax laws.

Home schooling

RELEVANT ISSUES: Education; Parenting and family relationships

SIGNIFICANCE: Home schooling is education offered at home by parents who choose educational materials, methods, and materials that they feel are appropriate for their children

To a certain extent, home schooling has always existed in the United States. Early settlers in sparsely populated areas had to take responsibility for their children's education. Parents often had to teach young children at home, although some wealthy parents, such as the plantation owners in the Virginia colony, hired tutors to teach their children at home. Thomas Jefferson and other early leaders of the United States were home schooled by tutors.

Reasons for Home Schooling. In the latter part of the twentieth century, home schooling became popular for a variety of reasons related to social change. During the latter part of the 1960's and the 1970's people who objected to the authoritarian structures in society saw public schools as examples of those structures. When some of these people became parents, they chose to home school their children rather than send them to public schools. In the late 1970's and early 1980's some educators and writers called for "deschooling." These educators, chief among whom was John Holt, argued that public schools were poor places to learn, because public school teachers told children what to think and what to do rather than encouraging them to initiate their own learning. Some parents, taking their cues from Holt and other writers, decided to take their children out of public schools and offer them home schooling. This particular group of home schooling parents has generally offered their children a curriculum guided by their children's interests. The parents, sometimes called "unschoolers" serve as guides and resources, while the children initiate what is studied and how it is studied.

The U.S. Department of Education estimated that in the early 1980's some 15,000 children were home schooled in the United States. By the early 1990's the Department of Education's estimate had risen to 350,000, while other sources placed the number at 500,000. Since the 1980's, home schooling has also seen a dramatic increase in Canada, where it is legal in all provinces and territories.

The rapid increase in home schooling in the 1980's and 1990's can be attributed primarily to parents' concerns about moral and values education in the public schools. Generally, values education in the public schools has considered moral issues from a relative rather than from an absolute viewpoint. Many home-schooling parents, particularly those who are Christians, believe that certain moral questions have right and wrong answers. These parents prefer to teach their moral values to their children rather than to have their children attend public schools, where moral questions may be debated but no final answers offered. Parents' concerns about moral education in the public schools have been supplemented by their concerns about safety. The incidence of children bringing knives, guns, and drugs to school has caused many parents to feel that their children should stay at home in a safe environment.

Although applicable only to the Amish, the 1972 Supreme Court case of *Wisconsin v. Yoder*, in which the Supreme Court found that Amish families could not be forced to send their children to public schools in Wisconsin, has caused many home-schooling families, particularly those who home school for religious reasons, to feel comfortable challenging compulsory attendance laws.

Requirements. Home schooling is legal in all U.S. states, the District of Columbia, and all provinces and territories of Canada. In some states, however, home schooling is permitted only under private school status. Requirements for teaching credentials and student achievement vary from state to state. Some states, such as North Dakota, require parents offering instruction to pass a "teacher's test" or to have a college degree, whereas other states, such as Idaho, have no requirements for home-school teachers. In West Virginia, home-schooled students must annually score at least in the fortieth percentile on standardized tests. In Oregon, students have to score in only the fifteenth percentile on such tests. Some states (for example, New Jersey) have no achievement requirements. Requirements change from time to time, but as all states have compulsory attendance laws, states generally have some sort of system whereby parents who home school have to report that they do so to local or state superintendents of instruction. Failure to report could cause parents to be found in violation of school attendance laws.

Every state has home-schooling organizations composed of parents who provide information to other parents who wish to know how to comply with home-schooling and compulsory education laws. The Home School Legal Defense Association has helped home-schooling parents to solve problems that have arisen from conflicts with local or state education authorities.

In Canada, home-schooling laws vary from province to province. However, parents generally are required to provide "satisfactory" or "equivalent" instruction in order to have their children exempted from compulsory school attendance. In British Columbia and Alberta provision is made for home schoolers to have access to school facilities and materials. In Canada, as in the United States, laws related to home schooling have changed as more parents have chosen this option for educating their children. Throughout Canada there are organizations of home-schooling parents, which provide information to help other parents comply with compulsory attendance laws. The Home School Legal Defense Association of Canada provides legal services to home schoolers who may have conflicts with school authorities.

Home School Curricula. The curriculum offered in home schools varies depending on the requirements of school law and the goals and philosophies of home-schooling parents. States requiring home schools to operate under private school statues generally have specific curricular requirements. Other states may ask parents to submit a curriculum plan but may not dictate the provisions of the plan as long as students demonstrate adequate achievement as assessed by state-mandated tests. Some parents are concerned about offering their students a structured program. Such parents generally feel that their children learn best and become most disciplined if they adhere to a daily schedule complete with goals and objectives much like those offered by the public schools. Other parents, particularly those who have been influenced by "deschooling" philosophy, contend that the structure of the public schools is one of the reasons why they have chosen to home school their children. These parents are more likely to allow their children to pursue their own interests, believing that they will learn naturally and initiate projects that help them to achieve, in an enjoyable manner, the goals and skills they require.

While home schoolers often develop their own curriculum plans, there are commercial plans available for those who do not feel comfortable about developing their own. Many commercial plans offer moral and values education for those who want it. At the high school level some home schoolers choose correspondence high-school programs for their children. Such programs offer high-school students a chance to register credits for transcripts so that they may qualify for admission to college. Generally, however, home schooled students who do well on college entrance exams have little problem being admitted to public or private colleges and universities, whether or not they present traditional high school transcripts to admissions boards.

Public Concerns. The public at large has shown some concern about home-schooled students. Particularly, some have wondered whether these students' parents are truly being held accountable for seeing that their children achieve, and they have also wondered whether these children are being properly socialized. A 1990 study showed that home-schooled children scored higher in mathematics, reading, science, language, and social studies than 80 percent of children taught in the public schools. As for worries about socialization, many home schooling parents feel their children are better socialized than public school children because home schooled children do not encounter many of the negative influences that public school children encounter. Such home-schooling parents feel that their children are well socialized, because the parents have opportunities to help them develop character as they deal with their daily activities and help them develop social skills as they interact with a variety of people each day, not just people they meet during school activities. —*Annita Marie Ward*

BIBLIOGRAPHY

Gorder, Cheryl. *Home Schools: An Alternative.* 3d ed. Tempe, Ariz.: Blue Bird, 1990.

Hendrickson, Borg. *Home School—Taking the First Step: The Complete Program Planning Guide.* Rev. ed. Sitka, Ala: Mountain Meadow Press, 1994.

Holt, John. *Teach Your Own.* Cambridge, Mass.: Bell Books, 1981.

Wade, Theodore E., et al. *The Home School Manual.* Niles, Mich.: Gazelle Publications, 1998.

See also Bedtime reading; Educating children; Mennonites and Amish; Moral education; Private schools; Public education; Religion; Schools.

Home sharing

RELEVANT ISSUES: Aging; Health and medicine

SIGNIFICANCE: Providing younger people with a place to live in exchange for payment or services benefits many older homeowners who are willing to lose a certain amount of privacy

Home sharing is an arrangement in which two or more unrelated persons live together in a single dwelling. Each resident has a private area, such as a bedroom, and shares common areas such as the kitchen, with other residents. Many types of arrangements can be considered home sharing, ranging from students sharing a rented home to several older people living in a group home provided and maintained by a government agency. In the United States one of the most important forms of home sharing occurs when elderly homeowners offer lodgings to younger persons in exchange for money or services. Although most such situations are arranged by the persons involved, an increasing number of government agencies bring people together for this purpose.

Agency-assisted home-sharing arrangements can be classified into three basic groups, depending on the degree of personal care required by elderly homeowners. In about half of agency-assisted home sharing arrangements, homeowners require no services or only occasional help with heavy household chores or repairs. In such situations homeowners are primarily interested in receiving income and lodgers are primarily interested in finding relatively inexpensive, temporary places to live. The relationships among residents is stable and formal, with little personal interaction. In slightly less than half of agency-assisted home-sharing arrangements, homeowners require help with routine household chores because of health problems. In such situations lodgers perform these chores instead of paying rent. Such an arrangement is likely to be unstable, as homeowners' declining health requires more services than lodgers can provide. The relationships among residents are informal but not extremely intimate. In a small number of agency-assisted home-sharing arrangements, homeowners require both household help and personal services because of ill health. In such situations lodgers receive payment for services rendered. The relationships among residents are intimate, and they are likely to consider themselves family.

Homeowners benefit from home sharing by being able to remain in their homes. Healthy homeowners receive income that allows them to maintain their homes, while homeowners with health problems receive services they would otherwise need to obtain outside the home. Home sharing may also provide homeowners with companionship and a sense of security. The primary disadvantage to homeowners is loss of privacy. The primary advantage of home sharing for lodgers is financial, either in the form of low or free rent or in the form of income. A possible disadvantage is that as homeowners grow increasingly ill they may require more and more help. Society benefits from home sharing by avoiding the need to provide special housing for the elderly.   —*Rose Secrest*

See also Aging and elderly care; Home ownership; Nursing and convalescent homes; Retirement communities.

Homeless families

RELEVANT ISSUES: Economics and work; Parenting and family relationships; Sociology
SIGNIFICANCE: According to the United States Conference of Mayors, families with children make up 39 percent of all homeless persons in the United States and are the fastest growing segment of the homeless population

In the mid-1990's the Children's Defense Fund (CDF) estimated that the number of homeless children ranged from 50,000 to 500,000, not including an estimated 500,000 to 1,300,000 "unaccompanied youth," who were runaway or "throwaway" adolescents. It is more difficult to estimate the incidence of adolescent homelessness, because few shelters or services are designed to accommodate unaccompanied minors and because adolescents often avoid services so that they are not returned to their homes or to institutional care (for example, group homes and foster homes). Estimates of the numbers of homeless families do not include "marginally housed" families, such as those who live in unsafe housing, "double up" with friends or relatives, or live in their cars.

Causes of Homelessness. Historically, homeless rates have paralleled general economic trends. Low-income families have been most affected by economic trends, including declines in real earnings, increases in housing costs, changes in the low-income housing ratio (the number of low-rent residences compared to the number of low-income families), and the transfer of financial burden from the federal to the state level. People on waiting lists for public housing must wait several years for apartments in most cities. Middle- and upper-income families are less affected by stagnating wages, because they are less dependent on wage income. Most of the families living in poverty are "working poor," including the homeless. Although approximately one-third of homeless families include an employed person, wage income is insufficient to provide basic necessities. In the 1980's and 1990's housing costs outstripped wages, while rents increased more than home-ownership costs.

Changes in appropriations for low-income housing have exacerbated homelessness. Between 1980 and 1988 federal housing funds were cut by 80 percent, compounding the impact of the increase in housing costs. Families in the late 1990's spent a much greater proportion of their income on housing costs than in past generations, and this contributed to the largest increase in homelessness since the Great Depression. Children make up 40 percent of the population in poverty and are the poorest demographic group in the United States.

Demographic trends can contribute to increased poverty and homelessness. Changes in family structure, such as loss of a wage earner, addition of family members, domestic violence, and separation or divorce often precipitate homelessness. Single parents, female-headed households, and young families are more vulnerable to poverty and homelessness in part because of factors contributing to the feminization of poverty.

Effects on Family Life. Homelessness strains family interactions. Parents preoccupied with meeting the basic needs of their families often spend their days going to different offices to obtain information and assistance. The stressors associated with homelessness negatively impact parents' physical and mental health, thereby increasing the probability of irritable and negative interactions with their children. Shelters offer little privacy for family interactions, and they dictate routines.

Family members are sometimes separated from one another in order to be sheltered, because many shelters are restricted by gender and age. Older boys—sometimes as young as eight years of age—may be separated from their mothers and sisters. Similarly, fathers may be sheltered separately. Sometimes parents decide that their chil-

Homeless families headed by mothers are much more common than those headed by men. (Ben Klaffke)

dren must stay with friends or relatives. However, homeless families have a difficult time maintaining social ties because of their transience. The fact that their children stay with friends or relatives may cause other family members to be evicted because of the lack of space.

Effects on Children's Development. Homeless children evidence deficits in health, education, and social and emotional adaptation. For example, homeless women often receive no prenatal care, and infant mortality, low birth weight, and underimmunization rates are significantly greater than among housed poor children and children who do not live in poverty. Compared to housed children, homeless children suffer from more health problems, such as upper respiratory infections, ear infections, asthma, and anemia. Preven-

tive health care is largely inaccessible to homeless children, and they are exposed to more environmental toxins, such as lead. Inadequate nutrition compromises immune functioning, making children more vulnerable to infection as well as to less efficient excretory system function, which exacerbates the difficulty in removing ingested toxins. Poor nutrition also contributes to lower energy and attention levels, challenging children's ability to benefit from school attendance. Psychosocial difficulties experienced by homeless children include sleep disorders, shyness, aggression, depression, and anxiety.

Almost half of the families eligible for food stamps do not receive them, and families that have received federal assistance through the Aid to Families with Dependent Children (AFDC) pro-

The problems of the homeless are aggravated by the fact that almost half the people eligible for food stamps do not receive them. (CLEO Freelance Photography)

gram lose a significant portion of their grants if they are homeless, because they do not pay rent. Prices at inner-city grocery stores are higher than at large supermarkets, and the range of food choices is limited. Homeless families often eat fast food, because they lack utensils and staples necessary for the preparation of more nutritious foods, because many shelters do not have facilities for cooking or storing food, and because many shelters prohibit cooking.

Estimates of school attendance rates among homeless children range from 43 to 70 percent, because homeless children change schools frequently or must travel long distances from shelters to schools. Attention deficits and language delays are more frequently observed in homeless chil-

dren than in housed poor children. Between 33 and 43 percent of homeless children have repeated a grade and 25 percent have been enrolled in special education classes, compared with 10 percent of children in the general population. Homeless children score lower than housed children in reading and math, and almost half receive failing grades.

It is often difficult for homeless parents to enroll their children in school, because they lack the necessary records (for example, birth certificates and immunization records) and because it takes a long time to have records transferred to new schools. Homeless children frequently lack appropriate clothing and are often teased by other children because of their appearance or dress. Home-

In 1990 the U.S. Census Bureau made its first effort to count all the homeless persons in the United States. (AP/Wide World Photos)

less children's lack of safe and developmentally appropriate places to play contributes to delays in motor skills, language, and social and emotional development. Thus, homeless children are often disadvantaged before they even begin school.

Efforts to Address the Problem. Causes of homelessness and the lack of family sustainability emanate from all levels of the social system: family, community, and local and federal governments. Therefore, efforts to successfully address the incidence of homelessness among families (and individuals) must address potentiating factors at all systemic levels and be coordinated. For example, welfare programs are administered by state governments, but housing programs are administered by local governments. When families' welfare benefits are reduced, their self-sufficiency is significantly hindered, because it takes months for them to save enough money for security deposits on rental units. Rather than coordinating resources for sustainability, many programs inadvertently maintain family instability.

A large proportion of funding for low-income housing and homelessness is allocated for emergency shelters. Effective strategies to address homelessness must include measures to prevent homelessness, provide emergency shelter, and promote self-sufficiency. Only a fraction of families eligible for housing assistance receive it, and every day precariously housed families are evicted because there is no system of prevention. The cost of reestablishing residence once a family is homeless is much greater than the cost of preventing homelessness in the first place—in economic, social, and human capital.   —*Julia C. Torquati*

BIBLIOGRAPHY
Bassuk, E., L. Rubin, and A. Lauriat. "Characteristics of Sheltered Homeless Families." *American Journal of Public Health* 76 (1986).
Kryder-Coe, J., L. M. Salamon, and J. M. Molnar, eds. *Homeless Children and Youth: A New American Dilemma.* New Brunswick, N.J.: Transaction Publishers, 1991.
McChesney, K. Y. "Family Homelessness: A Systemic Problem." *Journal of Social Issues* 46 (1990).
Molnar, J., W. R. Rath, and T. P. Klein. "Constantly Compromised: The Impact of Homelessness on Children." *Journal of Social Issues* 46 (1990).
Rafferty, Y., and M. Shinn. "The Impact of Homelessness on Children." *American Psychologist* 48 (1991).
Waxman, Laura DeKoven. *A Status Report on Hunger and Homelessness in America's Cities.* Washington, D.C.: United States Conference of Mayors, 1994.
Wright, J. D. *Address Unknown: The Homeless in America.* New York: Aldine de Gruyter, 1989.
———. "Poor People, Poor Health: The Health Status of the Homeless." *Journal of Social Issues* 46 (1990).

See also Abandonment of the family; Child abandonment; Elder abuse; Family economics; Feminization of poverty; Habitat for Humanity International (HFHI); Home ownership; McKinney Homeless Assistance Act; Poverty; Social capital.

Household

RELEVANT ISSUES: Demographics; Sociology
SIGNIFICANCE: The household is the most basic social and economic unit in North American society and the family is the most common type of household

The governments of the United States and Canada define a household as all the persons who occupy a single housing unit. Housing units include apartments, houses, mobile homes, or other types of common living quarters. Households may consist of one person living alone, one family, two or more families living together, or unrelated people living together.

A family is defined as a group of people who are related by birth, marriage, or adoption. Members of families who live together constitute a family household. Canada recognizes two people of the opposite sex who live together in a husband-and-wife relationship as related by marriage under common law, even if they have not been formally married. The United States, following the marriage laws of most of its states, recognizes only people who have been legally married as belonging to the same family. Thus, in the United States unmarried men and women who live together are not considered a family household.

Nonfamily households include one person living alone, groups or boarders, or roommates, people who live together in order to share expenses.

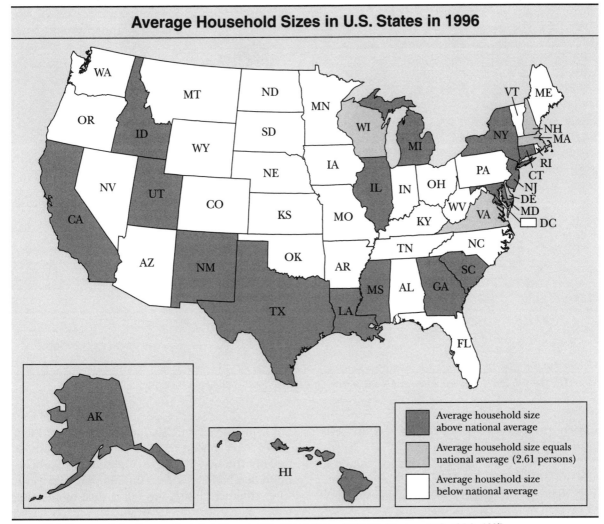

Average Household Sizes in U.S. States in 1996

Legend:
- Average household size above national average
- Average household size equals national average (2.61 persons)
- Average household size below national average

Source: U.S. Bureau of the Census, *Statistical Abstract of the United States: 1997.* Washington, D.C.: GPO, 1997.

In the United States two unrelated persons who live together in a close personal relationship are classified as an unmarried partner household.

The family is the most common type of household. The U.S. Bureau of the Census, the agency in charge of collecting and maintaining statistics on the U.S. population, reports that there were 99,627,000 households in the United States in 1996. Of these, 69,594,000, or 70 percent, were family households. The United States Census has two basic classifications of family households: "married-couple families" and "other families." The category "other families" includes "male householder, no wife present" and "female householder, no husband present." The Canadian census recognizes "husband-wife families" and "lone-parent families." "Husband-wife families" include "families of married couples" and "families of common-law couples." "Lone-parent families" include "female-parent families" and "male-parent families."

Most family households are husband and wife households. In the United States 77 percent of family households in 1996 were married-couple households. In Canada 74 percent of family households in 1996 were families of married couples. The female householder or lone female parent family is the most common other-family type. Among family households that were not based on married couples, 78 percent were headed by

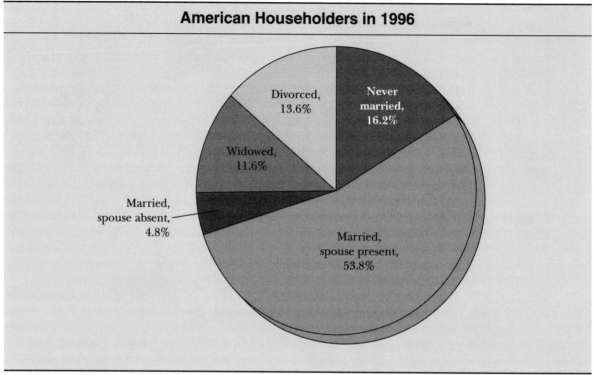

American Householders in 1996

Divorced, 13.6%

Never married, 16.2%

Widowed, 11.6%

Married, spouse absent, 4.8%

Married, spouse present, 53.8%

Source: U.S. Bureau of the Census, *Statistical Abstract of the United States: 1997.* Washington, D.C.: GPO, 1997.

women in the United States and 83 percent were headed by women in Canada.

People living alone make up the most common type of nonfamily household. In the United States in 1996 people living alone made up an estimated 83 percent of nonfamily households.

—*Carl L. Bankston III*

See also Alternative family types; Cohabitation; Disabilities; Family: concept and history; Family demographics; Family size.

Hull House

DATE: Founded on September 18, 1889, in Chicago, Illinois, as the Jane Addams Hull House Association

RELEVANT ISSUES: Children and child development; Economics and work; Education

SIGNIFICANCE: A prominent historical force in the organization of activities and human services for poor families in the United States, Hull House strived to create a better life for the disadvantaged

On September 18, 1889, Jane Addams and Ellen Gates Starr opened Hull House in a westside neighborhood of Chicago, Illinois, a neighborhood that had earned a reputation for its poverty. The settlement house was established in an aging mansion named for its original owner, Charles Hull. The purpose of Hull House was to ease the pain and suffering of poor persons by improving their social situations. Hull House supported many social reforms in the early twentieth century, providing a model for other settlement houses throughout the United States.

The lives of many urban families were improved as a result of the leisure and educational activities Hull House provided. Its founders believed that opportunities for a decent life should not be based on race, ethnic background, or gender. Hull House worked toward achieving social justice by involving neighbors in clubs, lectures, debates, classes, art, and music and in providing meals, a pharmacy, and child-care services. In engaging in these activities, people tried to solve the problems affecting their families.

Preventing juvenile delinquency was a primary

concern of Hull House. Lacking places to play and congregate, neighborhood children played in the streets. They were exposed to the dangers of the city, including unsanitary conditions, gangs, and criminals. To combat this problem, Hull House built a playground and gymnasium and established boys' and girls' clubs. Summer school, art exhibits, music lessons and performances, reading groups, and many other activities were provided for the children of area families.

Families near Hull House lived in intensely crowded, ramshackle tenements. They had no plumbing or sewage disposal, irregular garbage pickup, poor lighting, and vermin. Hull House played a role in exposing the conditions of the tenements so that laws were passed to regulate the quality of tenement housing. Another concern at

Hull House was labor reform. Men, women, and even children worked long, hard hours in factories under unsafe conditions and for little pay. Because of the long work hours, families were kept apart and children did not attend school. Bad working conditions created many health problems. Siding with the labor unions that were emerging, Hull House provided meeting places and mediated for union groups who were negotiating for better working conditions, shorter working hours, fair wages, and child-labor laws. Child-labor laws were passed, prohibiting young children under fourteen years of age from working in factories. Laws were also passed to limit the length of the working day, so that families could spend time together.

In 1997 two original Hull House buildings operated as a museum, while the Hull House Associa-

An immigrant woman entering Hull House with her children in 1903. (University of Illinois at Chicago, The University Library, Jane Addams Memorial Collection)

tion operated programs in more than forty different Chicago locations for disadvantaged families. Hull House's services include emergency assistance, foster care, job training, arts programs, counseling, home-delivered meals, literacy programs, and child care. —*Karen L. Barak*

See also Addams, Jane; Community programs for children; Lathrop, Julia C.; Settlement houses; Social workers.

Human Genome Project

RELEVANT ISSUES: Children and child development; Health and medicine
SIGNIFICANCE: The Human Genome Project involves medical research that could alter unwanted genetic traits in families and eliminate many diseases

The genome of an organism is the totality of genes constituting its hereditary makeup. The identification and study of genes is of great medical importance in determining particular genes involved in unwanted hereditary traits or diseases.

In 1990 an internationally coordinated effort called the Human Genome Project was initiated to characterize the entire human genome. One of the primary goals of the project is to determine the exact location of all the human genes, numbering approximately 50,000 to 100,000, on their respective chromosomes. An estimated four thousand of these genes are probably associated with diseases. Another primary goal of this project is to establish the sequence of nucleotides, numbering about six billion pairs, of all the genes. Achieving both goals, which is possible, would be of great medical benefit to all humanity.

The Human Genome Project has been greatly assisted by the ability of scientists to clone large fragments of deoxyribonucleic acid (DNA) into yeast for further analysis and by the automation of numerous genetic techniques, such as DNA sequencing. Under the direction of the geneticist and Nobel Prize winner James Watson and with assistance from the National Science Foundation and the Howard Hughes Medical Institute, the Office of Human Research within the U.S. National Institutes of Health and the Department of Energy have been centrally involved in the project. —*Alvin K. Benson*

See also Birth defects; Eugenics; Genetic counseling; Genetic disorders; Health problems; Heredity.

Hutterites

RELEVANT ISSUES: Demographics; Religious beliefs and practices
SIGNIFICANCE: The Hutterites are a religious group known for sharing all their property equally and for having more children than most other groups because of their antibirth-control stance

The Hutterian Brethren are one of three Anabaptist religious groups—along with the Amish and the Mennonites—that began in Central Europe in the 1520's. The Hutterites take their name from Jakob Hutter, their charismatic leader who was burned at the stake for heresy in 1536. All three Anabaptist groups oppose infant baptism, but the Hutterites are distinguished from the others by practicing communalism. Continually persecuted for their pacifism and their opposition to public education, they moved from Russia to the United States in the 1870's and then to Canada after World War I. In the 1990's they lived in agricultural colonies called *bruderhofs* (from the original German they still speak meaning "communal farms") that are primarily located in the Western prairie provinces and Montana.

Hutterite families live together in apartments that surround a community dining hall. Children remain with their families until the age of three, at which time they attend the community kindergarten. Government teachers provide public education at Hutterite colonies through the eighth grade, while German teachers provide religious and cultural instruction. The fact that the colonies are physically isolated from cities helps to preserve the Hutterite way of life.

Persons are considered adolescents from the age of fifteen until they are baptized, at which time they become marriage-age adults. The Hutterites developed a coupling practice whereby marriageable youths were assembled about twice a year and preachers gave each male a choice of three females from whom to select a wife. Males who did not want to marry the available females were forced to wait until the next coupling period. Following the uproar caused when a young girl refused to marry an older man in 1830, personal choice was instituted. However, Hutterites must marry Hutterites, and since most colonies are like large extended families, in which persons either are or feel like relatives, most young people go outside their particular colonies to find spouses. Western romantic notions are not considered important and divorce is extremely rare.

In the 1950's scholars declared the Hutterites to be the demographic standard for maximum possible fertility. The Hutterites had grown from only 443 people in 1880 to 8,542 in 1950, which appeared to be the world's fastest natural population growth rate. Families had an average of ten children, but since Hutterite women did not marry until they reached the age of about twenty-two, it was estimated that women could bear up to fourteen children if they start when they are young. There is virtually no premarital sex among the Hutterites, and all methods of birth control are considered to be sinful. Studies since the 1950's have indicated that the birth rate has been declining among the Hutterites, as Hutterite women have had their doctors prescribe contraceptives for medical reasons. This has been seen as the beginning of a women's movement in a patriarchal society.

—*Bron B. Ingoldsby*

See also Birth control; Courting rituals; Family size; Matchmaking; Mennonites and Amish; Patriarchs; Religion.

Imaginary friends

RELEVANT ISSUES: Children and child development; Parenting and family relationships

SIGNIFICANCE: A part of normal childhood development, imaginary friends are creations of children's imaginations that help them cope with social and emotional issues

Imaginary friends are imagined playmates, animals, siblings, or creatures created by children. They usually have a specific name, physical description, and preferences. Children openly play with and talk to their imaginary friends, sharing feelings and stories. Children also commonly ask others to interact with their imaginary companions, such as by having them come on trips or participate in meals.

Most often children do not assume that anyone can see their imaginary friends. Instead, such friends are assumed to be invisible to everyone but the children themselves. Indeed, for some children their companions are only pretend friends whom even the children do not see. Other children, however, actually visualize their imaginary companions. In particular, children who are especially good at visualization may provide highly detailed descriptions of these friends.

Not all children have imaginary friends, but 12 to 31 percent of children ages two through nine and a half do. Such friends are most common in only children and those who might be lonely. Imaginary friends are no more common in children with emotional problems than in those without such problems. Bright children are more likely to create imaginary friends than slow children, and the brightest sometimes have several imaginary companions whom they imagine to be twins or triplets.

Parents' apprehension is normal when they learn about their chil-

Invention of imaginary friends is a normal part of childhood development. (James L. Shaffer)

dren's imaginary friends, but there is no immediate reason for alarm. Imaginary companions are most often created by children as a coping strategy to deal with feelings or to experiment with new social skills. They have meaning to children and allow them to gain greater self-confidence, decreasing fears related to approaching new situations. More generally, imaginary friends help children engage in emotions, facilitating empathy and perspective taking. While children sometimes blame imaginary friends for occurrences, such as taking or breaking things, more often than not imaginary friends are associated with positive emotional expression.

Children talk freely and openly about their imaginary friends. Children may also use their friends to express feelings that are otherwise difficult for them to express directly. Thus, it is especially important for parents to accept their children's imaginary friends, as they may represent a part of their children's emotional selves. Parents should avoid rejecting their children's imaginary friends and instead treat them with the same respect and privacy they show to their children.

If parents feel apprehensive about imaginary friends, they may consult with therapists. If imaginary companions interfere in normal peer relationships or play, are related to traumatic events, or if children more generally have trouble separating fantasy from reality, consultation may be helpful. In most cases, however, imaginary companions are merely a part of children's normal development and will disappear before they reach their preteen years just as quietly as they appeared in childhood. —*Nancy A. Piotrowski*

See also Birth order; Childhood fears and anxieties; Only children; Parenting.

In loco parentis

RELEVANT ISSUES: Children and child development; Law; Parenting and family relationships
SIGNIFICANCE: To the extent that families fail to perform the socializing role that traditionally has been expected of them, other institutions and individuals are called upon to fill the void *in loco parentis*

In loco parentis (literally, "in the place of a parent") is a legal concept indicating the usually temporary assumption by nonparents of parental rights and responsibilities over juveniles. It concerns both narrow legal questions about who possesses "parental" powers over individual minors and broader social questions about the extent to which children and juveniles should be controlled, socialized, and cared for by persons other than their parents. In the narrow legal sense, *in loco parentis* has been taken to mean that individuals or organizations may assume temporary guardianship of juveniles in the absence of supervision by their natural or adopted parents. Boarding schools, for example, have assumed such status. Establishing a legal claim to a relationship of *in loco parentis* at times can be a contentious, disputatious matter resolved only by courts. The broader question of the extent to which children and juveniles should be subjected to control and socialization and placed in the care of persons other than their parents often sparks contentious public policy debates concerning societal rights and responsibilities. —*Steve D. Boilard*

See also Foster homes; Guardianship; Orphans; Private schools.

In re Baby M

DATE: Ruling issued on February 3, 1988
RELEVANT ISSUES: Law; Parenting and family relationships
SIGNIFICANCE: A state supreme court ruled for the first time in the case *In re Baby M* on whether a surrogate-parenting contract was enforceable

Baby M raised questions regarding contract law, reproductive rights, and social and sexual equality. At issue was whether a contract signed between Mary Beth Whitehead, a "surrogate" mother, William Stern, a sperm donor, and the Infertility Center of New York (ICNY), the surrogacy broker, was enforceable. The New Jersey Supreme Court's decision affirmed in part, reversed in part, and remanded for further proceedings a lower trial court's decision. Citing the "best interests of the child," the lower court had granted the Sterns custody of Baby M. Finding that only a state-approved agency can terminate parental rights, the New Jersey Supreme Court identified Whitehead as the natural mother, revoked the term "surrogate mother," and restored her parental rights. The

New Jersey women demonstrating support for Mary Beth Whitehead's custody claim to the child she bore as a "surrogate" mother. (AP/Wide World Photos)

surrogacy contract was declared unenforceable and illegal because of multiple conflicts with New Jersey's laws and public policies—for example, laws against baby selling. Furthermore, the court found that by privileging the father's rights over the mother's, the contract violated the state's laws regarding equal parental rights. While the court did not declare surrogacy itself criminal, it did find that an exchange of money for surrogacy services was illegal, thus rendering surrogacy contracts unenforceable and potentially undesirable. By 1992 eighteen states had outlawed or restricted surrogacy operations.   —*Dyan E. Mazurana*

See also Alternative family types; Family law; Surrogate mothers.

In re Gault

DATE: Ruling issued on May 15, 1967
SIGNIFICANCE: The *Gault* decision was the first juvenile decision ever reviewed on constitutional grounds by the U.S. Supreme Court

Toward the end of its 1966-1967 term the U.S. Supreme Court handed down what has become the bellwether case in juvenile justice in the twentieth century. The long road of fifteen-year-old Gerald Francis Gault to the Supreme Court began in Gila County, Arizona, on June 8, 1964. Gault was taken into custody and charged with delinquency for allegedly making a lewd telephone call to a neighbor living in his trailer park. He was sub-

The In re Gault *decision ensured that juvenile offenders would not be denied the procedural rights customarily granted to adults.* (James L. Shaffer)

sequently found guilty of delinquency and sentenced to the state reformatory until age twenty-one, or a total of nearly six years.

After unsuccessful appeals in state courts, the U.S. Supreme Court granted review of the case. In an exhaustive 8 to 1 opinion authored by Justice Abe Fortas, the Court reversed Gault's delinquency conviction, ruling that Gault's incarceration violated four principles of constitutional due process and fundamental fairness. The Court ruled that henceforth in cases in which juveniles are charged with delinquency and a possible loss of liberty, such juveniles must be given adequate notices of the charges, be afforded the right to counsel at delinquency adjudicatory proceedings, be afforded the right to confront and cross-examine witnesses, and be afforded the right to remain silent and not be subject to compulsory self-incrimination. This case essentially revolutionized juvenile court practice in the United States.

—John C. Watkins, Jr.

See also Children's rights; Family law; Generation X; Juvenile courts; Juvenile delinquency; Parental divorce.

Incest

Relevant issues: Children and child development; Health and medicine; Kinship and genealogy; Parenting and family relationships; Violence

Significance: Sexual relations between blood relatives, incest has long been considered taboo and is often regarded by modern society as a form of violence that has severe short-term and long-term consequences for its victims

Incest has always been regarded as deviant. Indeed it is the universal taboo. Yet, in the past incest was seen as nonviolent sexual deviance. By the late 1970's and early 1980's this view began to shift, as at least cross-generational incest began to be viewed as a type of rape and hence an act of violence. This has had the effect of placing the issue of incest within a drastically new frame of reference.

Abusive and Nonabusive Incest. There are two types of incestuous relations, those that take place between age equals and those that are initiated by older family members against younger ones, or cross-generational incest. A distinction is thus made between sexual victimization that involves older and considerably younger relatives and incest that involves sexual relations between close relatives who are peers. The latter is usually consensual and therefore seen as nonabusive, although deviant.

One example of nonabusive incest is boys' sexual relations with female cousins. This was found by one researcher to be the most common form of incest (thirty-three out of sixty cases). The same study found that sexual relations between brothers and sisters is the next most common form (sixteen out of sixty cases). A very close third is homosexual relations between brothers (fifteen out of sixty cases). Of the 151 women in this study who reported having had incestuous experiences, 5 had such experiences with their biological fathers and 2 with their stepfathers.

Types of Incestuous Relations. The most common incestuous experience for females is with their brothers (72 out of 151 cases). It should not, however, be assumed that these are nonabusive or consensual relationships. Quite often a high degree of sexual victimization occurs. It is common for brothers to be at least five years older than their sisters, whereby physical coercion often plays a prominent role. It has been estimated that the average age discrepancy between brothers and sisters when incest occurs is about seven years: Brothers are on average age 19.9 years old and sisters 10.7 years old. This type of age discrepancy is considered sufficient to qualify as sexual victimization. It should be noted that in one study half the women who experienced sibling incest never married.

The type of incest that receives the most attention is that between fathers and daughters. Because children are usually accepting of parental authority and because they regard their parents as role models, they exist in a relationship of dependency and trust with respect to their parents. Consequently, father-daughter incest cannot be seen as voluntary in any meaningful sense of the term. Therefore, the general consensus among researchers in the 1990's has been to view this type of incest as a form of rape, like all forms of child molestation. The average age of female victims is estimated to be slightly older than ten years. The average age of fathers is between thirty-five and thirty-seven years old.

In the case of intrafamilial, cross-generational incest, there appears to be a pattern of abuse. The most common type of abuse for both girls and boys is genital fondling. This is accompanied by exhibitionism and mutual masturbation. The process may culminate in oral intercourse. In the case of girls, vaginal penetration is rarely involved if the perpetrator is a natural father. In one study, it was found that intercourse occurred in 4 percent of the cases as opposed to genital fondling, which occurred in 38 percent of the cases, while exhibitionism occurred in 20 percent of the cases.

In situations where girls are abused by family members, a common pattern entails a progression in levels of victimization. It typically begins with affectionate fondling during the preschool years, progressing to mutual masturbation and oral sex during middle childhood and then vaginal penetration which occurs, if at all, in preadolescence or early adolescence. Because children are generally docile when confronted with adult authority and are emotionally dependent on parents, coercion is seldom used in the case of girls.

Most of the research on incest consistently reports that mother-son incest is extremely rare. In those rare cases in which it does occur, it generally involves sons sexually assaulting their mothers. In these instances the sons are usually either psychotic or mentally retarded. Boys are actually much more likely to be victimized by either their fathers or their stepfathers. In the case of father-son incest, the levels of physical coercion employed are significantly higher than in the case of girls.

Principal Victims of Incest. Although it is thought that incest with boys may be seriously underreported, the general consensus is that girls are the principal victims of incest. Diana Russell, in her San Francisco study, found that uncles made up the largest category of incest perpetrators, whereby nieces were the clear victims. Uncles made up 25 percent of abuse perpetrators. Fathers made up the next most common category of perpetrators at 24 percent. In this category, 14 percent were biological fathers, 8 percent were stepfathers, and 2 percent were adoptive fathers. In Russell's study, stepfathers were, relative to their numbers, seven times more likely to abuse their stepdaughters sexually than were natural fathers. One-sixth of all the women studied in her sample who had stepfathers were sexually abused by them by the age of fourteen.

It has been observed that stepfathers demonstrate a far greater willingness to engage in vaginal penetration with their stepdaughters than do biological fathers. Moreover, stepfathers abuse their stepdaughters with far greater frequency than do natural fathers. Stepfathers are more than three times as likely to have abused their stepdaughters twenty or more times (41 percent of the sample) than biological fathers (12 percent of the sample). Stepfathers are one-third as likely to have abused their stepdaughters only once (18 percent of the sample) as compared to 48 percent in the case of natural fathers. This is why incest has increased with the growth of blended families.

Causes of Incest. Because of the predominance of fathers in the cross-generational incest pattern, it is reasonable to conclude that one important causative factor is patriarchy. It has been argued that this type of abusive incest is a function of male dominance and the socialization that attends it. Males are often taught that their will in all matters concerning their families should be unopposed.

It should be noted that most fathers do not engage in incest even in strongly patriarchal cultures. Other contributing factors must be involved besides this background variable. Generally, father-daughter incest occurs in dysfunctional families. Women who have been subject to incestuous abuse report very poor relations with their mothers. Mother-daughter estrangement has repeatedly been found to be a key factor in father-daughter incest. Moreover, mothers of such daughters may be deceased, suffer from prolonged illnesses, be victims of alcoholism, or suffer from other incapacitating conditions. In these situations, daughters increasingly assume the role of "woman of the house," which may lead to abuse from their fathers.

It appears that incest offenders bear many striking similarities to child molesters in general. Although child molestation is a form of rape, the perpetrators can be contrasted with the rapists of adult victims in a number of ways. Molesters tend to be older than rapists; molesters are more sexually repressed and less sexually aggressive than are rapists; molesters have significantly greater difficulty in getting along with members of the opposite sex than do rapists; molesters are less violent than rapists and they are more willing to admit guilt than are rapists. One characteristic that incest perpetrators do not share with molesters in general is that they experience greater social isolation.

Effects of Incest. One study of female victims of abusive incest cluster the aftermath effects under four headings: traumatic sexualization, through which children's sexual identity is shaped in inappropriate and dysfunctional ways, often resulting in precocious sexuality; betrayal, or the discovery by abused children that someone whom they trusted caused them harm, often resulting in the inability of women to form trusting relationships in the future; powerlessness, or the process by which children's will, desires, and sense of personal competence are completely negated, often with lasting effects; and stigmatization, or feelings of shame and guilt that children incorporate into their identity, often assuming responsibility for their own abuse and leading them to replicate victimizing relationships throughout their lives.

It should be noted that boys who have been subject to abusive incest do not typically respond with feelings of guilt. The socialization of boys is such that they are permitted to express their anger at abuse by directing this anger outward. By contrast, the socialization of girls induces them to deflect their anger inward and express it in the form of depression, including suicidal depression.

—*Richard S. Bell*

BIBLIOGRAPHY

Finkelhor, David. *Child Sexual Abuse: New Theory and Research.* New York: Free Press, 1984.

Goode, Eric. *Deviant Behavior.* 5th ed. Upper Saddle River, N.J.: Prentice Hall, 1997.

Herman, Judith L. *Father-Daughter Incest.* Cambridge, Mass.: Harvard University Press, 1981.

Russell, Diana E. H. *The Secret Trauma: Incest in the Lives of Girls and Women.* New York: Basic Books, 1986.

Siegel, Larry J., and Joseph J. Senna. *Juvenile Delinquency: Theory, Practice, and Law.* 6th ed. St. Paul, Minn.: West, 1997.

See also Child abuse; Child molestation; Domestic violence; Dysfunctional families; Exogamy; Father-daughter relationships; Mother-son relationships; Sexuality and sexual taboos; Stepfamilies.

Infanticide

RELEVANT ISSUES: Parenting and family relationships; Violence
SIGNIFICANCE: Infanticide began in prehistoric times and has remained in both developed and underdeveloped nations as a major societal problem afflicting those least able to defend themselves

Infanticide, the intentional killing of infants or young children, is as old as humanity itself and exists in many cultures. Prehistoric hunters widely used infanticide to space their offspring and thus guarantee survival of older siblings, especially when food supplies were low. For early humans, no other means of birth control or prenatal abortion existed. The killing of female newborns, in particular, limited the number of future child bearers, providing the needed balance between population, food, and other resources. These practices existed until modern times among Eskimo and aboriginal hunting communities. Infanticide was less pronounced among African tribal communities, although twins were often considered as bad omens and were frequently put to death.

Infanticide in Ancient and Medieval Civilizations. As humanity slowly shifted from hunting and gathering societies to agriculturally-based civilizations, infanticide remained the main means of limiting family size. Egyptian civilization remained fairly free from infanticide until after 1000 B.C.E. because of sufficient food supplies and the sacredness of the family unit. However, many other Middle Eastern peoples practiced infanticide by suffocation or abandonment. Infants were also sacrificed in religious worship to gods such as Baal and Marduk. The first great world conqueror, Sargon of Assyria, started life as an abandoned child as did the biblical Moses. The biblical account of Abraham being stopped from sacrificing his first-born son Isaac probably symbolizes an early Hebrew break with other Semitic peoples in the practice of child sacrifice. Thereafter, Jewish culture treated newborns as having the same rights to life as adults. Until Muhammad strictly forbade the practice of female infanticide, Arabic peoples continued the practice, because females were of minimum value in the caravan trade. Those cultures

Tombstone of the murdered Smith brothers. (AP/Wide World Photos)

that continued infanticide developed clearly defined longevity rights for membership in the family group lasting from several days to several years. Such rites served as a defense mechanism against guilt for killing family members.

Overcrowding in ancient Greece and Rome caused infanticide to become a common practice. In both civilizations the average family did not have room for more than one daughter and three or four sons. Moreover, surplus children added to complications in family land divisions. Hence, in the ancient Greek city-states unwanted newborns were either smothered or abandoned. In addition, many city-states had laws requiring that imperfect infants be destroyed. Only after ten days were infants accepted as family members and thus protected. In Rome, founded according to legend by the two bothers Romulus and Remus, who were raised by a she-wolf, the power of fathers was supreme in determining the life or death of their offspring. As Christianity spread in the crumbling Roman Empire, there was still no major effort to stop the practice of infanticide. It was not until 787 C.E. that the Roman Catholic Church established the first asylum for the care of abandoned babies. Infanticide continued throughout the Middle Ages, as tales of abandoned children and evil stepmothers gave grist to countless folk tales.

The Non-Western World and Infanticide. In the non-Western world the killing of newborn females was quite common to curb the cost of dowries. Through the late twentieth century female infanticide has remained a major problem in rural India, in spite of government efforts to stop it. A more indirect policy, neglect of females, also guarantees that male infants have a much better chance of surviving than female infants. In Japan infanticide was widely practiced, particularly among impoverished peasants, as a means of birth control. The practice was called *mabiki* (thinning-out). Newborns were suffocated before they first cried to prevent an ancestral spirit from entering their bodies. Infanticide was frequent in China during times of famine. The agricultural nature of Chinese society, however, favored large families in normal times. Moreover, strong reverence for ancestors and tight extended family structures acted as a deterrent to infanticide. Female infanticide has become more prevalent in modern China because of its one couple, one child policy. As a

result of this policy, which was adopted to reduce overpopulation, many Chinese infants meet with accidents so that first surviving children are male.

From Early Modern to Modern Times. With the growth of cities infanticide also grew. Unwanted newborns were abandoned or disposed of by either being thrown in rivers or sewers by increasing numbers of prostitutes and unwed mothers. An indirect way of terminating unwanted newborns was "the wet nurse system," first developed in Italy during the Renaissance. Wet nurses were notorious for nursing more babies than they could possibly handle or for neglecting infants in their care when higher-paying parents could be found. In England during the nineteenth century, wet nurses were nicknamed "angel makers." By using wet nurses, parents removed the stigma of directly killing their infants. Another "death sentence" for infants involved their abandonment in front of churches, hospitals, and foundling homes. Eighteenth century Paris was notorious for its ill-run foundling homes, in which few infants or young children survived.

Infanticide received little attention in modern times until a pediatrician, C. Henry Kempe, coined the term "battered child syndrome" in an article published in 1962 in *The Journal of the American Medical Association*. Kempe related the killing of young children to the larger societal problem of child abuse. By the late 1960's all fifty U.S. states had passed laws requiring professionals such as teachers, doctors, and social workers to report cases of child abuse. In the 1980's an average of one million abuses were reported each year, 40 percent of which were substantiated. In the 1990's the average was three million abuse reports and 2,000 deaths per year resulting from abuse.

Paradoxically, many child abusers were themselves abused children or individuals with low self-esteem and high levels of frustration. Infants fall victim to violent fits of parental rage, in which a few seconds of violent shaking or pummeling may result in death. Newborns are thrown into dumpsters by young teenage mothers or starved to death by drug addicted, alcoholic, or mentally ill mothers. Dysfunctional families, the drug problem in the United States, the steady rise of women and children living in poverty, continual cutbacks in government services, the violent nature of American society, inadequate child-care services,

In October, 1994, Susan Smith (pictured with her husband) horrified the nation by reporting that carjackers had kidnapped her two infant sons. However, police soon suspected Smith herself, and she was later convicted of murdering her own children. (AP/Wide World Photos)

postpartum depression, and out-of-control boy-friends left to care for infants fathered by other men are all given as partial answers to explain the rising tide of child mortality.

Risk of Infanticide in the United States. Unfortunately, infants and young children are at much greater risk in the United States than in any other advanced industrial country. The United States ranked twentieth in infant mortality in 1987. Unlicensed and inadequate child-care centers for working mothers inadvertently play a role similar to that of the "wet nurses" of old. To make minor inroads into problems associated with the raising of infants, the Family and Medical Leave Act was enacted in 1993 after it was urged by child-advocate groups such as the Children's Defense Fund (CDF).

The U.S. media are filled with horror stories, such as the Susan Smith case of 1994. Susan Smith was convicted on two counts of murder for drowning her baby boys (one three years old and the other fourteen months) by driving her car into a lake. The case became an intense, unfolding drama. Yet, few stories appear in the popular media about the general problem of child abuse. One such story of note in 1994 was the Diane Melton case, in which nineteen children living in horrific conditions in a Chicago slum were taken by the state from their mother to prevent further neglect. The Melton case clearly gave precedence to the rights of children over that of preservation of the family.

On the international level, the United Nations passed the United Nations Declaration of the Rights of Children in 1989, which mandated that "the child shall be protected against all forms of neglect, cruelty, and exploitation." Nevertheless, infanticide is still not considered a crime worldwide. Premarital pregnancies in traditionalist nations often lead to infanticide. Throughout the world, the bulk of infant and child murders go unreported and unnoticed. —*Irwin Halfond*

BIBLIOGRAPHY

Best, Joel. *Threatened Children: Rhetoric and Concern About Child Victims.* Chicago: University of Chicago Press, 1990.

Breiner, Sander J. *Slaughter of the Innocents: Child Abuse Through the Ages and Today.* New York: Plenum Press, 1990.

Kohl, Marvin, ed. *Infanticide and the Value of Life.* Buffalo: Prometheus Books, 1978.

Korbin, Jill E., ed. *Child Abuse and Neglect: Cross-Cultural Perspectives.* Berkeley: University of California Press, 1981.

Piers, Maria W. *Infanticide.* New York: W. W. Norton, 1978.

Zeigler, Edward F., et al., eds. *Children, Families, and Government: Preparing for the Twenty-first Century.* New York: Cambridge University Press, 1996.

See also Abortion; Birth defects; Child abuse; Domestic violence; Euthanasia; Poverty; Teen mothers.

Inheritance and estate law

RELEVANT ISSUES: Law; Parenting and family relationships

SIGNIFICANCE: People have a legal right to decide who gets their property when they die, but the legal rules governing this right are complex and can be expensive and time-consuming to pursue

Inheritance and estate law concerns how property is transferred at death. The property may be real estate, personal property, investments, or money. State laws, as opposed to federal laws, generally govern such transfers. These laws may differ in important respects between states.

Wills. The standard way to transfer property at death is by wills. Persons who make wills are called "testators." The requirements for valid wills are governed by state statutes. These statutes vary from state to state, but they share certain common features. The Uniform Probate Code has been enacted in many states to make the rules on wills more uniform.

Wills must almost always be in writing. A few states recognize nuncupative, or oral, wills, which dispose of some items of personal property at or near death. Many states recognize holographic wills, which must be written in the handwriting of testators but without witnesses.

Certain topics are covered in nearly all wills. First, wills state the name, residence, and testamentary capacity of the testators. Second, they usually provide for the payment of taxes and debts of the deceased. Third, they appoint persons to administer the estate. This person is called the "administrator," "executor," or "personal representative." Fourth, wills dispose of the property of the testators. These dispositions may be called devises or legacies. Finally, wills are signed by testators and witnesses. Most statutes require only two witnesses.

Testators must have testamentary capacity at the time they sign their wills. Testators must be of a minimum age, which is usually eighteen years old. They must also be of sound mind at the signing of their wills. This, in turn, is based on two general propositions pertaining to whether testators can form a rational plan for the distribution of their property upon their death. First, it must be established that testators know and understand the nature and extent of the property covered in their wills. Second, testators must be able to recognize the natural objects of bounty—that is, the people who normally receive property through wills, such as spouses and children. This does not mean, however, that testators must will their property to such people. In all but a few states it is possible to disinherit and leave no property to all relatives except spouses. Testamentary capacity is a weak legal requirement. A person can have testamentary capacity and still not be able to enter into contracts or conduct daily affairs.

Intestacy. People die intestate if they leave no wills and do not otherwise dispose of their property. Others die intestate if they do not leave wills that are considered valid by probate courts. Probate is a legal proceeding whereby property is transferred at death. Probate courts decide the validity of wills and determine who receives property either under wills or otherwise. Probate courts appoint persons to collect the property of the deceased, pay debts and taxes out of the property, and transfer the remaining property to the correct people. In many states, some property is not probated. This includes joint tenancy property, life insurance proceeds, and similar items. Courts may be prohibited from probating wills if such wills do not meet the requirements of validity, if testators lacked the testamentary capacity to make them, or for other reasons. Persons may leave valid wills that fail to dispose of all their property. Such people die partially intestate.

Every state has an intestacy statute that directs who will get the property of intestates. While the statutes vary significantly, each is based on the family status of the deceased. If the deceased leaves a surviving spouse, the spouse usually gets all or most of the property. If there is a surviving spouse and children, some states divide the property between them while others still leave all the property to the spouse. If there is no surviving spouse, property goes to descendants such as children and grandchildren. If there are no descendants, property goes to ancestors such as parents and grandparents. If there are no descendants or ancestors, the property escheats, or goes to the state.

Will Substitutes. There are alternatives to transferring property by will. Some can be less expensive than wills and may not have to be probated. Two or more persons may own property as joint tenants with rights of survivorship. If joint tenants die, their interest in the property automatically goes to the surviving joint tenants. No legal proceeding is normally required for such a transfer to be effective. Tenancy by the entirety is a form of joint tenancy recognized in some states between husbands and wives. Homes, automobiles, bank accounts, investments and many other forms of property can be held in joint tenancy or tenancy by the entirety.

Trusts can also be used to transfer property at death. A trust is created by a transfer to a trustee of legal title in property. The trustee holds the property for people called beneficiaries. The documents creating the trust can specify who gets the property when the beneficiaries die. A living trust is a form of trust into which people put all their assets to be managed for their own benefit by a trustee. The living trust then tells the trustee who gets the property when the beneficiary dies. This can be a substitute for a will which avoids probate and the attendant publicity.

There are other ways to transfer special assets at death without a will. Upon proof of a person's death, money from a life insurance policy is paid to a designated beneficiary outside probate in most states. Pensions and other retirement plans often provide for a joint and survivor annuity. A retired person purchases such an annuity under which retirees receive income for life and other persons, such as a spouses, receive the income when the retiree dies.

Married Couples. Married people normally leave most of their estates to a surviving spouse. If the estate is particularly large, property may also

John F. Kennedy, Jr. (center rear) and Caroline Kennedy Schlossberg (right rear) at the funeral of their mother, Jacqueline Kennedy Onassis, most of whose estate was sold at auction to benefit her heirs. (Reuters/Jim Bourg/Archive Photos)

be left to children, charities, and others. However, surviving spouses have important legal rights that wills cannot ignore. It is possible in most states to disinherit children and other relatives, but not spouses.

A number of states in the southwest United States are community property states. While community property statutes differ from state to state, they share common features. All money, property, and other assets acquired during marriage are presumed to be marital property. Each spouse is the owner of an undivided one-half interest in all marital property regardless of who earned or acquired it. Upon the death of one spouse, the one-half interest owned by the surviving spouse remains in the ownership and control of the survivor. Only the one-half interest owned by the deceased can be transferred by will. Community property states also recognize separate or individual property, which is wholly owned and controlled by one spouse. Any property brought to the marriage is usually classified as separate property. Some property acquired during the marriage may be separate property, as is property acquired by gift or inheritance by a single spouse. Separate property can usually be left in a will to persons of testators' choice.

The remaining U.S. states base their inheritance and estate laws on the common law inherited from England. According to common law, wives had a dower interest in one-third of their husbands' real property. Similarly, husbands had a curtesy right to all real property owned by their wives, provided they had children. With respect to dower and curtesy, surviving spouses had control of the property only for the duration of their lives as a means of support for themselves and their children. The will of the deceased spouse could not vary dower or curtesy rights unless the surviving spouse consented. States which still use dower and curtesy have changed these rights in some respects, such as equalizing the rights of men and women and giving survivors absolute ownership instead of a mere life interest.

Many states have replaced the common law rules with comprehensive statutory schemes such as the Uniform Probate Code. Under these statutes, surviving spouses have a right to a forced or elective share of the property of the deceased. The statutes differ in the amount of the share. Some states use proportional amounts, such as one-third, while others use absolute dollar amounts. Still others require that surviving spouses be given certain assets such as the homestead. As with most inheritance laws, surviving spouses may choose to waive their forced share. —*David E. Paas*

BIBLIOGRAPHY

Anderson, Patricia. *Affairs in Order: A Complete Resource Guide to Death and Dying.* New York: Macmillan, 1991.

Goodman, Jordan. *Everyone's Money Book.* Chicago: Dearborn Financial, 1994.

Shae, Irving. *Nolo's Everyday Law Book.* Berkeley, Calif.: Nolo Press, 1996.

See also Children born out of wedlock; Intergenerational income transfer; Prenuptial agreements; Primogeniture; Son preference; Tax laws; Uniform Marital Property Act (UMPA); Wealth; Wills and bequests.

In-laws

RELEVANT ISSUES: Children and child development; Divorce; Kinship and genealogy; Law; Marriage and dating; Parenting and family relationships

SIGNIFICANCE: In most marriages, spouses must interact with a myriad of in-laws, which can be a major source of problems in couples' social, economic, and psychological family development

The nuclear family, in whatever combination of individuals, is greatly influenced by interactions with in-laws, including mothers-in-law, fathers-in-law, sisters- and brothers-in-law, and uncles- and aunts-in-law. These new relatives, by their very presence and family histories, provide unsolicited, though well-intentioned, opinions, advice, traditions, and expectations with which new couples must come to terms. When couples do not share ethnic, social, economic, or educational backgrounds, their marriages must adjust to the differences in lifestyle and customs that in-laws bring to the equation.

Problem Areas. Counseling that focuses on relationships with in-laws and extended family is a relatively new branch of psychotherapy. Most therapy techniques center on developing healthy com-

Three generations of any family produce multiple pairs of in-law relationships. (James L. Shaffer)

munication skills, focusing on unreal expectations, and healing damaged relationships among couples and their in-laws. Research shows that it is easier to build healthy relationships than to heal the damaged emotions of unresolved conflict.

When couples and their in-laws lack effective communication skills, unresolved emotions and problems arising as early as courtship and marriage can affect family relationships for years. In-law relationships that become unhealthy early in marriage are the major causes of marital discord

and divorce. Couples must tackle problems in dealing with siblings-in-law, arranging holidays, and handling family crises. Additionally, couples, married or unmarried, must learn to negotiate conflicts that arise over family loyalties, overinvolvement, and legal and financial differences.

Research shows that there is more in-law conflict when new couples do not integrate their relationships into in-laws' families before marriage. Meeting and getting to know prospective family member—even if briefly—helps establish emotional bonds and gives in-laws time to get to know those who want to be a part of the family. Couples who choose not to marry tend to experience more conflicts with in-laws than couples who marry.

When couples' in-laws belong to different religions, one side of the family may openly refuse to officially recognize their children's partners as a part of the family. This is more often true when in-laws hold fundamentalist religious beliefs or when those wishing to marry are of different cultures. Some religions require parents to declare children dead if they marry outside the faith. Some parents refuse their children any family inheritance if they do not marry into the family's religion. Couples who experience conflicts with in-laws over religion experience higher than normal rates of divorce.

Couples choose each other as partners in a relationship. However, they do not have the luxury of choosing their in-laws. Even mentioning issues in parenting styles or economic choices often sounds like criticism. Since in-laws are family, criticism is unexpected and unappreciated. Issues such as arranging holidays can become explosive when in-laws on either side of the family are more demanding, less understanding, or ethnically different. Research shows that both husbands and wives have more trouble with mothers-in-laws. However, husbands have a higher disapproval rate with fathers-in-law when there are differences in their economic or educational status.

In-Law Visitation Rights. While many families grant visitation rights to in-laws at holiday time and invite them only to certain family events, the issue of grandparents' visitation rights is now a matter of litigation in many U.S. states and Canadian provinces. Men most often feel neglected and abused by the courts when child custody and visitation schedules are decided, because primary custody is awarded to women in most cases. There-

The 1979 film The In-Laws *spoofed the often-uncertain obligations that in-laws feel for each other.* (Museum of Modern Art, Film Stills Archive)

fore, grandparents-in-law are most often neglected in informal visitation schedules.

In child-custody cases all in-law rights to children are often forgotten by parents going through the stress and emotional conflicts of changes in the family structure. When grandparents' rights are overlooked, grandparents themselves must protect their interests. There are four main categories of litigation concerning grandparents: disputes involving parents' divorce, cases in which the legal custody of children has been assigned to persons other than the children's parents, cases involving the death of the children's parent who is the child of the grandparents, and cases in which living parents, for whatever reasons, deny visitation rights to grandparents.

Most requests for in-law visitation rights are settled out of court through mediation. However, some requests result in motions that must be decided in court. Divorce decrees of parents with minor children do not routinely establish visitation rights of grandparents or in-laws. In some instances, such as proven cases of abuse, grandparents may enjoy formal visitation rights even though one or both parents may be denied rights to see their own children.

When one parent is granted sole custody of minor children in a divorce, the courts are naturally reluctant to interfere with custodial parents' wishes concerning grandparents' visitation rights. During separation, before child custody is determined, most states refuse to hear cases requesting visitation rights by grandparents.

When child custody is granted to persons other than natural parents, grandparents may have to file motions in court to have access to their grandchildren. However, in the case of adoption natural parents revoke all rights to their minor children. Since parents are the only persons with legal responsibility for their own children, they are the only parties whose visitation rights are considered. Permission to adopt children legally revokes all rights of biological grandparents.

The Best Interest of the Child. In Canada and the United States the courts base their decisions on what is in the "best interest of the child." In most cases, one parent is designated as the custodial parent in divorce cases and the other enjoys visitation rights. Visitation schedules typically include all weekends, alternating holidays, and shared summer vacations. In the case of joint custody, each parent shares equal time with the children. Custodial parents can object to any form of visitation by noncustodial parents or grandparents or they may object to the visitation schedule. If noncustodial family members' visitation schedules upset the nuclear family to the point that these schedules are not in the best interest of the children, courts are inclined to rule in favor of custodial parents. Additionally, the visitation rights of noncustodial parents and grandparents usually cannot stop custodial parents from moving to other states for employment purposes.

Courts grant visitation rights to grandparents because they recognize the unique bond between grandchildren and grandparents. In cases in which parents are from different cultures or different religions, the courts understand the special role in-laws play in passing on family customs and history. Usually, courts will intervene only after family mediation fails.

Since divorced custodial parents are no longer related by marriage to their former mothers-and fathers-in-law, many custodial parents fear that grandparents and other in-laws may spend their time negatively influencing or emotionally upsetting the children, playing them against their custodial parent. The relationship between grandparents and custodial parents usually determines whether in-laws are granted visitation rights without seeking legal help. For the sake of the children, all in-laws must make every effort never to downgrade custodial parents in the children's eyes. This only complicates in-law relations and may lead to the termination of in-law visitation rights.

—*Thomas K. McKnight*

BIBLIOGRAPHY

Averick, Leah. *Don't Call Me Mom: How to Improve Your In-Law Relationships.* Hollywood, Fla.: Lifetime, 1996. Appropriate for new couples, couples of first or second marriages, parents, and grandparents, this how-to guide offers concrete techniques designed to make peace between in-laws.

Horsley, Gloria Call. *The In-Law Survival Manual: A Guide to Cultivating Healthy In-Law Relationships.* New York: John Wiley and Sons, 1996. Describes how to build healthy in-law relations from the beginning of couples' lives together and examines how to resolve problems resulting from power struggles, intergenerational misunderstandings, and financial difficulties.

_____. *In-Laws: A Guide to Extended-Family Therapy.* New York: John Wiley and Sons, 1995. Reference manual of methods and procedures for examining and ameliorating the major issues in in-law relationships.

Kincaid, Ron, and Jorie Kincaid. *In-Laws: Getting Along with Your Other Family.* Downers Grove, Ill.: InterVarsity Press, 1996. Discusses nine key principles for handling financial, parenting, holiday, and communications problems among in-laws.

Truly, Traci. *Grandparents' Rights: With Forms (Take the Law into Your Own Hands).* Clearwater, Fla.: Galt Press, 1995. Written by a family-practice attorney, this book presents a guide for the average person with no legal background and discusses laws from all states relevant to grandparents' visitation rights.

See also Blended families; Death; Divorce; Extended families; Kinship systems; Visitation rights.

Institutional families

RELEVANT ISSUES: Economics and work; Sociology
SIGNIFICANCE: Sociologists use the term "institutional family" to refer to situations in which the primary role of the family is to ensure economic stability

Until new patterns of family life emerged in the twentieth century, one of the most important functions of the traditional family was to provide a stable structure for economic production. This stability was most often provided by institutional families. The economic activities of institutional families are generally less formal than the more organized businesses associated with corporate or company families. Institutional families may be engaged in agricultural production on family-owned land, they may run small, informal businesses, or they may practice particular trades.

Institutional families are characterized by an emphasis on loyalty to the extended family, close connections to the local community, and respect for the authority of fathers. Marriage is seen as a practical partnership rather than a romantic relationship. Children are expected to continue the economic activities of parents. Institutional fami-

lies have the advantage of stability, but they offer little in the way of individual freedom.

The institutional family was the traditional family structure for most of humanity from the beginnings of civilization until the twentieth century. It is still the primary pattern of family life in less industrialized societies. Alternatives to the institutional family arose with the decline in the number of families involved in small-scale agricultural production in urbanized societies. Marriages based on emotional needs replaced those based on economic necessity. The importance of the nuclear family increased as the importance of the extended family declined. A new family structure, known as the "psychological family," placed more emphasis on the desires of the individual and less on loyalty to the family. Psychological families have the advantage of greater individual freedom, but they are much less stable than institutional families. Although adults may welcome the possibility of ending unsatisfactory marriages, the consequences of divorce may be detrimental to children.

Just as the psychological family began to replace the institutional family in the early twentieth century, some sociologists believed that a new pattern of family life was emerging in the late twentieth century. This new pattern, known as the "pluralistic family," arose with the changes in industrialized societies that promoted greater equality between the sexes and more acceptance of a variety of lifestyles. Pluralistic families emphasize tolerance and flexibility. The structure of pluralistic families may be influenced by such nontraditional factors as divorce and remarriage, cohabitation, and homosexuality.

Many sociologists believe that the ideal family structure should incorporate values of the institutional family, the psychological family, and the pluralistic family. The family loyalty and community connections of the institutional family, the emotional concerns and individual freedom of the psychological family, and the gender equality and diversity of the pluralistic family could be combined to result in a stable and rewarding family structure. —*Rose Secrest*

See also Alternative family types; Corporate families; Extended families; Family businesses; Family economics; Nuclear family; Retirement communities.

Interfaith marriages

RELEVANT ISSUES: Marriage and dating; Religious beliefs and practices

SIGNIFICANCE: Since the 1960's the institution of marriage in North America shifted from one in which individuals selected partners of the same religious tradition to one in which partners increasingly came from diverse religious faiths

During the 1970's many Americans were introduced to the concept of interfaith marriage, the joining of two individuals from different faith traditions, when they watched the Emmy Award-winning television show *All in the Family*, in which Gloria Bunker, a Protestant, and her husband Michael Stivik, a Polish American Roman Catholic, were portrayed. In one episode, Archie Bunker, Gloria's father, met Michael's uncle as they prepared for the wedding ceremony. When Archie was confronted by the fact that Michael's relatives desired a traditional Roman Catholic ceremony Archie responded: "Wait just one minute. I ain't going through no ceremony with all that mumbo-jumbo and some priest sprinklin' incest all over everybody!"

Although certainly intended as an overstatement, the fictional Archie Bunker's reaction to the interfaith relationship of his daughter exemplified the deep-seated mistrust and lack of understanding of religious traditions in American culture. Americans and Canadians historically sought homogeneity in their marriage institutions and often developed religious and civil laws to enforce the practice of religious endogamy. Changing economic patterns in the latter half of the twentieth century, coupled with increased mobility and new emphases on the importance of the individual, led to a rapid rise in the number of people marrying outside their religious traditions. These interfaith marriages have dramatically altered how couples relate to their families, children, and their cultural communities.

Development of Interfaith Marriages. In the first half of the twentieth century, individuals rarely chose mates outside their faith traditions. Since the end of World War II economic and social forces have enabled individuals to choose mates outside the ethnic and religious communities that once closely guarded the faith of their children.

Economic gains by individuals within religious minority groups, the increased mobility of the American populace, the weakening of ethnic ties, the triumph of individualism, and the emerging tolerance of divergent religious views have produced a radical shift in marriage patterns in North America. Particularly, persons within the Roman Catholic and Jewish traditions have improved their economic status and have moved from cities in which their ethnic communities enforced the traditions and expectations of their religious and cultural groups to the suburbs in which they often live with Protestants of similar social and economic status. Surveys conducted in the United States in the late-1980's suggested that more than half of all Roman Catholics chose non-Roman Catholic mates. Similarly in the Jewish community, roughly 40 percent of all Jewish marriages have been regarded as interfaith relationships, the vast majority of which involve Christians.

In an era of increased tolerance and the perceived triumph of societal pluralism, the question has been raised as to why interfaith marriage should be a cause for concern. Society has underestimated the role that religious traditions play in guiding people through transitional periods in life: birth, death, holiday celebrations, and weddings. Even though many individuals may not identify strongly with their historic faith traditions, the vast majority of North Americans understand their movement through the stages of life by way of unique religious and ethnic traditions. Different religious traditions often vary greatly in their ritual practices related to birth, death, and even basic holiday celebrations. Individuals who have failed to practice their faith may not recognize the significant pull that their religious traditions have on them.

Faith and Marriage. Marriage is the primary method by which religious groups ensure their existence. Indeed, at one time interreligious marriages were the single greatest source of Roman Catholic converts, but by the late twentieth century they had increasingly become the major cause of defections from Roman Catholicism. Forty percent of interfaith marriages in Roman Catholicism result in departures from the faith. Both Roman Catholic and Protestant groups express concern that the growing number of interfaith marriages will ultimately lead to the dissolu-

Marriages between Christians and Jews are often solemnized in carefully orchestrated interfaith wedding ceremonies. (James L. Shaffer)

tion, or at the very least, to a watering down of their faith traditions.

Many in the Jewish community have viewed interfaith marriage as a direct attack on the Jewish population. Far more than Roman Catholics and Protestants, Jews tie religious identity to the cultural and ethnic identity of a unique group of people. Traditionally, Orthodox and Conservative Judaism tried to preserve the community of culture and faith through Jewish law, or *Hallachah.* Jewish law defines marriage as a partnership between two Jews and further defines a Jew as an individual born to a Jewish mother. Children born to non-Jewish women are therefore not considered Jews unless they participate in conversion ceremonies according to Jewish law. Thus, many Jewish leaders view interreligious marriage as a direct challenge to the continuation of the Jewish

people, because it leads to the birth of children who are outside the community.

Finally, studies have estimated that more than two-thirds of all interfaith marriages end in divorce. Interreligious couples must overcome the prejudices of their faith communities, their parents, and the challenges of raising children in dual-faith homes. Even blended partners who enjoy the support of the extended family in the religious community face difficulties. When these institutions withdraw their support from the marriage union, the conflicts may be too difficult to overcome.

Protestant and Roman Catholic Policy. Historically, most religious groups have promoted endogamy either through law or sanction within their communities. Since the mid-1960's organized religious groups have begun to make some modifications in the way they treat couples of interfaith marriages. As a result of Vatican II (1962-1965), Protestant or Jewish spouses in Roman Catholic marriages no longer sign documents pertaining to the raising of children but are usually reminded of their obligation to raise their children in the Roman Catholic faith. Furthermore, marriage ceremonies may be held in Roman Catholic churches, Protestant churches, or synagogues. Nevertheless, the Roman Catholic Church takes the official position that a non-Roman Catholic cannot take the Sacrament of the Eucharist.

Through canon law, the Roman Catholic Church urges mixed-faith couples to abstain from communion as a sign of the division among Christians. Protestant spouses may worship in the Roman Catholic tradition, but they are not considered equal participants. Generally, Canadian Roman Catholics have been much more tolerant of interreligious marriages than their Roman Catholic counterparts in the United States. In the late 1980's, both the Roman Catholic Church and the Anglican Church of Canada adopted new guidelines to promote interfaith harmony. Protestant churches, many with local congregational forms of government, have usually responded to such relationships according to local custom.

Jewish Policy. The Jewish community has been severely divided over the issue of interfaith marriage. The division was exemplified by the reaction of a portion of the New York Jewish community to Cheryl Krause, a Presbyterian married for nine years to a Jewish man. Krause was shocked by the decision of a Jewish newspaper to ban announcements of interfaith marriages. The editor of the newspaper, Jonathan S. Tobin, argued in an editorial that interfaith marriages were not cause for celebration in the Jewish community. The Conservative and Orthodox communities praised the editorial and reiterated their opposition to interreligious marriages. In contrast, the Reform Jewish community repeated its stand presented in the patrilineal descent resolution of 1983, which stated that the child of one Jewish parent is presumed to be of Jewish descent regardless of whether the Jewish parent is the father or mother. The Reform position, similar to that of the Roman Catholic Church, has recognized interfaith marriages and encouraged the continuation of Jewish religious status through the education of the children and appropriate ritual acts tying individuals to the Jewish faith and people.

Living in an Interfaith Relationship. Most scholars agree that interreligious marriages present challenges that need to be addressed by couples before they formalize their relationships. Many couples seem to marry without some basic understanding of the unstated assumptions that undergird their life choices. When asked to identify their religious preference in public opinion polls, more than 90 percent of Americans have classified themselves as belonging to particular religions. Individuals may not be religious in practice, but their faith traditions are often active in determining their life patterns. A thorough understanding of the faith traditions of marriage partners is vital to the success of interreligious marriages. Couples must also confront the fact that children of interfaith marriages are much more likely to have difficulty with their identities and are much less likely to be involved in or linked to institutionalized religions than children of same-faith marriages. Psychologists suggest that couples contemplating interfaith marriage should carefully weigh the challenges they will face relating to each other, their children, and their communities.

—Robin E. Baker

BIBLIOGRAPHY

Cowan, Paul, and Rachel Cowan. *Mixed Blessings: Marriage Between Jews and Christians.* New York: Doubleday, 1987.

Mayer, Egon. *Love and Tradition: Marriage Between Jews and Christians.* New York: Plenum Press, 1985.

Rosenbaum, Mary Helene, and Stanley Ned Rosenbaum. *Celebrating Our Differences: Living Two Faiths in One Marriage.* Boston, Ky.: Ragged Edge Press, 1994.

Schiappa, Barbara D. *Mixing: Catholic-Protestant Marriages in the 1980's.* New York: Paulist Press, 1982.

Schneider, Susan Weidman. *Intermarriage: The Challenge of Living with Differences Between Christians and Jews.* New York: Free Press, 1989.

See also Couples; Cultural influences; Holidays; Jews; Muslims; Religion; Roman Catholics; Weddings.

Intergenerational income transfer

RELEVANT ISSUE: Economics and work

SIGNIFICANCE: The movement of wealth between generations is a powerful economic force both within individual families and within society at large, in which it may have important political consequences

Economists use the term "intergenerational income transfer" to refer to any situation in which wealth possessed by members of one generation is given to or used by members of another generation. Such transactions may take place within individual families or within society as a whole.

Within individual families, intergenerational income transfers take place whenever parents pay for the economic needs of children. Although this is probably the most common form of intergenerational income transfer within families, it has rarely been studied in detail by economists. In many economic studies, it has been assumed that each member of a family receives an equal share of the family's total income. According to one study published by economists Edward P. Lazear and Robert T. Michael in 1988, the average child within a family actually received only about 40 percent as much of the family income as adult members of the same family.

Another important form of intergenerational income transfer within families takes place when members of older generations give wealth to members of younger generations in the form of gifts when the elders are still alive or bequests after they die. In 1981 economists Laurence J. Kotlikoff and Lawrence H. Summers claimed that inheritances were responsible for about 80 percent of all household wealth in the United States. Although other economists have disputed this claim, it remains clear that intergenerational income transfers are an important part of the U.S. economy, a fact reflected in the importance of inheritance tax laws.

Intergenerational income transfers within families also occur when members of younger generations provide for the economic needs of older generations. This usually occurs when the elders are retired or otherwise no longer earning their own incomes. In the United States the passage of the Social Security Act in the mid-1930's reduced the expectation that younger family members would be the primary source of income for elderly family members, but this form of financial support still remains vital to many older Americans.

In society as a whole, intergenerational income transfers take place when taxes paid mostly by one generation are used to pay for programs that primarily benefit members of another generation. In the United States the most important such programs are Social Security and Medicare, which are primarily paid for by younger generations and which mostly benefit the elderly. Debates over the fairness of these programs and the ability of the United States government to continue paying for them as the percentage of elderly Americans increases demonstrate the political importance of intergenerational income transfers.   —*Rose Secrest*

See also Family economics; Generational relationships; Inheritance and estate law; Retirement; Sandwich generation; Social Security; Tax laws; Wealth; Wills and bequests.

Interracial families

RELEVANT ISSUES: Demographics; Marriage and dating; Race and ethnicity; Sociology

SIGNIFICANCE: Although mixed-race families became much more common in North America during the second half of the twentieth century, couples and children in such families continued to face problems of social disapproval and problems of racial identity

Throughout much of American history, marriages between members of different racial groups were rare; they were even illegal in many places in the United States. Most southern states, for example, had laws forbidding miscegenation, or marriages between people of different races, until 1967, when the U.S. Supreme Court ruled that laws prohibiting interracial marriage were unconstitutional in its *Loving v. Virginia* decision.

Although many racially mixed children were born during and after the era of slavery, which ended in 1865, these children were usually born out of wedlock to white fathers and African American mothers. They were seldom publicly acknowledged by the fathers. Children with both African American and white ancestry were generally re-

After this Native American man and non-Indian woman married each other in the late nineteenth century, the woman's family attempted to destroy evidence of the husband's racial identity. (Arkent Archive)

garded as African American and rarely lived in racially mixed family units.

After World War II some forms of interracial marriage became common and widely accepted. For example, many of the 150,000 interracial unions on record in 1960 involved American servicemen and Asian war brides. Marriages of Asian Americans to members of other races increased in the decades that followed. By the 1990's a majority of all marriages involving Japanese Americans were to members of other groups. Members of most other Asian American groups also showed high rates of interracial marriage. Similarly, most Native Americans married either whites or African Americans.

In contrast, marriages between whites and African Americans—the two largest racial groups in the United States—continued to be comparatively few in number. However, these unions also increased fairly rapidly throughout the late twentieth century. In 1963 fewer than 1 percent of African American marriages were to white spouses,

according to data from the National Center for Health Statistics. Only seven years later, nearly 3 percent of new African American marriages were to white persons. By 1980 this figure had increased to nearly 7 percent. In 1990 more than 12 percent of new African American marriages involved white husbands and wives.

This growth in interracial marriage in the United States reflected changing American views on racial relations. However, while societal attitudes were becoming more tolerant, racially mixed families still faced some forms of prejudice. Moreover, the children of such marriages faced questions of their personal identity as they questioned to which groups they "belonged." Interracial marriages also created difficulties for governmental agencies in classifying people by race and ethnicity.

Attitudes Toward Interracial Families. Interracial families emerge from marriages among members of different racial groups. Public approval has strongly influenced how many of these unions

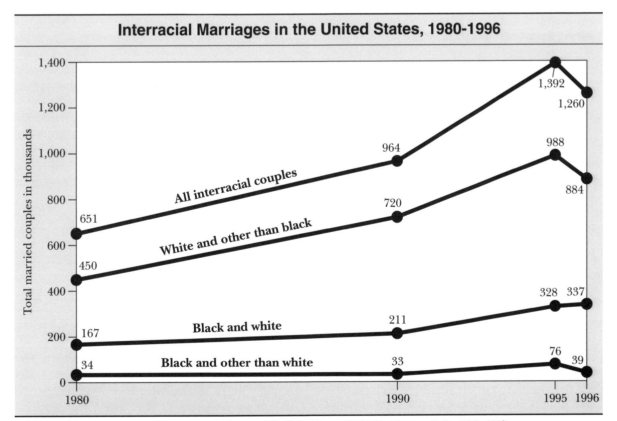

Interracial Marriages in the United States, 1980-1996

Source: U.S. Bureau of the Census, *Statistical Abstract of the United States: 1997*. Washington, D.C.: GPO, 1997.

there will be and what difficulties members of these families will face. By the 1990's popular disapproval of marriages between white and Asian Americans or between African and Asian Americans was almost nonexistent. Opposition to the formation of African American-white families continued to be strong through the end of the twentieth century, but this was also changing rapidly.

According to data for 1963 cited by Stephan Thernstrom and Abigail Thernstrom, 90 percent of white parents objected to their children dating African Americans that year. By 1994 only 35 percent of white parents objected to interracial dating and most parents who continued to express disapproval were older people. Among African American parents, the percentage of those who condoned their children dating whites increased from 72 percent to 88 percent between 1987 and 1994.

Acceptance of interracial marriage lagged behind acceptance of interracial dating, but attitudes toward marriages across racial lines also became much more tolerant. In 1963 a 62 percent majority of white Americans favored laws making interracial marriage illegal. In 1994 only 16 percent of whites and 3 percent of African Americans favored such laws. In 1968, 17 percent of whites and 48 percent of African Americans expressed approval of marriages between members of different races. In 1994, 45 percent of whites and 68 percent of African Americans said that they approved of such marriages.

Popular tolerance of interracial families increased in almost all regions of the country but varied among regions. California, with its highly diverse population, showed more interracial families and greater acceptance of them. According to a 1994 study in Orange County, California, 60 percent of persons between 18 and 34 years of age reported having dated members of races other than their own. Although about 4 percent of couples in the entire United States were in mixed-race marriages, this figure was nearly 10 percent in California; more than a fourth of all interracial marriages in the United States in 1990 were in California.

Problems of Interracial Families. Despite increasing popular acceptance of interracial families, people in these families have still encountered disapproval and discrimination. Parents and friends often exert pressures on single people to discourage them from dating those of another race. One growing source of opposition to interracial families is the increase in feelings of racial solidarity among African Americans. Some African Americans believe that marriages between African Americans and whites undermine the racial unity needed to overcome racial inequality. African Americans who have married whites have occasionally been accused of "deserting" their race. The percentage of African Americans approving interracial marriages actually decreased from 76 percent in 1983 to 72 percent in 1991 and 68 percent in 1994.

African American women were especially prone to disapprove of interracial marriage. Two-thirds of all marriages between African Americans and white Americans in the 1990's were between African American men and white women. Because African American men as a group also had relatively high rates of unemployment and imprisonment, this led some African American women to believe that marriage outside the group was making the shortage of available men worse.

Classifying Multiracial Children. Race has often been an important part of the self-images of Americans. Children in interracial families have often faced questions of their own identity. Traditionally, children born of unions between white and nonwhite parents were classified as members of the minority race. For example, a child with a white mother and an African American father was automatically regarded as African American. However, as racial lines began to blur, and as children with multiple racial backgrounds became more numerous, issues of identity became more complicated.

Until 1989 birth registration rules in the United States required that children of one white parent and one African American parent be classified as "black." For other racial groups, such as Asians or Native Americans, children were usually classified according to the race of the mother. During the 1990's, however, multiracial persons who refused to be racially classified became increasingly vocal as their numbers grew.

The U.S. Census Bureau, the government agency that maintains counts of the American population, divided all people into mutually exclusive racial categories: white, black, Asian/Pacific Islander, and Native American. In 1995, in re-

During the mid-1990's multiracial golfing star Tiger Woods confounded journalists and critics anxious to assign him to a racial category by refusing all single-race labels. (AP/Wide World Photos)

The late twentieth century saw a dramatic increase in the numbers of marriages between African Americans and whites, as well as an even greater rise in public acceptance of such marriages. (AP/Wide World Photos)

sponse to demands from the offspring of interracial families, the federal government considered introducing a "multiracial" category. This change of official classification enjoyed much support.

A 1995 pilot study conducted by the Census Bureau found that more than 4 million persons—nearly 2 percent of the nation's entire population—would classify themselves as multiracial if they were given the opportunity to do so. In July, 1996, supporters of the new census category staged the Multiracial Solidarity March in Washington, D.C. However, introduction of a new category also met with opposition. Affirmative action programs and other race-based programs to address racial inequality depended on the ability to classify people according to race. Many supporters of approaches such as affirmative action feared that a multiracial category would lead to a decrease in people recognized as belonging to racial minorities and thereby undermine efforts to redress racial inequalities.   —*Carl L. Bankston III*

BIBLIOGRAPHY

Cretser, Gary A., and Leon J. Joseph. *Intermarriage in the United States*. New York: Haworth Press, 1985.

Davis, F. James. *Who Is Black? One Nation's Definition*. University Park: Pennsylvania State University Press, 1991.

Hacker, Andrew. *Two Nations: Black and White, Separate, Hostile, Unequal*. New York: Charles Scribner's Sons, 1992.

Johnson, Walter, and D. Michael Warren, eds. *Inside the Mixed Marriage: Accounts of Changing Attitudes, Patterns, and Perceptions of Cross-Cultural and Interracial Marriages*. Lanham, Md.: University Press of America, 1994.

Spencer, Jon Michael. *The New Colored People: The Mixed Race Movement in America*. New York: New York University Press, 1997.

Thernstrom, Stephan, and Abigail Thernstrom. *America in Black and White: One Nation, Indivisible*. New York: Simon & Schuster, 1997.

Tizard, Barbara. *Black, White, or Mixed Race? Race and Racism in the Lives of Young People of Mixed Parentage*. New York: Routledge, 1993.

See also Adoption issues; Amerasian children; Antimiscegenation laws; Exogamy; *Loving v. Virginia*; Mail-order brides; Sexuality and sexual taboos; War brides.

Japanese Americans

RELEVANT ISSUES: Kinship and genealogy; Race and ethnicity; Parenting and family relationships

SIGNIFICANCE: The first Japanese immigrants came to North America in the latter part of the nineteenth century, and their descendants, who are generally very well educated and prosperous, numbered about 700,000 in the United States and about 45,000 in Canada in the late twentieth century

Although Japanese immigrants were among the most discriminated against people in the histories of the United States and Canada, they managed to remain in North America, prosper, and raise families. At the turn of the twenty-first century Japanese Americans were among the best educated and most prosperous ethnic groups in North America.

Background. Immigration from Japan to the United States, which was originally destined for Hawaii, began in the late 1860's but remained insignificant until the 1890's. From 1900 until 1910 more than 100,000 Japanese immigrated to the American mainland, settling mainly in California. Eventually Japanese immigrants settled in Oregon, Washington, and British Columbia. The Japanese are perhaps the only immigrant group in North America that chose to clearly differentiate members of each generation by giving them distinct names, designating characteristics which they believed the members of each generation would exhibit. They did this by naming each generation according to an ordinal number system. *Issei* (Japanese for "first generation") were members of the first generation of Japanese who came to America. The *Issei Nisei* are the children of the *Issei* (*ni* is Japanese for "two"). *Sansei* are the grandchildren of the *Issei* (*san* is "three" in Japanese). *Yonsei* are the great-grandchildren of the *Issei* (*yon* is one way of saying "four" in Japanese).

The *Issei*, who arrived between 1890 and 1910, were generally young male agricultural workers who, while not generally highly educated, were literate. The members of this group brought to America a deep respect for education, the willingness to work hard, a love of family, and the Japanese value of conforming to the wishes of the group. These early immigrants were met with hatred and discrimination in America, particularly in California, where the majority of them settled. The first Japanese immigrants were not allowed to own land or to marry non-Japanese persons. Because the ratio of Japanese males to Japanese females in North America was twenty-four to one in the early twentieth century, many of the *Issei* allowed their families in Japan to arrange marriages for them, seeing their wives only in a photograph before the wedding. The fact that Japanese immigrants accepted "picture brides" angered their white neighbors, who nevertheless made it impossible for young Japanese immigrants to marry most of the women with whom they came into contact.

The *Issei* who married settled down with their brides to raise families, often working as tenant farmers on land they were not permitted to own, as gardeners, or as houseboys in the homes of the wealthy. They raised families that were generally larger than average pre-World War II American families. They sent their children to public schools, where the youngsters did well, although in some parts of California the *Nisei* were not allowed to attend public schools with white children. The *Issei* believed very much in education, and they made great personal sacrifices to provide well for their children. *Issei* parents were guided by the philosophy of *kodomo no tame ni* (for the sake of the children).

The *Issei* generally wanted their children to receive a good education and worked hard to provide funds for this. Because they also wanted their children to know the Japanese language and culture, many *Nisei* children were sent after school or on Saturdays to Japanese school. However, the *Nisei*, who were born in North America, were Americans who mainly wanted to be as Americanized as

Community centers make it easier for many Japanese Americans to observe traditional customs. (Ben Klaffke)

possible. In general, they were not interested in the Japanese language and culture and looked forward to adulthood, when they would be able to own land and exercise their rights as citizens.

World War II Internment. By the start of World War II two generations of Japanese Americans lived in the United States and Canada. However, with the start of the armed conflict between the United States and Japan, the American and Canadian governments claimed that the Japanese immigrants and their descendants posed a threat to security. Thus, on February 19, 1942, President Franklin D. Roosevelt issued Executive Order 9066, requiring persons of Japanese origin or descent living in the western part of the United States (California, Oregon, Washington, and the southern part of Arizona) to be placed in internment camps. This order affected 110,000 people but did not apply to the large number of Japanese Americans living in Hawaii, where the Japanese attack on Pearl Harbor had occurred. In Canada the 1942 War Measures Act placed Japanese noncitizens and Japanese Canadians in camps that actually required them to pay for their housing. Those who objected to living in these camps were placed in prisoner of war camps in northern Ontario along with captured German soldiers. Although Japanese in North America were considered a security risk, in 1943 an all-*Nisei* army group was

formed, which distinguished itself in combat during the last two years of World War II.

Those who lived in the camps accepted life there, which was made possible by the Japanese idea of *shikata ga nai* (it cannot be helped). This idea holds that humans must accept things about which they can do nothing and they should not resist. Those who lived in the internment camps spent their time working, gardening, attending high school, planning community dances, participating in Boy Scout troops, and generally trying to pass the time as normally and productively as possible. In January, 1945, Japanese noncitizens and Japanese Americans were allowed to leave the camps. Prior to 1945 about 35,000 people had

After World War II many Japanese American families returned from internment camps to find their homes vandalized by racists. (AP/Wide World Photos)

A Japanese American father and his daughter prepare for a traditional Japanese New Year celebration in Los Angeles's Little Tokyo district. (Diane C. Lyell)

been granted permission to leave the camps. Unable to live in the western United States, they and their families settled in the East. Soon after the United States released the detainees from the camps, the Canadians followed suit.

Post-World War II Years. The *Sansei* were the generation of Japanese Americans born just after or during World War II. They and their children, the *Yonsei*, have had very little direct contact with Japanese culture, although they have been influenced by their *Issei* and *Nisei* ancestors. The tremendous emphasis that Japanese Americans place on education is evidenced by the fact that about 90 percent of *Sansei* have attended college. Japanese American homes have one of the highest average family incomes of any ethnic group, surpassed only by Jewish families.

Japanese Americans have left their agricultural heritage behind them. Ninety percent now live in urban areas. In the United States one-third live in Hawaii and one-third in California. In Canada most Americans of Japanese descent live in British Columbia or Ontario. About 18 percent of married men of Japanese descent are married to women of another race, while 35 percent of married women of Japanese descent have intermarried. In California and Hawaii these percentages are far higher.

Japanese Customs and Celebrations. Persons of Japanese heritage, particularly those living where there are large numbers of Japanese Americans, continue to celebrate some traditional Japanese customs. Japanese New Year, *O-Shogatsu*, is a three day celebration in which *mochi*, or rice cakes, are eaten and a pair of bamboo reeds is placed over the front door to celebrate fidelity in marriage and to symbolize the Japanese family's ability to bend but not break. Some *Issei* and *Nisei* families still observe *O-Bon*, the Buddhist festival of the dead, in which ancestors are remembered and their graves cleared. May 5, Children's Day, which was originally called Boy's Day, is celebrated by flying carp flags. To the Japanese, carp is a symbol of good luck, courage, and endurance. Traditionally, Japanese families fly one carp flag for each son in the family.

Japanese American families continue to eat traditional Japanese foods such as sushi, tempura, sashimi, and sukiyaki—all of which have become part of the mainstream American diet. Some Japanese Americans share their culture with other Americans by teaching flower arranging (ikebana) and by demonstrating and teaching the tea ceremony. American school children learn origami, or paper folding, which is a traditional Japanese art. In some cities, where there are large numbers of Japanese Americans, there are *Nisei* parades in which persons of Japanese descent wear traditional Japanese dress and demonstrate aspects of Japanese culture. —*Annita Marie Ward*

BIBLIOGRAPHY

Chalfen, Richard. *Turning Leaves: The Photograph Collection of Two Japanese Families.* Albuquerque: University of New Mexico Press, 1991.

Hoobler, Dorothy, Thomas Hoobler, and George Takei. *The Japanese American Family Album.* New York: Oxford University Press, 1996.

Iida, Deborah. *Middle Son.* Chapel Hill, N.C.: Algonquin Books, 1996.

Kitano, Harry. *The Japanese Americans.* New York: Chelsea House, 1987.

Ng, Franklin, ed. *Asian American Encyclopedia.* 6 vols. New York: Marshall Cavendish, 1995.

Yanogisako, Sylvia Junko. *Transforming the Past: Tradition and Kinship Among Japanese Americans.* Palo Alto, Calif.: Stanford University Press, 1985.

See also Chinese Americans; East Indians and Pakistanis; Filipino Americans; Korean Americans; Pacific Islanders; Religion; Southeast Asian Americans; Vietnamese Americans; War brides.

Jews

RELEVANT ISSUES: Parenting and family relationships; Race and ethnicity; Religious beliefs and practices

SIGNIFICANCE: The family has been the single most important social and religious institution for the maintenance of Judaism

The origins and framework of Judaism lie in the patriarchal, agricultural societies of the Middle East. Two of the defining events in early Jewish history were the destruction of both Temples in ancient times and the subsequent forced exile of the Jewish people from the Holy Land. The Temple in Jerusalem represented the pinnacle of religious practice. In order to substitute for this central holy place, synagogues began to sprout up elsewhere and prayer replaced animal sacrifice. Most important, rabbis located the fundamental seat of religious practice in the family, calling it *mikdash m'at* ("miniature sanctuary").

Judaism and the Home. Most of the seminal rituals of Judaism are centered in the home. The beginning and end of life are marked by home rituals: circumcision for boys and *shiva*, the seven days of mourning for which prayers are preferably said at home. On the anniversary of deaths, candles are lit not in synagogues but at home.

The major holidays and their attendant rites are celebrated in the home: the Passover seder,

Important Jewish rituals, such as lighting Hanukkah candles on the mennorah, are observed mostly in the home. (Long Hare Photographs)

Sukkoth, the lighting of the Hanukkah candles, and Sabbath meals. Rituals around the meal—sacramental wine, ritual hand washing, and pouring salt on bread—are all reminders of rituals that were performed at the Temple altar. On Friday nights, husbands recite special biblical praises to their wives (Prov. 31:10-31) and fathers bless their children.

Rabbinical Law. Jewish law pervades all of religious life, especially the family. The first commandment in Genesis (1:28) reads: "be fruitful and multiply." The rabbis prescribed that every man have at least one son and one daughter. More offspring were better, although the rabbis also recommended limiting reproduction during periods of famine and crisis. Although Jewish law strongly promotes having children, it also makes allowance for the practice of birth control (for women only) and, under some conditions, for abortion. In general, the rabbis strongly disapproved of abortion because it takes away a potential life. Yet the law not only allows for but also insists upon abortion if the fetus threatens the life of the pregnant woman—even until the moment when the fetus breaches the womb. Moreover, the law allows for abortion if the fetus threatens the psychological health of the expectant mother. This standard, however, is difficult to apply and thus leads to a great deal of leeway and disagreement.

Marriage is a highly desirable institution; remaining single and celibate is unacceptable. Following the Scriptures, which state that a man should leave his parents and cling to his wife (Gen. 2:24), one rabbi in the Talmud says simply: "Every Jew who has no wife lives without joy, without blessing, and without goodness." Marriage is a serious proposition. The traditional Hebrew and Aramaic word for betrothal is *kiddushin*, the same word used for "holiness." However, some scholars argue that the word in this context means "separateness," that is, setting women aside for their husbands.

Within the boundaries of their own cultural norms, the rabbis wanted to encourage stable, happy marriages, especially for the economic protection of women, since sons inherited the land. Daughters were much better off being married, since the law mandated that husbands make at least three provisions for their wives: food, clothing, and sexual attention (Ex. 21:10). Whatever

dowries women brought to their marriages they reclaimed upon widowhood or divorce.

The Hebrew Scriptures allow for divorce. Although the Talmud stated that only men must consent to divorce, in the eleventh century rabbinical scholar Gershom ben Judah decreed that wives also could not be divorced without their consent. Jewish law thus allows for divorce by mutual consent. In general, Judaism opposed divorce, but it made allowances to prevent very unhappy marriages. One folk idiom asks: "Why should two cry when four can laugh?"

According to folk tradition, fathers spent a good deal of energy worrying about marrying off their daughters. However, the rabbis also placed upon fathers the obligation to find suitable brides for their sons. Even until the end of the nineteenth century, marriages were arranged by parents or matchmakers. The matchmaker role reflected the gender segregation typical of many traditional religious societies. After about the age of five, boys and girls had limited contact outside their own families. For boys, Torah learning was extremely important. Young men were urged to become scholars, and the most successful among them became rabbis and teachers. Girls were domesticated at a very early age. They learned to run the household and, when they got older, normally helped raise their younger siblings. Since money was invariably in short supply among the Jews of Eastern Europe, Jewish women often worked outside the home, typically selling in the marketplace to provide their families with an income. Some worked in order to allow their husbands to continue to study the Torah. Although a religious ideal, full economic support by wives, which often consisted of money they received from their fathers, was limited to a few families for economic reasons.

Gender differences were pervasive in religious culture. For newborn girls, there was no ceremony comparable to the covenant of male circumcision. No record exists of any major Jewish community anywhere practicing ritual circumcision of teenage girls. Only boys publicly marked the transition to the first stage of adulthood at the age of thirteen by having Bar Mitzvahs. Only men were required to engage in daily prayer or to say the *kaddish*, the prayer of mourning. Only men counted in forming a quorum of ten (*minyan*). Except for two specific holiday rites, women were

Study of the Torah under rabbis remains an important part of the upbringing of Jewish boys. (James L. Shaffer)

intentionally excused from the obligations of daily prayer. The rabbis, all of them men, believed that women's main job was taking care of children, whose needs could not always wait. Wives were required to observe the laws of "family purity": to refrain from sexual contact during menstruation and for seven subsequent days, after which they immersed themselves in a ritual bath.

Women were clearly shunted aside in public religion. Nevertheless, because of their roles as managers of the household and as prime socializ-ing agents, women were the main religious force in the home. In many Jewish societies, women maintained the traditions even as their husbands and brothers abandoned them. Their sexism not-withstanding, the rabbis recognized the impor-tance of women in the religious arena. They thus established the immensely important rule that the determination of children's religious identity as Jewish or non-Jewish depended completely on mothers, ordaining that fathers simply did not count in determining children's religious identity.

Jewish infants are defined as the children of a Jewish mother. Persons whose mothers were not Jewish could always convert.

Ashkenazic and Sephardic Families. The major cultural division in Judaism has been between the Ashkenazim, which includes most North American Jews and whose roots are to be found in Central Europe, and the Sephardim, who settled in the Middle East and North Africa and many of whom were expelled from Spain in the late fifteenth century. Although Jews often lived relatively ghettoized lives, they almost always maintained contact with and borrowed from the surrounding world. The two Jewish subcultures changed in ways which reflected the cultures around them. This is most clearly seen in music, food, and family matters, especially the role of women.

Sexual propriety and barriers to illicit sexual interaction were even more rigid in Muslim than in Christian cultures. The full-body covering, including the veil, in Islamic societies attests to this extreme separation of women. Practically, this meant that Middle Eastern Jewish women, like Islamic women, were much more socially secluded than women in the West. They were much less likely to work outside the home or even to be seen outside the home than Western women. They were less educated. Because most Arab cultures were patrilocal, women left their parents' homes and lived with their husbands and often with their in-laws. Another major difference between Ashkenazic and Sephardic Jews, which was more theoretical than real, was that like their Muslim neighbors Jews in Arab countries permitted polygyny. Although the Scriptures note the taking of more than one wife, by the Talmudic period it was clearly in serious disrepute and not heavily practiced. Among the Ashkenazim, Gershom ben Juddah issued a universally accepted decree in about the year 1000 that banned polygyny. Among the Sephardim, polygyny existed more on paper than in real life, although even in the twentieth century occasional cases of polygyny have been reported.

Nineteenth Century Eastern European Jewry. By far the largest and most important wave of Jewish immigration to North America was from Eastern Europe between 1881 and 1923. By the end of the nineteenth century the Enlightenment had reached Eastern Europe. Science, the ideas of equality and liberty, and the beginnings of industrialization turned Jewish life upside down.

Eventually, Jewish religion and family structure had to weaken, a development already foreshadowed in Germany. East European orthodoxy looked and felt old fashioned. Thus, German Jews introduced changes based on their own society: a more formal decorum in the synagogue, the recitation of some prayers in German, and greater openness to the formal education of girls.

Traditional authorities, such as small-town rabbis, could not compete with the enticing ideas to be found in the cafés of Warsaw, Budapest, and Odessa. The medieval world of the yeshiva—schools for talmudic study—paled in contrast to the excitement of science, revolutionary politics, and romantic love. The life of the itinerant milkman offered little hope of anything beyond an impoverished subsistence. At the end of the musical "Fiddler on the Roof," the protagonist Tevye sees his family split apart, as some of his daughters leave and marry secular Jews or even non-Jews and he himself prepares to leave his small town for America. Indeed, Sholem Aleichem (Sholem Yakov Rabinowitz), the author of the Tevye stories, actually left Russia to live out his days in New York.

Immigration and Change in America. The changes that affected Jewish life in Germany were magnified in the United States. Many early German Jewish immigrants were Americanized, and the Reform movement proceeded much more rapidly in America than in Germany. Although early Eastern European Jews lived ghettoized lives in the United States, even first-generation Jews experienced important changes. Because of severe economic pressures, many young boys worked. Few boys took religious education seriously, especially in the face of work pressures and competing attractions like sports and vaudeville. The passion for learning was transferred to secular studies, which offered the hope of good jobs.

One of the distinguishing characteristics of Jewish immigrants to the Untied States was that they came as families, which often included grandparents. These ethnic families faced many problems. Fathers lost prestige because their skills in the "old country" were often unappreciated in the New World. More than a few men deserted their families, seeking their fortunes elsewhere. Child delinquency, crime, and prostitution increased.

By the second generation, however, Jews were upwardly mobile. Educational levels rose dramatically, although boys were much more likely than girls to go to college. Marriages remained overwhelmingly endogamous, and they were surprisingly stable. Concurrently, however, change was under way. Social dating increased and young people selected their mates based increasingly on American standards. Matchmakers virtually disappeared. Status was based on money, a secular education, and jobs, not on traditional Torah learning. Because women, as well as men, married later, most young women entered the workforce before marriage and childbearing.

The dynamics of the second generation were reflected clearly in its children and grandchildren. American Jews in the period following World War II were educated and successful. Many postponed marriage, and increasing numbers did not marry at all. By 1990 the proportion of Jews who did not marry was higher than that in the non-Jewish population. Intermarriage rates exploded. Between 1985 and 1990, 52 percent of those Jews who married were wedded to non-Jews. Divorce rates approached those of the population at large, and in Canada they were slightly higher. Jews were less likely than non-Jews to have children—too few to replace their numbers.

One of the consequences of low fertility rates and good health practices was that longevity among Jews was much higher than among other Americans. As a result, the Jewish community was forced to spend more of its resources tending to the needs of its elderly than other sections of the population. Like many traditional cultures, Judaism has always urged that elders be respected. For example, in Israel many buses feature signs from the Scriptures that read: "Thou shalt rise up before the hoary head" (Lev. 19:32). That reverence has been put to a monetary test in late twentieth century North America.

Very little incidence of pregnancy has occurred among single Jewish teenagers. Because most Jews have engaged in family planning—a function of education—the number of unwanted pregnancies has been relatively small. Domestic abuse has not been unknown, and although it has probably been noticeably lower than in the population at large, its incidence has been significant.

Denominational Differences. The effects of Americanization on Jewish family life in North America have been reflected in the differentiation between Jewish denominations. Although historically Reform Judaism has been the most accommodating to American life, since the return to ethnicity in the mid-1960's it has moved to reclaim tradition by observing some neglected holidays and by placing more emphasis on Hebrew, Torah study, and Israel. On family matters, however, Reform Judaism has continued to move in the opposite direction—toward prevailing progressive American norms, especially on gender issues. Although it granted religious equality to women earlier than other denominations—for example, the right of girls to have a Bas Mitzvah—the first

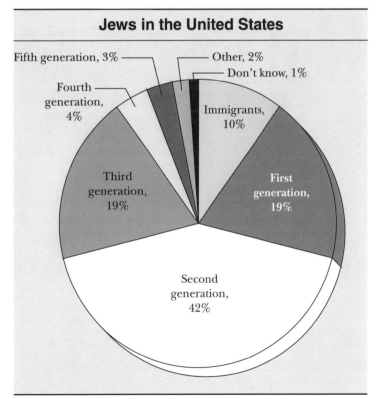

Source: *Los Angeles Times* (April 22, 1998)

Since the early 1990's most Reform rabbinical students have been women. (James L. Shaffer)

woman Reform rabbi was not ordained until 1972. By the 1990's, however, more than half of Reform rabbinical students were women. Reform has been strongly prochoice on the issue of abortion. Both Reform and Reconstructionism pressed for rituals to celebrate women's life cycle events, such as birth, giving birth, and the menopause.

Probably the most radical shift in ritual was the proposal in Reform Judaism to allow Jewish identity to pass through either mothers or fathers. Although this proposal received a mixed reaction even among Reform Jews, it reflected their concern with family and their willingness to change. An issue that has even more seriously divided Reform rabbis has been whether they should officiate at mixed marriages. Both proposals reflected the reality that Jews have been intermarrying and that their numbers have been declining. Many Reform positions have been forcefully rejected, especially by Orthodox Jews, leading to growing tensions between the major Jewish denominations.

Those most resistant to change have been the Orthodox Jews. They have maintained the strictest gender separation, capitulating to the extremists in eliminating mixed dancing at public celebrations, even for married couples. Yet, Orthodoxy has also been affected by life in the United States. Orthodox Jews have been increasingly sensitive to the involvement of women in study, prayer, and home rituals. However, they still insist on gender separation, even in study. Nevertheless, American Orthodoxy has been more open and more successful than previous Orthodox communities in other countries in teaching women to study traditional Jewish texts. A number of Orthodox women's minyans have been formed in large cities. Whereas Orthodoxy as a whole pronounced Bas Mitzvahs as anathema in the late 1960's, thirty years later it generally accepted them, although among Orthodox Jews the performance of Bas Mitzvahs was not equivalent to the performance of Bar Mitzvahs. Nevertheless, Bas Mitzvahs have allowed girls to study, share their knowledge, and achieve some form of public acknowledgment.

—*Alan M. Fisher*

BIBLIOGRAPHY

Baker, Adrienne. *The Jewish Woman in Contemporary Society*. New York: New York University Press, 1993. Insightful look into feminist-based changes in Jewish life in the United States and Great Britain.

Biale, Rachel. *Women and Jewish Law*. New York: Schocken Books, 1984. Thorough examination of major family issues affecting women in the context of Jewish life.

Cohen, Steven M., and Paula E. Hyman, eds. *The Jewish Family*. New York: Holmes & Meier, 1986. Articles dealing with the diversity of Jewish families going back to the eighteenth century.

Epstein, Louis M. *Marriage Laws in the Bible and the Talmud*. Cambridge, Mass.: Harvard University Press, 1942. Comprehensive source for acceptable and unacceptable forms of marriage among Jews as stated in the Bible and the Talmud.

Feldman, David M. *Marital Relations, Birth Control and Abortion in Jewish Law*. New York: Schocken Books, 1974. Examines the rabbinical legal tradition of marriage, sex, and procreation.

Goitein, Solomon D. *A Mediterranean Society. Vol. 3: The Family*. Berkeley: University of California Press, 1978. The most comprehensive picture of medieval Jewish life in the Arab world.

Kraemer, David, ed. *The Jewish Family*. New York: Oxford University Press, 1989. Interesting set of essays covering two thousand years of Jewish life.

See also Bar Mitzvahs and Bas Mitzvahs; Circumcision; Endogamy; Eugenics; Interfaith marriages; Matchmaking; Middle Easterners; Religion; Sexuality and sexual taboos.

Juvenile courts

RELEVANT ISSUES: Children and child development; Law; Violence

SIGNIFICANCE: Although the juvenile court system was established as a humane alternative to adult courts for the adjudication of juvenile crimes, because of a startling increase in violent crimes committed by young people juvenile justice has become more concerned with punishment than rehabilitation, including even the prosecution of parents for their delinquent children's crimes

The juvenile court system, which operates at the local, state, and federal levels, is composed formally of police, courts, probation, parole, corrections, and schools and informally of citizens' groups, parents, and such institutions as churches. It is designed to arrest criminal suspects, determine their culpability, punish or rehabilitate the guilty, and supervise their reentry into society.

Function of Juvenile Courts. The passage in 1899 of the Illinois Juvenile Court Act saw the establishment of the Cook County Juvenile Court, the first juvenile court in the United States, which became the model for juvenile courts throughout the country. In 1938 the Federal Juvenile Court Act was passed, which incorporated Illinois's provi-

sions, and by 1945 every state had instituted its own juvenile court system. The U.S. juvenile court system accommodates five groups of children: delinquents, or violators of the criminal code; undisciplined juveniles who habitually flout adult authority; children without parents or legal guardians; neglected or abused children; and status offenders, or those who violate laws specifically covering children, such as truants and vagrants.

Aside from stressing the welfare and reform of children, juvenile courts differ from adult courts

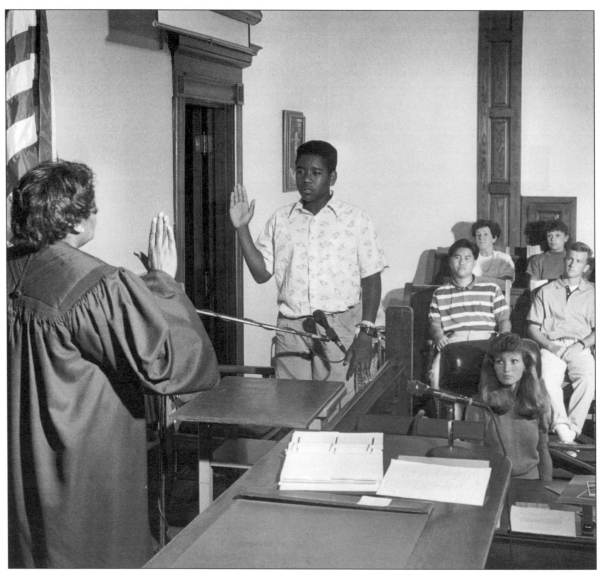

Separate juvenile court systems have been established in most states to provide less intimidating alternatives to adult courts. (James L. Shaffer)

by ensuring offenders' right to privacy, giving more consideration to the testimony of psychologists and psychiatrists than legal precedents in determining sentences, limiting periods of imprisonment, providing corrections facilities for juveniles separate from those for adults, giving a wide latitude to discretionary judgments, and withholding delinquents' right to jury trials. The traditional system of juvenile justice makes certain philosophical assumptions: that the state is the "ultimate" parent of all children within its jurisdiction, that all children are worth rehabilitating, that in view of juveniles' immaturity and corrigibility their antisocial acts should be interpreted as behavior problems rather than criminal behavior, and that the due process appropriate to adults may be suspended in the interest of rehabilitation.

Juvenile court jurisdiction is determined by offenders' conduct and age. The upper age-limit for juvenile court jurisdiction varies: It can be as low as sixteen or as high as eighteen. Juvenile court jurisdiction may take one of three forms, depending on the state. It may be "exclusive," meaning that certain juvenile infractions—typically status offenses like truancy—may be tried only in juvenile court, whereas violations of the criminal code may not be tried in juvenile court. All the states, the District of Columbia, and the federal government permit judicial waivers allowing especially violent delinquents to be remanded to adult criminal courts for trial. Alternatively, jurisdiction may be "original," which means that juvenile courts alone have the authority to initiate legal proceedings against juvenile offenders. Original jurisdiction covers most cases of delinquency and all status offenses. Finally, jurisdiction may be "concurrent," whereby adult courts have the authority to initiate proceedings against delinquents in such cases as homicide and rape. Some communities have made innovative provisions of their own for governing the operation of their juvenile courts. For example, Dela-

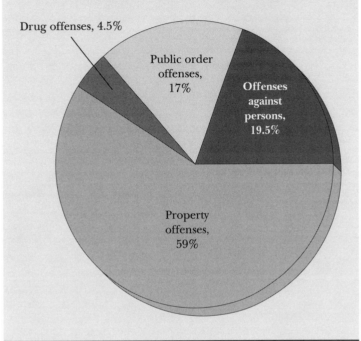

Juvenile Offenses Disposed by U.S. Juvenile Courts in 1991

Drug offenses, 4.5%

Public order offenses, 17%

Offenses against persons, 19.5%

Property offenses, 59%

Source: U.S. Department of Justice, Bureau of Justice Statistics, *Sourcebook of Criminal Justice Statistics—1993.* Washington, D.C.: U.S. Government Printing Office, 1994.

Note: Total juvenile offenses disposed by juvenile courts, 1991, was 1,338,100.

ware County in Pennsylvania has instituted "Youth Aid Panels," made up of private citizens who serve voluntarily, as an alternative to juvenile court; and Odessa, Texas, established Teen Court in 1983 in which judicial participants, except the judge, are carefully selected juveniles from the town.

Impact of the Juvenile Court System on Families. One effect of the juvenile court system on families is that since the 1980's, because of the staggering increase in violent crimes committed by children, parents have been held legally liable. Thus, under California's Street Terrorism and Enforcement and Prevention Act, Gloria Williams was cocharged with her fifteen-year-old son for the rape he committed. In 1989 Florida passed a law imposing a $5,000 fine and five-year sentence of imprisonment on parents who neglect to keep firearms safe from their children. In 1985 Wisconsin passed legislation making even both sets of grandparents financially responsible for

Alarming rises in violent juvenile crime have tended to shift emphases in juvenile justice from rehabilitation to punishment. (James L. Shaffer)

the children born out of wedlock to their minor grandchildren.

The domestic intervention of the juvenile justice system may be rehabilitative and therapeutic in aim rather than disciplinary. The trend is toward early intervention by juvenile authorities to prevent child abuse and neglect. This may take the form of either voluntary or court-ordered parent education or counseling programs, which seek to train parents in controlling their anger and frustration. On the other hand, in extreme cases parental rights may be terminated and children removed from their homes. However, punishment of parents may result in the fracturing of the family bond, which, if it occurs in enough families, may have deleterious social effects. In an effort to balance punitive and rehabilitative measures, an incest program in California's Santa Clara County put perpetrators on probation and committed entire families to a rehabilitative program. Cases of suspected child-abuse permit the authorities to invade domestic privacy in ways that other criminal and civil cases do not. If the police suspect abuse, they may enter a home without a warrant, remove children, and arrest parents. The evidence they obtain under such circumstances is admissible in court.

Demand for Reform of Juvenile Justice. Since the 1970's there has been a marked increase in violent crimes committed by children— some of them very young children. The number of murders committed by youths between the ages of fifteen and twenty-four more than doubled between 1968 and 1993. The young were also victims of violence in unprecedented numbers. In 1992 Charles Everett Koop, surgeon general of the U.S. Public Health Service from 1981 to 1989, declared that gunshot wounds had replaced infectious diseases like small pox and syphilis as the chief cause of death among adolescents.

Juvenile offenders thus posed as great a threat to the community as their adult counterparts, and their victims suffered no less grievously than the victims of adult crimes. Consequently, in 1985 Alfred Regnery, administrator of the U.S. Office of Juvenile Justice and Delinquency Prevention, recommended that juvenile justice should emphasize deterrence, leave their court records unsealed when juveniles reach adulthood, and blur the distinction between juvenile and adult criminals. In 1995 the International Association of Chiefs of Police, among others, called for the reform of juvenile justice in the direction of favoring punish-

Juveniles Held in U.S. Juvenile Facilities in 1991

Reason Held	Total	Male	Female
Total juveniles	**57,661**	**51,282**	**6,379**
Delinquent Offenses[a]	95%	97.3%	80.7%
Offenses against persons			
Violent[b]	19	20.5	10.3
Other[c]	12	12.1	9.4
Property offenses			
Serious[d]	24	24.4	17.1
Other[e]	12	12.5	12.9
Alcohol offenses	1	1.0	1.0
Drug-related offenses	10	10.4	5.3
Public-order offenses[f]	4	4.4	5.4
Probation/parole violations	8	7.2	12.9
Other	5	4.8	6.4
Nondelinquent Reasons	5%	2.7%	19.3%
Status offenses[g]	3	1.8	12.9
Nonoffenders[h]	1	0.7	4.2
Voluntary commitments	1	0.2	2.2

Source: U.S. Department of Justice, Bureau of Justice Statistics, *Sourcebook of Criminal Justice Statistics—1993.* Washington, D.C.: U.S. Government Printing Office, 1994.

[a] Offenses that would be criminal if committed by adults.

[b] Includes murder, nonnegligent manslaughter, forcible rape, robbery, and aggravated assault.

[c] Includes negligent manslaughter, simple assault, and sexual assault.

[d] Includes burglary, arson, larceny/theft, and motor vehicle theft.

[e] Includes vandalism, forgery, counterfeiting, fraud, stolen property, and unauthorized vehicle use.

[f] Includes weapons offenses, prostitution, commercialized vice, disorderly conduct, minor traffic offenses, curfew or loitering law offenses, and offenses against morals and decency and the like.

[g] Offenses that would not be considered crimes if committed by adults.

[h] Dependency, neglect, abuse, emotional disturbance, retardation, and other.

ment over rehabilitation. This punitive trend is reflected in state legislation. In 1995, for example, Texas passed legislation that lowered from fifteen to fourteen the age at which juveniles can be tried as adults, relaxed restrictions on photographing and fingerprinting juvenile suspects, made most juvenile hearings public, and opened the way to sentencing delinquents convicted of exceptionally violent crimes to as much as forty years in prison.

Juvenile Rights. There have been landmark Supreme Court decisions concerning delinquents who were tried as adults. One involved Morris Kent, Jr., who was charged with rape and burglary when he was sixteen years old. He was indicted in an adult criminal court and sentenced to a lengthy prison term. However, in 1966 the Supreme Court overturned his sentence (*Kent v. United States*), arguing that he should have had a fuller hearing in juvenile court. By so doing, the Court laid the precedent for a minimum of due process in juvenile court hearings. In *Breed v. Jones* (1975), Jones had been found delinquent by an adjudicatory hearing in juvenile court and was remanded to adult court for trial. There he was found guilty of first-degree robbery and committed to the custody of the California Youth Authority. He appealed to the U.S. Supreme Court on the grounds of double jeopardy, since he had been adjudicated in juvenile court prior to his conviction in adult court. The Court agreed with Jones, thereby curtailing the conditions under which a juvenile could be transferred from juvenile to adult court.

Some moral and legal issues raised by the juvenile court system are whether the punishing of status offenses like truancy with incarceration and detention is a violation of juveniles' due process rights, since they are not strictly criminal offenses; whether punishing parents for their children's crimes is legal and moral; whether juveniles can legally waive their Miranda rights (the right to remain silent when arrested and the right to an attorney); whether the disproportionate number of minority juveniles appearing in juvenile court constitutes a form of discrimination; whether it is morally and legally permissible to try juveniles as adults; and whether it is appropriate to incarcerate delinquents in correctional institutions, which have been found to be "schools" for crime.

—*Richard A. S. Hall*

BIBLIOGRAPHY

Currie, Elliott. *Dope and Trouble: Portraits of Delinquent Youth.* New York: Pantheon Books, 1991.

Humes, Edward. *No Matter How Loud I Shout: A Year in the Life of Juvenile Court.* New York: Simon & Schuster, 1996.

Kenney, John P., et al. *Police Work with Juveniles and the Administration of Juvenile Justice.* 7th ed. Springfield, Ill.: Charles C Thomas, 1989.

Mennel, Robert M. *Thorns and Thistles: Juvenile Delinquents in the United States, 1825-1940.* Hanover, N.H.: University Press of New England, 1973.

Miller, Maryann. *Coping with Weapons and Violence in Your School and on Your Streets.* New York: Rosen Publishing Group, 1993.

Prothrow-Stith, Deborah. *Deadly Consequences.* New York: HarperCollins, 1993.

Schmalleger, Frank. *Criminal Justice Today: An Introductory Text for the Twenty-first Century.* 4th ed. Upper Saddle River, N.J.: Prentice Hall, 1997.

See also Child abuse; Child Abuse Prevention and Treatment Act (CAPTA); Children's rights; Family courts; Family Violence Prevention and Services Act; *In loco parentis*; *In re Gault*; Juvenile courts; Juvenile delinquency; Legal separation; Systematic Training for Effective Parenting (STEP).

Juvenile delinquency

RELEVANT ISSUES: Children and child development; Law; Parenting and family relationships; Violence

SIGNIFICANCE: Children are treated differently from adults under the law, and laws have changed to reflect differences between children and adults and to protect the rights of children

Delinquent acts committed by minors can be divided into acts that would be illegal if committed by an adult and status offenses, which are illegal only by virtue of the offender's status, that of being a minor. Children and adolescents who leave the residence of their parents or other legal guardians—called runaways—without permission are status offenders.

Historical Background. The Puritans who settled in New England in the seventeenth century brought with them a religious philosophy that emphasized "original sin," the idea that people are born with evil desires and inclinations that must

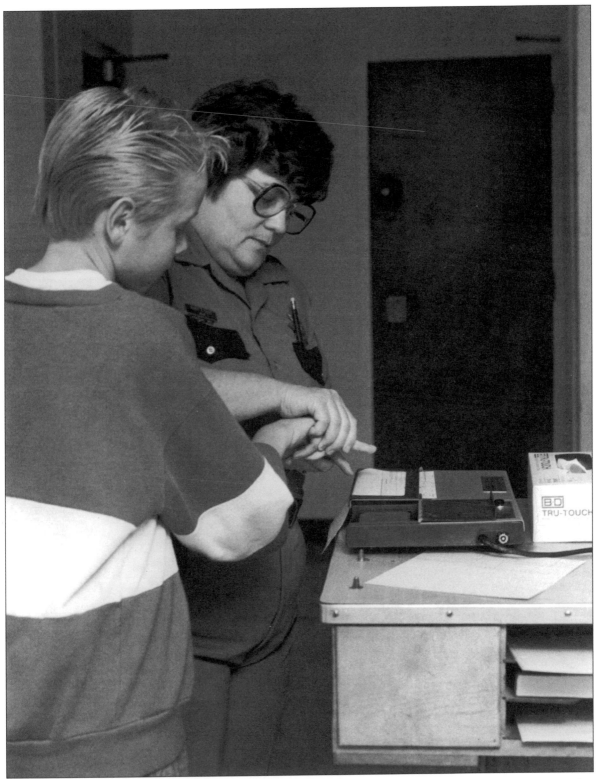

Decisions about whether young offenders are to be treated as juveniles or as adults after they are arrested often depend on the seriousness of their crimes. (James L. Shaffer)

Restitution—such as painting a house defaced by graffiti—is often made part of sentences imposed on youthful offenders. (Mary LaSalle)

be ruthlessly eradicated. They thought this essential, not merely to mold children into socially acceptable adults but also to save children's souls from eternal damnation. The punishment of youthful offenders therefore was harsh. The punitive fervor that pervaded Puritan culture was exemplified by the Salem witch trials, when presumed witches as young as fourteen years of age were burned at the stake.

Parents in colonial New England had absolute power over the lives of their children, who owed them unquestioning obedience. When the judicial arm of the colonial government intervened between parent and child, it was at the behest of a parent, claiming that a child could not be controlled.

During the seventeenth and eighteenth centuries, the colonies, which succeeded in overthrowing British rule and became the first thirteen states of a new federal republic, continued to try juveniles as adults and incarcerate them with adults. In the nineteenth century, the new republic underwent major changes that resulted in new concepts and practices with respect to delinquent youth. Westward expansion provided an opportunity for those who were likely to come into conflict with the law to move to areas where civil authority had not yet been established. There was a vast migration of people from different parts of Europe, whose cultures and customs were different from those of the original settlers.

The women's movement, which borrowed both rhetoric and membership from the abolitionist movement, promoted increased involvement in spheres typically reserved for men, particularly politics and the workforce. Women, increasingly accepted as public speakers, became advocates for the young, the poor, and the foreign born. They were at the center of the temperance movement, the struggle to improve conditions in prisons and mental hospitals, and the settlement house movement. The latter part of the nineteenth century

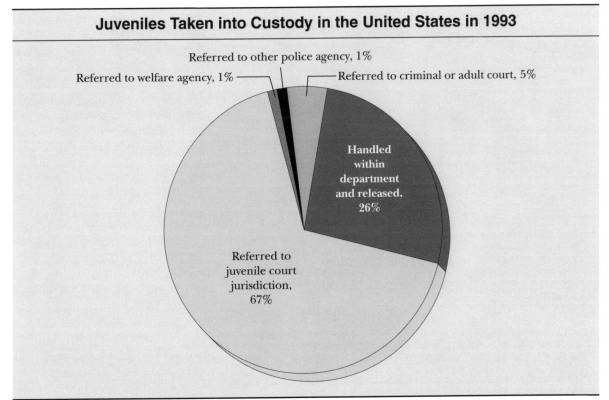

Juveniles Taken into Custody in the United States in 1993

Referred to other police agency, 1%

Referred to welfare agency, 1%

Referred to criminal or adult court, 5%

Handled within department and released, 26%

Referred to juvenile court jurisdiction, 67%

Source: U.S. Department of Justice, Federal Bureau of Investigation, *Crime in the United States* (Uniform Crime Reports). Washington, D.C.: U.S. Government Printing Office, 1994.

Note: Total number of juveniles taken into custody in cities was 1,091,890.

was known as the era of the Progressive movement because of the prominence of these causes and others aimed at improving the human condition.

Reforms in Juvenile Justice. One area in which reformers challenged the status quo was the field of juvenile justice. Reformers thought that delinquency was the result of improper child rearing. Instead of locking up juvenile lawbreakers with adult criminals, which would tend to reinforce their delinquent tendencies, they believed that efforts should be made to rehabilitate them through the right kind of care and education. These sentiments culminated in the establishment of a separate system of juvenile justice in almost every state during the first quarter of the twentieth century.

The new juvenile courts had jurisdiction over delinquent minors as well as those considered "wayward" or "incorrigible," such as runaways and truants, whose acts would not be criminal if they were adults. The new courts were informal and nonadversarial. Judges relied on social workers rather than lawyers to inform and advise them. The standard of proof required for a conviction was "preponderance of evidence" as in civil court, rather than "guilt beyond a reasonable doubt," as in adult criminal courts. Misbehaving children frequently were incarcerated with those convicted of crimes, and sometimes for even longer periods of time, because the criteria for duration of incarceration was not that of punitive justice used in adult courts, but rather the judge's idea of what would be in the best interests of the child and of society.

The purpose of this new system was to transform delinquent and difficult children into moral and productive members of society. That goal rarely was attempted in juvenile jails, which, for the most part, simply warehoused young people. The reformers nevertheless had accomplished two of their objectives: There were separate jails, often called reformatories, for minors, and juvenile miscreants could not be detained past the age of twenty-one. In addition, there was a fundamental change with respect to the relationship between parents and the state. The state, through the juvenile court system, had placed itself in a *parens patriae* role, meaning "in the parents' stead." The state was now the final protector of the young and could intervene when it saw fit. Parents no longer had absolute power over their children under law.

Juvenile courts were legally empowered to return runaway minors to their parents, but in practice, if a child took up residence in another state, it was difficult for parents to force their return. This problem was resolved by the Interstate Compact on Juveniles, a federal law enacted in 1954. Under the compact, a parent could use the juvenile court of another state to compel a child's return without actually traveling to the other state and appearing before the court. They could file an Interstate Requisition, to be handled by the compact administrator in the child's home state.

U.S. Public Opinion on Punishing Juvenile Offenders

Source: CNN/*USA Today*/Gallup Poll

Note: In 1994 a cross-section of Americans were asked how society should deal with persons under age eighteen who commit crimes. This table summarizes their responses.

Delinquency Cases of Boys and Girls in the United States in 1994

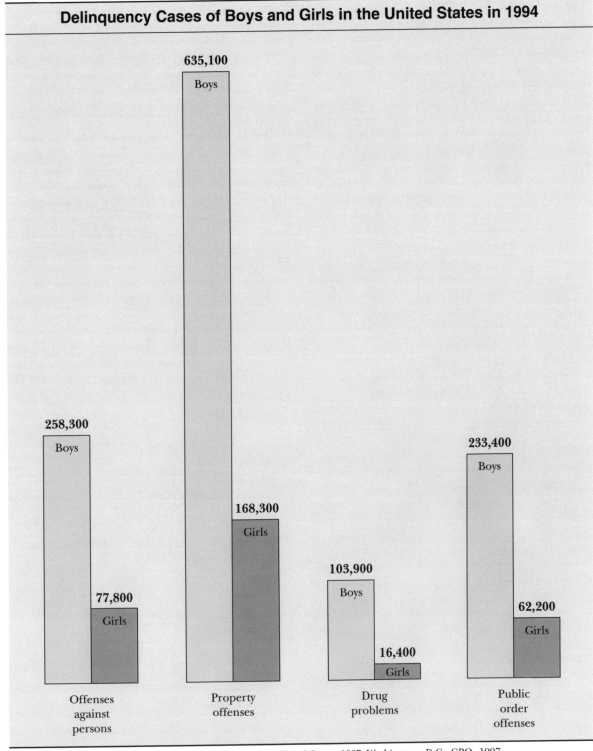

Source: U.S. Bureau of the Census, *Statistical Abstract of the United States: 1997.* Washington, D.C.: GPO, 1997.
Note: In 1994 juveniles were charged with 1,555,400 delinquency offenses in the United States. Such offenses are defined as those for which adult offenders would be tried in criminal courts. Boys were charged with a total of 1,230,700 offenses, girls with 324,700 offenses.

Rights of Children. The age at which a runaway is no longer a minor depends on the law in the child's home state, not the state to which he or she has moved. The compact cannot be used to detain minors whose parents or legal guardians have not requested their return, or those considered emancipated minors, which in most states means that parents and children have mutually severed the rights and responsibilities of the parent-child relationship. The major flaw in the compact is that it does not require that a hearing be held in either state to determine whether it is in the child's best interests to be returned. The judge in the receiving state can, at his or her discretion, hold such a hearing if there is a question of abuse or neglect.

The state, rather than parents or guardians, had been the ultimate authority with respect to children since formation of the juvenile justice system by the states early in the twentieth century. That authority had been ratified by Congress with the passage of the Interstate Compact on Runaways. The compact, paradoxically, had underscored parental rights.

Rights of children were not addressed in the law until a series of decisions by the Supreme Court in the 1960's radically changed juvenile courts in concept and practice. The decade of the 1960's was notable largely for the struggle of African Americans to secure civil rights. The success of the Civil Rights movement inspired other racial minorities, women, gays, and disabled persons to demand first-class citizenship. The demand for equal justice also led people to question the propriety of the informal practices of juvenile court and to demand civil rights for minors.

In 1966, in *Kent v. United States*, the Supreme Court maintained that a juvenile accused of a serious crime could not be remanded to an adult court without the effective assistance of a lawyer at a formal hearing. In 1967, in *In re Gault*, the Supreme Court effectively invalidated the informal practices of the juvenile courts. Gerald Gault was a sixteen-year-old accused of making an obscene phone call and given a five-year sentence by a juvenile judge. The Court went much further than simply invalidating the inappropriate sentence. It ruled that a minor charged with a crime must be given a precise statement of the charges; has the right to legal counsel, which the court must provide, if necessary; and must be able to confront his or her accusers. The standard of proof for conviction was changed to guilt beyond a reasonable doubt, as in adult criminal trials, and not preponderance of evidence, the standard in civil trials that also had been the standard in juvenile criminal trials. The only right the accused juvenile now lacked in comparison to an accused adult was the right to a trial by jury.

Public concern over a precipitous increase in juvenile crime, especially violent crime, led Congress to pass the Juvenile Justice and Delinquency Prevention Act in 1974. The purpose of the act was to deal with the problem of juvenile delinquency on a national scale by providing states with a mandate to set up delinquency prevention programs and to train workers for such programs. The act makes a clear distinction between juvenile crime and status offenses, such as running away or truancy, and prohibits states from incarcerating status offenders as a condition for receiving funds under the act. The principal effects of the act have been the formation of a national network of runaway shelters and an upsurge of neighborhood-based delinquency prevention programs. *—Jenifer Wolf*

BIBLIOGRAPHY

Bode, Janet. *Hard Time: A Real Life Look at Juvenile Crime and Violence.* New York: Delacorte Press, 1996.

Connors, Patricia. *Runaways: Coping at Home and on the Street.* New York: Rosen Publishing Group, 1989.

Edwards, Richard L., ed. *Encyclopedia of Social Work.* 19th ed. Washington, D.C.: National Association of Social Workers, 1995.

Museck, David. *An Introduction to the Sociology of Juvenile Delinquency.* Albany: State University of New York Press, 1995.

Paradise, Emily. *Runaway and Homeless Youth: A Survey of State Law.* Washington, D.C.: ABA Center on Children and the Law, 1994.

Rothman, Jack. *Runaway and Homeless Youth: Strengthening Services to Families and Children.* New York: Longman, 1991.

See also Child abduction; Children's Bureau; Children's rights; Curfews; Disciplining children; Family courts; Gangs; *In re Gault*; Juvenile courts; Latchkey children; National Center for Missing and Exploited Children (NCMEC).

Kagan, Jerome

BORN: February 25, 1929, Newark, N.J.
AREA OF ACHIEVEMENT: Children and child development
SIGNIFICANCE: Best known for his work on shyness in children, Kagan demonstrated how some early childhood behaviors are similar to behaviors in teenagers and adults

After earning a bachelor's degree from Rutgers University and a Ph.D. from Yale, Jerome Kagan focused his career on studying children's temperaments and inherited emotional capabilities. In the course of his career he taught at Ohio State University and the Fels Research Institute in Yellow Springs, Ohio. In 1964 he became the Daniel and Amy Stark Professor of Psychology at Harvard University, where he studied human development.

Kagan extensively studied and contrasted two groups of children: shy, timid, cautious children and sociable, bold, outgoing children. While his work does not discount the importance of environmental and cultural influences, it underscores the importance of a genetic basis for emotional, cognitive, and social development. In fact, his work has demonstrated how early behavior in children from six to ten years of age can often closely resemble later behavior, such as the passive withdrawal from stressful situations, dependency on the family, the ease with which anger is aroused, intellectual mastery, social anxiety, sex-role identification, and patterns of sexual behavior, including sexual preference.

In 1987 Kagan was honored with an Award for Distinguished Scientific Contribution by the American Psychological Association. Subsequently, he began to explore the cross-cultural aspects of this work as applied to children from Guatemala.

—*Nancy A. Piotrowski*

See also Childhood fears and anxieties; Heredity; Stranger anxiety.

Kinship systems

RELEVANT ISSUES: Kinship and Genealogy
SIGNIFICANCE: Human culture is characterized to a large extent by the rules governing kin relations, which regulate sexual norms, marriage practices, affiliation, and the inheritance of property

The notion that "blood is thicker than water" is expressed in the complex and varied processes by which human beings identify and behave with their kin. Early studies of kinship focused on descriptions of the names various cultures used to describe kin relationships. However, the question "why" was inevitably raised, and explanations reflect the varied contributions of economic theory, anthropological data, sociology, and sociobiology. In the context of of the rules governing kin relations, practices of naming children and the names women assume (or do not assume) upon marriage are of interest. Finally, while some have argued that industrialization effectively precluded the maintenance of extensive kinship ties, the work of several historians suggests this has not been the case.

History of Kinship Study. Many date the study of kinship and families to the 1861 publication of Johann Jakob Bachofen's *Das Mutterrecht* (*Mother Right*). In this work Bachofen suggested that humans originally lived in a state of promiscuity, in which descent could only be traced along the female line. He suggested that women held a position of respect and honor that was surrendered with the transition to monogamy.

Several years later, in 1886, John Ferguson McLennan published *Studies in Ancient History* in England. McLennan had never heard of Bachofen's work. Instead, he emphasized a process he called "exogamy." Under this system, tribes acquired brides by capturing women from other tribes. This method, which he called "marriage by capture," contrasted with the marital practices of "endogamous" tribes, or groups who required marriage within the tribe.

Anthropologists' early efforts to study kinship patterns involved detailed examination of the use of language to describe human relationships. For example, Lewis Henry Morgan's pioneering work, *Systems of Consanguinity and Affinity of the Human Family*, published in 1871, included two hundred pages of tables listing the diverse names cultures in the Americas, Europe, the Near East, and Africa used to describe kin. Morgan thought his research would illuminate the Asiatic origins of Native Americans. His work was criticized (most notably by Sir John Lubbock in his 1875 work *Origin of Civilization*) as not addressing the more profound question—namely, the source of the idea of kinship. He argued that Morgan's classification system "is a system of mutual salutations merely." Indeed, Lubbock argued that more important

than the "system of address," or what people call each other, is the system of blood ties and the methods by which people determine the importance of these ties. He went on to describe what he called "communal marriage," in which a group of men are married to a group of women. The argument about the appropriate focus of study continued in the work of Alfred Louis Kroeber and William Halse Rivers, both of whom published papers debating the importance of terminology in anthropology's understanding of kinship.

Claude Lévi-Strauss entered the debate with his enormously influential work, translated into English in 1969 under the title *Elementary Structures of Kinship*. Lévi-Strauss saw a strong relationship between kinship systems and marriage rules. He went beyond description to suggest that marriage

Claude Lévi-Strauss, author of Elementary Structures of Kinship. (Micha Bar-Am/New York Times/Archive Photos)

is essentially an exchange in which wives are a commodity. His analysis went on to discuss the system of exchange between "wife-givers" and "wife-takers."

This analysis reflected themes introduced in *The Origin of the Family, Private Property, and the State* (1884) by Friedrich Engels, who, together with Karl Marx, founded scientific socialism. Engels linked the rise of the family to the development of private property and the need for an orderly system of inheritance. Drawing on Morgan's observations, Engels argued that the development of human families proceeded in a more or less orderly fashion from "group marriage" or "herd," in which a group of men and women were essentially married to one another and shared children and resources, to the atomic monogamous relationships of modern times. He described the "overthrow of mother right," in which matrilineal systems of inheritance were replaced by patriarchal ones, as "one of the most decisive [revolutions] ever experienced by humanity," linking this development to the increased importance of wealth and the gender-based division of labor. In brief, Engels felt that as the surplus value of a man's labor outside the home increased, so did his desire for that value to be inherited by his children rather than by his maternal relatives.

Friedrich Engels, author of The Origin of the Family, Private Property, and the State. (Archive Photos)

Pierre L. van den Berghe moved the analysis from economics to sociobiology in his work, which culminated in the 1990 publication of *Human Family Systems: An Evolutionary View.* In this book he argued that kinship is not unique to humans. Noting that animals have some affinity for blood relations, he suggested that there is an evolutionary basis to patterns of marriage and family. Van den Berghe identified three fundamental processes that define human society: kin selection, reciprocity, and coercion. He observed that kin selection, or the preference for kin, is an attribute humans share with many other species and noted that this undoubtedly improves the genetic prospects of individuals. Van den Berghe's observations about reciprocity stem to a large extent from the work of exchange theorists such as George Simmel. Finally, van den Berghe suggested that the use of coercion to exploit members of the same species is a distinctively human trait linked to the rise of ever-larger and more complex societies held together by ever-increasing degrees of coercion and inequality. He notes that this feature has been observed in primates, but "organized coercion exercised over conspecifics who are neither kin nor mates, for the purposes of extracting the product of their labor, has been elaborated in humans to a degree incommensurable with any other animal societies."

Sexual Norms and Marriage Practices. Early anthropologists were intrigued by the sexual norms and marriage practices in cultures they considered "primitive." The study of these cultures was often initiated by missionaries. Thus, missionaries in Australia described (and no doubt tried to change) the sexual practices of aboriginal groups in which tribes were divided into large groups, or moieties, and sexual intercourse within the moiety was forbidden while every woman in one moiety was by birth a wife of every man in the other. This arrangement has been termed "group marriage." Morgan spent much time studying the Iroquois in New York State. There, he found a system of monogamy in which pair relationships were easily terminated by either participant. He termed this the "pairing family." Patterns of "polyandry" (in which a woman is married to more than one man) and "polygny" (in which a man is married to more than one woman) were also observed and described among foreign or "exotic" cultures.

Some have argued that the development of monogamous marital relationships interferes with tribal or community solidarity, facilitating the dominance of men over women. In "group marriage," children may be unsure about their paternity, but they cannot doubt the identity of their mothers. Thus, accumulated property can more logically be inherited along maternal lines. Furthermore, when men do not possess individual women but have an attachment to all or several women in a group, opportunities for jealousy are limited. Monogamy involves a jealous attachment to only one member of the group and necessarily involves a couple retreating from the community for both sexual and emotional gratification.

Incest and First-Cousin Marriage. The incest taboo has a strange fascination, with poor Oedipus the most striking example of Western interest in the sexual relations of intimate family members. The source of this taboo—whether cultural or biological—has been the subject of great debate. Lévi-Strauss argued for the cultural source. He thought that the incest taboo was the very foundation of human society—that it alone differentiated humans from animals. In contrast, van den Berghe argued for biology. He suggested that natural selection has established an erotic disinterest resulting from familiarity in childhood. As evidence, van den Berghe offers the observation that unre-

lated children raised together in an Israeli kibbutz seldom marry or have sexual relationships. Of course there are well-documented exceptions to the incest taboo in the history of Hawaiian, Incan, and Egyptian royal families. Under some circumstances kings were permitted or even expected to marry their sisters to preserve the purity of the royal line.

Cultures and groups vary in the extent to which first-cousin marriage is tolerated. Where it is permitted, first-cousin marriage can reflect a desire to maintain the cohesiveness and exclusivity of a kin group. Thus, first-cousin marriage has been common among the royal families of Europe. But this practice can be divisive in two ways. The first relates to inheritance. If inheritance comes from grandparents and the offspring of a set of grandparents marry, their union can create inequities in the division of property. The married cousins might arguably be entitled to a double share of the inheritance; otherwise they may be penalized because of their marriage. In either case, such marriages can foster discontent and inequalities within family groups. First-cousin marriage can be disruptive in a second, more political way. Families often use marriage to establish strong ties to other groups. This is to the advantage of both families. In this context, first-cousin marriage deprives families of an opportunity to establish strategic alliances through marriage.

Rules of Descent. Rules of descent can determine the inheritance of property as well as the names assumed by spouses and children. Van den Berghe identified four patterns: bilateral, patrilineal, matrilineal, and double descent. He suggested that the most common pattern is patrilineal, in which only the male line is recognized, with bilateral descent next in frequency. Bilateral systems recognize all ancestors along both paternal and maternal lines. Next in frequency are matrilineal systems, in which ancestry is traced only along mothers' lines. In double descent, only fathers' male ancestors and mothers' female ancestors are recognized. American society is considered to use a bilateral system, with surnames traditionally transmitted patrilineally.

Matrilineal cultures are distinguished from "matriarchal" groups in that in matrilineal cultures *lineage*, not authority resides with the mothers. Thus, while individuals trace their inheritance along maternal lines, authority over family members typically resides with the fathers. This can create a confusing situation for women, in which the role of wife and sister imply responsiveness to different men. The authority of a husband in matters involving the nuclear family may conflict with that of the brother in matters of lineal relations. The Ashanti of West Africa, and the inhabitants of Guadalcanal in the Solomon Islands both have matrilineal kinship groups.

Kinship in Industrial Society. It is popular to bemoan the demise of the extended family and blame urbanization, industrialization, the women's movement and other social ills for its loss. On the other hand, as Tamara Hareven and other historians have demonstrated, the nuclear household has been the preferred form of family organization for centuries. Furthermore, industrialization, rather than eliminating the role of kin, changed it. Hareven's study of workers in a Massachusetts textile mill underscored the role of extended kin in providing assistance during crucial life situations. Thus, when workers immigrate, they often call on extended kin for information and assistance. Similarly, during economic downturns, individuals in industrial settings often seek out kin for support. Thus, rather than eliminating the ties of kinship, industrialization seems to have offered new ways for these ties to be expressed.

In an interesting extension of the traditional understanding of kinship, members of the Church of Jesus Christ of Latter-day Saints (Mormons) believe that kinship is forever. Church doctrine includes the promise that Mormon families will be united in the afterlife. Founded by Joseph Smith in 1830, the church is relatively young and has grown tremendously through conversion. As a result, many ancestors of modern Mormons were not themselves members of the church. Mormons have developed the practice of posthumous baptism to ensure that Mormons will be united with their ancestors in the hereafter. As a result, the most extensive collection of genealogical documents in the world is found in the headquarters of the church at Salt Lake City, Utah.

The underlying need for systems of relationships transcends economic structures and is not undermined by changing gender roles. Humans need affiliation today as much as they ever did. Modern families integrate and adopt traditional kinship patterns to support themselves as they face challenges in the new millennium.

—*Amanda Smith Barusch*

BIBLIOGRAPHY

Bamberger, J. "The Myth of Matriarchy: Why Men Rule in Primitive Society." In *Women, Culture, and Society*, edited by M. Rosaldo and L. Lamphere.: Palo Alto, Calif.: Stanford University Press, 1974. Bamberger argues that stories about an earlier time when women ruled serve to justify why men must dominate.

Engels, Friedrich. *The Origin of the Family, Private Property and the State*. International Publishers, 1942. This work merits consideration as a classic articulation of Marxist theoretical perspectives on the family, offering a fascinating analysis of the status of women in families and in the economy.

Farber, B. *Comparative Kinship Systems: A Method of Analysis*. New York: John Wiley and Sons, 1968. An interesting and useful description of kinship systems, including American and Soviet patterns, as well as patrilineal and matrilineal approaches.

Hareven, Tamara K. *Family Time and Industrial Time*. Cambridge, England: Cambridge University Press, 1982. This book examines the role of the family in the adaptation of immigrant laborers to work and life in an industrial setting. Using life-history interviews, Hareven examines the experiences of workers in a textile factory.

Trautmann, T. R. *Lewis Henry Morgan and the Invention of Kinship*. Berkeley: University of California Press, 1987. This work has been described as "an indispensable guide for understanding the course of Morgan's research."

Van den Berghe, Pierre L. *Human Family Systems: An Evolutionary View*. Prospect Heights, Ill.: Waveland Press, 1990. With its roots in sociobiology, this book examines the evolutionary roots of kinship among humans as well as other animals, offering interesting comparative material on selected preindustrial societies as well as the United States and Japan.

See also Affinity; Endogamy; Exogamy; Extended families; Family albums and records; Inheritance and estate law; In-laws; Native Americans; Nuclear family; Parallel cousins; Polyandry; Polygyny; Primogeniture.

Kohlberg, Lawrence

BORN: October 25, 1927, Bronxville, N.Y.
DIED: January 17, 1987, Boston, Mass.
AREAS OF ACHIEVEMENT: Children and child development; Education
SIGNIFICANCE: In his pioneering work, Kohlberg extended Jean Piaget's work on cognitive development to study individuals' reasoning in making moral decisions

After a brief appointment at Yale University as assistant professor, Lawrence Kohlberg returned to teach at the University of Chicago, his alma mater. While there, he instituted the Child Psychology Training Program and was a popular but demanding supervisor. In 1968 he joined Harvard's Graduate School of Education, where he established the Center for Moral Development and Education.

Kohlberg's experimental method was to present people with a moral dilemma, such as whether they should break the law to steal medicine for a loved one, and note what they said in justifying their decisions. He described six basic moral stages and together with colleagues devised a sophisticated scoring procedure for ascertaining individuals' moral stages. He and his followers conducted much research, including a twenty-year longitudinal study of his dissertation subjects. Not simply content with discussions of hypothetical dilemmas, Kohlberg also developed a vision of a "just community," which he put into practice in an Israeli kibbutz school and in others schools and prisons.

At the age of forty-six, while on a trip to Central America, Kohlberg contracted a disease that ruined his health and sapped his energy. Henceforth, he suffered from constant dizzy spells, nausea, frequent pain, disability, and depression. At the age of fifty-nine, he apparently committed suicide by drowning. —*Lillian M. Range*

See also Child rearing; Moral education.

Korean Americans

RELEVANT ISSUES: Demographics; Race and ethnicity; Religious beliefs and practices
SIGNIFICANCE: Korean American families face the challenge of balancing the conservative, traditional principles of Korea with the more liberal, egalitarian beliefs of the American family

Most Korean Americans have strong family ties to South Korea. Confucian principles influence social and familial behavior. A patrilineal system dominates the traditional Korean family, which means that husbands are the commanders of their wives and families. Wives are expected to obey their husbands and serve husbands' parents and families. Wives must bear children to perpetuate their husbands' family lineage.

According to Confucian philosophy and centuries of tradition, Korean women obey their fathers until their marriage, at which time they must obey their husbands. After their husbands die, they must obey their sons. These strong patrilineal beliefs have posed difficulties when Koreans emigrate to the United States and attempt to adapt to mainstream American culture, which encourages gender equality. On the other hand, these unique traditional values enable Korean Americans to maintain their cultural identity and focus on the rich traditions of their native country.

Historical Overview. Koreans came to America after 1882, when the Korean-American trade and travel treaty was signed. American missionaries traveled to Korea to convert Korean Buddhists to Christianity. Sheltered and submissive Korean women found that church work offered them some freedom and was socially rewarding. From 1903 to 1905 seven thousand Koreans emigrated to the United States for political and financial reasons. Some of the first Korean immigrants were men working on Hawaiian sugar plantations. Emigrating to the mainland, they searched for better conditions in agricultural areas and for opportunities in the professions they had learned in their native Korea. Some Americans resented the fact that Korean immigrants took jobs in the United States and excluded them from participating in those professions. As a result, Koreans often started their own businesses in city districts where Korean families clustered.

The influx of Koreans to America slowly grew. By 1940 there were 8,568 Korean Americans. The Korean War, which ended in 1953, increased Korean immigration. Many U.S. servicemen returned home from the Korean War with Korean brides, while Korean students enrolled in U.S. col-

As a group Korean Americans are among the most recently arrived Asian immigrants, but because most of them are Christians they have adapted to North American life comparatively quickly. (Ben Klaffke)

The Reverend Sun Myung Moon, leader of the Korean-based Unification Church, has enjoyed success in the United States, where he is well known for conducting mass wedding ceremonies that join thousands of couples. (AP/Wide World Photos)

leges and American families adopted Korean infants. The 1965 Immigration and Nationality Act also contributed to the increase in Korean Americans by easing immigration restrictions. The 1990 United States Census Bureau reported that there were almost 800,000 Koreans in the United States.

The Canadian Employment Equity Act of 1986 classified Korean Canadians as a "visible minority." This act allowed the Canadian government to collect data on Korean Canadians as well as on other minorities and ethnic immigrants in Canada during the 1980's. About one third of Korean Canadians emigrated to Canada in the 1980's.

Demographics. Korean Americans and Canadians live primarily in urban areas. In the United States, Honolulu, Los Angeles, Chicago, and New York are important cities with substantial Korean populations. In some cities geographic areas have developed which have come to be known as "Koreatowns." Approximately 50 percent of Korean Canadians lived in the Toronto vicinity in 1991.

Education of males and females, which is valued in Korean culture, stems from historical Confucian beliefs. Koreans believe that success, power, and respect are attainable with education.

Some 57 percent of Korean Canadians had university degrees in the late 1990's, more than any other visible minority group. The high educational levels that Koreans have attained are evidenced by the large percentages of Korean professionals, managers, and entrepreneurs. In the United States, 40 percent of Korean men own businesses, such as grocery stores or dry cleaners. Many Korean medical professionals are forced to work in high-crime, inner-city areas because of the difficulties they face in finding jobs. In spite of such problems, unemployment rates among Koreans are low. They accept difficult working conditions and set themselves the goal of acquiring enough capital to improve their situation. The success of Korean-owned businesses has been attributed to the fact that Koreans work long hours, have strong work ethics, and make sacrifices for their families.

Family Interaction with Mainstream Society. The business success of Korean immigrants has caused resentment among other ethnic groups. In some cities African American and Korean relations have suffered because of cultural differences. The 1992 Los Angeles riots seriously affected local Korean businesses. Many were vandalized, looted, or burned. Korean Americans have better relations with Latinos. Both are entrepreneurial ethnic groups, and many Korean Americans speak Spanish as a second language.

Some Korean youth feel that they play dual roles as immigrants. They believe that being Korean American is a high-maintenance ethnic status. Even Korean children born in the United States are often expected to speak Korean and English, know Korean geography, and marry other Koreans. The majority of Korean Americans speak the Korean language at home. Korean American teenagers face some difficulties at school because of the language barrier that isolates their parents. The limited English proficiency of many parents is a cause for concern among both parents and children.

Traditional Korean culture is significantly different from American culture. Traditional Koreans place high value on filial piety. This devotion to older family members and particularly to husbands' families is lacking in American culture. Aging Korean parents expect that their children will respect them, and parents are frustrated when their children do not.

Korean American wives are burdened by double roles, while husbands are frustrated by the Americanization of their wives. Women must balance the role of traditional Korean wives, whose goal is to serve their husbands' families, with the role of employed American wives, whose goals are gender equality, personal satisfaction, and independence. Korean American husbands, influenced by filial piety, may fear their wives' challenges to male dominance at home. They feel that the gradual lessening of their wives' obedience is a problem that stems from American culture.

Maintaining Cultural Identity. In fulfilling social and religious roles, Korean churches adhere closely to traditional Korean beliefs. They encourage fellowship among Korean immigrants; provide social services for their congregations and the community, such as helping immigrants adjust to the new culture; and provide their members opportunities for leadership and status among Korean Americans. Sundays are often filled with activities sponsored by Korean churches. After Sunday services, congregations may have Love Feasts, at which traditional Korean foods are served.

Churches teach children Korean culture in Sunday afternoon workshops or summer camps.

Korean American churches preserve and promote traditional customs and festivals, as well as adapt customs to American ways. The Korean Lunar New Year's Day festival, called Sol-Nal, occurs in January or February. Like New Year's Day in the West, Lunar New Year's Day is a time to celebrate and make resolutions. Korean families gather for memorial services honoring ancestors or visit living elders. New clothes, special foods, candles, and incense are important to this festival.

The Harvest Moon Festival is celebrated in September or October on the fifteenth day of the eighth lunar month. Its purpose is to give thanks for successful harvests and is thus similar to Thanksgiving in the United States. Ancestors are honored during the Harvest Moon Festival. Festive foods, such as fruits, vegetables, zucchini pancakes, meat, rice, and wine are served. Crescent-shaped rice cakes filled with sweet sesame seeds or bean paste are the highlight of the harvest Moon festival. Moon-viewing is important to the festival and has inspired Korean poetry.

In Korea, traditional weddings were arranged by brides' and grooms' parents. Often, brides and grooms met for the first time at their wedding. In the late twentieth century, Western traditions of dating, love, engagements, and white wedding gowns have become the cultural norm among Korean Americans. Some Korean Americans have two wedding ceremonies, a Christian and a Buddhist one. Wedding feasts may be held in honor of brides and grooms, because food is an important part of such ceremonies. Tables are laden with traditional Korean foods such as kimchi, or spicy preserved cabbage; pulgolgi, or spicy beef; fish; rice; noodles; and vegetables.

Korean American families have managed to retain some of the cultural norms of traditional Korea while adapting to their modern life conditions in the United State and Canada. They have found ways to synthesize Korean and American values by adapting both. Unique values will eventually emerge, allowing Korean Americans to balance change with continuity. —*Celia Stall-Meadows*

BIBLIOGRAPHY

Auerbach, Susan, ed. *Encyclopedia of Multiculturalism*. Vol. 4. New York: Marshall Cavendish, 1994.

Kim, Kwang Chung, and Won Moo Hurh. "The Burden of Double Roles: Korean Wives in the USA." *Ethnic and Racial Studies* 11 (April, 1988).

Koh, Frances. *Korean Holidays and Festivals*. Minneapolis: EastWest Press, 1990.

Moffett, Eileen. *Korean Ways*. Seoul, Korea: Seoul International Publishing House, 1986.

Ng, Franklin, ed. *Asian American Encyclopedia*. 6 vols. New York: Marshall Cavendish, 1995.

Park, Eun-Ja Kim. "Voices of Korean-American Students." *Adolescence* 30 (Winter, 1995).

Skabelund, Grant, ed. "Culturgram for the 90's: South Korea." In *Culturgrams*. Provo, Utah: Brigham Young University, 1991.

Suyenaga, Ruth, et al. "Korean Children's Day: Teacher's Guide." In *Multicultural Celebrations*. Boston: The Children's Museum, 1992.

See also Amerasian children; Chinese Americans; Cultural influences; Dual-earner families; Family businesses; Filial responsibility; Filipino Americans; Japanese Americans; Pacific Islanders; Southeast Asian Americans; Vietnamese Americans; War brides; Women's roles.

Kübler-Ross, Elisabeth

BORN: July 8, 1926, Zurich, Switzerland
AREAS OF ACHIEVEMENT: Health and medicine; Religious beliefs and practices; Sociology
SIGNIFICANCE: Elisabeth Kübler-Ross pioneered the understanding of the terminally ill and conceptualized five psychological stages persons experience in facing their own deaths

Educated in Switzerland, Kübler-Ross won recognition while serving as a professor of psychiatry at the University of Chicago's Billings Memorial Hospital. Her innovative questioning of schizophrenic patients about what would help them in their own treatment led a group of theology students to ask her for help in counseling terminally ill patients. In response, Kübler-Ross developed a series of seminars in which dying patients agreed to talk with her about their feelings and needs while audiences observed and listened behind a one-way window. The enormous impact of these sessions on health care providers, social workers, and theology students focused attention on the unmet needs of the terminally ill. In 1969 Kübler-Ross published *On Death and Dying*, and later that year

Elisabeth Kübler-Ross at her Virginia farm in 1987. (AP/Wide World Photos)

Life magazine featured an article about her. As a national best-seller, *On Death and Dying* popularized her theory of the five stages experienced by the terminally ill or those suffering from significant loss: denial, anger, bargaining, grieving, and acceptance. Blunt, compelling, and compassionate as a writer and lecturer, Kübler-Ross became an inspiring champion of the hospice care movement with its program of psychological, social, and spiritual support along with symptom and pain control. Public approval of Kübler-Ross's philosophy of terminal care and the five-stage theory remained high in the late twentieth century, but controversy surrounded her later research into the question of life after death.   —*Irene N. Gillum*

See also Aging and elderly care; Family caregiving; Family life cycle; Grief counseling.

Latchkey children

RELEVANT ISSUES: Economics and work; Parenting and family relationships

SIGNIFICANCE: In an era of rising crime rates and frequent discussion about the loss of "family values," discussion about latchkey children, who spend time on a regular basis without parental supervision, has increasingly become a society-wide phenomenon

The issue of latchkey children fundamentally involves the socioeconomic status of women in society. The traditional concept of the family was one in which the man went into the workforce while the woman remained at home to care for the children and the household. The safety and the security of the family were her primary responsibilities. During the nineteenth and twentieth centuries a "cult of domesticity" developed. It held that a woman's natural place was in the home as caregiver. Motherhood was exalted by society. World War II, however, accelerated the process of moving women out of the home and into the workplace.

Latchkey Children in World War II. "Latchkey children," or "latchkey kids," refers to children who spend part of the day unsupervised by their working parents. These children carry their own house or "latchkeys." Although latchkey is a British term, the concept of latchkey children appears to have originated in North America. Although it undoubtedly existed in different forms as far back as the nineteenth century, when working-class children were perceived as being prone to delinquency because of inadequate parenting, the concept of latchkey children arose in Canada and the United States during World War II. Canada entered the war in September 1939, while American participation did not begin until December, 1941. The demand for men to serve in the war produced a civilian labor shortage, especially in important war-related industries. The governments of Canada and the United States turned to women as an untapped labor supply in order to fill jobs. In the United States, female participation in the workforce rose by 50 percent between 1940 and 1945. A problem immediately arose as to what child-care provisions would be made for those women who wanted to work and yet had young children at home. Some companies handled this dilemma by refusing to hire any women with children. Many mothers turned to grandparents and other family members to care for their children. In Canada and the United States certain companies began to provide limited day care. Private day care also appeared, but there was no guarantee that mothers' shifts would neatly coincide with day-care center hours.

Backlash Against Working Women. A backlash of public opinion quickly developed, primarily against mothers. By 1942, in Canada, there was widespread fear that juvenile delinquency was on the rise because children lacked adequate parental supervision. Three Canadian provinces—Ontario, Quebec, and Alberta—signed an agreement to establish state-run day-care facilities for women involved in the war effort. These centers remained until the end of the war when, in an effort to free up positions for returning male soldiers, they were closed.

In the United States, the backlash was even more intense. With mothers gone from the home, people publicly expressed the fear that crime, immorality, and disease, along with other vices, would increase among children. Women, who had been told that it was their patriotic duty to get involved in the war effort, were now derided as unpatriotic because they were neglecting their children. Newspapers described children by themselves at playgrounds with latchkeys hanging around their necks. In press releases, J. Edgar Hoover, the director of the Federal Bureau of Investigation (FBI), warned that child rearing was being neglected and that a rising tide of lawlessness was the result. In June, 1943, the Italian Mothers' Club of Greenwich House held a meeting on the perceived problem of latchkey children. It ended with a reading of a poem containing senti-

Although "latchkey" is a British term, the concept of "latchkey children" appears to have originated in North America. (James L. Shaffer)

ments that would remain long after the war had
ended:

> My mom goes out to work all day
> to help to win the fight,
> But who will look after us
> Till she comes home at night.
> Though your country needs you mom
> Your children need you too
> We're the future of the land
> It's really up to you.

The U.S. government made only a limited effort
to deal with the lack of proper child care. In 1940
it enacted the Lanham Act, which was designed to
provide funds for communities during wartime.
Child care was one funding priority. By the end of
the war, close to 600,000 children had received
some care in a center funded by the Lanham Act.
Nevertheless, there was strong opposition to gov-
ernment-run day care; it was believed that such
enterprises would encourage women to work, ac-
celerating the destruction of the family and thus
making the problem of latchkey children that
much worse.

Latchkey Children After the War. The fear of
latchkey children and what they represented did
not end with the conclusion of World War II.
While female employment in the United States
took a dip after 1945, by 1947 the level was higher
than in 1940, and it continued to increase. A wave
of American feminism, best exemplified by Betty
Friedan's *The Feminine Mystique* (1963), made its
appearance in the 1960's. It challenged the notion
that women were fulfilled by staying home as
mothers. Women continued to work and they began to move into male-dominated professions
such as medicine and law.

The problem of latchkey children remained,
however, and it only grew worse as American economic fortunes declined in the 1970's. Having a
stay-at-home parent became a luxury that few
families could afford. Both parents needed to
work in order for families to maintain a reasonable standard of living. The growing number of
latchkey children also increasingly reflected economic divisions in American society. Whereas
wealthy Americans could afford quality day care or
live-at-home nannies, an increasing number of
working-class and middle-class parents could not.
Other demographic factors contributed to the rise

in latchkey children. These included the rapidly
increasing number of single-parent families, the
decline in extended families that eliminated the
presence of other adults who might have shared in
child care, and the shrinking size of families,
which meant that older siblings were not available
to look after younger ones.

A 1990 national survey by the United States
Department of Education recorded that 44 percent of children between the ages of five and
twelve with working mothers had no child care
whatsoever. By 1993 *Time* magazine estimated that
as many as ten million children in the United
States qualified as latchkey children since, on a
regular basis, they spent part of their day unsupervised. Such statistics prompted church, school,
and parental organizations to try to fill the apparent void. One response was to create a service
called "PhoneFriend," which allowed lonely children to contact the outside world. Other concerned citizens published books on safety and activities for children who were on their own.

**Latchkey Children in the Era of "Family Val-
ues."** By the 1990's the issue of latchkey children
increasingly took on political overtones. On one
side were those who argued that latchkey children
symbolized the decline of the family. The media in
the United States and Canada carried stories listing potential dangers for latchkey children, including having access to firearms stored at home;
being potential victims of assault, including molestation; watching violent television programs; and
having unlimited access to the Internet (which
could lead to encountering sexually explicit materials or even potential child abusers). Even popular culture played upon parents' fears for their
children's safety. *Home Alone*, one of the most
popular Hollywood films of 1990, was a comedy
about a small child who was inadvertently left behind by his parents when they went on vacation.
While they were away, the family home, with the
boy in it, was invaded by thieves.

On the other side of the debate were individuals, including many feminists, who argued that the
latchkey problem was being exaggerated, since according to the U.S. Census Bureau the actual
number of latchkey children in 1990 was about 1.6
million, or approximately 7.6 percent of grade-
school children. These critics viewed the emphasis
on the problem of latchkey children as an attempt

to return women to the home, and that, in some cases, more freedom for children could be beneficial instead of harmful, since such a situation allowed children greater independence and encouraged them to be responsible at an early age. A 1986 study even found that most children enjoyed being home alone. In Canada and the United States, critics also pointed out that all levels of government had remained uninvolved with the problem, even though they could have helped ensure that affordable and quality child care was available to all those who needed it. Whatever the number of latchkey children, the problem of child welfare and child care is one that has been present in both Canada and the United States for more than a half century.   —*Steven R. Hewitt*

BIBLIOGRAPHY

Friedan, Betty. *The Feminine Mystique.* New York: W. W. Norton, 1963.

Hartmann, M. Susan. *The Home Front and Beyond: American Women in the 1940's.* Boston: Twayne, 1982.

O'Brien, Kenneth Paul, and Lynn Hudson Parsons. *The Home-Front War: World War II and American Society.* London: Greenwood Press, 1995.

Padilla, Mary. "Latchkey Children: A Review of the Literature." *Child Welfare* 68 (July/August, 1989).

Pierson, Ruth Roach. *They're Still Women After All: The Second World War and Canadian Womanhood.* Toronto: McClelland and Stewart, 1986.

Robinson, Bryan. *Home-Alone Kids: The Working Parent's Complete Guide to Providing the Best Care for Your Child.* New York: Lexington Books, 1989.

See also Child abandonment; Child care; Child safety; Childhood history; Community programs for children; Day care; Juvenile delinquency; Single-parent families; Substitute caregivers; Work.

Lathrop, Julia C.

BORN: June 29, 1858, Rockford, Ill.

DIED: April 15, 1932, Rockford, Ill.

AREA OF ACHIEVEMENT: Children and child development

SIGNIFICANCE: Committed to improving life for women and children, particularly immigrants, delinquents, and the poor, Lathrop helped implement broad-ranging reforms, becoming the first woman to head a U.S. government bureau

Daughter of attorney William Lathrop and the woman suffrage advocate Sarah Potter Lathrop, Julia Clifford Lathrop graduated from Vassar College in 1880, later reading law in her father's office. In 1890 she joined reformer Jane Addams at Hull House in Chicago. In 1893 Illinois governor John P. Altgeld appointed her to the Illinois Board of Charities. In her reports, based on visits to 102 Illinois institutions and published in *Hull-House Maps and Papers* (1895) and *Suggestions for Visitors to County Poorhouses and to Other Public Charitable Institutions* (1905), she argued for the reform of mental institutions and hospitals and for separation of children in such facilities. Convinced of the need to separate adult and juvenile criminals, she joined with Addams and others to create the first U.S. juvenile court system, established in Cook County (Chicago) in 1909. From 1908 until her death, she worked with the Illinois Immigrants' Protective League, which she helped found.

On April 17, 1912, President William Howard Taft named her as first head of the newly formed Children's Bureau of the U.S. Department of Commerce and Labor. This, the first national agency to focus on the problems of children, was given responsibility for enforcing the 1916 Keating-Owen Child Labor Act, the first U.S. child-labor laws. Under Lathrop, the bureau undertook studies of such problems as infant and maternal mortality, nutrition, delinquency, and illegitimacy. In 1921 Lathrop resigned because of poor health. She later helped investigate conditions at the Ellis Island immigration center and became an assessor for the Child Welfare Committee of the League of Nations, winning international honors for her work on behalf of child war victims.

—*Betty Richardson*

See also Addams, Jane; Children's Bureau; Hull House; Juvenile courts; Settlement houses.

Latinos

RELEVANT ISSUES: Children and child development; Demographics; Parenting and family relationships; Race and ethnicity; Religious beliefs and practices

SIGNIFICANCE: Although new roles and traditions are emerging within Latino families, many Latinos continue to find satisfaction in following traditional practices, viewing the family as a lifetime source of stability, protection, and support

Because the historical and cultural experiences of the various groups known collectively as "Latinos" differ widely, it is impossible to discuss a monolithic tradition. There are no universal customs or lifestyles that can fully reflect Latino family life. Nevertheless, there is a strong tradition among Latinos of emphasizing the importance of family, kin, and neighborhood ties.

As with other ethnic and cultural groups, the Latino family functions as a conduit for transmitting social skills and cultural values from one generation to the next. It is important to remember that cultural traditions based on ancestral customs and national origins exert long-lasting influence on Latino family structure and behavior. Family life among Mexican Americans is not identical to that found among Puerto Ricans, Cuban Americans, or Dominican Americans, in part because of such factors as variations in economic and social status; urban versus rural origins; distinctions between professionals, skilled laborers, and unskilled laborers; and differences between persons with high literacy skills and levels of education and those with limited literacy and education. Although members within a particular Latino extended family may share the same cultural origins, the length of time each member has lived in the United States is often very different. Individual family members may not share the same beliefs about what is important in life. Latino families often find themselves forging delicate compromises when their traditional values clash with mainstream American attitudes.

La Familia. There are probably more similarities than differences between the various Latino groups when it comes to basic family characteristics and values. The concept of *la familia* is central to Latino identity, since individuals are considered to be representatives or symbols of the families who raise them. The actions of family members are commonly viewed as bringing honor or shame to the entire family, not solely to individual members.

The extended Latino family includes all the members of the nuclear family plus aunts, uncles, cousins, grandparents, and even godparents. Whether extended family members are related by blood, marriage, or close friendship, they play an important role in improving the economic status of the family. The ability to call upon extended family members for assistance allows for greater flexibility in sharing caregiving responsibilities, giving mothers and younger women the opportunity to add to their families' economic resources by working outside the home.

Eating together is an activity that gives family members an opportunity to strengthen their ties to one another, to share news, and to discuss important family decisions. In preparing family meals, many Latinos include traditional foods and use recipes that have been handed down from generation to generation. Extended family members often participate in these family meals.

Family Loyalty and Size. Because Latinos have traditionally defined themselves in terms of their obligations to their families, they are willing to set aside other demands in order to fulfill such obligations. If a close family member or relative needs assistance of some kind—whether financial, physical, or emotional—most Latinos consider this more important than their own personal desires and plans. It is not uncommon for Latinos to take time off from work or school if another family member needs help when visiting a doctor, registering a car, or consulting a lawyer. Especially among immigrant families, Latino children are expected to serve as translators for their Spanish-speaking elders and facilitate families' contact with the broader English-speaking society.

Although large Latino families are not as common as they once were, Latinos continue to outpace other American ethnic groups in terms of birth rates and family size. Although changing attitudes toward divorce and family planning methods have had some effect on family size, Latinos have historically placed great value on having large families. Their reverence for traditional ways has made many Latinos reluctant to have smaller families with fewer children. Many Latinos face a conflict of cultural values when making the decision to have children, since their cultural tradition of placing family responsibilities first contradicts the tradition of individualism that is encouraged by mainstream American society. Even the most enduring reasons given for having children, such

Three generations of Puerto Rican women. (Hazel Hankin)

Quinceañeras play an important and unique role in Latino culture in bringing families and community members together. (James L. Shaffer)

as a desire to carry on the family name or to ensure that family members will be cared for in old age, reflect a mixture of selflessness and self-interest.

According to the 1990 U.S. Census, nearly 70 percent of all Hispanic families were headed by married couples. While 76 percent of Cuban American and 73 percent of Mexican American and South American families were headed by married couples, this was the case for only 56 percent of Puerto Rican and 50 percent of Dominican American families. Central American families had the highest percentage of families headed by fathers whose wives were absent (14 percent), while families headed by females were highest among Dominican Americans (41 percent) and Puerto Ricans (36 percent). Figures from 1990 show that 65 percent of Hispanic families had children under the age of eighteen as compared to 48 percent for all American families.

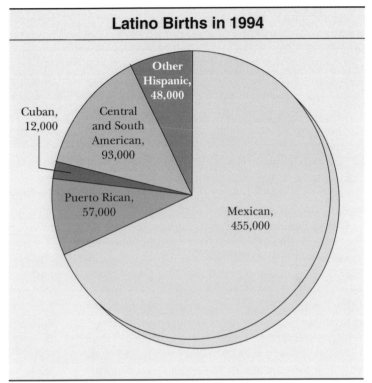

Latino Births in 1994

Other Hispanic, 48,000

Cuban, 12,000

Central and South American, 93,000

Puerto Rican, 57,000

Mexican, 455,000

Source: U.S. Bureau of the Census, *Statistical Abstract of the United States: 1997.* Washington, D.C.: GPO, 1997.

The Bureau of the Census has estimated that the Hispanic population will increase to 88 million (a fourfold increase over the 1990 population) and will represent 60 percent of the U.S. population by the middle of the twenty-first century. Such growth is expected to occur because of a natural increase within Hispanic families already living in the United States rather than because of a rise in immigration. This projected growth will widen the median age gap between the Hispanic and non-Hispanic white populations. According to the 1990 census, Hispanics' median age was 25.4 years, whereas non-Hispanic whites' median age was 34.8 years. By the middle of the twenty-first century the median ages are projected to reach 32.1 years and 54.2 years, respectively.

Traditional Family Roles. Certain cultural expectations persist among Latinos regarding appropriate roles for family members. It is expected that Latino parents will make whatever personal sacrifices are necessary to improve the welfare of and opportunities available to their children. Such demands are intergenerational, since young adults

are expected to make similar sacrifices to assist their elderly relatives and parents, as well as younger siblings. The demand for self-sacrifice is accompanied by an expectation that family members will maintain their pride and dignity. Among Latinos, self-worth and self-respect are defined in terms of how behavior reflects upbringing and reinforces the community's regard for the family. It is often considered disrespectful and ungrateful to place individual needs above the welfare of the family as a whole, and betraying the family's esteem and public image is considered more shameful than to bring shame upon oneself.

Historically, Latinos have vested men with ultimate authority to make family decisions. The patriarchal structure that resulted was based on the assumed superiority of men, producing a cultural tradition known as *machismo*. While defining desired traits and behaviors for Latinos as providing leadership, protection, and economic security for the family, *machismo* also dictated reciprocal traits and behaviors for Latinas. Women were expected to respect male authority, to take responsibility for domestic duties, and to honor the family reputation by seeking social relationships and recreation among friends and extended family members. Despite the negative characteristics often associated with the concept of *machismo*, it arose from the expectation that men earned respect within the Latino community by exercising their authority in the family in a just and fair manner. As traditional stereotypes have given way to a more modern view of family structure and relationships, Latinos have acknowledged the equally important role that women have played in shaping family life and making important decisions.

Latino families encourage children to have respect for authority. Children are expected to express reverence toward their elders, including grandparents and other older relatives. Obedience is valued, yet discipline within the family is increasingly affected by parental absence. Although they can call upon members of their extended family, many Latino parents who work multiple jobs to earn enough money to support their children find it difficult to ensure that their children are always under adult supervision.

Family Naming Customs and Celebrations. Many families recognize Latino heritage by using the surnames of both parents. In Spanish, this combination of surnames is called *el nombre completo*, or "full name." First and middle names are followed by the father's and mother's first surnames. Although most Latino families have assimilated the mainstream American custom of adopting one surname for legal purposes, many Latinos identify themselves to each other by their full names as a sign of respect for their kinship ties and cultural origins.

Baptism is an important event in many Latino families. Among Roman Catholic Latinos, this ceremony celebrates the birth of infants and welcomes them as part of the Church family. Godparents, or *padrinos*, are chosen from among close relatives or family friends to help care for children and serve as role models in guiding them to adulthood. Other family events with religious dimensions include first Communion and the quinceañera (part of the fifteenth birthday celebration that marks the end of childhood and the beginning of womanhood for young Latinas). Special family traditions mark the observance of saints' and holy days, including *Semana Santa* (Holy Week

before Easter) and *Navidad* (Christmas). The Christmas procession known as *Las Posadas* revolves around the family theme of Joseph and Mary's search for lodging in Bethlehem before the birth of Jesus.

Some Latinos observe other family-related holidays or celebrations. Mexican Americans observe *Día de los Muertos* (Day of the Dead) to honor deceased relatives. There are also family traditions associated with patriotic holidays celebrated in Latinos' countries of origin—particularly *Dieciseis* for Mexican Americans, *Día de la Raza* for Puerto Ricans and Dominican Americans, and Independence Day for Cuban Americans.

Blending the Old and the New. Although the child-centered focus of *la familia* persists, many Latino parents share family responsibilities instead of holding tightly to their traditional family roles. Many Latinos and Latinas take advantage of educational and career opportunities, choosing to postpone marriage until later in life. When they marry, many husbands and wives find it easier to share family responsibilities that were formerly defined either as male or female. While families acknowledge that their members have individual goals, many Latinos find comfort in honoring their attachment to their families as a positive cultural attribute and reaffirm the tradition of pulling together to provide mutual assistance in times of need. While such values are hardly unique to Latino families, they do serve to reaffirm cultural roots and ties within the Latino community.

—Wendy Sacket

BIBLIOGRAPHY

Acosta-Belén, Edna, and Barbara R. Sjostrom, eds. *The Hispanic Experience in the United States: Contemporary Issues and Perspectives.* New York: Praeger, 1988. Collection of essays reflecting the research interests of sociologists and cultural anthropologists who have explored issues relating to Latino family life.

Carrasquillo, Angela L. *Hispanic Children and Youth in the United States: A Resource Guide.* New York: Garland, 1991. In addition to directing readers to resource material on family life, language, education, health care, justice, and other social issues, Carrasquillo offers a useful introduction to the history, culture, and diversity of Latino children.

Día de los Muertos celebrants in Austin, Texas. (Diane C. Lyell)

Hoobler, Dorothy, and Thomas Hoobler. *The Mexican American Family Album*. New York: Oxford University Press, 1994. Focusing on the experiences of Mexican Americans, the Hooblers have gathered a broad range of first-person accounts—including personal recollections, diary entries, and letters—to accompany the photographs that comprise this chronicle of family life.

Moore, Joan, and Harry Pachon. *Hispanics in the United States*. Englewood Cliffs, N.J.: Prentice-Hall, 1985. Although its statistical information is somewhat dated, this work offers an informative portrait of the Latino community and its attitudes toward the family.

Shorris, Earl. *Latinos: A Biography of the People*. New York: W. W. Norton, 1992. Drawing on extensive primary research as well as life portraits of his own family and friends, Shorris offers a lively social history of various Latino groups and their experiences in the United States.

Zambrana, Ruth E., ed. *Understanding Latino Families: Scholarship, Policy, and Practice*. Thousand Oaks, Calif.: Sage Publications, 1995. Among the most useful essays in this collection are "Variations, Combinations, and Evolutions: Latino Families in the United States," by Aida Hurtado; "The Study of Latino Families," by William A. Vega; and "Contemporary Issues in Latino Families," by Douglas S. Massey, Ruth E. Zambrana, and Sally Alonzo Bell.

See also Baptismal rites; Compadrazgo; Cultural influences; Extended families; Family gatherings and reunions; Gangs; Gender inequality; Godparents; Holidays; Names; Native Americans; Quinceañera; Roman Catholics.

Learning disorders

Relevant issues: Children and child development; Education; Parenting and family relationships

Significance: Confusion over the nature and causes of learning disabilities has led specialists to use different terms to describe similar symptoms, adding to the frustration felt by parents seeking help for their learning-disabled children

The term "learning disabilities" covers a wide range of learning disorders. The federal Education for All Handicapped Children Act (EHA) of 1975 provided a general definition of learning disabilities that has served as a guideline for federal funding. Nevertheless, the term has continued to remain open to various interpretations. Consequently, some school districts have established their own standards for identifying students with learning disabilities. The criteria they have used for identifying learning disabilities have not specified exactly what learning disabilities are. Instead, they have essentially described associated symptoms and behaviors. This lack of specificity has caused confusion in the diagnosis and treatment of learning disabilities over the years.

Background. Several different models have been used to study learning disabilities. Initially, learning disabilities (and hyperactivity) were viewed from a medical standpoint. The medical model influenced many theorists to explain learning disabilities in terms of abnormalities in neurological and mental functioning. Explanations based on neurological dysfunction gave rise to theories of minimal brain damage that were first described by Alfred A. Strauss in 1940. These theories provided a model for theory, research, and treatment throughout the 1950's.

A number of expressions have been used over the years to describe the wide range of learning disabilities: the clumsy child, the dyslexic child, the hyperactive child syndrome, the hyperkinetic syndrome, the perceptually handicapped child, and learning disorders. While these terms led to inaccurate assessments, they nonetheless focused attention on the existence of learning disorders. Parents who for years had endured the frustrations of raising children who struggled to adjust socially and perform academically were finally given a tangible reason for their children's problems.

The inability to confirm the theory of brain damage among the learning disabled and the hyperactive led to a reevaluation of the causes and new terminology: "brain dysfunction." Brain dysfunction was eventually replaced by the term "learning disabilities," which was coined in 1963 by Samuel Kirk.

Learning Disabilities. Children were said to be "learning disabled" if they exhibited significant underachievement in one or more academic areas, despite having at least average scores on standardized intelligence tests; if they exhibited no major behavior disorders; if they did not suffer from environmental deprivation; and if no uncorrected sensory handicap existed. Children were diagnosed as "hyperactive" if they exhibited excessive motor activity, impulsivity, or distractibility to the point that these problems interfered with learning. Learning disabilities are not a single condition, but a wide range of specific disabilities that are the result of dysfunctional activities in the brain or central nervous system.

Learning disabilities can typically be classified into three broad categories (which in some instances can be further divided into subcategories): developmental language (speech) disorders, academic (skills) disorders, and other disorders (difficulties not classified under developmental and academic disorders). Language and speech difficulties may be the first indication that a problem exists. Parents should be alerted to this possibility if their children have problems producing speech sounds, using language, or understanding others. However, articulation, expressive, or receptive disorders may also be present. Other learning disabilities include motor skills disorders, specific developmental disorders, and attention disorders. The latter can range from daydreaming to impulsivity and distractibility.

Diagnosis and Treatment. There are no definitive explanations for specific learning disabilities. Brain damage, neurological impairment, disease, malnutrition, infection, and genetic factors are all possibilities that have been considered. Learning disabilities are not categorized by cause but by

An important principle established by court decisions has been the right of children with learning disorders to have a free public education. (Don Franklin)

In 1995 this seven-year-old Pennsylvania child was a member of a group of children with learning disabilities admitted to regular classrooms. (AP/Wide World Photos)

symptoms. However, the improper diagnosis of students with learning disabilities may lead to inappropriate treatment strategies. In addition such a diagnosis may confound the results of research on the phenomenon of learning disabilities, thus limiting the effectiveness of potential treatment. Educators should be alert to students who have poor academic performance when indicators such as intelligence tests suggest that higher results should be expected. While poor academic performance is not the defining characteristic of learning disabilities, it does serve as an indicator for concern. Poor academic performance is evidenced by difficulties in mastering reading, writing, and mathematics.

A number of tests, such as the Detroit Tests of Learning Aptitude (DTLA) and the Diagnostic and Statistical Manual of Mental Disorders (DSM), have been developed to help identify learning-disabled children. The DTLA focuses on general intelligence and the psychological processes involved in learning and remembering. The DSM is typically used when applying for health insurance coverage and treatment services.

Not all learning difficulties are products of learning disabilities. Instances of mild to moderate retardation, developmental lag, and emotional and behavioral problems can account for much of the low achievement among some students. Proper diagnosis is the first step in attending to the problem. Pediatricians and parents should monitor their children as early as possible for certain developmental milestones. Failure to achieve these milestones should alert parents to the need for more detailed investigation. Parents should, however, allow their children sufficient time for development. Because children develop differently and at different rates, developmental delays may be normal. However, if there is a history of learning disability in a family, a professional evaluation may be warranted. Parents have the right to request an evaluation by the school if they believe learning delays are evident.

Dumping Ground. Children diagnosed as having learning disabilities constitute the largest population of students with special needs in North America. They represent approximately 5 percent of all students in U.S. public schools. However, the label "learning disabilities" has become a dumping ground for intellectual-developmental problems that have no identifiable organic bases. Parents tend to feel less stigmatized when their children are "learning disabled" than when they are "mentally retarded" (or "slow learners"). In 1992-1993 the U.S. Department of Education indicated that of all students classified with disabilities, 57.1 percent were identified as having specific learning disabilities. A major task facing parents and educators is to differentiate between children who are actually learning disabled, those who are mildly mentally retarded, and those who are nondisabled low achievers. General characteristics of students with learning disabilities include discrepancies between capability and performance, hyperactivity or impulsiveness, poor motor coordination, poor grasp of spatial relations, delays in achievement, attention deficit, normal intelligence (even giftedness), specific memory disorders, immature social skills, anomalies in perception, lack of self-motivation and self-regulation, and disorganization.

Familial Concerns. Many parents of learning-disabled children seek to know what has caused their children's problems and if there is something that they could have done to prevent them. Instead of seeking causes, parents should focus on seeking the proper educational services once their children have been diagnosed as learning disabled. Having a child with learning disabilities affects not only the child but also the entire family. Strategies to help learning-disabled children may require restructuring familial priorities and routines. Special attention may be required in the explanation of instructions, personal organization (skills), time management, and study habits (time, place, and duration). Parents of learning-disabled children often experience guilt, anger, despair, self-blame, or simply denial. Siblings may be embarrassed to have brothers or sisters labeled as "exceptional." They may also be jealous over the special attention given to their learning-disabled siblings.

—*Charles C. Jackson*

BIBLIOGRAPHY

Braswell, Lauren, and Michael L. Bloomquist. *Cognitive-Behavioral Therapy with ADHD Children: Child, Family, and School Interventions.* New York: Guilford Press, 1991.

Lahey, Benjamin B. *Behavior Therapy with Hyperactive and Learning Disabled Children.* New York: Oxford University Press, 1979.

Lefrancois, Guy R. *Psychology for Teaching.* Belmont, Calif.: Wadsworth, 1997.

Millichap, Gordon J. *Learning Disabilities and Related Disorders: Facts and Current Issues.* Chicago: Year Book Medical Publishers, 1977.

Neuwirth, Sharyn. *Learning Disabilities: Decade of the Brain.* Washington, D.C.: National Institutes of Health and National Institute of Mental Health, 1993.

See also Attention-deficit hyperactivity disorder (ADHD); Behavior disorders; Disabilities; Educating children; Education for All Handicapped Children Act (EHA); Genetic disorders; Mental health; Schools.

Least interest principle

RELEVANT ISSUES: Marriage and dating; Parenting and family relationships; Sociology

SIGNIFICANCE: In relationships, indifferent persons who care least about issues or others tend to hold more power than those who care deeply and are highly committed

The principle of least interest involves a discrepancy between commitment and power. The roots of this principle can be traced to E. A. Ross, who discussed the law of personal exploitation in *Principles of Sociology* (1921). Ross noted that persons who care least can readily exploit those who are deeply committed. In *The Family: A Dynamic Interpretation* (1938), sociologist Willard Waller adapted this idea to the field of marriage and the family, calling it "the principle of least interest."

Some brief examples illustrate how this principle operates in typical family lives. Friends may negotiate for power by threatening to go home if they are not allowed to play with a child's new toys. Teenagers may issue ultimatums to their parents by declaring that they will not complete their homework or do household chores unless they are allowed to meet their friends at the movies or have the use of the car on Friday night. Parents often threaten to withhold rewards in order to encourage children to improve their behavior. In a 1982 study, sociologist F. Ivan Nye defined the key ideas behind the principle of least interest in terms of exchange theory, arguing that those who find relationships less rewarding or more costly than their partners may ask for additional rewards beyond the relationships themselves, such as expensive entertainment or sexual favors.

The work of J. Ross Eshleman and John Scanzoni suggest that relationships are more stable when power and resources are in balance or are equally shared. Equals have a much lower probability of being used or exploited in a relationship. Traditionally, women have desired marriage and parenthood more highly than men and have thus been more committed to these institutions. Men have generally invested less commitment in these institutions and, as a consequence, have tended to wield more power within marital and family relationships than have women. The principle of least interest holds that the most loving and committed persons in relationships are more vulnerable and less powerful in daily activities than partners who are less committed.

Many scholars have used the principle of least interest to explain the dynamics of marriage and family relationships. Because the principle of least interest helps to explain the dynamics of male-female and other interpersonal relationships, research dealing with gender relations, power, and feminism have emphasized this concept.

—*Jay D. Schvaneveldt*

See also Disciplining children; Family life education; Gender inequality; Generational relationships.

Legal separation

RELEVANT ISSUES: Divorce; Law

SIGNIFICANCE: Legal separation is a formal arrangement by which married partners live apart prior to or in lieu of obtaining a divorce

Legal separation is often a half-way house between marriage and divorce. In some states a period of separation is a requirement for divorce, and a formal legal separation of spouses for a specified period of time satisfies this requirement. However, married couples can separate without ever obtaining a divorce, and—at least in some jurisdictions—they can secure a divorce without having first separated. Moreover, not every separation is a "legal" one. Married partners may separate informally as a result of discord. For separations to be legal the details of the separation must be spelled out either in a contract or by a court order. This, in fact, is the key purpose of a legal separation: to specify formally the rights and obligations of separated married partners in matters of child custody, visitation rights, and financial support. Although informally separated partners may agree to some resolution of these matters, a legal separation makes these agreements binding and enforceable.

Separation as an Alternative to Divorce. Some married partners, for moral or religious reasons, reject divorce as a means of resolving marital discord. In such cases, they may perceive separation to be an appropriate alternative to divorce. If they separate, couples cease living together while remaining married. Just as in the case of divorce, however, separating partners must frequently formalize their living arrangements by such means as contracts or court decrees. Legal separation provides this measure of formality. Other married partners may "try on" a divorce by separating for a period of time before actually divorcing. Such separations may lead to divorce, to reconciliation, or conceivably to a permanent separation that is never formalized by divorce.

In many ways, legal separations are the functional equivalent of divorce. The key difference between legal separation and divorce, however, is that partners who are divorced can remarry, while partners who are merely separated—even legally separated—cannot remarry without obtaining a divorce. In addition, legal separation agreements or court decrees generally do not bring about the division of marital property or disturb rights to inheritances or pensions that arise out of the marriage relationship. Parties seeking a judicial resolution of these issues must generally obtain a divorce.

Separation Agreements. Many of the same issues confronting married partners seeking a divorce face partners contemplating separation. Questions to be resolved include who will have custody of the children, what visiting rights noncustodial parents will have, or whether one spouse will provide spousal or child support to the other. Partners seeking to formalize their separation must address these issues, and they typically do so by entering into a contract with each other. Such contracts spell out the details of separate living arrangements and are generally enforced by courts. Additionally, should separated marriage partners subsequently seek a divorce, the terms of

their separation agreement as to such matters as child custody and support are often merged into the final divorce decree.

In many contexts, courts grant parties great latitude in specifying the terms of their agreements. However courts refuse to enforce contracts obtained as a result of fraud or coercion. Additionally, courts sometimes decline to enforce contracts viewed as grossly unfair to one of the parties to the contract. Such contracts are typically referred to as "unconscionable." Separation agreements are subject to similar limits. Courts generally enforce such agreements as long as they are not obtained by fraud or coercion, are not grossly unfair to one of the marriage partners, and do not violate the best interest of the children.

If anything, courts tend to be more willing to upset the provisions of separation agreements thought to be unfair than to upset commercial contracts. This greater willingness to police separation agreements is not without reason. It arises out of an abiding conviction by many courts that society has an interest in assuring that children and the economically weaker of two marriage partners be provided for when a marriage terminates (as in divorce) or when married couples separate. In general, separation agreements are more likely to be enforced if both spouses are represented by attorneys who aid in negotiating and drafting such agreements. Moreover, when agreements deal with financial issues such as support payments by one spouse to another, they are more likely to be enforced when married partners fully disclose their respective financial affairs.

Separation Decrees. In some states, married partners wishing to formalize their separation arrangements by obtaining court orders may do so. Just as courts may finalize divorces with decrees that provide for matters such as child support, alimony, and visitation rights, separation decrees can deal with the same matters. The difference between separation agreements and separation decrees is that separation agreements can be more readily modified than court decrees. Couples obtain decrees by filing an action with the appropriate court asking the court to grant them legal separation.

Some jurisdictions require couples seeking a legal separation decree to prove that there are grounds for the separation. The more common trend is to grant legal separations without having to provide such proof. This trend is in keeping with the fact that divorces are more acceptable in the late twentieth century than in the past. Generally, courts issue decrees that accord with whatever agreements married partners reach concerning issues such as custody and support.

Advantages and Drawbacks. On one hand, separations—whether legal or informal—can offer spouses an opportunity to resolve marital difficulties short of divorce. Separations may create a temporary breathing space that gives married couples the perspective needed to surmount difficulties that might otherwise propel them to divorce. In cases in which separations evolve into divorce, however, they may also prepare spouses for the emotional turmoil of marital dissolution. Separations in such cases lengthen the process of terminating the marital relationship and spread the frequent emotional turmoil accompanying this termination across an extended period of time. In some cases, this gives marriage partners a greater period of time to adapt to the termination of their marriages. Moreover, separation agreements are generally easier to enter into and modify than divorce decrees. In jurisdictions that require proof of grounds for separation and divorce, it is generally easier to present proof sufficient to obtain a separation than to obtain a divorce.

On the other hand, legal separation may simply postpone the inevitable and increase legal fees. Negotiating and drafting separation agreements or obtaining separation decrees generally involves the assistance of attorneys. Since spouses generally consult attorneys to obtain a divorce, the end result may be to pay lawyers twice—once for the separation and once for the divorce. In addition, separation agreements and decrees do not generally alter certain legal rights based on the marriage relationship, such as inheritance and pension rights. A separated spouse may still be entitled to certain benefits upon the death of the other spouse. Finally, separation agreements or decrees usually do not contain provisions for a final division of marital property.   —*Timothy L. Hall*

BIBLIOGRAPHY

Crumbley, D. Larry, and Nicholas G. Apostolou. *Handbook of Financial Planning for Divorce and Separation.* New York: John Wiley & Sons, 1989.

Harwood, Norma. *A Woman's Legal Guide to Separation and Divorce in All Fifty States.* New York: Charles Scribner's Sons, 1985.

Price, Sharon J., and Patrick C. McKenry. *Divorce.* Newbury Park, Calif.: Sage Publications, 1988.

Sack, Steven Mitchell. *The Complete Legal Guide to Marriage, Divorce, Custody, and Living Together.* New York: McGraw-Hill, 1987.

Weiss, Robert S. *Marital Separation.* New York: Basic Books, 1975.

See also Alimony; Child custody; Child support; Divorce; Marriage laws; Separation anxiety; Visitation rights.

Life expectancy

RELEVANT ISSUES: Aging; Health and medicine; Sociology

SIGNIFICANCE: Life expectancy has had an enormous impact on how families function, and as life expectancy has dramatically increased in industrialized societies, family life and the care of the old and young has changed

Changes in life expectancy have had a dramatic impact on the rhythms of family life. With increased longevity have come changes in the timing of family events such as marriage, birth of a first child, departure of a last child, and grandparenthood. Longevity may also influence the strength of emotional bonds, making possible long-term attachments that were unheard of in colonial times. Conversely, the extended life span demands more of relationships. Marriages that might once have ended with a death are more likely to end in divorce. Golden anniversaries, once rare, have become commonplace. In colonial times, blended families were typically the result of death, most often of the mother. Modern blended families more often result from divorce. The resulting presence of noncustodial parents both extends and complicates family dynamics. These changes have produced tremendous variation in family histories and structures.

Life Expectancy: Gender and Ethnic Differences. Human life expectancy at birth has increased in both developing and developed nations. This is largely attributable to the widespread application of public health measures such as immunization and rehydration therapies for child-

Rapid increases in the number of older persons have imposed unprecedented demands on family caregivers. (James L. Shaffer)

hood diarrhea. These gains have clearly been most striking in developed nations. In the United States, for example, life expectancy during the colonial era is estimated to have been under forty years. By 1996 life expectancy in the United States was seventy-six years. That year Canadians enjoyed a somewhat higher life expectancy of seventy-nine years. Japan now enjoys the longest life expectancy, at just over seventy-nine years. Notably, life expectancy at age sixty has not increased dramatically. This suggests that the most significant health gains of this century have resulted in more people surviving childhood, not in an extension of the human life span.

Modern women enjoy longer life expectancy than men. In the United States and Canada this gender differential has consistently been about seven years. In 1997 the life expectancy for women born in the United States was 78.6 years and for men 71.8. Men once enjoyed longer life expectancies than women. This gender difference was reversed when the development of antibiotics and modern delivery techniques reduced women's risks of dying in childbirth.

The life expectancy of ethnic minorities has consistently lagged behind that of whites. In the United States the 1990 life expectancy for minorities was 72.9 years compared to 77.6 for whites. The gap is particularly striking when white men are compared to African American men. In 1980 white men had a life expectancy of 69.5 years at birth compared to 63.7 for African American men, a difference of 5.7 years. By 1990 that difference had increased to 8.2 years. That year white men had a life expectancy of 72.7 years compared to 64.5 for African American men. This dramatic increase has been attributed to homicide and other risks faced most often by African American men. It

Infant and Maternal Mortality Rates in the U.S., 1970-1989

Source: Bureau of the Census (1992)

has led community leaders to call on African American families to provide guidance and support to men.

With increased life expectancy most developed nations have also seen declining fertility rates. Indeed, the baby boom that affected the United States and Canada after World War II might be seen as more of a "blip" in a long-term trend of declining fertility. The Canadian fertility rate (the number of children a typical woman would have during her lifetime) dropped from 3.9 in 1960 to a 1990 low of 1.8. Figures for the United States are comparable, with a 1960 fertility rate of 3.4 that by 1990 had declined to 2.1, the replacement rate at which population equilibrium is maintained.

There are dramatic differences in fertility rates between developed and developing nations. In the less developed regions of the world fertility rates can be as high as 6 to 8 children per woman of childbearing age. In 1991 the highest fertility rate in the world was in Rwanda, an East African nation with 8.5 children per woman of childbearing age. Singapore (1.6) and Japan (1.8) have some of the world's lowest rates. Taken together, increased longevity and declining fertility rates have significant implications for family life.

Colonial Families: Short Life Expectancy in a Hostile Environment. On November 11, 1620, the *Mayflower* reached the coast of Cape Cod at the beginning a colonial period that would extend well into the following century. Any discussion of family life in this period must take into account class, region, and ethnicity. In their detailed examination of the history of family life in America, Steven Mintz and Susan Kellogg identified three subgroups among colonial families: Native Americans, African Americans, and European immigrants. All three groups faced the challenge of maintaining family ties in a hostile environment with short life expectancies.

Although all Native American groups used kinship as the basis for social organization, there was tremendous variation. Some tribes, like the Chey-enne, were patrilineal, with land-use rights and identification flowing through fathers. Others, like the Pueblo, were matrilineal. In these groups identification and inheritance came from moth-ers. Typically, Native American girls married early, between the ages of twelve and fifteen. Because of high infant mortality and the common practice of nursing babies for two or more years, most families were small. Contact with European immigrants radically decreased Native American life expec-tancy by exposing them to diseases and war.

African Americans under slavery experienced uneven gender ratios and suffered from extremely short life expectancy. In the early years of the slave trade three men were enslaved for every two women. A slave's life expectancy has been esti-mated at twenty-eight to thirty-two years. These two factors virtually precluded family life in the early years of slavery. However, women born in America had longer life expectancies than those born in Africa and thus had more opportunities to bear children. Although slave marriages lacked legal sanction in most areas, many couples estab-lished long-term bonds with immediate family and extended kin. Often these bonds did not require blood relationships. When children were sepa-rated from all blood relatives, they were raised by unrelated adults. Slave children were often taught to refer to adult slaves as "aunt" or "uncle." Thus kin and community were maintained. These strong ties enabled slaves to survive poverty, over-work, disease, and physical abuse, and they did not interfere with strong emotional ties to blood rela-tions. For decades after the end of the Civil War newspapers in the South ran lists of former slaves trying to reunite with their spouses and children.

Life expectancy and uneven sex ratios also marked the lives of European immigrants. Men greatly outnumbered women and, particularly in the South, life expectancies were extremely short. In seventeenth century Maryland only one third of all marriages lasted a decade. Parental death was more the norm than the exception, as George Washington's life illustrates. His father died when George was eleven, leaving the child to be raised by his half-brother. In the Chesapeake colonies two-thirds of all children lost one parent before their eighteenth birthdays; one-third lost both.

Despite their vast differences, these groups of families had some things in common. Marriages were strongly preferred, and monogamy the domi-nant form of relationship. However, marriages were short-lived. Infant mortality was high, so that families remained small despite the high birth rate. Parents who survived spent their entire adult lives raising children. A woman's first grandchild was frequently born before her last child, and her last child typically left home when the mother was in her early sixties, a little beyond her adult life expectancy. Thus, the generational transitions of modern times were not the norm. Parents were parents for the bulk of their adult lives and did not anticipate or fear the modern "empty nest."

Children and parents were more often sepa-rated by death in the seventeenth and eighteenth centuries. Both children and mothers were vulner-able. Surviving children of that time were less likely than modern children to be raised by a bio-logical parent. Thus, although divorce was uncom-mon, many children were raised in blended and stepfamilies or by maiden aunts.

Greater parental authority, particularly among Europeans, may have resulted from the agrarian economy. Prior to the industrial revolution a fam-ily's farm or property was the key source of income for parents and their children. Following the En-glish rule of primogeniture, the oldest son usually stood to inherit this property and with it a guaran-teed income for life. However, this inheritance depended on his not alienating his parents.

During the colonial era there were few elderly people. Benjamin Franklin lived well into his eighties. When he died in 1790, however, he had very few age peers. When Mother Theresa died in her eighties in 1997, she was part of a large and rapidly expanding age group.

Between Here and There: A World of Differ-ence. Since the colonial era, families have faced and adapted to a wide range of social and eco-nomic upheavals. While few of these were directly linked to the steady increase in human longevity, a brief review offers insight into how families might adapt. It is popular to blame the Industrial Revolu-tion for the destruction of the extended family. However, as Tamara Hareven argued in her book *Family Time and Industrial Time*, extended family households were more the exception than the rule in preindustrial times. Families often coped with the challenges of industrialization by calling upon the resources of extended kinship networks. The same applied to World Wars, depressions, and other major changes. Families tended to reside in nuclear households and call on extended kin for assistance in crises.

The 1950's stands out as an era of distinctly nuclear families. Amid unprecedented economic prosperity and with memories of the Great Depression and World War II, Americans and Canadians married in unusually high numbers and bore many babies. This baby boom has affected all major social institutions as it progresses along its life course. The 1950's were also unusual because of the low divorce rate. In essence, although they are now romanticized as "the way families should be," the 1950's were an anomaly. They were followed by an era during which gender roles were reexamined, wives and mothers entered the work force, sexual norms were hotly debated, and individual fulfillment surpassed family well-being as

the hallmark of success. In that context, human life expectancy has extended to unforeseen and unprecedented length.

Changing Rhythms and Varied Forms. As people live longer and have fewer children, the face of the modern family has changed. Simply put, the family is older. In place of dependent children, families now have dependent elders. Modern women can expect to spend more years of their lives caring for the elderly than they do for their children. Thus, whereas women may have focused previously on the education of the future generation, this focus has shifted to the care and sustenance of the previous one. Whereas retirement security once came from children, in recent times it comes from Social Security.

Increased longevity affords both women and men greater flexibility in the timing of major family events. In the 1990's a growing number of professional women chose to postpone the birth of

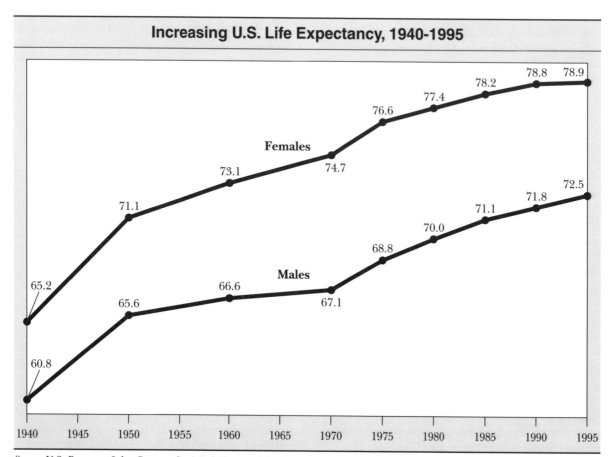

Increasing U.S. Life Expectancy, 1940-1995

Source: U.S. Bureau of the Census, *Statistical Abstract of the United States: 1997.* Washington, D.C.: GPO, 1997.

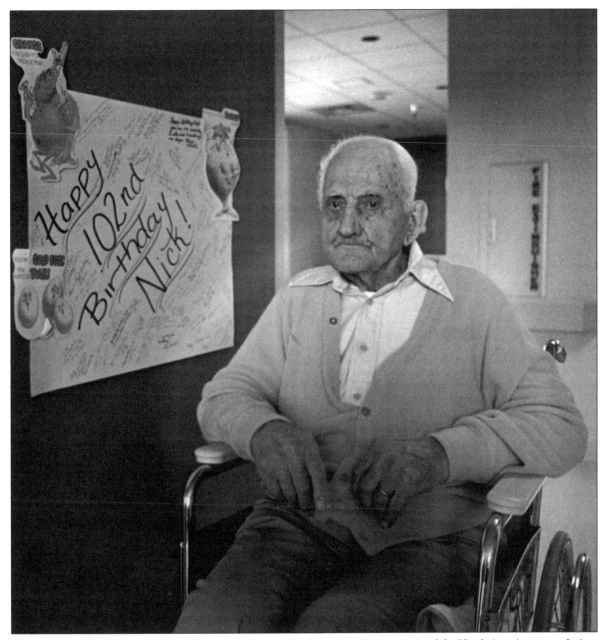

Persons more than a hundred years old make up one of the fastest-growing segments of the North American population. (James L. Shaffer)

their first child until their late thirties and early forties. At the same time other women bear children in their early twenties. Some women are becoming grandparents while their age peers are rearing toddlers, and a growing number elect to remain childless or "child-free." In recent years the proportion of women who remain childless has increased dramatically. In the United States in 1996, 42 percent of women aged fifteen to forty-four had no children. These women and their partners have made it necessary to reconsider what constitutes a family.

The modern family, like that of colonial times, is characterized by diversity. Individuals who do not live in traditional nuclear families often include unmarried partners and children of friends. This strategy is reminiscent of the bonds that enabled African Americans to survive slavery and oppression.

Increased longevity challenges families to care for the elderly and provide them with meaningful roles. It also forces marriages that might once have ended in death to close with divorce. Its net effect is the presence of more adults (grandparents and noncustodial parents) in the lives of children. Whether those adults will drain resources away from children or offer support and guidance to the young will depend on individual and cultural factors yet to be determined.

—*Amanda Smith Barusch*

BIBLIOGRAPHY

Bould, S., B. Sanborn, and L. Reif. *Eighty-Five Plus: The Oldest Old.* Belmont, Calif: International Thomson Publishing, 1989. Reports on an ethnographic study conducted in a home for the elderly in London and offers a detailed description of the needs and abilities of the fastest-growing population group in developed nations: the very old.

Caplow, Theodore, et al. *Middletown Families: Fifty Years of Change and Continuity.* Minneapolis: University of Minnesota Press, 1982. Reports on a follow-up study of a small industrial city first investigated in the mid-1920's and describes the continuity and change in family life while refuting the myth that families have deteriorated.

Cherlin, A. J., and F. F. Furstenberg. *The New American Grandparent: A Place in the Family, A Life Apart.* New York: Basic Books, 1986. Examines how the role of grandparenting is experienced in the context of modern families, based on hundreds of interviews with grandparents.

Haber, Carole. *Beyond Sixty-Five: The Dilemma of Old Age in America's Past.* New York: Cambridge University Press, 1983. Examines the status of the elderly in colonial times and identifies changes in the patterning of individual life transitions such as marriage, birth, and death.

Hareven, Tamara K. *Family Time and Industrial Time: The Relationship Between the Family and Work in a New England Industrial Community.* Cambridge, England: Cambridge University Press, 1982. Explores family and work in the social history of the Amoskeag mills in Manchester, New Hampshire, refuting the notion that industrialization destroyed the three-generation family while demonstrating how families adapted to and helped shape industrial development.

Mintz, Steven, and Susan Kellogg. *Domestic Revolutions: A Social History of Domestic Family Life.* New York: Free Press, 1987. Presents a detailed review of the values that influenced family life in the United States from the arrival of the Mayflower to the present and argues that modern families are characterized by their diversity and a lack of unified ideals or standards.

Moody, H. R. *Abundance of Life: Human Development Policies for an Aging Society.* New York: Columbia University Press, 1988. Argues that the aging of society need not be a gloomy prospect and details alternatives to modern policies that address the needs of the elderly.

See also Death; Euthanasia; Family demographics; Gender longevity; Social Security; Widowhood.

Lineage

RELEVANT ISSUES: Kinship and genealogy; Marriage and dating

SIGNIFICANCE: Lineage is a relationship of ongoing, small groups of relatives who claim descent from a common ancestor, from whom they trace themselves through genealogies

Lineage groups usually trace their ancestors through unilineal genealogies, which—as the name implies—trace ancestry through a single patrilineal or matrilineal line. In patrilineal genealogies sons trace their ancestry from their fathers to their fathers' fathers and so on. In matrilineal genealogies daughters trace their ancestry from their mothers to their mothers' mothers and so on.

Lineage groups are corporate in that they continue on after the deaths of their elder members. Consequently, these groups can accumulate and pass down property, coordinate activities of their members, assign status to individuals within the group, and negotiate with other groups. They are typically exogamous—that is, their members marry outside the group, thus curbing competition for marriage partners within the lineage and building alliances with other groups. They may exist within larger kin groups called clans, in which case a lineage is the smallest unit. They typically live close together.

As lineage groups grow, they may split into clans. Clan members may or may not be able to say how they are related. When they attempt to do so, they may employ a second type of genealogy, called a segmentary lineage. Segmentary lineages attempt to rank various families or clans covered by the genealogy. They do so by tracing not only persons' direct ancestors, but their ancestor's siblings back to a real or fictional common ancestor.

Four generations of a matrilineal line. (James L. Shaffer)

In Western societies, lineage is traced through both parents. In theory, one is equally related to all family members on mothers' and fathers' sides of the family. Relatives go back lineally to all eight great grandparents and reach out laterally to distant cousins. In just a few generations, a person's family tree contains many branches. Because such groups are too unwieldy to function socially, families reduce their active kin to smaller groups of maternal and paternal relatives, rarely stretching beyond first cousins once removed and second cousins. Such groups usually correspond to the relatives one might invite to a North American wedding.

In North American society many people have begun to trace their maternal and paternal lineages. Computerized birth, marriage, and death records have facilitated information gathering, analysis and storage. The geographical spread of modern families may have contributed to this interest in family genealogies, because this spread curbs or in some cases renders impossible the transmission of family traditions from generation to generation. Simple curiosity or the death of a parent or sibling may spur persons' interest in discovering their family past. Membership in voluntary organizations, such as the Daughters of the American Revolution or the Church of Jesus Christ of Latter-day Saints, may also prompt people to trace their lineage.   —*Paul L. Redditt*

See also Bilateral descent; Clans; Extended families; Family albums and records; Family History Library; Family trees; Matrilineal descent; Moiety; Parallel cousins; Patrilineal descent; Tribes.

Literature and families

RELEVANT ISSUES: Marriage and dating; Parenting and family relationships; Race and ethnicity

SIGNIFICANCE: In American literature the family has mirrored the development of an American identity, the effects of slavery and racism on society, the assimilation of immigrants, and the stress of modern life on the traditional family structure

The idea of the family has been a central image throughout the history of American literature. In keeping with the individualistic nature of the American character, the family has often been the confine against which protagonists must rebel or from which they must escape in order to find their own identity. However, the literary depiction of the family unit and individuals' place in it also reflect certain philosophical and social constructs of the culture and time during which literary works have been written.

Native American Creation Myths. The literary traditions of the indigenous peoples of North America were oral in nature: They were sung and recited in long narratives at rituals and ceremonies. The words arose from the community and were preserved and modulated from generation to generation and from storyteller to storyteller. One type of North American creation story is the gestation myth. In the Iroquois creation story, the Earth Diver, a woman of the celestial world, conceives twins. When they are near birth, her body sinks down into the lower world of dark waters, where a turtle offering her a seat grows into an island of earth. The twin brothers, the good mind and the bad mind, are the active agents of creation, but the story requires the participation of the mother and the turtle as well as the twins. The central role of the mother reflects the matrilineal orientation of the Iroquois, while the importance of the turtle in the creation of the earth underscores the familial connection between animal persons and human persons and the interaction of the twins reveals both the creative power of the human mind and its limitations. Similarly, the Navajo creation myth, the *Diné Bahane*, although an emergence myth rather than a gestation myth, emphasizes the interaction of the animal people families with the holy people to create the first man and the first woman from two ears of corn. Their daughter, Changing Woman, produces her own set of twins, who slay the monsters that plague the people on this earth. In the Native American tradition the interconnection of all living things on earth is almost always seen within the context of familial relationships.

Colonial Literature. The earliest works of American literature arising from the European colonization of the Americas were accounts of exploration, descriptions of discovered lands and their inhabitants, and reports of encounters with the indigenous peoples. In the Pocahontas story by Captain John Smith, included in his *General*

Idealized portrait of Pocahontas made during her visit to England. (Library of Congress)

History of Virginia (1624), a young Indian princess defies her father, Chief Powhatan, to save the English explorer. Smith's account may well have been modeled on Garcilaso de la Vega's story of Juan de Ortiz, who, seventy years earlier, had been captured by hostile Indians on the Gulf Coast of Florida and saved from death by the cacique's daughter. He lived among the Indians for eleven years, learning their language, until Hernando de Soto's expedition rescued him in 1539. Whether the rescues of Ortiz and Smith were true or invented, the motif of the Indian princess preserving the European explorer has provided powerful imagery for the American imagination. It symbolizes two interwoven shifts in familial identification: Native Americans' rejection of traditional familial

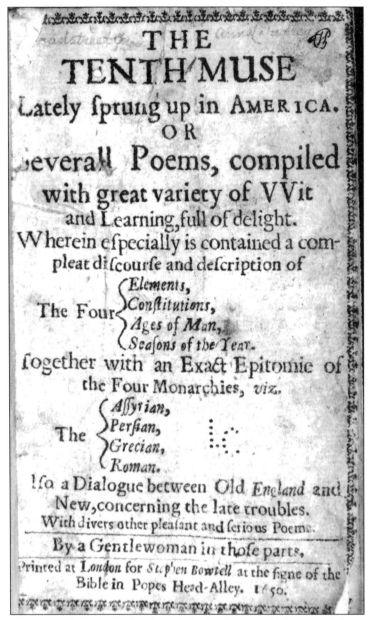

Title page from Anne Bradstreet's book of poetry. (Library of Congress)

Anne Bradstreet came with her family and husband in 1630 to join the Puritan settlement in the Massachusetts colony. Although a member of the ruling elite, Bradstreet, as a woman, was subject to the strongly patriarchal orientation of the Puritans, which disapproved of strong-minded women expressing their views. A devoted daughter, wife, and the mother of eight children, as well as the first significant American poet, she combined theological and domestic inspiration to chronicle her new life in America. In her best known poem, "The Author to Her Book" (1650), she laments that her book is "an ill-formed offspring of my feeble brain," which was snatched from her side by unwise but well-meaning friends and thrust upon the world. Upon the "child's" return to its mother, she attempts to clean it up but is dismayed by the flaws she cannot rectify. Bradstreet's rather sardonic summary both reflects and rebels against the Puritan tenets regarding children. She sees her book as flawed, hobbling, and dirty (as a child born into sin) and in need of parental correction. However, despite her protests the reader senses a strong affection for it on its wayward path. "In Reference to Her Children, 23. June, 1656" more directly recounts her vigilant care and concern for the well-being of her four daughters and four sons. Bradstreet broke the silence imposed upon women by the patriarchal Puritan tradition while conforming to her society's religious traditions. She insists upon the importance of the mother's nurturing role, going so far in her *Meditations* to liken God's care for humankind to that of a mother for her children.

In a particularly American literary genre, the Captivity Narrative, the authors relate their experiences at the hands of Indian captors. There is a major dichotomy between Providence Tales, in authority by embracing the new civilization (wish fulfillment on the part of the Europeans) and Europeans' adoption of a new motherland as represented by the Indian princess. These stories underline a basic American belief in identity by consent rather than descent: The family or identity into which one is born is less important than the family or identity one chooses.

which the captives praise God for their deliverance from the heathen savages and for their return to their Christian families, and white Indian Tales, in which the captives remain with their captors, choosing to become part of their adoptive Indian families. In the first published story, *A Narrative of the Captivity and Restoration of Mrs. Mary Rowlandson, Or The Sovereignty and Goodness of God* (1682), Mary Rowlandson relates the capture of herself and her three children from Lancaster, Massachusetts, in 1676. For eleven weeks they traveled with Wampanoag warriors and their families during King Philip's War. During their captivity, Rowlandson was separated from her two elder children, and her youngest daughter died in her arms. Eventually ransomed, Rowlandson attributed her return to her community and family to the power of God, but she also saw in her experience the chastising hand of God calling her, her family, and society to dependence and obedience.

Nearly as popular as Rowlandson's narrative was *The Redeemed Captive, Returning to Zion* (1707) by fellow Puritan John Williams. During a 1704 Iroquois raid on Deerfield, Massachusetts, Williams's wife and two youngest children were killed, and he and five of his children were captured and brought to Canada. Williams was held captive by Indians for eight weeks and by the French for two years. Like Rowlandson, Williams and his children, except for the youngest daughter Eunice, were ransomed. When Williams tried to reclaim Eunice, she refused to leave her adoptive Indian family, and by 1713 she had converted to Roman Catholicism and married an Indian. Throughout his narrative, Williams continually emphasizes his attempts to regain his children and complains both about the efforts (and frequent successes) of the Jesuits to convert the captives to Roman Catholicism and the strong affection that many captives felt for their adopted Indian families.

Early American Literature. Post-Revolutionary literature often uses the paradigm of the family as a tool to explore the emergence of an American identity and posit an ideal of the American character. The subject of relationships between white Americans and Native Americans continues to be an important one, as does an examination of the plight of African Americans.

Although James Fenimore Cooper's *The Last of the Mohicans* (1826) is set during the French and Indian Wars, the central problem of the novel is more closely related to the issue of European American domination of the new country and President James Monroe's policy of Indian removal, formulated in 1824. More than seventy novels were published between 1812 and 1860

James Fenimore Cooper. (Library of Congress)

dealing with Indian-white relations. In almost all of them, whites marry whites, bad Indians are destroyed, and good Indians fade away with no descendants. The theme is both elegiac and triumphant: The noble savage gives way to the civilized Christian. Thus, in Cooper's novel the daughters of the Scottish Colonel Munro cannot marry Indians. Alice is rescued from Huron captivity to marry Heywood. Cora is loved by Uncas, son of the Mohican Chingachgook, and is captured by the Huron-turned-Mohawk Magua to replace his dead wife. When faced with death or marriage to Magua, Cora leaps from a cliff. Both Uncas and Magua die in the subsequent battle. Buried separately, Cora and Uncas can only be united in imagination. Cooper respects the native American traditions and culture but insists that relative harmony in the new republic can only succeed upon the recognition of the traditional distinctions between races, nationalities, sexes and religions.

Unlike *The Last of the Mohicans*, Catharine Maria Sedgwick's novel *Hope Leslie* (1827) countenances marriage between whites and Indians. The protagonist's sister, Faith Leslie, captured in childhood by Mohawks, marries an Indian and refuses to return to the Puritan community when offered the chance. Throughout her novels, which include *Redwood* (1824) and *The Linwoods, Or "Sixty Years Since in America"* (1835), Sedgwick's sympathies lie with prisoners, slaves, and members of minority groups—not only Native Americans, but also members of such religious groups as the Quakers and Shakers. A single woman, she creates independent female protagonists who exhibit bravery and generosity toward their siblings, yet who almost always find marriage as their goal and reward.

Slave Narratives. The European explorations—from Christopher Columbus's voyages to the expeditions of Vasco Núñez de Balboa, Juan Ponce de León, Hernán Cortés and Pedro Menéndez de Avilés—and the French excursions into the Great Lakes region included both white and black explorers. However, the horror of slavery arrived in Jamestown, Virginia, in 1619, with the arrival of twenty Africans who were classified as indentured servants. By the 1620's the system of the enslavement of African captives had taken hold in the British colonies. The captive Africans, torn away from their families in Africa and separated from their families at the whim of slaveholders in the United States, resisted their enslavement by creating an African-based culture in the New World that allowed them to affirm their humanity and create possibilities for escape, both actual and spiritual. To rouse antislavery support from white Americans and sway their white audiences, educated African-Americans turned to European forms, incorporating biblical rhetoric and symbolism.

In the mid-nineteenth century, accounts of successful escapes from slavery became the most popular features of newspapers and magazines, and slave narratives filled hundreds of books. These stories, published to elicit abolitionist sympathy and outrage, not only informed the public

Abolitionist Frederick Douglass. (Library of Congress)

about the conditions of slavery and gave a voice to the oppressed, but also became the foundation of the modern African American novel. Central both to the description of slavery and the slaves' desire for freedom was the condition of the family under the slave system as practiced in North America. In *Narrative of the Life of Frederick Douglass: An American Slave* (1845), Frederick Douglass relates the disruption of any family life under a system that viewed childbearing as analogous to animal breeding, useful only for increasing the wealth of the slaveholders. He describes his own early separation from his mother and the nearly insurmountable difficulties he faced in sustaining familial relationships and nurturance under economic conditions driven by slavery.

Harriet Jacobs, using the pseudonym of Linda Brent, details in *Incidents in the Life of a Slave Girl, Written by Herself* (1861) the sexual pressures facing even a somewhat privileged and educated female slave. When she refused the sexual advances of her master, he denied her request to marry a free black man. Revengeful and seeking to escape from her master's unwanted attentions and his wife's jealousy, "Linda" became the mistress of another white man, who, she hoped, would protect her children from the fate of slavery. In a desperate attempt to protect her two children from the clutches of her jealous master and mistress, "Linda" ran away and spent years hiding in the crawl space of her grandmother's house, where she could hear her children and sew for them, although they were ignorant of her presence. She eventually escaped to New York and recovered her children, who had been purchased by their father. Jacobs's account, borrowing from the traditions of the nineteenth century domestic novel and the popular slave narrative, was written to convince an audience of white women to become involved in the abolitionist movement.

From Domestic Literature to Realism. The early nineteenth century New England Transcendentalist intellectuals and writers, heavily influenced by the English Romantics, tended to find inspiration and value in individuals' own encounter with nature and their own inner enlightenment. They opposed the rampant materialism of Jacksonian democracy and experimented with communal forms of living. As Henry David Thoreau became a hermit at Walden Pond, Bronson Alcott attempted

to establish a communal utopia at Brook Farm, which Nathaniel Hawthorne satirized in *Blithedale Romance* (1852). Meanwhile, Ralph Waldo Emerson preached "self-reliance." Although the notion of individualism seems to have triumphed in nineteenth century America, the concept was not without its critics, who feared that too much individualism easily led to selfishness and a disregard for the public good. Alexis de Tocqueville, author of *Democracy in America* (1835-1840), warned that such democratic individualism could

> make every man forget his ancestors, it hides his descendants and separates his contemporaries from him; it throws him back forever upon himself alone and threatens in the end to confine him entirely with the solitude of his own heart.

Such is the individualism of Herman Melville's Captain Ahab in *Moby Dick* (1851), who not only leaves his wife to search for the white whale, but also separates himself from the ship's family to follow his obsession. The question of how to balance the claims of individualism and community has been central to the development of American culture and philosophy.

The domestic literature of the nineteenth century, written mainly by women for a female audience, is often dismissed from the literary canon. However, these novels—based on the everyday experience of American families and reflecting modern concerns about the stability of families, the role of women in society, and the care of orphaned children—not only were extremely popular (more so than the novels of Hawthorne or Melville), but also paved the way for the literary realism and naturalism of the late nineteenth and early twentieth centuries.

Harriet Beecher Stowe's novel *Uncle Tom's Cabin* (1852) sold 10,000 copies in the first few days and 300,000 copies in the first year. The stage versions made it the most performed story in the nineteenth century, both in the United States and throughout the world. The popularity of Stowe's novel rests on its affirmation of two cherished beliefs in North American culture: the sanctity of the family and the possibility of redemption through Christian love. Because slaves were treated as property rather than as human beings, the system of slavery implicitly denied their possession of souls. Such denial not only steeped the slaveholders in sin, but also destroyed the foundation of human society, which rested upon the institution of the family. The image of Eliza, with her babe in her arms, running away from the slave catchers across the ice floes of a river, proved a powerful weapon in the battle to convince the American public of the evils of slavery.

Countering Stowe's antislavery stance and defending the agrarian, communal life of Southern plantations, Southern domestic novelists such as Caroline Gilman, Caroline Hentz, Maria McIntosh, and Augusta Evans contrasted the coldness of Northern industrial wage slavery with the noblesse oblige of Southern planters. In these novels the system of slavery resembles an idealized feudal system in which the master and mistress of the plantation assume the responsibility of civilizing, Christianizing, and caring for a "subservient and benighted race." This carefully constructed social and class structure prevented the Northern plague of individualistic greed from infecting the South. An idealized version of the extended family of the Southern plantation, the Southern domestic novel was revived with the twentieth century success of Margaret Mitchell's *Gone with the Wind* (1936).

After the Civil War domestic novelists set their sights on the negotiations of women and children with the larger society. The plight of the orphan became a staple, particularly in literature that targeted younger readers as well as adults. Louisa May Alcott played on this theme in many of her novels, often contrasting orphans being raised by wealthy relatives with those less fortunate, who were thrown to the mercies of charity or forced into the labor market. Rose, the orphan-protagonist of *Eight Cousins* (1875), has been taken in by her two doting great aunts and a bachelor doctor uncle, who have modern ideas about raising girls to be well educated and physically strong. However, in the kitchen of this privileged household, Phoebe, a girl of about the same age as Rose, toils as a housemaid.

Mark Twain's *The Adventures of Tom Sawyer* (1876) and *Adventures of Huckleberry Finn* (1884) also contrast the cared-for, somewhat domesticated orphan Tom with his less fortunate and wilder friend Huck. Thoroughly nurtured by Aunt Polly, Tom is happy to return home from his adventures while Huck, abused and abandoned by

his father, finds temporary companionship with the escaped slave Jim, while resisting the attractions of numerous mother surrogates who want to take him in and "sivilize" him. Huck seems destined to remain the eternal orphan, skirting the edges of society as he "lights out for the Territory."

A different kind of orphaning, imposed by white American society upon Indian children, was described by Zitkala-Ša (Gertrude Simmons Bonnin) in three autobiographical essays titled "Impressions of an Indian Childhood," "The School Days of an Indian Child," and "An Indian Teacher Among Indians," published in the *Atlantic Monthly* in 1900. Brought up on a Sioux reservation until she was eight years old, Zitkala-Ša was sent to a Quaker missionary school for American Indians in Wabash, Indiana. At this boarding school, which, like others, was founded to educate Indian children, the students were forced to have their long hair cut, to wear white society's clothing, and to give up their own language for English. Separated from their families and their cultures, the children faced overwhelming disorientation; many pined away and some even committed suicide. Zitkala-Ša survived, spending a short time teaching at another such school, but she became indignantly aware of her estrangement both from her mother and from the dominant white society in which she remained an outsider. Her experiences led her to social activism to improve the lot of Native Americans and to preserve Native American culture.

Traditional family responsibilities and social demands conflict with the need of both men and women to live as discrete and independent individuals in the novels and stories of authors conveying local color, such as Sarah Orne Jewett, Mary E. Wilkins Freeman, Kate Chopin, and Charles Chesnutt; of social realists such as William Dean Howells and Hamlin Garland; of psychological realists such as William James and Edith Wharton; and of naturalists such as Stephen Crane and Theodore Dreiser. This conflict played itself out against the backdrop of radical shifts in American culture: from a rural, agrarian lifestyle to an urban, industrialized one; from a society dominated by a patriarchal system to one in which women claimed their voices and legal place; from a country in which the frontier seemed nearly limitless to one whose spacious vistas were being filled with a growing population fed both by increasing prosperity and massive immigration; and from a nation whose international presence was minor to one that was becoming a major world power. All of these shifts impacted the dynamics and stability of the family as reflected in modern literature.

Immigrant Families. The pattern of immigrant family novels most often follows that of generational conflict. Parents come to America searching for prosperity while trying to preserve traditional ethnic values. The children, more fluent in English than their parents, often have to serve as translators and bridges to the new world but are restrained by their parents from adopting its values. The children rebel, yet feel the loss of their rich cultural heritage. The path of assimilation is fraught with contradictions and ambivalence. Anzia Yezierska's *Bread Givers* (1925), subtitled "A Struggle Between a Father of the Old World and a Daughter of New," chronicles the struggle of a young Eastern European Jewish woman to free herself from the bonds of a patriarchal family to become educated. Children of Chinese immigrants, such as Maxine Hong Kingston, who wrote *Warrior Woman* (1976), and Amy Tan, who wrote *The Joy-Luck Club* (1989), counterpoint immigrant mothers' memories with daughters' difficulties in integrating into mainstream American life. Born in Cuba, exiles from Fidel Castro's regime such as Virgil Suarez, who wrote *Latin Jazz* (1989), and Christina Garcia, who wrote *Dreaming in Cuban* (1992), explore how the dislocation and frustrations of political exile interweave with the fabric of family life. Becoming American while retaining ethnic identities is the common thread stitching together immigrant literature.

Family Sagas. The history and discovery of ancestors defines the American family saga. The television adaptation of Alex Haley's *Roots* (1976), which traces his family back to the captured Afri-

Maxine Hong Kingston in 1991. (San Francisco Chronicle)

can Kunta Kinte, held Americans transfixed in front of their television sets when the miniseries was broadcast in 1977. *Roots* is, perhaps, the most popular example of this type of literature, but more complex and less celebratory versions have been crafted by such writers as William Faulkner, Toni Morrison, and Louise Erdrich. Faulkner's Yoknapatawpha County families, including the McCaslins, Comptons, Snopses, and Sartorises, reveal the depth, breadth, and confusion of the American experience, particularly as it was lived in the South. As Faulkner reveals hidden incest, miscegenation, and exploitation in his white, Native

Toni Morrison in the early 1990's. (Maria Mulas)

kind of self-murder, Toni Morrison requires her characters and readers to contemplate such horrific acts as a mother's murder of her child in *Beloved* (1988) and the desecration of a teenage girl's corpse by the crazed wife of the girl's middle-aged lover-murderer in *Jazz* (1992). In Morrison's novels, it is only through the reaffirmation of familial bonds and love, through self-examination and truth-telling that salvation can be found. Louise Erdrich's quartet of novels, *Love Medicine* (1984), *The Beet Queen* (1986), *Tracks* (1988), and *The Bingo Palace* (1994), which employ traditional techniques from the Native American storytelling cycle, depicts the lives of three generations of Chippewa families living on the Turtle Mountain Reservation in North Dakota. She weaves together ancient tribal knowledge with ongoing twentieth century oppression to reveal the paths of survival for Native American families. Each of these authors uses multiple viewpoints and relies on oral traditions to invite the reader into the family of listeners. To participate in each particular familial experience, one must enter the storyteller's world and understand its conventions.

Another invitation to participate in the drama of American families is extended from the stages of American theaters all across the country. With the rise of realistic theater at the end of the nineteenth century, the stage became the venue for domestic drama. Eugene O'Neill recast tragic Greek family dramas into homespun American clothes. O'Neill resets Aeschylus's *Oresteia*, a cycle of family murder and revenge in the aftermath of the Trojan War, as *Mourning Becomes Electra* (1931) at the end of the Civil War. Euripides' *Hippolytus*, the tale of a queen's illicit passion for her stepson, becomes *Desire Under the Elms* (1924), in which a young New England wife seduces her stepson, hoping to conceive a child. O'Neill also used the stage to explore

American, and African American familial histories, he forces both his characters and readers to examine the social, historical, and personal forces that have defined them as individuals. Only in the recognition of these forces can individuals make moral choices. Thus, when Isaac McCaslin in *Go Down, Moses* (1942) discovers his grandfather's African American descendants, he rejects his claim to the family plantation and the guilt of slavery attached to it.

In the framework of historical oppression and the dissolution of familial support that leads to a the failure of his own family in *Long Day's Journey into Night* (1941, 1956) and *A Moon for the Misbegotten* (1943, 1952). He described his one light-hearted play, *Ah, Wilderness!* (1933), which celebrates the American family, as the story of "a boyhood I never had."

Following O'Neill's success, Arthur Miller and Tennessee Williams used family dynamics to explore the tensions tearing away at twentieth century family life. In *Death of a Salesman* (1949) and *All My Sons* (1947), Miller reveals the fatal effects of materialistic ambition on the integrity of the family. Williams reveals how loneliness, sexual anxiety, and hypocrisy inhibit family members from communicating with each other in such plays as *The Glass Menagerie* (1944) and *Cat on a Hot Tin Roof* (1955).

Racism and the struggle for civil rights challenge the families in the dramas of Lorraine Hansberry and August Wilson. Hansberry's landmark *A Raisin in the Sun* (1959) tells the story of an African American family integrating a white Chicago neighborhood during the Civil Rights era. Wilson, in a series of plays set in different decades, continues to record the twentieth century African American experience, especially as it has been lived by working-class families. In *The Piano Lesson* (1987) the focus is a piano with the carved image of Boy Willie and Bereneice's slave ancestors, who had been traded for the piano. Carved by their great-grandfather and retrieved by their father, the piano becomes a source of conflict between the siblings. For Wilson, it represents the memory, culture, and heritage essential to the integrity of the African American family.

When one examines American literature, Leo Tolstoy's maxim in *Anna Karenina* (1875-1877) that "All happy families are alike, but an unhappy family is unhappy after its own fashion," does not really hold true. The varieties of happiness and unhappiness are rivaled only by the varieties of families and their experiences. What does hold true is that through the eyes of literature one sees that the family, despite its strains, remains the cornerstone of social discourse. —*Jane Anderson Jones*

BIBLIOGRAPHY

Baker, Houston A., Jr., ed. *Three American Literatures: Essays in Chicano, Native American, and*

Playwright Arthur Miller in the late 1980's. (Inge Morath/ Magnum)

Asian-American Literature for Teachers of American Literature. New York: The Modern Language Association of America, 1982. Collection of essays with overviews of cultural literary traditions and a detailed analysis of particular works.

Hill, Patricia Liggins, et al. *Call and Response: The Riverside Anthology of the African-American Literary Tradition.* Boston: Houghton Mifflin, 1998. Comprehensive and chronological anthology of African American literature emphasizing a distinct African American literary aesthetic grounded in African oral traditions and preserved through the experience of slavery in America.

Owens, Louis. *Other Destinies: Understanding the American Indian Novel.* Norman, Okla.: University of Oklahoma Press, 1992. Critical analysis of the novels written between 1874 and 1990 by Native Americans, dealing with their relationship to traditional oral literature and how they differ from mainstream American literature.

Perosa, Sergio. *American Theories of the Novel: 1793-1903.* New York: The Gotham Library of New York University Press, 1985. Traces the history of the American novel from its first appearance at the end of the eighteenth century through attempts to nationalize the form in the nineteenth century to its place in the early twentieth century as the premier literary form.

Sollors, Werner. *Beyond Ethnicity: Consent and Descent in American Culture.* New York: Oxford University Press, 1986. Posits that the conflict of self-identification by descent (heredity, ethnic background) versus consent (marriage, assimilation) has welded Americans into one people, despite the periodic exaggeration of differences.

Tompkins, Jane. *Sensational Designs: The Cultural Work of American Fiction 1790-1860.* New York: Oxford University Press, 1985. Reexamination of the works of such authors as Charles Brockden Brown, James Fenimore Cooper, Harriet Beecher Stowe, and Susan Bogert Warner in the light of their impact upon societal attitudes.

See also Art and iconography; Childhood history; Children's literature; Cultural influences; Family: concept and history; Film depictions of families; Haley, Alex; Moral education; Myths and storytelling; Television depictions of families; Vengeance in families.

Living wills

RELEVANT ISSUES: Health and medicine; Law
SIGNIFICANCE: A living will is a directive to physicians giving directions as to what methods of life-prolonging medical treatment should or should not be used when individuals have a terminal condition and become unable to make their wishes known

Living wills are not wills in the traditional sense. Traditional wills do not take effect until after persons die. Living wills come into effect while individuals are still alive but are unable to make their wishes known (for example, if they are in a coma) or when they do not have the mental ability to legally make their wishes known (for example, if they have Alzheimer's disease or dementia). Living wills are also known as medical directives or directives to physicians. Living wills are directives to physicians and other health care personnel to perform or not to perform certain life-sustaining medical treatments that artificially prolong life, such as resuscitation, force feeding, or breathing assistance. Persons may also say that they want drug therapy to alleviate pain. Living wills are valid only in the case of terminal illnesses in most states, and in some states doctors are permitted only to withhold treatment.

Over the years the right to die with dignity and without the expense of large medical bills has been discussed by federal and state legislators. The U.S. Supreme Court in *Cruzan v. Director, Missouri Department of Health* (1990) decided that individuals have the right to control their medical treatment. Individuals' desires come first, even if they choose to forgo life-prolonging medical treatment while family members or physicians want to prolong life. Sometimes individuals can make such decisions themselves. For example, they can ask to be discharged from the hospital and return home. However, when persons near the end of an illness or are involved in severe accidents, they are often no longer capable of making their wishes known. It is in such circumstances that living wills take effect, directing physicians to take or not to take action. Physicians who are not willing to abide by individuals' wishes must turn such cases over to other physicians.

Because accidents can happen to persons of all

ages, living wills are not just for the elderly. It is easy to make a living will. Most hospitals and physicians have standard forms that have been approved by the state. When people are admitted to the hospital, they are usually asked if they have a living will. If not, they will be given the opportunity to make one. If they have specific wishes, they may decide to have attorneys draw up a living will.

One of the problems with living wills is that persons must decide in advance, without taking

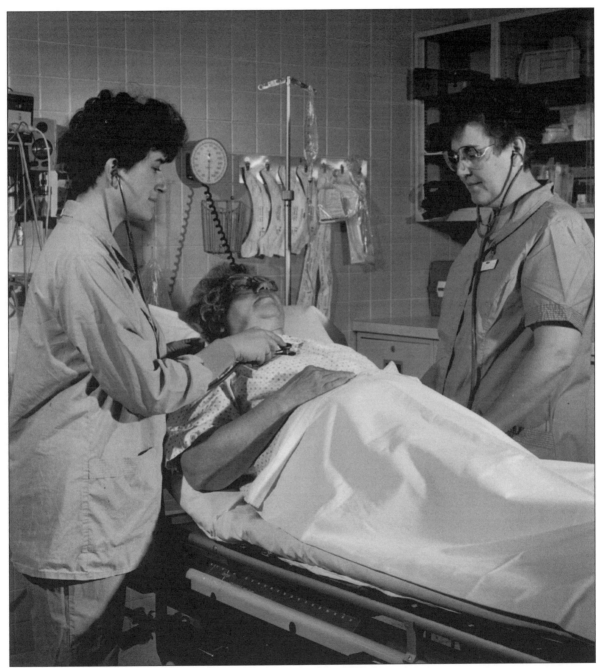

One problem of living wills is that patients must make life-or-death decisions in advance of receiving treatments, without knowing what circumstances may develop. (James L. Shaffer)

future circumstances into account. Another problem with them is that they only take effect when patients' condition is terminal. Persons in the early stages of Alzheimer's disease, although not terminally ill, may not be mentally fit to make health care decisions. A durable power of attorney for health care or health care proxies allows individuals to deal with all these problems.

—*Celia Ray Hayhoe*

See also Aging and elderly care; Alzheimer's disease; Family caregiving; Family law; Health problems; Nursing and convalescent homes; Sandwich generation; Wills and bequests.

Love

RELEVANT ISSUES: Divorce; Marriage and dating; Parenting and family relationships

SIGNIFICANCE: Love affects the psychological and physical development of children and adolescents and profoundly influences the course of individual adult and family life

Love can be discussed from any number of perspectives, drawing upon investigations in anthropology, philosophy, psychoanalysis, psychology, sociobiology, and sociology. It can be studied by analyzing the myths, sagas, poetry, drama, novels, and song which throughout history have chronicled how the power of love unites and sometimes divides people. As early as the sixth century B.C.E. the Greek poet Sappho wrote love lyrics which, in turn, inspired Ovid (43 B.C.E. to 18 C.E.) to create his erotic love poems. The tales of historic lovers, tragic lovers, and great love affairs continue to fascinate us and inspire creativity.

Forms of Love. The word "love" is derived from the Old English word *lufu*. Love assumes many forms. To distinguish between them the ancient Greeks used several words: *eros*, for erotic or romantic love; *agape*, for altruistic and unselfish love; *philia*, for love between friends; *pragma*, for logical love; and *storge*, for affectionate love. The view of love depicted in Plato's ancient work *Symposium* has profoundly influenced the Western world. Plato argued that love is always directed toward what is good, and in loving something a person seeks to possess the goodness in it. Plato distinguished between love and sex. For him, the highest form of love was predominantly intellectual, employing the senses of sight and sound rather than touch or smell. Hundreds of years later this attitude was expressed in courtly love. By the time of the Italian Renaissance, "platonic love" had come to signify a pure, spiritual relationship.

Between 1985 and 1986 broadcast journalist Bill Moyers interviewed the anthropologist Joseph Campbell for a television series called *The Power of Myth*. He asked Campbell where they should begin a discussion about love. Campbell replied, "With the troubadours in the twelfth century," explaining that the troubadours were the first people in the West who thought of love in the way modern people do—as a person-to-person relationship. Campbell was referring to *amor*, or romantic love, "the kind of seizure that comes from the meeting of the eyes," as opposed to "lust, or passion, or a general religious sentiment." Historically documented in various societies, romantic love became, and remains, the ideal for the Western world. Cross-cultural research has shown, however, that romantic love is not limited to, nor solely the product of, Western cultures.

Besides the feelings of desire, attraction, and sexual passion of romantic partners, love is also reflected in the deep affection and solicitude felt within families and among friends. Love is apparent in the care, interdependence, and lifelong commitment of family members to each other, in people's con-

---

Valentines

Modern Americans associate St. Valentine's Day, February 14, with romantic love. Traditionally, however, the date commemorates the martyrdoms of two Christian figures of the same name. Historical details are sketchy and even contradictory, but the first Saint Valentine appears to have been a priest who was beheaded in Rome in 269 C.E. The second Valentine was also beheaded in Rome during the same period. It is believed that February 14 was chosen as the date for celebrating Christian martyrs to divert attention of early Romans from an ancient pagan celebration around the same time. In modern times the unofficial holiday became an occasion for exchanging gifts and cards with affectionate messages.

Human love takes many forms, including the love of pets. (James L. Shaffer)

cern and willingness to provide help in their communities, and in times of war or peril, when they sacrifice their lives. People love their family pets, their work, their interests, personal possessions, places that hold a special meaning for them. People also love themselves. As opposed to narcissistic love, which implies self-aggrandizement and self-ishness, a healthy self-love involves respect for one's own integrity and uniqueness coupled with self-understanding. Theologians use love to describe God's benevolence toward the world and people's devotion to God, besides depicting how

Love profoundly affects the psychological health of the family and the development of children. (James L. Shaffer)

people should behave toward one another—"Thou shalt love thy neighbor as thyself."

Freudian View. Throughout the twentieth century researchers from a number of disciplines attempted to redefine love in order to make it measurable to scientific investigation. Sigmund Freud's psychoanalytic theory has greatly influenced the psychological interpretation of love. Freud considered the combination of sexual and mental love as one of the most important aspects of life, with the essence of love being sexual desire. A healthy adult was a person successful in the areas of love and work. Using the technique of psychoanalysis, he examined how an "object of love" is chosen and concluded that both normal and neurotic love develop from a "fixation of the infantile feelings of tenderness for the mother." Freud believed that a "neurotic" man could compulsively choose maternal surrogates as love objects—that is, women who would replace the mother—whereas a normal attitude toward love would involve tender, affectionate feelings combined with sensual feelings. He believed that because mothers are the primary satisfiers of an infant's needs for food and sucking during their first year of life, infants become emotionally attached to them. Fifty years later, in experiments using rhesus monkeys with surrogate cloth and wire mothers, Margaret and Harry Harlow showed that feeding was less crucial to psychological development than Freud had postulated. Although the rhesus monkey was fed by a "wire mother," it spent most of its time clinging to a soft, cuddly "terry-cloth mother." From this result the Harlows concluded that the need for comfort contact in monkeys, and possibly humans, is as basic as their need for food.

Post-Freudian View. Post-Freudian theorists such as Karen Horney, Melanie Klein, and Harry Stack Sullivan built upon Freud's premises. Klein, for example, associated mature love with emancipation from infantile dependence. Sullivan saw a strict division between sexuality and love, which he described as "a situation of collaboration." Erich Fromm's typology of love included motherly love, brotherly love, erotic love, the love of God, and love of one's self. What mattered, according to Fromm, was the particular quality of loving, not the object of love: "Love is a union with somebody, or something, outside oneself, under the condition of retaining the separateness and integrity of one's own self." In *The Art of Loving* (1956) he states that love "is an art," and to learn how to love people must apply themselves as they would to learn any other art. Fromm emphasized that an individual's deepest need is to overcome the feeling of separateness metaphorically described in the story of Adam and Eve. This is attained through love, the interpersonal union or fusion with another person. Differentiating between symbiotic union and a mature union, in which one's individuality is preserved, Fromm wrote, "Love is the active concern for the life and growth of that which we love." A similar view is expressed by philosopher Irving Singer, who defines love as a way of valuing something. Fromm considered brotherly love and erotic love as love between equals, whereas motherly love is a relationship defined by its inequality and an unconditional affirmation of the child's life and its needs. He believed that care, responsibility, respect, and knowledge were common to all forms of love, and the affirmation of one's own life was rooted in one's capacity to manifest these elements.

Erik Erikson's stage theory of development differs from that of Freud in that Erikson's emphasis is socially rather than sexually based. Each of Erikson's eight stages involves a psychological conflict that requires resolution before an individual can progress to the next stage. During young adulthood a person wants and needs intimacy and seeks deep personal commitments. Having successfully resolved their adolescent identity crises and no longer confused about their roles in life, young adults need to involve themselves in intimate relationships rather than remain in social isolation. Erikson proposed that when people can make commitments, achieve intimacy, and express devotion, they will experience love.

Humanists stress the human potential for healthy development and the ability of people to take charge of their own lives and be creative. Abraham Maslow's hierarchy of human needs indicates that the lower level needs of physiological survival and safety must be met before a person can begin seeking the higher level needs of love and acceptance. In turn, love and belongingness must be present before the needs of self-esteem can be met through achievement and competency. Humanistic psychotherapists emphasize the value of demonstrating love through empathy and acceptance as a means to individual psychological growth.

Love as Attachment and Bonding. Often conceived of as the purest form of love, against which other types are measured, is the unconditional love of mothers for their children. Yet not all mothers love their children, or if they do, they are able to treat them with the type of love that allows them to grow into healthy adults. For children reared in such institutional settings as orphanages, in which families or primary caretakers are lacking, love is frequently absent during early childhood. Many such children fail to develop the capacity to empathize. Bonding between mothers and their children is a complex and prolonged process. Problems arising in early mother-child interactions can interfere with infants' physical growth and health and contribute to later developmental, behavioral, and emotional problems. When children are deprived of primary caregivers after the age of three months, major developmental problems can develop. Only if later individual attention and environmental stimulation are provided can the results of such conditions be corrected.

During the 1960's psychologists began extensively to investigate emotional bonding. Preeminent in this area were researchers Mary Ainsworth and John Bowlby. Love was interpreted as an emotional tie formed between one animal or person and another specific individual. Ainsworth and Bowlby introduced the concept of "attachment" in order to clearly specify the loving behavior they were investigating. Attached individuals seek close contact with one another and, especially at young ages, become distressed when they are separated. Bowlby observed infants and young children in residential nurseries and hospital wards who were separated from their mothers. He discovered that the children who had a secure relationship with their mothers displayed a predictable pattern of behavior upon separation: First they protested, then they felt despair, and finally they moved to a state of detachment.

Ainsworth and Bowlby's studies showed that young children have a special attachment to their mothers. Although acknowledging the importance of other family attachments, they considered them less important. Nevertheless, cross-cultural research has shown that multiple, simultaneous attachments can occur when caregiving is a shared responsibility in the family.

Bowlby and Ainsworth maintained that love (attachment) is essential to an infant's survival. Bowlby argued that behaviors like crying, smiling, and clinging elicit protective caregiving responses from parents. Babies, as well as children, try to maintain contact with caregivers to whom they are attached by engaging in eye contact, pulling and tugging at them, and by asking to be picked up. When they are unsuccessful they thrash about, whine, cry, or screech—behaviors that suggest separation anxiety.

In the United States about 65 to 70 percent of middle-class babies are securely attached to their mothers. These mothers respond sensitively to their babies' smiles and cries and are more likely to be affectionate, cooperative, reliable, and predictable caregivers than mothers of unattached babies. Traditionally, fathers have been less involved than mothers in the caregiving of babies, but when infants are observed in their homes they seek out their fathers about as often as they do their mothers. Babies attach themselves to fathers at about the same time as they do to mothers. Secure attachments in infancy are related to secure attachments with the same people twenty years later, which in turn is found to relate to attachments in romantic relationships.

In the 1950's it was shown that infants deprived of human physical contact became seriously ill. Results published in 1997 of a forty-year longitudinal study at Harvard University showed a similar influence on health in adults. Boys and young men who experienced close relationships with their parents were less likely to develop certain illnesses in midlife, whereas 91 percent of the men who had not enjoyed close relationships had coronary artery disease, duodenal ulcers, high blood pressure, or suffered from alcoholism.

Each year in the United States nearly three million children experience unloving parental behavior. They are victims of physical, sexual, and emotional abuse and physical and emotional neglect. The incidence is probably actually higher, as many cases remain unreported. The reported rate of child abuse in 1990 was four times that reported in 1970. Abused children are more likely to be unattached to their parents and are more withdrawn from their peers. They are angrier, more aggres-

It has been argued that love increases along with mutual rapport and dependency. (James L. Shaffer)

It has also been argued that love tends to decrease along with a diminution of rapport, communication, and dependency. (James L. Shaffer)

sive, and more noncompliant than other children. Rarely expressing positive emotion, they have lower self-esteem and more cognitive problems, and as they grow older they are at greater risk of developing emotional and behavioral difficulties and of failing academically. They are also more likely to become abusive parents themselves.

Parenting. Children learn how to love from parents who express their love to their children in different parenting styles. How these styles influence children's development was investigated by Diane Baumrind in 1971. Authoritative parents set clear boundaries and demand adherence to rules, yet they reason with and respect their children's points of view. Because they give their children strong support and feelings of love, their children are self-reliant, independent, and have high self-esteem. They are highly active and motivated to achieve; they do well academically and are socially competent. If their parents should divorce, their children exhibit fewer behavior problems, better school performance, and better relationships with other children than the children of either authoritarian or permissive parents.

Children learn social skills and competency through play and interaction with their peers. As early as one year of age infants begin to show a capacity for sharing, and by two years of age they can relate to others with empathy. Friendships become increasingly more important as they grow older. By the time children reach middle childhood, parents tend to spend less time with them. Striving for greater independence, adolescents spend even less time with their families, but they continue to feel a great deal of love, loyalty, and respect for their parents. Adolescents who feel close to their parents are more likely to show greater independence, self-reliance, and higher self-esteem than adolescents who are distant from their parents.

Friendship throughout adolescence is extremely important. Best friends are usually of the same gender. Intimacy and closeness are more central in girls' friendships than in boys'. When sexual interest and romantic strivings emerge, adolescents typically demonstrate concern for their physical appearance. In early adolescence dating is more often than not casual and short-lived. By late adolescence romantic relationships involve love, trust, and commitment and are more

stable. Early love affairs are sometimes passionate and tempestuous.

Theories of Love. As love became a focus of psychological research during the 1960's, it reflected a growing popular interest in the quality of intimate relationships. Attachment theory was extended into the study of adult interpersonal and emotional relationships, showing that people who had experienced loving, affectionate attachments as children were more likely to have similar experiences in their adult relationships. In 1960 Ira Reiss proposed that in adult relationships love increases when rapport, self-revelation, and mutual dependency develop and both partners' personal needs are met, while it decreases when rapport, communication, and dependency lessen and a couple's needs remain unmet.

Romantic love was rarely investigated until the 1970's. Harold Kelley suggested there were three types of love: passionate love, which develops suddenly, lasts only briefly, and emphasizes need-related issues such as sex, loneliness, and self-esteem; pragmatic love, which develops slowly from trusting and satisfying interactions, as when friendship develops into love, and which emphasizes trust and tolerance; and altruistic love, which consists of internally motivated caring. Altruistic love is independent of responses from other persons and, as Kelley suggested, is long lasting, like "mother love."

In 1986 Robert L. Sternberg unified many of the descriptions of love in a triangular theory composed of three elements: intimacy, passion, and a decision/commitment component. When the elements are differently combined, they form eight possible types of love. Liking involves intimacy alone. Romantic love involves intimacy and passion, while infatuation involves solely passion. Fatuous love consists of passion plus commitment, whereas companionate love consists of intimacy plus commitment. Empty love exists where there is only commitment. Consummate love includes intimacy, passion, and commitment, while nonlove exists when none of these elements is present.

Love and Marriage. While psychologists addressed the components of love, sociologists directed their attention to the relationship between marriage and love. Until the late nineteenth and twentieth centuries marriage in the middle and upper classes within the Judeo-Christian tradition in the West was either a political or a social arrangement. It was sanctified by the churches and involved a transfer of wealth, property, and legal status. In prearranged marriages the partners' love for one another was expected to develop throughout the course of marriage, meaning that an absence or diminishing of love was insufficient reason to terminate marriage. Historically and in the modern world, civil law, social ritual, and religious ceremony attest to the high value placed on marital union. Religiously sanctioned and recognized as a civil union, modern marriages usually take place because couples have fallen in love. A series of rituals, including courtship, engagement, and the exchange of betrothal gifts, culminates in wedding ceremonies witnessed by friends and family, during which vows of undying love and tokens—usually rings, symbolizing the love shared by the couples—are exchanged. As a consequence of the gay rights movement, same-sex marriage became a hotly debated issue in the 1990's in the United States and Canada. Despite increased public acknowledgment of homosexual love and commitment, insufficient pressure was placed on legislators to legalize same-sex marriages.

Loss of Love. In *The Way We Really Are: Coming to Terms with America's Changing Families* (1997), sociologist Stephanie Coontz noted that marriage is a changed institution, playing a smaller role in organizing social and personal life in the late twentieth century than previously. In explaining this she cited higher divorce rates and the delaying of marriages that were no longer expected to last a lifetime. Few socially proscribed rituals, except the obligatory newspaper announcement, accompany divorces. In contrast, when death intervenes in love relationships, including marriage, social and religious rituals exist to acknowledge the loss to the surviving partner, family, friends, and community. Publicly, funeral rites serve to observe and honor the loss of a loved one, while privately they help to assuage the emotional pain of the bereaved, thereby serving to acknowledge the profound meaning and central importance of love in a person's life. Whole nations mourn the deaths of beloved leaders or heroes.

Sociologist Robert S. Weiss and his colleagues at Harvard University studied the experiences of marital partners following separation and divorce.

Their work revealed that the social support of friendships did not mitigate the loneliness of the emotional isolation felt after losing a committed relationship, thus demonstrating the enormous impact marital relationships have on husbands and wives. In 1993 Karen Kayser investigated love from the different perspective of how and why people fall out of love with their partners. She uncovered three distinct phases of marital dissatisfaction. The first involves disappointment, as partners feel angry, hurt, and disillusioned. The second is the transition from disappointment to disaffection, as partners feel intensely angry and hurt. The third is the phase of disaffection, as couples make plans and act to end their marriages, feeling anger, apathy, and hopelessness. Kayser echoes Stephanie Coontz's remark that people in the late twentieth century have unrealistically high expectations of love. The causes of disaffection are interrelated. They include a lack of mutuality, unfulfilled intimacy needs, and unresolved conflicts. Women tend to experience marital disaffection more frequently than men, a finding consistent with earlier studies in which men were shown to be generally happier in their marriages than women.

When passion dissipates, it is harder to remain in love. In the final volume of his 1987 trilogy, Irving Singer discusses falling in love, being in love, and staying in love. Staying in love involves a "cherishing of the joint experience which is one's life with another person as well as a cherishing of the particular person who has lived through it with us."

Chemistry of Love. During the 1980's and 1990's the biological sciences provided increased understanding of the chemical aspects of love. Oxytocin, which has been called the love hormone, is released into the blood stream not only during the birth process and lactation, but also during sexual arousal and orgasm. It has been proposed that endorphins, the natural opiate of the body, are present in both mothers and infants during and immediately following birth, thus creating a mutual dependency or attachment relationship. A similar state exists between sexual partners. Low levels of endorphins are associated with unpleasant feelings, while high levels kill pain and induce a state of happy relaxation. Researchers have suggested that the opposite of love is not

One measure of the strength of love is how long it endures. (James L. Shaffer)

hate, but grief. Phenylethylamine, popularly known as "the molecule of love," is an amphetamine-like substance that evokes a mind-altered state. Found in the bloodstream of lovers, it plays a critical role in the limbic system.

In his presidential address to the American Psychological Association in 1958, Harry Harlow stated, "The little we know about love does not transcend simple observation, and the little we write about it has been written better by poets and novelists." At the end of the twentieth century research on love had burgeoned into mammoth proportions, with investigators from almost all disciplines joining the fray. —*Susan E. Hamilton*

BIBLIOGRAPHY

Bowlby, John. *Attachment and Loss.* 3 vols. New York: Basic Books, 1969-1980. A psychoanalytic interpretation of children's attachment to their mothers and the grief following temporary and permanent separation. Incorporates cognitive psychology and human information processing theory, thus creating a new paradigm of personality development and psychopathology.

Campbell, Joseph, with Bill Moyers. "Tales of Love and Marriage." In *The Power of Myth*, edited by Betty Sue Flowers. New York: Doubleday, 1988. Interview with Bill Moyers that draws upon Campbell's vast knowledge of cultural myth to trace the development of love through time.

Coontz, Stephanie. *The Way We Really Are: Coming to Terms with America's Changing Families.* New York: Basic Books, 1997. A sound interpretation of statistical information and research findings discussing underlying issues pertinent to change in family structure, values, and tradition, including those of marriage, divorce, and single parenting.

Freud, Sigmund. *On Creativity and the Unconscious.* New York: Harper & Bros., 1958. Contains three important essays, *Contributions to the Psychology of Love*, written in 1910, 1912, and 1918, presenting Freud's insights and theoretical observations on love objects, erotic life, and virginity.

Fromm, Erich. *The Art of Loving.* New York: Harper & Row, 1956. A psychoanalytic theory of love applied to different love objects and an examination of the disintegration of love in Western society, with a prescription for how to practice love.

Jankowiak, William, ed. *Romantic Passion: A Universal Experience.* New York: Columbia University Press, 1995. A collection of essays by anthropologists examining modern romantic passion as a private experience and cultural expression and presenting relevant biological, psychological, and cultural factors.

Kayser, Karen. *When Love Dies: The Process of Marital Disaffection.* New York: Guilford Press, 1993. Examines the deterioration of marital love based on clinical experience and research interviews with spouses who no longer loved their partners.

Singer, Irving. *The Nature of Love.* 3 vols. Chicago: University of Chicago Press, 1987. A vast and detailed historical and philosophical examination of the ideas of love from classical times to the twentieth century.

Smolak, Linda. *Adult Development.* Englewood Cliffs, N.J.: Prentice Hall, 1993. A college-level text presenting research and discussion concerning family and social relationships across the life span and including an examination of marriage from a sociobiological perspective.

Sternberg, Robert J., and Michael L. Barnes, eds. *The Psychology of Love.* New Haven, Conn.: Yale University Press, 1988. A collection of essays discussing theories of love and relationship maintenance.

See also Adultery; Bonding and attachment; Child rearing; Couples; Courting rituals; Erikson, Erik H.; Family unity; Freudian psychology; Marriage; Maslow, Abraham; Puberty and adolescence; Tough love.

Loving v. Virginia

DATE: Ruling issued on June 12, 1967
RELEVANT ISSUES: Law; Marriage and dating; Race and ethnicity
SIGNIFICANCE: This Supreme Court decision struck down the antimiscegenation laws of several states that prohibited interracial couples from marrying or living together while not married

In 1958 Virginia and several other states outlawed interracial marriage and sex between unmarried interracial partners. All such laws prohibited whites and African Americans from intermarry-

Mildred and Richard Loving at the time they challenged Virginia's antimiscegenation law. (AP/Wide World Photos)

ing; some also applied to members of other races.

Richard Loving, a white man, and Mildred Jeter, an African American woman, lived in Virginia and wanted to be married. They went to the District of Columbia, where they were married legally. When they returned to their home in Virginia, however, they were arrested. The circuit court of Caroline County, Virginia, found them guilty and sentenced them to one year in jail, a sentence which would be suspended if they agreed to leave the state.

The Lovings moved to Washington, D.C., and filed an appeal against the Virginia court decision. In 1967 the case reached the U.S. Supreme Court. The Court's justices unanimously sided with the Lovings, overturning the Virginia statute and those similar to it. By denying interracial couples the right to do something that other couples were allowed to do, antimiscegenation laws violated these citizens' right to the equal protection of the laws as guaranteed by the Fourteenth Amendment of the U.S. Constitution. This decision removed the legal stigma some states had attached to interracial unions, and it prohibited states from punishing people as criminals for loving someone of a different race.
                                                    —*Roger D. Hardaway*

See also Antimiscegenation laws; Cohabitation; Family law; Interracial families; Marriage laws.

Lynd, Robert

Born: September 26, 1892, New Albany, Ind.
Died: November 1, 1970, Warren, Conn.

Lynd, Helen

Born: March 17, 1896, La Grange, Ill.
Died: January 30, 1982, Warren, Ohio

Area of achievement: Sociology

Significance: The Lynds were pioneers in using the objective techniques of cultural anthropology to analyze a modern city

Written by the husband-and-wife team of Robert and Helen Lynd, the studies *Middletown: A Study in Contemporary American Culture* (1929) and *Middletown in Transition: A Study in Cultural Conflicts* (1937) are considered classics in the field of urban sociology. Rather than using an impersonal quantitative and statistical approach in their analysis of Muncie, Indiana, the Lynds examined all aspects of daily life among individuals, families, and groups in this midwestern American city. After spending a year and a half gaining firsthand experience from living in the city, the Lynds focused much of their attention on the nuclear family. Middletown children were expected to marry and to produce families. Childbearing was considered to be a moral obligation. Men were expected to be good providers; women were to be good housewives and rear the children.

Returning to the city some ten years later during the Great Depression, the Lynds found few substantial changes, even though its population had grown from 36,000 to 50,000. Family concerns were still paramount, although young residents of Muncie were delaying their marriages and raising smaller families. Some residents felt that the Depression actually had positive effects on family life, because it directed the attention of individual families inward to face their problems. Other factors that helped strengthen family bonds included government policies that favored families over individuals in the distribution of federal relief funds and legal costs that encouraged many couples to work out problems rather than seek divorce.

—*Nis Petersen*

See also Communities; Family values; Home ownership.

McKinney Homeless Assistance Act

DATE: Enacted on July 22, 1987
RELEVANT ISSUES: Economics and work; Law
SIGNIFICANCE: Pushed through Congress by Representative Stewart B. McKinney of Connecticut, the McKinney Homeless Assistance Act provides funding for emergency, transitional, and permanent housing and for supportive, preventive outreach programs for America's homeless

Stewart McKinney was a liberal Republican who played a major role in shaping federal housing and urban development programs. In his final years, he took up the cause of homelessness.

Funds providing assistance to homeless families

Congress passed the McKinney Homeless Assistance Act in 1987 to assist homeless families and individuals throughout the United States but slashed its budget eight years later. (James L. Shaffer)

and individuals under the McKinney Act are distributed via several federal agencies, with the bulk of the monies administered by the U.S. Department of Housing and Urban Development (HUD). Opponents of federal assistance for the homeless argued that the McKinney Act was nothing more than another welfare program, an extension of the welfare state. There were other concerns, however, as one of the most controversial elements of the legislation was the right of homeless organizations to access underused federal facilities. Many communities trying to ease the economic impact of military-base closings by promoting commercial redevelopment opposed such action, arguing that the presence of the homeless hindered economic development potential.

Beginning in 1995 Congress slashed HUD funding and specifically eliminated allocations for the McKinney Adult Education for the Homeless Program. The following year funding for the McKinney Education for Homeless Children and Youth Program was reduced substantially as well. The push in the 105th Congress was to continue this trend with a move toward distribution of HUD McKinney funds to states via block grants. Supporters of the McKinney Act defend the legislation, arguing that the housing and service programs it provides have done much to address the problems of the homeless.

—Donald C. Simmons, Jr.

See also Aid to Families with Dependent Children (AFDC); Family-friendly programs; Welfare.

Mail-order brides

Relevant issues: Marriage and dating; Race and ethnicity

Significance: Thousands of marriages in the United States and other countries are arranged by mail through international dating and introduction services

Mail-order brides, a term used to describe women who meet their husbands through the mail, are an old part of the American social landscape. During the nineteenth century there were relatively few women in the Canadian and U.S. West. Newspapers in the West routinely carried advertisements for wives placed by lonely farmers or ranchers. While little is known about how many marriages were formed through the mail or how successful they were, this was apparently a fairly common form of courtship.

Modern Mail-Order Brides. During the twentieth century, finding a mate by mail became a rare occurrence in North America. After mass transportation and the automobile became common, dating became the primary form of courtship. American cultural values placed heavy emphasis on romantic love as a motivation for marrying. The ideal of romantic love required that men and women develop intense emotional intimacy before marriage, and intimacy can rarely be created at a distance.

Despite the cultural emphasis on dating and romantic love, mail-order marriages began to become more common in the period following World War II. Sociologists, psychologists, and anthropologists have often noted that men and women tend to look for different characteristics in mates. Men are more likely to look for youth and physical attractiveness. Women are more likely to look for mates who are financially secure. As worldwide transportation and communications have improved, men in relatively prosperous countries could make contact with younger women in comparatively low-income countries. Between 1968 and 1981, for example, more than seven hundred women emigrated to France from the island of Mauritius, a former French colony, as mail-order brides for lonely middle-aged French farmers.

During the 1970's Asia, and especially the Philippines, became an important source of mail-order brides for men in the United States. Because the Philippines was an American colony from 1898 to 1945, Filipinas are often able to speak English and are familiar with American culture. Filipino and American entrepreneurs set up introduction services to put American men searching for wives in contact with Filipinas searching for financially stable husbands. Most often, international introduction services put potential spouses in contact with one another by marketing catalogs containing the photographs of women with their addresses and personal information. By the late 1990's several of these catalogs were available through the Internet as well as by regular mail.

It has been estimated that by the 1990's approximately nineteen thousand mail-order brides left

Japanese mail-order brides arriving in San Francisco Bay around 1915. (National Archives)

the Philippines each year to join husbands and fiancés abroad, with the United States as their primary destination. In 1997 the social scientist Concepcion Montoya identified Filipina mail-order brides, who often established social networks among themselves, as a rapidly emerging American community.

With the collapse of the Soviet Union in 1991, Russia and Eastern Europe became another major source of mail-order brides for the Americas and Europe. The difficulties of the Russian economy during the 1990's caused many young Russian women to seek more prosperous lives abroad. As in the Philippines, catalogs served as the primary way in which men initially made contact with potential brides. One of the best-known of these catalogs was *European Connections*, a quarterly containing photographs of women in Russia and Eastern Europe. For $8.00 to $15.00, American men could order the addresses of women in the catalog. European Connections and other introduction services also arranged expeditions to Russia for American and Western European men.

Stereotypes and Negative Views. Many Americans hold unfavorable views of men who marry foreign women whom they have met through the mail. Popular opinion often holds that men who seek brides abroad are looking for obedient wives whom they can easily dominate. Many people see husbands of mail-order brides as such undesirable mates that they cannot find mates by more conventional means. Women who become mail-order brides are often seen either as exploited victims or as opportunists selling themselves for comfortable lives.

A number of widely publicized incidents have reinforced the negative views many people hold about introductions and marriages by mail. Some mail-order brides have indeed suffered at the hands of their husbands. According to news reports, for example, sixteen Filipina mail-order brides between 1980 and 1995 were murdered by husbands in Australia. In the United States a similar occurrence received national attention in 1995. A man in Seattle, Washington, had brought a Filipina wife he had met through the mail to the United States. The marriage did not work out and the wife sought a divorce. In response, the husband contacted the Immigration and Naturalization Service, claiming that his estranged wife no longer qualified for residence in the United States and should be deported back to the Philippines. The woman, who had become pregnant with another man's child, was sitting in a Seattle courthouse waiting for a hearing on her residency status when her husband drew a gun and killed her and several of her friends.

There is no doubt that mail-order brides are sometimes exploited by their husbands and that women in a new country can be vulnerable. Cultural conflicts and conflicts of expectations can also trouble international marriages. Women from the Philippines, for example, often expect to have full control over matters pertaining to the household and do not see themselves as imported servants. While there is little information on the success rates of mail-order marriages, available evidence suggests that the horror stories of wife abuse are the exception rather than the rule and that many of these marriages work out to the satisfaction of both parties.

Research on Mail-Order Marriages. The sociologists William M. Kephart and Davor Jedlicka have conducted extensive research on the mail-order marriage process. Kephart and Jedlicka conducted interviews with agents and clients of international introduction services and studied the advertisements in their catalogs. These researchers found that the process began when men selected photographs of women and sent the women photographs of themselves. Selection on the basis of appearance, however, was only a first step. Next, prospective partners began exchanging letters. Usually these letters were quite long and detailed and contained extensive information on the tastes, interests, values, and plans of both parties. By necessity, the exchange of letters meant that the women had good, if not excellent, English-language skills. Once couples decided to marry, the American men usually went abroad to meet their future wives. This step became a necessity after January, 1987, when the marriage-fraud provision of the 1986 Immigration Act prohibited foreigners from coming to the United States to marry people whom they had never met.

Kephart and Jedlicka found that the majority of American men who became involved in mail-order marriages had had some unfortunate experience with courtship and marriage in the United States. More than half of them had been divorced and 75 percent had been through some kind of traumatic experience with women in the United States. Most were at least thirty-seven years old. The men earned above-average incomes and were above average in educational attainment and occupational level.

Most of the women involved in mail-order marriages were twenty-five years old or less. Contrary to popular stereotypes, fewer than 10 percent came from the countryside or held menial jobs in their home countries. The majority were college students and about 30 percent held professional, managerial, or clerical jobs requiring fairly high levels of education. Marrying foreign men did not seem to be the choice of peasant women, but of middle-class women with aspirations that could not be easily satisfied in their native countries.

—*Carl L. Bankston III*

BIBLIOGRAPHY

Kephart, William M., and Davor Jedlicka. *The Family, Society, and the Individual.* 7th ed. New York: HarperCollins, 1991.

Larsen, Wanwadee. *Confessions of a Mail Order Bride: American Life Through Thai Eyes.* Far Hills, N.J.: New Horizon Press, 1989.

Montoya, Concepcion. "Mail Order Brides: An Emerging Community." In *Filipino Americans: Transformation and Identity,* edited by Maria P. P. Root. Newbury Park, Calif.: Sage Publications, 1997.

See also Arranged marriages; Bride-price; Couples; Domestic violence; Filipino Americans; Matchmaking; Women's roles.

Marital rape

RELEVANT ISSUES: Law; Marriage and dating; Violence

SIGNIFICANCE: Marital rape, as a new category of crime that does not recognize marriage as a bar to prosecution, has fundamentally affected the traditional understanding of marriage

Marital rape is unwanted sexual intercourse that occurs within the bounds of marriage. Because the victim of marital rape most often is a woman, it is sometimes referred to as wife rape. The concept of marital rape is new to most of the Anglo-Saxon world. Traditionally, unwanted sexual intercourse committed by a man with his wife was not considered a crime because of the common law doctrine of marital exemption. The doctrine held that marriage is a bar to prosecuting rape cases because marriage gives a man unconditional right to have sexual access to his wife. It was assumed that when a woman gives herself in marriage, she gives him unconditional and irrevocable consent to sex on demand. Submitting to a husband's sexual desires was nothing more than repaying a marital debt.

History. Marriage was understood as a legal contract by which a woman's separate existence and personal rights were totally merged with those of her husband, so that what existed after marriage was a single legal entity, represented by the husband. In this perspective, charging a man with raping his wife amounted to accusing him of raping himself, which made no legal sense.

The cultural source of the doctrine of marital exemption was the belief that a wife was a man's property. Feminist scholars have pointed out that all rape laws were based on the assumption that men enjoyed ownership over women. Rape was a crime not because it violated a woman's personal rights but because it defiled a man's (father's or husband's) property.

In the 1970's, under the influence of the feminist movement, rape was culturally redefined not as an act of defiling a man's property but as a violation of the victim's personal rights. The emergence of marital rape as a new category of crime was a natural extension of this new understanding of rape. Furthermore, many states replaced existing rape laws with sexual assault laws to make them broad enough to include all unwanted forms of sexual contact as well as to make sexual offenses gender neutral.

Marital Rape Laws. Marital rape laws are not peculiar to the United States. Several European countries including Poland, the Czech Republic, Sweden, Norway, and Denmark had marital rape laws in their criminal statutes long before such laws were introduced in England and the United States. Marital rape laws are now in force in many non-Western countries as well.

Recognition of marital rape as a crime affects the very understanding of marriage in modern societies. Marriage is no longer considered an act of unconditional and irrevocable surrender of a woman's rights to a man, and women no longer are treated as men's property. Rather, marriage is understood as a revocable contract freely entered into by two autonomous individuals with equal rights who do not surrender any of their fundamental rights as individuals.

Marital rape laws formally incorporate this new understanding of marriage. Because of its implications for changing the nature of the traditional marital relationship, the elimination of marital exemption initially was opposed by conservative religious groups such as the Moral Majority and by several prominent conservative politicians. Despite some opposition, every state in the United States has criminalized marital rape, although the severity of the punishment varies.

Legal Cases. In the United States, the first man to be indicted and tried for marital rape was John Rideout. Although he was acquitted of the charge

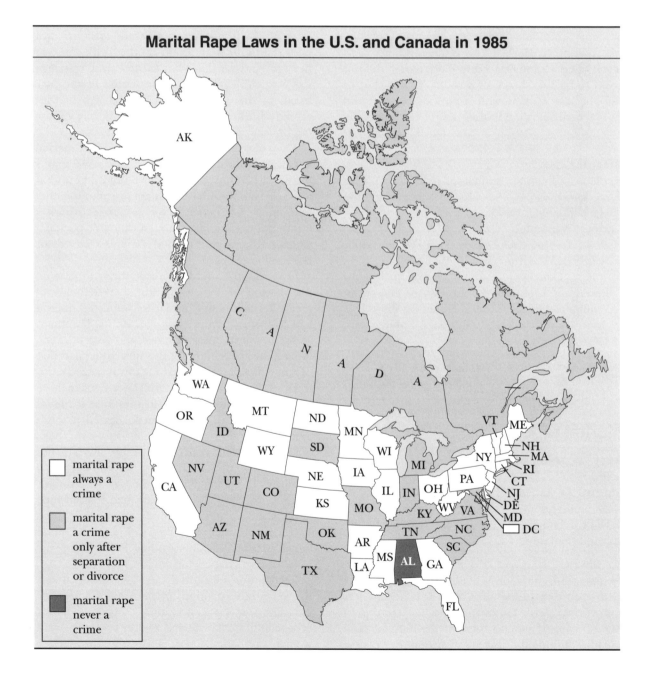

Marital Rape Laws in the U.S. and Canada in 1985

□ marital rape always a crime

▨ marital rape a crime only after separation or divorce

▓ marital rape never a crime

Supporters of Lorena Bobbitt demonstrating outside the courthouse during her January, 1994, trial for emasculating her husband. (AP/Wide World Photos)

of rape in 1978, his trial attracted national attention and stimulated much public discussion and research into the phenomenon of marital rape.

Perhaps the most publicized case of marital rape involved John Wayne Bobbitt and his wife Lorena Bobbitt. In 1994, Lorena Bobbitt cut off her husband's penis with a kitchen knife, claiming that she did so because she was tired of suffering years of physical and sexual abuse by her husband. She was acquitted of the charge of malicious wounding by a jury whose members believed that, at the time she mutilated her husband, she was temporarily insane. Although John Wayne Bobbitt eventually was acquitted of the charge of marital rape, the acquittal of Lorena Bobbitt was understood by

many as a message that marital rape may be resisted with force.

Extent of Marital Rape. For a variety of reasons, available studies do not provide an accurate account of the extent of marital rape. First, victims of marital rape are less likely to report victimization by their own husbands than if they were to be victimized by strangers. Second, most available studies are based on interviews with women who either have been estranged from their husbands or have been placed in shelters after being sexually and physically abused. Data collected on these women are not generalizable because they do not constitute a representative sample of the general population. Third, even when researchers have used representative samples, their survey instruments have employed a variety of terms with different meanings to describe marital rape, so that comparisons of these studies are difficult. A rough estimation indicates that approximately 14 percent of married women have experienced rape by their husbands.

Causes and Consequences of Marital Rape. Many men who rape their wives do not think of themselves as rapists. Rather, they believe that marriage entitles them to have sexual access to their wives whenever they desire. Some attribute the origin of this belief to the traditional patriarchal family structure in which men enjoy a relationship of domination and ownership over women. Although laws have changed, the cultural attitude toward and the traditional understanding of family relationships have not kept pace with these changes.

Some men use rape as a means of asserting their power over women. These men consider their ability to control and dominate others, particularly women, as essential to their masculine identity. Those who engage in sadistic rape probably suffer from serious emotional and psychological disorders. They associate sex with inflicting physical pain on one's partner.

Victims of marital rape react differently to their experience. Some women believe that it is a man's right to have sex on demand and a woman's obligation to provide it. Although very unhappy about their plight, these women helplessly accept the situation. Some wives submit to forced sex out of a desire to avoid greater physical harm or conflicts. These women use sex to appease their violent husbands. Some wives succeed in avoiding rape by staying out of the way when their husbands are angry, or by doing chores to placate them such as cooking their favorite meal or keeping the house clean.

Still others physically resist and take legal steps to prosecute their offending husbands. These actions usually result in putting an end to their marriages. To a large extent, the decision to leave or remain in the relationship depends on the wife's ability to financially support herself. Women who have the means to support themselves are more likely to leave the marriage than those who do not have such means.

Marital rape inflicts severe and long-standing trauma on the victim. Like stranger rape, marital rape diminishes a woman's self-esteem, as well as causing her to experience severe depression, long-term fears, anxieties, recurring nightmares, and, sometimes, a variety of psychosomatic reactions. It can cause serious physical injuries, miscarriages, stillbirths, bladder infections, and even infertility.

Community Support. In recent years, communities have made available a variety of support programs for victims of marital rape. Battered women's shelters are an immediate resource for many women who experience family violence, including rape. Rape crisis centers are another source of support for women as they look for legal, social, and emotional help to deal with their experiences.

Information on advocacy, treatment, and referral sources is readily available in most states. Some books on marital rape include such information. Numerous self-help groups and political activist groups such as the National Clearing House on Marital and Date Rape, the National Coalition Against Sexual Assault, State Coalitions on Domestic Violence, and Men Against Domestic Violence also provide information and support services to victims of marital rape. —*Mathew J. Kanjirathinkal*

BIBLIOGRAPHY

Alsdurf, J., and P. Alsdurf. *Battered into Submission.* Downers Grove, Ill.: InterVarsity Press, 1989.

Bergen, Raquel Kennedy. *Wife Rape: Understanding the Response of Survivors and Service Providers.* Thousand Oaks, Calif.: Sage Publications, 1996.

Brownmiller, Susan. *Against Our Will: Men, Women, and Rape.* New York: Simon & Schuster, 1975.

Buckborough, Anne L. "Family Law: Recent Developments in the Law of Marital Rape." *Annual Survey of American Law* (Summer, 1989).

Eskow, Lisa R. "The Ultimate Weapon? Demythologizing Spousal Rape and Reconceptualizing Its Prosecution." *Stanford Law Review* 48 (February, 1996).

Finkelhor, D., and K. Yllo. *License to Rape: Sexual Abuse of Wives.* New York: Holt, Rinehart, and Winston, 1985.

Russell, D. E. H. *Rape in Marriage.* Bloomington: Indiana University Press, 1990.

See also Cruelty as grounds for divorce; Cycle of violence theory; Dating violence; Divorce; Domestic violence; Dysfunctional families; Family law; Marriage laws; Men's roles.

Marriage

RELEVANT ISSUES: Divorce; Kinship and genealogy; Marriage and dating; Parenting and family relationships

SIGNIFICANCE: Marriage and family have long been important aspects of social life, but in the latter part of the twentieth century the traditional institution of marriage has changed

Since ancient times marriages have been performed to show the fidelity that couples have for each other, to protect the children that come from couples' unions, and to protect couples' property. At various times in world history marriages have been performed to join families who see their union as advantageous for various reasons. One

Marriage is the rite that traditionally creates a new family unit. (James L. Shaffer)

advantage ruling families have derived from marriage unions has been the establishment of closer relationships with other ruling families. However, in the United States in the twentieth century, couples generally married for four reasons: romantic attraction; family building; personal security; and companionship.

Civil and Religious Marriages. In modern America marriage has both a legal and religious basis. In all states of the United States and in all Canadian provinces marriage is regulated by laws. In all states and provinces people must obtain a license before marrying. Whereas some states mandate a waiting period of three to five days before marriage ceremonies can be performed, after which

couples obtain a marriage license, other states do not have such waiting periods. In order to obtain a license, individuals must be of a certain age (generally eighteen) or have parental permission to marry. They must take blood tests to determine whether they have certain sexually transmitted diseases. Family and marriage laws contain clauses pertaining to the protection of children born of marital unions and regulate couples' ownership of property, making them responsible for any debts they may incur. States have civil officials, such as judges, to perform marriage ceremonies, but many people prefer to be married by clerics, such as rabbis or priests.

If persons choose to have their marriage cere-

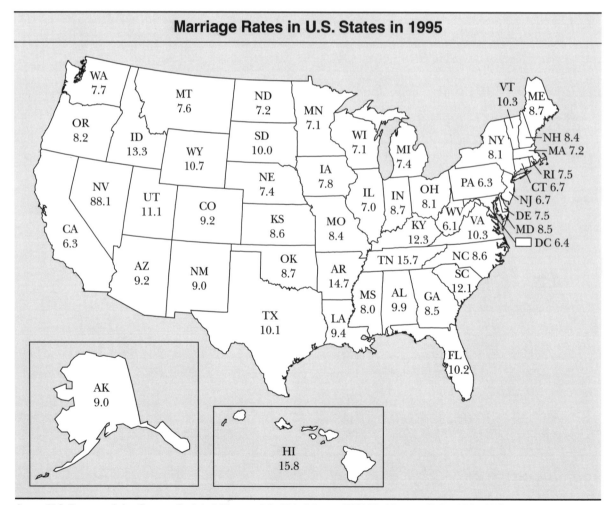

Marriage Rates in U.S. States in 1995

WA 7.7
MT 7.6
ND 7.2
MN 7.1
VT 10.3
ME 8.7
OR 8.2
ID 13.3
SD 10.0
WI 7.1
NY 8.1
NH 8.4
MA 7.2
WY 10.7
NE 7.4
IA 7.8
MI 7.4
PA 6.3
RI 7.5
CT 6.7
NV 88.1
UT 11.1
CO 9.2
IL 7.0
IN 8.7
OH 8.1
WV 6.1
NJ 6.7
DE 7.5
CA 6.3
KS 8.6
MO 8.4
KY 12.3
VA 10.3
MD 8.5
DC 6.4
AZ 9.2
NM 9.0
OK 8.7
AR 14.7
TN 15.7
NC 8.6
TX 10.1
MS 8.0
AL 9.9
GA 8.5
SC 12.1
LA 9.4
FL 10.2
AK 9.0
HI 15.8

Source: U.S. Bureau of the Census, *Statistical Abstract of the United States: 1997.* Washington, D.C.: GPO, 1997.
Note: Rates represent numbers of marriages per 1,000 residents. In some states—particularly Nevada—rates are high because of marriages of out-of-state residents. The rate for the United States as a whole in 1995 was 8.9.

Although more than half of marriages fail, weddings are almost invariably occasions for unbridled optimism. (Hazel Hankin)

monies performed by clerics rather than by civil officials, they must choose clerics who can legally perform marriages. Some clerics perform marriage ceremonies only for couples who have undergone certain types of marriage counseling. Some will not officiate at the marriages of couples who have ever undergone divorce. Sometimes couples must agree to raise their children as members of a certain faith before clerics will marry them. All major religions have certain beliefs about marital fidelity. These religions require that persons who wish to have religious weddings vow to be faithful to each other. They may also require that couples wishing religious weddings belong to

the religion for a certain period of time and agree that their children shall be raised as members of the religious denomination. Religions that stipulate whom their members can marry do not recognize the sanctity of interfaith marriages.

Marriage Statistics. During the twentieth century divorces increased dramatically in the United States. In 1920 one in seven marriages ended in divorce. In 1985 this ratio had increased to one in two. In the late 1990's the divorce rate had fallen from the 1985 high; nevertheless, in 1995 more than two out of five marriages ended in divorce. The high divorce rate did not, however, deter people from getting married. It is expected that 90

In 1964 the average age of grooms was twenty-four and that of brides twenty-one. Three decades later the average groom was twenty-seven and the average bride was twenty-five. (Hazel Hankin)

percent of all Americans will marry at least once in their lifetimes. In 1995 more than two million marriages were performed. Moreover, about 40 percent of all marriages involved at least one person who was marrying for the second time. Five out of six divorced men remarry as do four out of five divorced women. Of the more than two million brides who married in 1995, more than 17,000 were more than sixty-five years of age.

The age at which people marry has risen gradually over the last decade of the twentieth century. While in 1964 brides' average age was twenty-one and grooms' twenty-four, in 1995 brides' average age was twenty-five and grooms' twenty-seven. Divorced women who remarry do so at the average age of thirty-seven and divorced males at the average age of forty-one. In the United States the marriage rate of white women is 67 percent higher than that of African American women and the marriage rate of white men is 55 percent higher than that of African American men. In 1995, 85 percent of marriages involved white couples, 11 percent involved African American couples, 1 percent involved couples of other races, and 3 percent involved interracial couples.

Delaying Marriage. Over the last three decades of the twentieth century the age at which people married gradually increased. There are several reasons for this: the effects of the feminist movement, the sexual revolution of the 1960's and early 1970's, delayed childbearing, and longer life expectancy.

The feminist movement of the 1960's and 1970's made it more likely for young women to seek higher education and establish careers. Thus, women are more likely than previously to delay marriage until they have completed their education and established their careers. Also, since women are likely to work throughout their lifetimes, it is unlikely that they feel pressure to marry in order to ensure their financial support. Moreover, the feminist movement has contributed to a change in sex roles in the United States. This change has led women to be more independent, more likely to live on their own, and less likely to seek mates in their teenage years than women of previous generations. Thus, the feminist movement has contributed to encouraging persons to delay marriage until well into their twenties.

The sexual revolution of the 1960's and early 1970's also contributed to delayed marriages. Cohabitation between persons of the opposite sex became much more acceptable in American culture than it was previously. As a result, persons are able to achieve sexual gratification and companionship without marrying. Thus, the age at which people marry has gradually increased.

In the 1980's and 1990's women tended to delay childbearing into their thirties and early forties. This trend has probably been the result of young women's decision to work and establish their careers while they are in their twenties and early thirties. It has also been the result of medical techniques that have made later childbearing safer for mothers and their babies than it was previously. Since people choose to have children at older ages, younger people do not feel great pressure to marry while in their teens or early twenties. Delayed childbearing has contributed to the rise in the average age of brides and grooms.

Longer life expectancy has also caused people to feel less pressure to marry at early ages. In 1995 a twenty-five-year-old woman and a twenty-seven-year-old man could expect to spend nearly fifty years together as husband and wife if they both lived as long as predicted. It is possible that longer life expectancy has prompted many persons to consider whether they can actually spend fifty years with one particular partner.

Types of Marriages. Marriages can be classified in several different ways. First, they can be classified as either monogamous or polygamous. Monogamous marriages are those between only two people whereas polygamous marriages are those between more than two people. Polygyny, a type of polygamy, is the marriage of one man to more than one woman and polyandry is the marriage of one woman to more than one man. Polyandry has never been practiced in the United States, but polygyny has been practiced by several groups. One such group was the Oneida community of Oneida, New York, which was established in 1839. In the latter part of the nineteenth century and the early part of the twentieth century, members of the Church of Jesus Christ of Latter-day Saints (Mormons) practiced polygyny. In the late twentieth century all forms of polygamy were illegal in the United States and Canada. However, a few Mormons living in Utah and Colorado still practice it.

Marriages can also be classified according to the types of relationships between marriage partners. Marriages in the latter part of the twentieth century could be classified as traditional or egalitarian. In traditional marriages males are considered to be the heads of households and the chief decision makers. In these marriages men are generally the breadwinners while women are the homemakers and caretakers of children. Egalitarian marriages, on the other hand, consider husbands and wives as equals who play comparable roles and have comparable responsibilities and rights. At the end of the twentieth century marriages in North America tended to form on an egalitarian basis. However, some conservative groups such as the Christian Coalition and the Promise Keepers are committed to traditional marriage models.

Some sociologists classify marriages according to the communication patterns of couples. Thus, "conflict-habituated" marriages are those in which there is constant conflict and quarreling between spouses. "Devitalized" marriages are characterized by marital partners' indifference toward each

By the 1990's increases in life expectancy allowed the average newly married couple to look forward to fifty years of being together—if their marriages endured. (James L. Shaffer)

other. Many experts consider devitalized marriages to be the most common type of marriage in U.S. society. "Passive-congenial" marriages differ from devitalized marriages in that passive-congenial partners never had an exciting relationship to begin with. In "vital marriages" partners have a warm, loving relationship and are committed to each other. In "total" marriages partners have a close and loving relationship and are totally committed to sharing all parts of each others' lives. Sociologists think that marriage quality can change. Many factors spur change, such as the presence of young children or teenagers in the home, family illness, and financial problems.

Marriage Customs and Rituals. Among the ancient Saracens, peoples that lived on the fringes of the Roman Empire in what is modern Syria, brides carried sprigs of orange blossoms. As oranges were the most bountiful fruit in the region at that time, brides carried their blossoms to ensure fruitful marriages and childbearing. Modern brides have followed this custom by wearing orange blossoms in their hair, by carrying orange blossoms, or by using orange blossoms to decorate churches during weddings. In many early civilizations rice was considered to be a symbol of fruitfulness. Thus, rice was thrown at brides and grooms to ensure fruitful unions. This custom, too, has continued into modern times. The ancient Assyrians, Egyptians, and Hebrews traded sandals as a symbol of good faith when arranging marriages. Thus, modern spouses tie old shoes to the backs of their cars as they leave for their honeymoons, hoping to ensure that their partners will be faithful. Brides wear veils because Roman brides 2,000 years ago wore veils to signify their purity and to ward off evil spirits. For centuries rings have been part of wedding ceremonies, because they symbolize the permanency of the wedding vows and marriage partners' eternal love for each other.

Changes in the Marriage Relationship. Changes in the marriage relationship have come from several sources. The rising divorce rate has caused many couples to be anxious about sharing their worldly possessions, particularly if one spouse is much wealthier than the other. Thus, couples may decide to sign prenuptial agreements before marriage. Such agreements define how property will be divided in the event of divorce. Such agreements may also explain what spouses expect of

A Special Day for Marriage

Most people know February 14 as St. Valentine's Day—a special day for lovers. Around the same time of year, the second Sunday of every February is celebrated as World Marriage Day. The annual event generates parades, dinners, local contests, and other activities designed to encourage married couples to renew their wedding vows.

each other and the consequences if one person fails to meet the other's expectations. Prenuptial agreements may also specify how spouses will handle childbearing and child rearing. Having signed prenuptial agreements, persons may feel more secure about certain aspects of their relationships. However, such agreements may also remove an element of trust that is expected to be a part of the marital relationship.

A vocal gay community has led to changes in marriage customs. Homosexuals and gay rights activists have argued that employers and society at large should accord to gay and lesbian relationships the same legal status that they accord to heterosexual marriages, including granting partners in same-sex relationships pension and insurance benefits. In insisting on the recognition of same-sex marriages, homosexuals demand the right to raise children. The women's rights movement has also changed the nature of marriage. In general, marriage partners in the late twentieth century had more equitable relationships than marriage partners three decades before. Changes in marital relationships have evolved over a long period of time and have given wives a more equitable distribution of property, a greater opportunity to secure credit, and greater employment opportunities than previously. However, the more equitable relationships of late twentieth century North America also placed increased strains on marital relationships, as partners attempted to understand marital roles that evolved during their lifetimes.
                                    —*Annita Marie Ward*

BIBLIOGRAPHY

Coleman, James C. *Intimate Relationships: Marriage and Family.* 2d edition. New York: Macmillan,

1988. Extensive study of all aspects of marriage and of all topics relating to marriage.

Dicanio, Margaret. *Encyclopedia of Marriage, Divorce, and Family*. New York: Facts on File, 1989. Handy source of information on modern lifestyles, including on marriage and marital relationships.

Guteman, James. *Creating a Marriage*. Mahwah, N.J.: Paulist Press, 1994. Analysis of successful marriages.

Mintz, Steven, and Susan Kellogg. *Domestic Revolutions: A Social History of Domestic Family Life*. Brooklyn, N.Y.: The Free Press, 1989. Historical discussion of marriage and other domestic arrangements.

Oliker, Stacey J. *Best Friends and Marriage: Exchange Among Women*. Berkeley, Calif.: University of California Press, 1991. Book in which women share their experiences of marriage and marital relationships.

See also Arranged marriages; Civil marriage ceremonies; Cohabitation; Common-law marriage; Couples; Divorce; Domestic partners; Gay and lesbian families; Group marriage; Marriage counseling; Marriage laws; Matchmaking; Monogamy; Open marriage; Polyandry; Polygyny; Prenuptial agreements; Remarriage; Serial monogamy; Tax laws; Teen marriages; Weddings.

Marriage counseling

Relevant issues: Divorce; Marriage and dating
Significance: Marriage counseling can help partners resolve issues that cause an unhappy or dysfunctional relationship

In marriage counseling, a trained person helps those with courtship, marital, or family problems to understand themselves and to change in ways that promote healthier relationships. In contrast to psychotherapy, in which the focus is on the individual client, the focus in premarital and marital counseling is on the relationship between two people. Such counseling deals with the marital problems of married couples (financial, sexual, in-law, communication, role responsibilities, and so forth) and people considering marriage. This type of counseling emphasizes the sociological or psychosociological aspects of the relationship. It tends to remain at the couple's conscious level of functioning, as opposed to the psychodynamic models of counseling, in which the goal is to uncover some of the unconscious motives for behavior.

Goals of Marriage Counseling. For marriage counseling to be effective, both persons usually are counseled. Because change in one spouse will affect the relationship, both individuals must adapt to the new patterns of thinking and behaving. Marriage counseling is problem-centered so that it tends to be relatively limited in length. Persons are helped to explore, evaluate, and clarify the issues and feelings that bother them so that they more effectively communicate, both verbally and emotionally. They can learn courses of action that lead to some resolution of their problems. The counselor helps couples to make a realistic assessment of their situation and to accept facts that cannot be altered.

The counseling process may bring a final dissolution of a relationship that already has been destroyed, thus preventing any further damage to the people involved. The final resolution is decided upon by the couple (or at least one of the members), with the assistance of the counselor, and never by the counselor alone. The emphasis in marriage counseling is not on the perpetuation or dissolution of the relationship, but rather on the happiness, fulfillment, and growth of the individuals in the relationship.

The goals of marriage counseling depend on the problems the couple brings to counseling. When the problem is an issue in the marriage (for example, finances, in-laws, or alcohol and drug use), the assumption is made that the personality characteristics and needs of the interacting couple come together satisfactorily and that the cause of the difficulty is external to the marriage. It is not that the partners are fundamentally unhappy together, but rather that they face a situation that they cannot handle. When the problem is a case of marital conflict, then it is personalities or personal characteristics of the individuals that do not mesh, and a basic conflict develops.

In both cases, but particularly the second, one or both of the partners' attitude toward marriage is one of ambivalence: Someone is not happy with the state of the relationship but is not yet ready to give up on the marriage. The goal of counseling in such cases is to help the parties explore what they

Marriage counselors are trained to help couples—both those who are married and those considering marriage—to understand themselves better, with the goal of developing healthy and lasting relationships. (James L. Shaffer)

are getting from the marriage and whether they feel that there are irreconcilable differences. If so, the marriage counselor's role is to lend support to separation and eventual dissolution of the relationship.

Role of Past and Present Experiences. Another goal of marriage counseling is to help married couples recognize the connection between their present inappropriate behavior patterns and past experiences and attitudes. People are products of their past experiences. A person's personality, including feelings, attitudes, and the abilities to love and be affectionate and intimate, is formed as the person grows up. Two married people will have grown up differently and separately, so it is likely that they will have different ideas about marriage. These differences often are a contributing cause to the marital conflict. Knowledge and insight may not changes attitudes or emotions, but they help relieve some of the couple's intense feelings and attitudes about themselves and the other person.

The counseling process also helps to alleviate guilt and shame that the married people may feel about the present state of their relationship. One of the marriage partners may take the responsibility for the troubled state of the marriage. This is especially true if there has been emotional abuse and one of the individuals has been continually put down or has been told that the conflict is his or her fault. The marriage counselor facilitates better self-understanding, an understanding of the other person, and understanding of the marriage, and tries to relieve guilt and shame by reminding the couple that marital problems usually are the responsibility of both individuals. That is why counseling is more likely to be successful if both individuals are involved: There is a problem in the relationship that impacts both people, and both must change or adapt. Through increased self-awareness and awareness of the other, both partners come to recognize that each needs to change if the marital relationship is going to improve.

The Marriage Counselor. A trained marriage counselor has at least a graduate degree in marriage and family therapy, or in an allied mental health field with specialized work in marriage and the family. Both formal course work and supervised clinical experience are required for certification. The American Association of Marriage and Family Therapists is the leading clinical professional organization for marriage counselors, and only those who have been trained appropriately are allowed to join. Many states now require that marriage and family counselors be licensed by the state in which they practice, and licenses are granted only to those with appropriate credentials.

Marriage counselors perform several functions. They serve as an information source in situations requiring factual information, they help in making decisions about a present dilemma (such as moving or a wife going to work), they assist couples in relieving tension and stress brought on by a personal or situational crisis, and they help the partners change their inappropriate behavior patterns, such as abusive behavior, inappropriate spending, or infidelity. Marriage counselors develop a helping, trusting, and respectful counseling environment so that the married couple can improve their relationship, can express both positive and negative feelings and emotions, and can share with the counselor in an open and truthful manner.

Premarital Counseling. Another form of marriage counseling is premarital counseling. The basic aim of premarital counseling is to help engaged couples acquire a better understanding of what each partner is bringing into the marriage and what marriage entails. A basic difference between premarital and marital counseling is that premarital counseling is not necessarily problem-centered: It is more preventive in nature. By getting counseling before they get married, partners can learn to anticipate areas of conflict and see how their pasts may affect their lives together. Cohabiting couples can learn how marriage might change their relationships and resolve issues before they marry.

Premarital counseling not only helps the couple become aware of potential stress points in the marriage but also helps them develop problem-solving techniques to use when the relationship does get into trouble. Engaged couples often are so romantically attached and are so absorbed in making wedding plans that they neglect to look at and work on potential stress points in their marriage.

Couples often enter premarital counseling before experiencing day-to-day living in a cohabiting relationship, so there is a much heavier educational component. The partners learn what to expect in a marriage.

Family Counseling. Family counseling, another offshoot of marriage counseling, goes beyond the husband-wife relationship. As part of marriage counseling, the entire family may be asked to come to a counseling session so that the counselor and family can assess how the entire family is functioning and determine how the husband-wife relationship is affecting the entire family.

Sometimes family counseling reveals that a family member has special needs or emotional or behavioral problems that affect the family. Counseling may be necessary for this person as well as for other family members, who will explore their feelings about and relationships with this family member and discover ways to resolve problems with him or her. Family therapy often is appropriate when a family member is being rehabilitated for substance abuse or there are parent-child conflicts.

Like marital counseling, family counseling is problem-centered. It is short-term, and there are minimal attempts at changing people's personalities or discovering deep psychological roots of problems. The counseling primarily concerns the relationships within the family. It frequently involves individual sessions with family members to learn family secrets, to gather specific information, and to help with individual adjustments.

—*Sander M. Latts*

BIBLIOGRAPHY

Gordon, Lori. *If You Really Loved Me.* Palo Alto, Calif.: Science and Behavioral Books, 1996.

Gray, John. *Men Are from Mars, Women Are from Venus.* New York: HarperCollins, 1992.

Kirschenbaum, Mira. *Too Good to Leave, Too Bad to Stay.* New York: Dutton, 1996.

Napier, August, and Carl Whitaker. *The Family Crucible.* New York: Harper & Row, 1978.

Satir, Virginia. *The New People-Making.* Palo Alto, Calif.: Science and Behavioral Books, 1988.

Skidmore, Rex, Hulda Van Streeter, Garret Skidmore, and C. Jay Skidmore. *Marriage Consulting.* New York: Harper & Row, 1956.

See also Adultery; American Association for Marriage and Family Therapists (AAMFT); Couples; Cruelty as grounds for divorce; Divorce; Divorce mediation; Domestic violence; Ellis, Albert; Engagement; Family counseling; Masters, William H., and Virginia E. Johnson.

Marriage laws

RELEVANT ISSUES: Divorce; Law; Marriage and dating

SIGNIFICANCE: Marriage laws are those that define the requirements for entering into and terminating the marriage relationship

Because of the important role that marriage plays in the lives of individuals and the broader society, American law has traditionally viewed the marriage relationship as an appropriate subject of legal regulation. Consequently, one may neither marry nor cease being married without encountering the law at several points. Marriage laws govern who may be married and the formal steps one must take to become married or, conversely, to become unmarried through annulment or divorce.

Eligibility Requirements. Most people who marry do not need to contemplate whether they are, in fact, legally eligible to marry. The law's eligibility requirements for marriage do not pose a barrier to typical couples. Nevertheless, there are limits to who may marry. For example, persons must be above a certain minimum age to marry in most jurisdictions. Commonly, individuals seeking marriage must be at least sixteen years of age and have their parents' consent if they are not at least eighteen years of age. Similarly, persons must seek to marry eligible partners. In most states, this means that individuals seeking marriage must be of the opposite sex and that they must not be too closely related. All jurisdictions prohibit marriages between immediate family members and many prohibit marriages between first cousins, uncles and nieces, and aunts and nephews. Additionally, since bigamy remains a crime in virtually every jurisdiction, individuals currently married are not eligible to marry again. Finally, marriage is in essence a contract between two people, and, accordingly, the parties to this contract must be mentally competent to enter into the marriage contract.

Formal Requirements for Obtaining a Marriage. A minority of states allow individuals to undertake a "common law" marriage—that is, one which does not involve a formal marriage license and marriage ceremony. However, because society believes marriage to be a serious undertaking and not a fit subject for haphazard commitment, most jurisdictions impose legal requirements intended to formalize the marriage bond. Chief among these is the requirement that persons seeking marriage apply for and obtain a marriage license. The marriage application and license process serves a number of purposes. The application for the marriage license requires that applicants disclose information relating to their eligibility to be married—their ages, for example, and whether they are already married to someone else. These disclosures allow states to enforce marriage eligibility laws. For example, through the application process and related medical examination some states prevent marriages when one party has a venereal or other contagious disease that might infect spouses or children. The marriage license also serves the purpose of creating formal evidence of marriage. Whether parties are in fact married has many legal implications, and the license requirement allows the law to avoid swearing matches over the existence of a marriage. Finally, the application process serves as an information gathering device, which facilitates statistical record keeping.

In addition to the marriage licence, most jurisdictions also impose a waiting period between the application for a marriage license and its issuance. This period is intended to prevent marriages from occurring when persons are under the influence of alcohol or to prevent persons from marrying on a dare. Generally, waiting periods are designed to impress upon applicants the seriousness of their undertaking. Moreover, states attempt to emphasize the seriousness of the marriage commitment by requiring that some form of ceremony seal the marriage bond. Although states do not specify the contents of such ceremonies, which may be either civil, religious, or both, this requirement serves the purpose of lending a measure of gravity to the marriage commitment.

Ending a Marriage. The same legal impulse that formalizes the beginnings of the marriage union also formalizes its termination. Traditionally, marriage laws placed substantial barriers before married couples who wished to sever their relationship. Most states required that couples justify their desire to divorce by stating a significant reason,

such as physical or mental cruelty, desertion, habitual drunkenness, drug addiction, insanity, impotence, or infection with a venereal disease. Under traditional rules, one or both spouses sought a divorce on the grounds that their partner was at fault in one of these or in other respects. More recently, however, many states have adopted "no-fault" divorce laws. These laws allow persons to divorce without supplying proof that either spouse is particularly to blame for the marital breakdown. Commonly, a divorce will be granted in a no-fault jurisdiction on the basis of "irreconcilable differences" or "irretrievable breakdown."

Both fault-based and no-fault divorce systems require that divorces be finalized by a court order. Such orders not only declare that the parties to the divorce are no longer married and thus legally free to marry again if they choose, but they also deal with such matters as property division, child custody and visitation rights, child support, and spousal support. The participation of a court in the termination of a marriage, however, does not mean that most divorces are the subject of fierce court battles. The overwhelming percentage of divorces are the result of mutually agreed upon terms that courts routinely ratify.

The second common legal procedure for ending marriages is annulment. This procedure is applied in situations in which the law essentially denies that a marriage was ever valid. Thus, divorces terminate valid marriages while annulments end the facade of marriages that were not in fact marriages. Marriages procured by the fraud of one party upon another are common objects of annulment proceedings. Misrepresentations concerning criminal records, venereal diseases, and the ability to have sex or children may provide grounds for annulment. Additionally, marriages to ineligible partners—siblings or children, for example—may be annulled.

Modern Legal Developments. The trend of modern legal developments has been to relax the role of government in supervising the marriage relationship. The relaxed oversight of marriage is most visible in the increased ease with which couples may obtain a divorce. It is also witnessed by the diminished attention that the law pays to extramarital sexual activity by married couples. The handling of adultery, once a crime in most jurisdictions and solid grounds for divorce, is an example of modern perspectives. In many states, adultery is no longer a crime. In the states in which it is still a crime, it is seldom prosecuted. Moreover, adultery is no longer grounds for divorce in "no-fault" divorce states.

Emerging legal developments may also tend to lessen the legal significance of the traditional marriage relationship. Property settlements have long been a feature of divorce proceedings involving married partners. Recently, some cases have given nonmarried cohabiting individuals the same rights to a division of property as enjoyed by divorcing couples. Moreover, the U.S. Supreme Court in the last several decades of the twentieth century vigorously undermined the traditional significance of the marriage relationship by confer-

ring legal benefits on the illegitimate children of a marriage. Illegitimate children now enjoy substantial legal protections unknown in the past. Finally, sustained attacks have been made in recent years upon perhaps the most essential element of traditional marriage: that it be a relationship between a man and a woman. Advocates of gay and lesbian marriages have relied on state and federal constitutional provisions, such as the equal protection clause of the U.S. Constitution, to argue that laws prohibiting same-sex marriages are unconstitutional. These challenges have generally failed, but the possibility of their success in one state—Hawaii—prompted the U.S. Congress to enact the Defense of Marriage Act in 1996. Normally, marriages in one state are recognized in others. Many

In 1975 a Colorado county clerk (right) interpreted state marriage laws as empowering her to grant a marriage license to a gay couple (left). (AP/Wide World Photos)

opponents of same-sex marriage have feared that this normal practice would mean that the recognition of same-sex marriages in one state would force other states to recognize them. The Defense of Marriage Act provides that states are not required to give legal effect to same-sex marriages performed in other states. —*Timothy L. Hall*

BIBLIOGRAPHY

Clark, Homer H., Jr. *The Law of Domestic Relations in the United States.* 2 vols. St. Paul, Minn.: West Publishing, 1987.

Green, Joyce Hens, John V. Long, and Roberta L. Murawski. *Dissolution of Marriage.* Colorado Springs, Colo.: Shepard's/McGraw-Hill, 1986.

Harwood, Norma. *A Woman's Legal Guide to Separation and Divorce in All Fifty States.* New York: Charles Scribner's Sons, 1985.

Neely, Richard. *The Divorce Decision: The Legal and Human Consequences of Ending a Marriage.* New York: McGraw-Hill, 1984.

Sack, Steven Mitchell. *The Complete Legal Guide to Marriage, Divorce, Custody, and Living Together.* New York: McGraw-Hill, 1987.

Strasser, Mark Philip. *Legally Wed: Same-Sex Marriage and the Constitution.* Ithaca, N.Y.: Cornell University Press, 1997.

Weitzman, Lenore J. *The Marriage Contract: Spouses, Lovers, and the Law.* New York: Free Press, 1981.

See also Age of consent; Annulment; Antimiscegenation laws; Bigamy; Civil marriage ceremonies; Common-law marriage; Divorce; Family courts; Family law; Gay and lesbian families; Legal separation; *Loving v. Virginia*; Prenuptial agreements; Uniform Marriage and Divorce Act (UMDA).

Marriage squeeze

RELEVANT ISSUES: Demographics; Marriage and dating

SIGNIFICANCE: The marriage squeeze is the effect of an imbalance in the supply of marriageable males or females

The phrase "marriage squeeze" refers to the consequences of a shortage of men or women at the likely time of marriage. It happens when the sex ratio, the number of males per one hundred females, is high or low. Under such circumstances there are either more or less men seeking to marry than there are potential wives available.

The combination of variations in birth rates and the age difference between women and men at marriage can result in a low supply of potential partners. For example, increasing birth rates during the 1950's baby boom meant that cohorts of males and females entering adulthood were larger than the ones born earlier. Since American and Canadian women tend to marry men approximately two to three years their senior, "baby boomer" women found a shortage of older men to marry in the 1970's. Declining birth rates in the 1970's and 1980's subsequently remedied the marriage squeeze for females, since there were 99.2 men for 100 women in the group between ages twenty-five and forty-four in 1992.

Besides age, structural factors such as education, race, power, and employment have influenced the incidence of a marriage squeeze. In the 1990's African American women faced a marriage squeeze because of an absolute shortage of young African American males, whose low socioeconomic status further affected their desirability as husbands. Native American men have also faced a marriage squeeze because of the large number of Native American women who marry non-Native Americans. Many professional women who reached their thirties in the 1990's faced a marriage squeeze because, in addition to having to choose from a small supply of acceptable marriage partners, such women had careers and personal expectations that conflicted with traditional gender roles. —*Jacques M. Henry*

See also Baby-boom generation; Baby boomers; Family demographics; Gender longevity; Interfaith marriages; Interracial families; Marriage; Single life.

Marxist critique of the family

RELEVANT ISSUES: Economics and work; Parenting and family relationships

SIGNIFICANCE: Marxists and neo-Marxists attack the traditional nuclear family as an unnatural social organization and an instrument of oppression

Karl Marx and Friedrich Engels, the founders of scientific socialism, challenged a number of political, economic, and social institutions that had become associated with the industrializing countries of nineteenth century Europe. Among these institutions was the nuclear family (or "pairing family," as they sometimes called it). Since that time, Marxists and neo-Marxists have continued to attack the traditional family variously as a tool of societal oppression, as a means for facilitating capitalist production, as a structure of patriarchal domination, and as a symbol of heterosexual orthodoxy. Although Marxist critiques of the family have taken a number of different tacks, most treat the family either as an economic unit, as an instrument of societal control, or as a power structure.

Family as an Economic Unit. Early Marxist critiques of the family tended to focus on the family's function as an economic unit. Marx, Engels, and their followers were most concerned with economic production, and they viewed various social and political institutions in that context. The structure of the labor force and its relationship to the larger society was a particular concern.

Marxists typically view the most important social cleavages to be rooted in class, and class identity was

Karl Marx in 1881. (AP/Wide World Photos)

for them the most meaningful and politically powerful identity. Following this logic, divisions within a class—between national groups or clans or indeed families—were understood to obscure class identity and thus to postpone the proletarian revolution, which orthodox Marxists believe must eventually overthrow the capitalist system.

For this same reason, the Marxists have argued, the elites of the feudal and capitalist systems—those who own the "means of production"—surely have an interest in perpetuating the institution of the family for as long as possible. This presumably has influenced the structure of economic systems. Marxists have observed that the manorial system of agriculture organized land into plots to be

worked by individual men and their families. They have noted that plots were typically handed down through primogeniture (the right of the eldest son to inherit property), thus perpetuating and strengthening the significance of the family as an economic unit. Marxists have held up the arrangement of cities, the provision of health care, and various other aspects of everyday life as evidence of the institutionalization of the family.

Indeed, some Marxists have argued that the very institution of the nuclear family was invented by property-owning elites—that the modern family is an artifact of feudalism or mercantile capitalism. For example, it has been argued that the "family wage" made possible by the capitalist-driven industrial revolution made it possible for women to assume the role of homemakers. The linking of the nuclear family to relatively recent economic developments became an article of faith among nineteenth century Marxists and a subject for extensive scholarship. The theory, however, has subsequently been widely rejected by anthropological studies that trace family units of father, mother, and children to prehistoric times. Modern Marxist critiques nevertheless continue to argue that, irrespective of how it originally developed, the institution of the family has been pressed into the service of capitalism and the state.

To be sure, modern capitalist economic theory focuses on the "household" as a primary economic unit, although typically the relationships among the occupants of the household are not especially relevant to economic theory. Nevertheless, modern neo-Marxist critics argue that household-focused economics encourages overconsumption and fosters alienation, societal fragmentation, and other dysfunctions. In this sense, the neo-Marxist critique of the family springs from the same advocacy of communalism that undergirds its rejection of individualism.

Family as an Instrument of Societal Control. This leads to a second Marxist critique of the family—that it serves as an instrument of societal control. Once again, at one level this portrayal of the family is generally accepted. The family is widely regarded by mainstream sociologists and political scientists as a fundamental socializing agent. It is through the family that the basic elements of a society's culture are passed down to succeeding generations. Morals, mores, manners, tastes, religious beliefs, as well as historical memory and political values, are transmitted largely through the family. It is for this reason that Marxists have sought to supplant the family with the larger community when they have desired to weaken what they regard as capitalist, nationalistic, sexist, or otherwise "oppressive" cultures.

In the last half of the twentieth century in the West, homosexual rights movements adapted the Marxist critique to their cause. The institution of the traditional family, defined as a married man and woman with their children, is seen as a tool of society's heterosexual orthodoxy. By excluding same-sex marriages from the traditional definition of family, it is claimed, the state, through tax codes and other policies, seeks to marginalize homosexuals. It should be noted that such critiques treat the family primarily as a grouping for the distribution of political power and social sanction rather than as a social unit for the nurturing and rearing of children. On this score too, however, some neo-Marxists have called for the redefinition of family to include same-sex marriage and other "nontraditional" households, which allegedly would provide children with an adequate, or even superior, system of support and development.

Family as a Power Structure. Other critiques, popularized by Marx and Engels but reenergized by the late twentieth century feminist movement, address the family as a power structure. Instead of evaluating the institution of family as a unit of a larger economic or social system, this approach examines the relationships within the family unit itself.

For example, the traditional family is typically characterized as a patriarchal arrangement that places authority in the hands of male "breadwinners." As wives and mothers, women are depicted as being burdened with responsibilities while receiving little in the way of authority. Although early feminist movements attacked women's traditional role in the nuclear family as sexist—an attack that netted some results in the second half of the twentieth century in the form of court decisions and policies such as affirmative action and family leave—some Marxist strains of feminism attack the institution of the nuclear family as inherently patriarchal and unreformable.

Some apply the issue of unequal power relationships within the family to the situation of children, who might be portrayed as the helpless subjects of authoritarian family structures. Again, there is little dispute that the incidence of child neglect and abuse within the family is unacceptably high. Milder critiques note that the power relationships within families must be tempered by regard for the well-being of the individuals, the family, and society at large. Harsher critiques, however, view the traditional family as an oppressive and misogynist institution, one which nevertheless receives the sanction of the state and of society. Thus, affronts to Western notions of human rights and democracy, such as absolutism, rape, and slavery, are supposedly permitted within the power structure of the family.

If there is one theme that unites the Marxist critiques of the family, it is that the nuclear family is neither a natural nor an irreplaceable grouping for human societies. Although neither of these assertions has been conclusively proven, the various strains of the Marxist attack on the family continue to have resonance with some policymakers and various groups on the political Left.

—*Steve D. Boilard*

BIBLIOGRAPHY
Engels, Friedrich. *The Condition of the Working Class in England.* New York: Penguin, 1987.
_____. *The Origin of the Family, Private Property and the State.* International Publishers, 1942.
Farber, Bernard. *Kinship and Class: A Midwestern Study.* New York: Basic Books, 1971.
Rubin, Lillian B. *Families on the Fault Line: America's Working Class Speaks About the Family, the Economy, Race, and Ethnicity.* New York: HarperCollins, 1994.
Seccombe, Wally. *A Millennium of Family Change: Feudalism to Capitalism in Northwestern Europe.* London: Verso, 1992.
Stacey, Judith. *Brave New Families: Stories of Domestic Upheaval in Late Twentieth Century America.* New York: Basic Books, 1991.

See also Child rearing; Communal living; Dysfunctional families; Family: concept and history; Feminist sociology; Gay and lesbian families; Household; Patriarchs; Primogeniture.

Maslow, Abraham

BORN: April 1, 1908, Brooklyn, N.Y.
DIED: June 8, 1970, Menlo Park, Calif.
AREAS OF ACHIEVEMENT: Children and child development; Parenting and family relationships
SIGNIFICANCE: Maslow brought forth a theory of motivation and personality that highlighted striving for self-actualization

Known as the father of modern humanism, Abraham Harold Maslow developed a theory of motivation and personality. After receiving a Ph.D. in 1934, he concentrated his career on research, writing, and teaching, eventually becoming the chairman of the Psychology Department at Brandeis University in 1961 and later the president of the American Psychological Association.

Maslow's theory of motivation and personality was primarily developed from his work on normal and creative people. His approach was novel, because it focused on healthy psychology, as opposed to psychopathology and psychotherapeutic treatment. According to his theory, all individuals have a hierarchy of needs that must be met for physical and psychological survival. These include certain basic needs ranging from physiological needs (water, nourishment), safety (avoidance of harm and pain), belonging and love (intimacy, gregariousness, identification), and esteem (approval by self and others). Once these more basic needs are met, individuals can then go on to meet more complex needs, such as the need for self-actualization (recognizing one's special capabilities and potentials) and a need for understanding (emphasizing acquisition of information and a hunger for stimulation and experience). Throughout individuals' efforts to meet these survival needs, it is assumed that individuals push to develop their maximum potential, achieving unselfish love, creative living, unbiased understanding, and peak experiences.

—*Nancy A. Piotrowski*

See also Allport, Gordon; Love.

Masters, William H.

BORN: December 27, 1915, Cleveland, Ohio

Johnson, Virginia E.

BORN: February 11, 1925, Springfield, Mo.

AREAS OF ACHIEVEMENT: Health and medicine; Marriage and dating
SIGNIFICANCE: Noted for their research and understanding of human sexual behavior, Masters and Johnson were pioneers in the scientific study of sexual arousal and the treatment of sexual problems

After receiving his medical degree from the University of Rochester School of Medicine and Dentistry in 1943, William Masters, a gynecologist, began his laboratory studies of sexual behavior in 1954 while on the faculty of Washington University in St. Louis, Missouri. Virginia Johnson, who studied psychology and sociology at Drury College in Springfield, Missouri, and the University of Missouri joined him as a research associate in 1957. At that time, scientists knew little about human re-

William H. Masters and Virginia E. Johnson in 1970. (AP/Wide World Photos)

sponses to sexual stimulation. Masters and Johnson used motion pictures, electrocardiograms, electroencephalograms, polygraph-like instruments, and other scientific equipment to record physiological responses to sexual stimulations in men and women who volunteered to engage in sexual activity. In 1964 they established the Reproductive Biology Research Foundation in St. Louis, Missouri. In 1973 they became codirectors of the Masters and Johnson Institute in St. Louis, training thousands of workers in sex therapy. Their research stirred up much controversy and was met with much suspicion. Many critics have called them immoral and accused them of dehumanizing sex.

In 1966 the results of their eleven-year research project were published in *Human Sexual Response*,

which described the physiological responses during four phases of erotic arousal for males and females. Although written in technical language for physicians and other health scientists, the book became a best-seller. After counseling hundreds of married couples about problems dealing with sexual performance, Masters and Johnson published *Human Sexual Inadequacy* in 1970, dealing with the treatment of sexual problems, including impotence, premature ejaculation, and frigidity. This book is considered by many experts to be the first comprehensive study of the physiology and anatomy of human sexual activity under laboratory conditions.

Homosexuality in Perspective, a report on the clinical treatment of the sexual problems of homosexuals, appeared in 1979. Although they received much criticism for their views, Masters and Johnson claimed that they were able to change the sexual preference of homosexuals who wished to change. More controversy was sparked by their 1988 publication of *Crisis: Heterosexual Behavior in the Age of AIDS*, wherein they forecast an epidemic spread of acquired immunodeficiency syndrome (AIDS) among heterosexuals. Masters and Johnson were married in 1971 and have continued to collaborate since their divorce in 1993. Their other works include *The Pleasure Bond: A New Look at Sexuality and Commitment* (1975), *Ethical Issues in Sex Therapy and Research* (1977), and *Textbook of Sexual Medicine* (1979). Together with Robert C. Kolodny they coauthored *Human Sexuality* (1982) and *Heterosexuality* (1994). —*Alvin K. Benson*

See also Acquired immunodeficiency syndrome (AIDS); Fertility and infertility; Marriage counseling; Sex education; Sexual revolution; Sexuality and sexual taboos.

Matchmaking

RELEVANT ISSUES: Marriage and dating; Sociology
SIGNIFICANCE: While Western societies have seen a decline in the practice of matchmaking, by which marriages are arranged by third persons, expanding computer technology has made it possible for individuals to establish intimate relationships with each other via the Internet

Matchmaking is an age-old occupation, and the place of the matchmaker in human society ranges from that of honored and wise judge of human nature to neighborhood busybody and even pander. How matchmakers are perceived and the functions they perform are indissolubly connected with the social context in which mating relationships between the sexes take place.

Traditional Place of the Matchmaker. In traditional societies the matchmaker has filled a critical function in ensuring that appropriate and socially desirable matches take place while the contracting parties, particularly the parents, expend as little time, trouble, and money as possible. The skills of the matchmaker—who was usually, although not always, a woman—consisted in maintaining a network of contacts to potential matches, in having the ability to approach those concerned with tact

and discretion, and in understanding the implicit requirements in financial and social terms that would translate into a successful match. Her primary concerns were not romantic attraction, or even physical attractiveness, but property, dowry, family history, and social compatibility. These, more than any presumed love interest, were paramount in societies in which successful mating served to continue the social fabric of the family in perpetuity. The occupation of matchmaking has always been a critical one in societies in which honor and "face" are of great importance, since the object of matches may be to improve the position in society of one or the other participant or family, while ensuring that family dignity is preserved. For this reason, until relatively recently, matchmaking has been a common feature of Islamic, Japanese, and Jewish cultures, in which delicacy of feeling is important to social standing in the community. It is still practiced in more traditional families within those cultures, although not as exclusively as in the past. In India, where caste is still an important issue, matchmaking is a common practice. In the United States it is no longer considered a bona fide occupation.

The Romantic Age. The onset of romanticism around the turn of the nineteenth century set the stage for a change in prevailing myths about relations between the sexes, a change that was reflected in the novel, the new popular literary form that became and remained a major form of mass culture. The problematic nature of romantic attraction was explored in detail in such nineteenth century literary classics as Gustave Flaubert's *Madame Bovary* (1857) and Leo Tolstoy's *Anna Karenina* (1875-1877), both of which described family life in an atmosphere of unrestrained romanticism that collided with traditional values. A careful reading of these artistic and social documents reveals a great deal about the difficulty of choosing a mate based solely on romantic love. It seemed that the end result of the romantic impulse, if untempered by practicality and common sense, might be death and dissolution. On the other hand, the *o-miai*, the Japanese tradition of finding a mate through the ministrations of a matchmaker, which was depicted in Japanese novelist Jun'ichirō Tanizaki's *The Makioka Sisters* (1949), was subject to greater strains in the modern age. Here one sees the conflict between the ways of the past and the present, as three sisters of varying degrees of "modernity" seek to find suitable mates. The modern woman's desire to choose her own mate seemed to doom the role of the professional matchmaker.

The Sexual Revolution. Whether as a result of the failure of parental control, the loosening of family ties, the victory of romanticism, the ultimate emancipation of women, or simply the improvement of contraceptive devices, the demise of the function of matchmaker seemed almost certain with the arrival of the sexual revolution in the 1950's and 1960's. New freedom was in the air, and relations between the sexes seemed to be suddenly less difficult, more spontaneous, and certainly more promiscuous. The need for family attachments threatened to disappear forever with the frenetic acceptance—particularly by the young and overindulged baby-boom generation—of instant gratification and momentary pleasures, encapsulated in the motto: "Never trust anyone over thirty." The ultimate result of this new freedom, however, was a growing awareness of such attendant social evils as drug use, epidemic venereal disease, and a feeling of ultimate disconnectedness and impermanence. Yet, the desire for connectedness, through the discovery of a compatible and loving mate whom one might marry, has persisted. Personals columns in newspapers, magazines, and newsletters—all replete with advertisements that resonate with personal coded information, wit, and despair—appear everywhere. Loneliness is seemingly rampant, in spite of improvements in communication technology; psychological, physiological, and sociological studies of relations between the sexes; how-to books for every variety of potential relationship; and greater permissiveness among all social classes.

The Mating Game. Because of the perceived need for an improved methodology for mate selection as well as the time-honored entrepreneurial vision of money to be made a number of dating services began to appear and proliferated in the post-World War II period. These services have made use of advertisements and publicity venues to offer their services and find prospective clients. They are, in fact, a twentieth century form of the age-old matchmaking service. The modern introduction bureau, where for a few dollars one can get a long list of phone numbers of presum-

ably marriage-minded, or at least romance-minded, individuals, might or might not interview the persons who wish to be represented on its rolls. A panoply of dating and introduction agencies, ranging from expensive introduction clubs that put on exclusive social events to cheap fly-by-night newsletters run out of a garage, promise to make that important initial contact. A service called "It's Just Lunch," which arranges lunch dates for busy professionals in a number of cities, brings career professionals together for dutch-treat lunch dates in a nonthreatening and low-key atmosphere. Each service advertises its accomplishments by trumpeting the number of matches—hopefully marriages—it successfully consummates. Several mail-order services for obtaining foreign-born brides for marriage-minded men, particularly in the United States, Great Britain, and western Europe, cater to the desires of women in underdeveloped countries to find a better life in the First World. In most of these services there is a preponderance of men seeking women in the younger age brackets and a corresponding imbalance of women seeking men in the over-fifty age group.

The Binary Love Bite. The advent of the Internet as a pervasive influence in the 1990's has likewise resulted in a new twist on the matchmaking function. A number of sites on the Internet (Singles Alley, LoveSearch.com, Match.com) are designed to bring one partner, through the anonymity of the computer, into communication with another. They may take the form of profiles describing seeker and sought, chat rooms in which interested parties can initiate exploratory conversations, listserves where one can seek out persons who share one's interests and enthusiasms, and online personal ads. The glitzy and facile ease of entry onto the Web and the speed of online instantaneous communication have replaced the laborious and sensitive attention to personal qualifications of the traditional matchmaker. Once the prospective mates get beyond the computer interface, however, they are still at the mercy of physical limitations and fears, but without the intercession of the human matchmaker. Perhaps the problem is simply mathematical: One plus one does not equal two, and certainly not three, in the binary mathematics of the computer-turned-matchmaker.

—*Gloria Fulton*

BIBLIOGRAPHY

Batten, Mary. *Sexual Strategies: How Females Choose Their Mates.* New York: G. P. Putnam's Sons, 1992.

Clare, Anthony. *Lovelaw: Love, Sex, and Marriage Around the World.* London: BBC Publications, 1986.

Glodova, Mila, and Richard Onizuka. *Mail-Order Brides: Women for Sale.* Fort Collins, Colo.: Alaken, 1994.

Harris, Louis. *None But the Lonely Heart—Cupid in Business: The Story of Lonely-Heart Clubs, Marriage Brokers, Introduction Bureaus, Friendship Services, and Correspondence Clubs.* New York: Readers Press, 1943.

Kurian, George, ed. *Cross-Cultural Perspectives of Mate-Selection and Marriage.* Westport, Conn.: Greenwood Press, 1979.

Mullan, Bob. *The Mating Trade.* London: Routledge & Kegan Paul, 1984.

Small, Meredith F. *What's Love Got to Do with It? The Evolution of Human Mating.* New York: Anchor Books, 1995.

See also Arranged marriages; Couples; Courting rituals; Cultural influences; Dating; Jews.

Maternity leave

RELEVANT ISSUES: Demographics; Economics and work; Health and medicine; Parenting and family relationships

SIGNIFICANCE: As women comprised a larger and larger percentage of the paid labor force in the United States, their need for time off from work to care for their families without damaging their careers became more urgent

During the earlier part of the twentieth century, women were either not expected to be in the paid labor force or were expected to work only temporarily. Those who were or sought to be part of the paid labor force were, in fact, penalized for being out of the home. They were either not hired at all because they might one day become pregnant, were paid less because they were expected to be in the work force only temporarily before returning to the home, or were expected to remain single and childless. Women who remained in the paid labor force, especially in the professions, were expected to be like "nun scientists"—that is, married

to their work and not obligated to the nuclear family and the home.

Social Changes. Well into the second wave of feminism in the United States in the 1970's, resistance to maternity leave remained an indicator of resistance to women working outside the home. Women who went on maternity leave risked their health insurance benefits and seniority. In 1978 the passage of the Pregnancy Discrimination Act guaranteed insurance for women on maternity leave.

As society and economics changed, leading to an increase in the rate of divorce, single-parent households, and the need for two incomes to support families, women's requirements affected the requirements of the paid labor force. At the same time, notions of women's equality in personal and economic terms demanded of men that they share household and family duties and posed the question of fairness in career seniority. The increasing number of new mothers in the labor force accounted for much of the growth in female employment, with the largest increase during the 1960's and 1970's. In the 1970's discussions around the issues of maternity and paternity leave centered on the demand for fully paid leave and subsidized day care. Some insisted that day care should be provided at all workplaces, not simply at those companies employing large numbers of women, so that parents had a choice in day-care options and so that companies could not claim that it was too expensive to hire women. There was also discussion about the right of mothers to nurse their children on the job.

Legal Changes. During the 1990's the need for maternity leave and for time to care for family members combined with growing notions of gender equality. This resulted in the enactment of the Family and Medical Leave Act of 1993, the first act to be signed into law by President Bill Clinton. This federal law required employers to provide workers twelve weeks of unpaid leave in order to tend to personal illness, the birth and care of newborns, or the needs of workers' parents. It required companies with fifty or more employees to maintain workers' health benefits while they are on leave and to restore workers to their original jobs or jobs paying equivalent wages. The act was also an attempt to create family-friendly, high-performance workplaces.

The Family and Medical Leave Act not only attempted to stop the penalization of workers who took maternity and paternity leave but also had the larger effect of recognizing the need for family care. While the act mandated unpaid leave, some states such as Rhode Island, Hawaii, New Jersey, California, and New York provide partial pay benefits for maternity or paternity leave through temporary disability insurance plans. Some U.S. women work for companies that voluntarily offer their workers paid maternity leaves. The issue of paid maternity and family leave is a large one. For those women and men who cannot sustain the loss of salary or who have no other income options, maternity and family leave is, for all intents and purposes, unavailable to them.

International Considerations. U.S. policy toward maternity leave has been far less generous than that of other industrialized nations. By law, most industrialized nations offer more leave to employees than does the United States and pays them full or partial wages and benefits. They also grant extended unpaid leaves that do not jeopardize job security. The most generous countries offer 100 percent paid leave for up to twenty-eight weeks. Canada, for example, offers fifteen weeks of leave at 55 percent of workers' salaries. In fact, the International Labor Organization (ILO) of the United Nations has standards for maternity leave. According to a 1998 ILO report, maternity and nursing benefits in the United States were in fact the least generous in the industrialized world. The report points out that 80 percent of the 152 countries reviewed offered female workers paid maternity leaves and approximately one-third of these countries permitted workers to take leaves lasting longer than fourteen weeks. In at least 80 countries nursing mothers are legally provided with established breaks during the workday. The ILO also demonstrated that women were the primary source of income in 30 percent of the world's households, projecting that in the first decade of the twenty-first century 80 percent of all women in the industrialized countries will work outside the home during their childbearing years. The question of maternity leave benefits is related to that of parental leave benefits for those who are responsible for the care of their aging parents.

—*Frances R. Belmonte*

BIBLIOGRAPHY

Belmonte, Frances. *Women and Health: An Annotated Bibliography.* Lanham, MD: The Scarecrow Press, Inc., 1997.

Boston Women's Health Book Collective. *Our Bodies, Ourselves: A Book by and for Women.* New York: Simon and Schuster, 1976.

Frankenhaeuser, Marianne, Ulf Lundberg, and Margaret Chesney, eds. *Women, Work and Health: Stress and Opportunities.* New York: Plenum Press, 1991.

Lustbader, Wendy, and Nancy R. Hooyman. *Taking Care of Aging Family Members: A Practical Guide.* New York: The Free Press, 1994.

Miller, Dorothy C. *Women and Social Welfare: A Feminist Analysis.* New York: Praeger, 1990.

Spain, Daphne, and Suzanne M. Bianchi. *Balancing Act: Motherhood, Marriage, and Employment Among American Women.* New York: Russell Sage Foundation, 1996.

Weiner, Lynn Y. *From Working Girl to Working Mother: The Female Labor Force in the United States, 1820-1980.* Reprint. Chapel Hill: University of North Carolina Press, 1986.

See also Breast-feeding; Child care; Divorce; Family and Medical Leave Act (FMLA); Family-friendly programs; Mommy track.

Matriarchs

RELEVANT ISSUES: Kinship and genealogy; Parenting and family relationships; Sociology

SIGNIFICANCE: Used informally, "matriarch" may signify any strong maternal figure in a family, but in cultural history the term means rule by mothers or female social and political dominance

The term "matriarch" derives partially from the Latin word *mater* (mother) and from the Latin suffix *arch*, suggesting chief or ruler. Related terms in social science disciplines include "matriarchy" and "matriarchate," both of which indicate social systems in which women are the dominant authority figures. In less formal usage, the term "matriarch" may indicate any prominent maternal figure, whether a historical personage, such as Rose Kennedy, or literary characters, such as the mothers in Federico García Lorca's *Blood Wedding* (1933) and Bertolt Brecht's *Mother Courage and Her Children* (1941).

Rose Kennedy (left), one of the great matriarchal figures in U.S. history, with her son, future president John F. Kennedy, Cardinal Richard Cushing, and Mother Emile Ange in 1946. (Archive Photos)

In the nineteenth century, early anthropologists applied the Darwinian model of evolution to formulate broad general concepts about the development of human societies. Debates arose that centered on which gender ruled in early social organizations—males (patriarchs) or females (matriarchs). The matriarchal theory was formulated in J. J. Bachofen's *Mother Right* (1861) and Robert Briffault's *The Mothers: The Matriarchal Theory of Social Origins* (1927). These and other works argued that although patriarchy is the dominant social form in most known societies, all societies went through prepatriarchal stages in which women held primary societal and political authority.

In matriarchies the primary deities of society were female, and women served in high positions in both civil and religious institutions. Women had great social freedom and men held women, particularly their mothers, in great reverence. In addition, marriage proposals were initiated by females or their families, and genealogical descent was matrilineal, meaning that family names and inherited property passed through the maternal line. Marriage was also matrilocal, so that a husband lived in or paid conjugal visits to his wife's home.

By the 1950's the mainstream social science disciplines had turned away from the search for large, comprehensive explanations of social organization, and the term "matriarch" and the concept of matriarchy lost their former currency. Instead, mothers and motherhood became the focus of sociology and empirical psychology. The kinds of issues that came to prominence included natural childbirth and other maternal health matters, liberalized child-rearing techniques, attention to inequalities in divorce and child-support laws, abortion-law reform, and social services support for impoverished single and divorced mothers.

The simultaneous rise of feminist cultural theory since the 1960's has had a varied impact on the figure of the matriarch and the concept of matriarchy. Radical feminist theory holds that motherhood itself is an institution that oppresses women by subordinating them to their biological childbearing role. Nevertheless, the 1980's and 1990's have seen the resurrection of archaeologically based theories of prehistory, particularly in the work of Marija Gimbutas and Riane Eisler, who find hope for a kinder, gentler future in the matri-archal models of society derived from new archaeological findings and theories.

—Roger James Stilling

See also Feminist sociology; Freudian psychology; Kinship systems; Matrilineal descent; Motherhood; Patriarchs; Patrilocality, matrilocality, and neolocality; Polyandry.

Matrilineal descent

RELEVANT ISSUES: Kinship and genealogy; Parenting and family relationships

SIGNIFICANCE: In matrilineal cultures, only the mother's line is considered important for determining family ties, obligations, and inheritance

Societies that stress one side of the family over the other are called unilineal descent systems. Systems that give predominance to females on the mother's side of the family are called matrilineal descent systems. Kinship is probably the single most important principle of social organization in any society. Where people live, who they can and cannot marry, from whom they inherit status and property, whom they must take in or help in times of need, and other mutual rights and obligations are generally determined by kinship. Kinship ties are relatively weak in North America, but other, more traditional or less developed societies view kinship ties as more important than do North Americans.

Persons biologically descend from both their fathers and their mothers, but sometimes it is useful to emphasize one side of the family over the other. In matrilineal systems lineage is traced from children to their mothers to their grandmothers to their great grandmothers and so on. The father's side of the family is essentially ignored in determining such matters as inheritance.

Only about 20 percent of the world's cultures practice matrilineal descent, even though it has certain clear advantages over patrilineal descent. It is usually obvious who a child's mother is, but it is often not easy to determine paternity.

Matrilineal descent is more common in societies in which women control property and men settle near their in-laws after they marry in order to work in businesses or on the lands that their wives will inherit from their mothers. An example of this is the traditional Hopi culture in the southwestern

The three generations of women in this family are all members of the same matrilineage. (Hazel Hankin)

United States. When slavery was legal in the United States, the children of African American women inherited the slave or free status of their mothers, regardless of the status—or race—of their fathers. However, many societies mix different aspects of the various descent systems.

U.S. society has always been more patrilineal than matrilineal. However, the increase in never-married mothers beginning in the early 1970's was a movement toward matrilineality, since many children of unmarried mothers received their maternal family names. Moreover, children in the United States have always been able to inherit property from both mothers and fathers, signifying a tracing of family membership through both lines. If extended families continue to decrease in social importance in the United States, the tracing of descent may also become less important and the bestowing of mothers' surnames on children may become more common.   —*Glenn Canyon*

See also Bilateral descent; Clans; Extended families; Genealogy; Kinship systems; Lineage; Matriarchs; Moiety; Patrilineal descent; Patrilocality, matrilocality, and neolocality.

Mead, George H.

BORN: February 27, 1863, South Hadley, Mass.
DIED: April 26, 1931, Chicago, Ill.
AREAS OF ACHIEVEMENT: Children and child development; Sociology
SIGNIFICANCE: Mead, the founder of symbolic interactionism as a school of thought in social psychology, showed how self-identity is formed in childhood through interaction and language

George H. Mead received his bachelor's degree at Harvard University and completed his graduate studies at the University of Leipzig, Germany, where he studied under Wilhelm Wundt, the "father of modern psychology." During this period, Mead met G. Stanley Hall, a leading authority on the psychological study of children. Mead taught for two years at the University of Michigan, Ann Arbor, where he came in contact with sociologist Charles Horton Cooley. He also became acquainted with the philosopher John Dewey. When Dewey moved to the University of Chicago, Mead followed him. Mead taught in the philosophy department of the University of Chicago until his death. A brilliant lecturer, he had great difficulty writing. His reputation as a formative thinker in social psychology rests on the lecture notes compiled by his students and published posthumously in various works, notably *Mind, Self, and Society* (1934).

Mead contended that children acquire a sense of themselves as unique individuals through interaction with significant others, typically in a family setting. Children also acquire the language of their culture, which permits them to see themselves through the eyes of others. Mead believed that this capacity is essential for the development of empathy and moral restraint. He argued that in order to become competent social actors and possess a fully developed self-concept, children must go through several stages: the imitative stage, the play stage, and the game stage. As children advance through each of these stages, they learn how to play social roles and to evaluate their role playing by adopting the perspective of others in ways that are increasingly more sophisticated.

—*Richard S. Bell*

See also Child rearing; Dysfunctional families; Hall, G. Stanley.

Mead, Margaret

BORN: December 16, 1901, Philadelphia, Pa.
DIED: November 15, 1978, New York, N.Y.
AREAS OF ACHIEVEMENT: Children and child development; Sociology
SIGNIFICANCE: Mead, a cultural anthropologist in the United States, was a dominant force in the development of research into the relationship between culture and personality

Margaret Mead was born into a family with professional interest in education and the social sciences. Her paternal grandmother, Martha Ramsay Mead, was a pioneer in child psychology. Margaret's father, Edward Sherwood Mead, was a professor of economics at the University of Pennsylvania; her mother, Emily Fogg Mead, was a sociologist and advocate of women's rights. Margaret chose anthropology as a career after being a student of Franz Boas at Barnard College. A Phi Beta Kappa student, Mead received her bachelor's degree and married Luther Cressman. In 1924 she received her master's degree in psychology from Columbia University and in 1929 she received her Ph.D. from Columbia in anthropology, submitting a thesis entitled *An Inquiry into the Question of Cultural Stability in Polynesia.*

In 1925 Mead received a National Research Council fellowship to investigate technologically underdeveloped cultures. Her first field expedition was to Samoa to study the development of adolescent girls. Seeing that adolescence in Samoa was not an especially difficult period, Mead concluded that the structure of social relationships in some societies makes the transition to adulthood easy. This hypothesis was presented in her classic work *Coming of Age in Samoa* in 1928. Mead became assistant curator of ethnology at the American Museum of Natural History in New York City in 1926. She expanded her responsibilities at the museum during her forty-year tenure there.

With assistance from a fellowship granted by the Social Research Council, Mead investigated the thought patterns of young children in her next field work in 1929. In 1930 she coauthored *Growing Up in New Guinea* with her second husband, New Zealand anthropologist Reo Fortune. Twenty-five years later Mead returned to the village of Peri, where she had collected her original data, to investigate her prior subjects as adults. This research was presented in *New Lives for Old* in 1956. One of her most controversial works, *Sex and Temperament in Three Primitive Societies*, was published in 1935. This work examined the effects of social learning on the personality development of males and females.

While some scientists have criticized Mead's work for neglecting quantitative methods in favor of depth analysis and the "anecdotal" handling of data, her significant contributions to anthropology are evident. Mead and her third husband, British anthropologist Gregory Bateson, pioneered the extensive use of photography as a research technique to create a permanent record of ethnographers' observations.

After investigating food habits in the United States to assist the rationing program established during World War II, Mead became director of Research in Contemporary Cultures, an interdisciplinary project to investigate complex industrialized societies. She collected data and wrote on a variety of topics, including human survival under the threat of nuclear war, overpopulation, environmental destruction, the importance of education, the impact of technological change, and the institution of the family. —*Kathryn Dennick-Brecht*

See also Cultural influences; Educating children; Mental health; Pacific Islanders; Sheehy, Gail.

Mealtaking

RELEVANT ISSUES: Economics and work; Parenting and family relationships

SIGNIFICANCE: Mealtaking within a family setting characterizes daily life in most societies, and the rituals of mealtaking reinforce family cohesion and children's enculturation

Although food-related habits vary greatly across cultures, practicality and custom usually converge so that most meals are eaten in the household, in the company of family members and other intimates. Festivals, holidays, and rites of passage may involve more complex meals that are shared with a larger group or the entire community. Shared meals function to establish or maintain social bonds, however tenuous.

The American Ideal. Americans have developed a general ideal of what usual meals and mealtakings should be like. Although the details have varied by era and by ethnic and economic groups, in broad outline this ideal reflects the economic needs and the cultural values of the society.

The norm has been three meals a day—breakfast, lunch, and dinner—to be eaten at intervals marking the divisions of a typical workday. Ideally, each meal was prepared, served, and eaten within the nuclear family's home. Its preparation by the mother or other adult female relative emphasized her gender-ascribed responsibility for the physical and emotional nurturing of the entire family.

Serving arrangements, with all participants seated around the same oval or rectangular table, reflected the relative equality cherished by Americans. Food was brought to the table in full serving dishes, then passed around so diners could help themselves, echoing other values of abundance, individual choice, and self-sufficiency.

Meals might be hurried (weekday breakfasts) or more leisurely (evening dinners and weekend meals), but conversation always was expected to take place, so that meals served as forums for the family's concerns. Needed information on the day's activities was announced; family members' achievements and mistakes were noted—sometimes with admonitions to the junior members—and gossip was exchanged. Disagreements between family members might be aired at mealtimes and sorted out. Conversation might also involve "outside" news and topics, thus solidifying and reinforcing a family's social attitudes.

Televised situation comedies of the 1950's through the 1970's frequently illustrated the various dynamics of family meals. In *Leave It to Beaver* (1957-1963), for example, mealtime talk usually centered on children's worries or misdeeds, with the mother "speaking up for" the boys on topics they were reluctant to introduce, and the father gently probing the situation and then leading the boys to a solution that would set things right. In *The Brady Bunch* (1969-1974), mealtimes were occasions where the tensions among two lively sets of siblings in a blended family surfaced. *The Andy Griffith Show* (1960-1968) included mealtime discussions of everything from Opie's school problems to town problems that Andy had to resolve as sheriff. Aunt Bea, a substitute mother figure, often gave advice, showing how different generations and gender perspectives can contribute to problem solving. The satirical social-issue comedy *All in the Family* (1971-1979) featured raucous dinnertime arguments arising from the conflicts between Archie Bunker's knee-jerk chauvinism and his son-in-law's progressive "hippie" outlook. Although the two men never resolved their differences, Edith's peacemaking explanations and an underlying affection sustained family unity.

The Reality of Mealtaking. In reality, family mealtakings may have always fallen short of the ideal in some way. Families beset by poverty or extraordinary time demands could not offer bounteous home-cooked foods. Inelastic work schedules and the distances between work or school and home prevented many people from eating three daily meals at home. "Outside" lunches for factory workers and rural schoolchildren have been standard for many decades. Because of urban sprawl and the time-specific demands of employers, such lunches later became usual for most full-time employees and students everywhere. In Europe, the leisurely at-home lunch survives, even in such cities as Rome and Madrid. Willingness to spare time from the workday for family meals reflects differing cultural attitudes toward conflicting claims of home and business.

Family breakfasts are a more recent casualty of changing living patterns. Except on weekends and

Members of three generations sharing a family dinner. (James L. Shaffer)

Modern families have seen a growing tendency for meal-preparation tasks to be assumed by whichever adult arrives home first. (James L. Shaffer)

Busier lifestyles, increased disposable income, and proliferation of restaurants catering to families have combined to make family dinners out more common than in the past. (James L. Shaffer)

in families with toddlers and a stay-at-home mother, breakfasts typically are eaten "on the run" and involve ready-to-eat food, grabbed from a cupboard or purchased away from home at a fast-food restaurant or a workplace vending machine. Often, breakfast is skipped entirely.

The settings and attendees at family mealtakings also frequently vary from the ideal. Recent immigrant families may continue to serve adult males first and apart from the women and children, although both the spatial arrangements of most American houses and popular culture's influence undermine such practices as families become "Americanized."

Departures from the Ideal. Cooking as an exclusively female activity was challenged by the rising popularity of barbecuing beginning in the 1950's, with men serving as cooks. Family schedules also impact mealtaking. Food preparation tasks are now often divided or done by whoever arrives home first, replacing the earlier apportionment of duties by age and gender. Depending on their finances, family size, and lifestyle, some families take some meals together in restaurants. Others typically have mealtime guests, and others employ servants to prepare and serve the family meals. As long as mealtakings provide a regular opportunity for family members to eat and communicate with each other in a positive context, however, how, when, and where they take place seem to have little impact on family cohesion.

Some departures from the ideal, however, may be less benign. Some families have developed patterns of meals being eaten hurriedly in silence, or even in resentment. Meals are used as occasions for cutting reprimands on table manners or other behaviors, or as a backdrop for angry shouting matches and even physical threats. It is hard to see how such meals could contribute to good digestion or build long-term amity within the family.

Late Twentieth Century Trends. Surveys show that whereas the average American family shared two meals a day in 1970, by 1979 it shared only one. In 1991, only 54 percent of children aged nine through fifteen ate any meal daily with their family. It is generally agreed that children, teenagers, and adults are all obtaining a larger proportion of their food from snacks and other nonmeal occasions. These are often eaten hastily and alone. Most research noting these changes does so in terms of their impact on nutrition, but some analysts worry about the meaning for family life and social health as well.

Other studies show that teenagers whose families eat together at a table at least four times a week score significantly better on their Scholastic Aptitude Tests (SATs). Even in families with an alcoholic parent, a regular dinner ritual seems to serve as a buffer, lessening the chances of alcoholism or other major maladjustments occurring in the children's own adult lives. These findings do not prove a simple cause and effect relationship in which family dinners create good personal outcomes. Instead, the pattern of dining together probably indicates a certain degree of stability and shared purpose within the family.

Economic pressures, both within and outside individual families, are responsible for much of the shift in dining habits. Parents who add commuting to full-time employment may not have the time or energy to orchestrate daily family meal rituals. Family members' diverse schedules and outside affiliations, television, and a youth culture that lures adolescents away from home for their leisure hours are also often blamed.

Whether these trends signal the end of family mealtaking, or even the disintegration of the family, is far less certain. A shared restaurant meal, the African American custom of keeping a stew pot simmering to accommodate family members' comings and goings, and meals shared while parents and children watch and comment on television shows all may work to maintain a family's cohesiveness.

Much of the concern about the "vanishing family dinner" arises because the practical, ritualistic, and social aspects of family life all meet at the family dinner table. If the practical components change, the symbolic and interpersonal aspects do not disappear or even necessarily change in a predictable direction. —*Emily Alward*

BIBLIOGRAPHY

Camp, Charles. *American Foodways.* Little Rock, Ark.: August House, 1989.

Farb, Peter, and George Armelagos. *Consuming Passions: The Anthropology of Eating.* Boston: Houghton Mifflin, 1980.

Fieldhouse, Paul. *Food and Nutrition: Customs and Culture.* London: Croom Helm, 1985.

Mennell, Stephen, et al., eds. "The Sociology of Food: Eating, Diet, and Culture." *Current Sociology* 40 (Autumn, 1992).

Sharman, Anne, et al., eds. *Diet and Domestic Life in Society.* Philadelphia: Temple University Press, 1990.

See also Eating habits of children; Foodways; Holidays; Women's roles.

Megan's Law

DATE: Adopted on May 17, 1996, as an amendment to the Violent Crime Control and Law Enforcement Act of 1994

RELEVANT ISSUES: Law; Violence

SIGNIFICANCE: This law requires communities to be informed of the whereabouts of sex offenders

In some states persons convicted of sexual crimes were required to register their addresses with state or local police departments, but officials were not required to notify the community and those convicted of sexual offenses often failed to register. After seven-year-old Megan Kanka was kidnapped, raped, and killed in New Jersey on July 29, 1994, her parents and the nation were shocked that the person allegedly guilty of the crime was a two-time sex offender who lived across the street. As a result, New Jersey adopted the New Jersey Sexual Offender Registration Act of 1994, requiring prison officials to notify communities when a sex offender has been released to live or work in a neighborhood. Similar laws were adopted by the remaining forty-nine states between 1994 and 1996.

On September 13, 1994, Congress enacted the Jacob Wetterling Crimes Against Children and Sexually Violent Offender Registration Act as part of its omnibus crime control act. This federal legislation required state prison officials to notify local police when a person convicted of sex offenses moves into a neighborhood. On May 17, 1996, Congress strengthened the law by requiring local law enforcement officials to make this information available to the community. This amendment became known informally as "Megan's Law." States are allowed to decide how dangerous those accused of sexual offenses are and what type of notification is required. DNA, saliva samples, names, and addresses of convicted offenders are updated in a nationwide database system.

In some states the information on such persons is placed in a computerized online database, and journalists and photographers have accessed the information in order to provide publicity for the community. Nevertheless, some two thousand released sex offenders successfully challenged the constitutionality of the statute in U.S. District Court in New Jersey, and the district court ruling was appealed. *—Michael Haas*

See also Child abduction; Child molestation; Children's rights; Privacy.

Mendenhall, Dorothy Reed

BORN: September 22, 1874, Columbus, Ohio

DIED: July 31, 1964, Chester, Conn.

AREA OF ACHIEVEMENT: Health and medicine

SIGNIFICANCE: As a physician serving in the United States Children's Bureau, Mendenhall worked to improve health care during pregnancy, childbirth, infancy, and childhood

Dorothy Reed Mendenhall began a distinguished medical career in 1902 with the discovery of the Reed cell, an abnormal cell found in Hodgkin's disease. She temporarily left the medical field in 1906 to marry Charles Elwood Mendenhall. In 1907 her first child died a few hours after a difficult delivery, which left Mendenhall with injuries and a fever. This tragedy inspired her to strive to make childbirth less dangerous for mothers and children.

In 1914 Mendenhall began serving as a field lecturer for the University of Wisconsin. She educated residents of the state on maternal and infant health care and opened the first infant welfare clinic in Wisconsin in 1915. In 1917 she began serving as a medical officer in the U.S. Children's Bureau. Her contributions included writing educational publications, developing standards for child growth, and promoting proper nutrition for children and pregnant women. She also advocated adopting the methods used by Danish midwives to lower the rate of infant and maternal mortality during childbirth. In 1937, a year after she retired, her efforts resulted in the city of Madison, Wisconsin, having the lowest infant mortality rate in the United States. *—Rose Secrest*

See also Childbirth; Children's Bureau; Health of children.

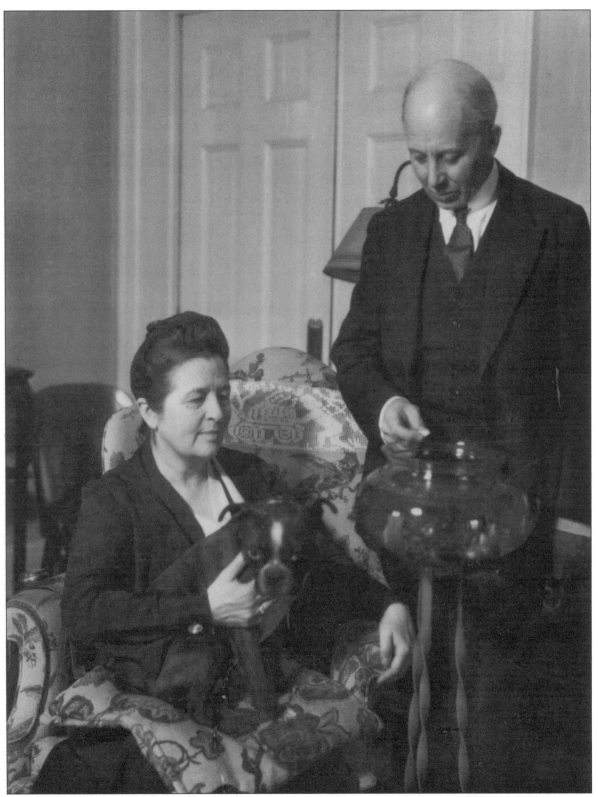

Dorothy Reed Mendenhall with her husband, Charles Elwood Mendenhall, in 1931. (Sophia Smith Collection)

Mennonites and Amish

Relevant issues: Aging; Marriage and dating; Parenting and family relationships; Religious beliefs and practices

Significance: Religion among the Amish and Mennonites is handed down from generation to generation and governs their values of work and life in general, setting them apart from the modern world

The Mennonites and Amish are religious groups that stem from the sixteenth century Anabaptist movement in Europe. Severely persecuted, the Anabaptists (which literally means "rebaptizers") split into many factions, some of which united in the mid-1500's behind the teachings of the Dutch Roman Catholic priest Menno Simons to form what came to be known as the Mennonites. Under the leadership of Jakob Ammann, a group that stressed even stricter discipline and separation

The old-fashioned horse-and-buggy rig has become a symbol of male Anabaptists in the United States. (James L. Shaffer)

from the world split off from the Mennonites in 1693 to form the Amish. Seeking to practice their religion in peace, Mennonites and Amish came to North America in several waves, settling first in Pennsylvania and later on the Midwestern plains and in the Canadian provinces.

Religious Practices. Beginning in the sixteenth century, the Mennonites and Amish rejected the practice of infant baptism. They refused to participate in military, police, or political activity, a pacifist stance that in twentieth century America has brought them into collision with governmental policy, especially during World War I. They also reject mandatory education of children past the eighth grade, believing that further education promotes worldly ideas and is irrelevant to their agrarian way of life.

The strict lifestyle of the Amish and Mennonites is reflected in their dress, buildings, and daily life. Mennonite and Amish clothing is dictated by their religious beliefs. Dresses may not be shorter than halfway between the knee and the floor; they must be of dark colors such as black, brown, gray or navy blue and they may be fastened only with straight pins. Shoes must be plain and black if for dress and socks must be black. Men may wear only suspenders without buckles and black hats with no less than a three inch brim. Women must wear prayer hats made very simply and must cover as much of their hair as possible. They must always wear aprons, shawls, bonnets, and capes when in public. Women may not cut or curl their hair; men may not part their hair, and the length should be at least halfway below the top of their ears. If possible, men and boys should wear a full beard before baptism.

The buildings of Amish and Mennonites may not be decorated inside or outside. Overstuffed furniture, pictures, large mirrors, and statues are forbidden. No bottled gas or electrical appliances may be used. The Amish and Mennonites are forbidden to have radios, attend films or fairs, or play cards or party games. Instead, they are encouraged to read, sing, play Bible games, and pay tithes (a proportion of income donated for religious purposes). They may not talk about sex or use obscene language. They may not buy or sell anything on Sundays, and they may not have insurance or receive government benefits. Twice a year, they collect money for widows and others who are unable to earn a living.

Courtship and Marriage. Courtship may begin at sixteen and is known as *rum springa*, or "running around." Males are presented with horses and buggies, and on Sunday afternoons they may be given the freedom from evening chores to attend singing events or to drive around the countryside looking at the young women. Courtship is kept a secret, and boys go to see girls only after girls' parents have gone to bed. Couples may sit and talk into the early hours of the morning. Some even practice "bundling"—that is, lying in bed together. Girls must keep their petticoats on and boys their shirts and trousers. The modern Amish do not practice bundling. Boys may escort girls home from singing events.

When a young couple decides to marry, the young man sends a male go-between to visit the parents of the bride-to-be to ask for her hand in marriage. Go-betweens do this in extreme secrecy and travel after dark. Once this is done, a minister travels to the home of the prospective couple and counsels them. This is also done in secrecy. If marriage plans are kept a secret until they are officially announced, the young man is considered a hero. Marriages take place two weeks after the banns are read and are usually held on Tuesdays and Thursdays in the months of November and December.

After the announcement of the pending wedding, the man moves in with bride's parents and helps prepare for the marriage. The entire farm must be cleaned up and ready for the ceremony. During this time, the groom also makes personal visits to those whom he wants to invite to their wedding. It is considered an honor to be called to weddings. The bridegroom kills chickens for the feast and aunts and uncles prepare the rest of the food.

Amish and Mennonite wedding ceremonies begin in the early morning and last into the early afternoon. Brides usually wear dresses of robin's egg blue and bridegrooms dress in black, brown, or gray. Wedding feasts may last until midnight. Couples then spend their wedding night in an upstairs room at the home of the bride's parents. The honeymoon consists of visiting relatives for two weeks and then returning to live with the groom's parents until the groom can buy land or take over one of the farms of their respective parents.

Couples never show affection in public toward each other and never use affectionate words to each other. Neither are allowed to wear wedding rings. Divorce is forbidden and remarriage is encouraged one to two years following the death of a spouse.

Aging. When men and women reach seventy years of age, they move to nearby small houses and hand over their farms to their sons, usually the youngest. These sons move into the main house with their families and take over all responsibilities. Elderly couples may perform light chores, help take care of the children, and help keep the yard and buildings looking neat. They are never sent to a nursing home; their children take care of them until they die. When they become ill or are on their death beds, families read the Bible and pray by their bedsides. Each night young girls sing hymns. After old people die, families construct simple coffins for them, which are brought to the cemetery by horse and wagon. Graves are dug by hand and the deceased are laid to rest. Families then go home to eat meals provided by members of the Amish community.

Family Relationships. Family organization in Amish and Mennonite communities is patriarchal. Fathers command the highest rank in the family and mothers the second. Sibling rank is based on age, with the older ones often disciplining the younger children verbally and physically. Children learn their roles in this social structure and learn how to respond to authority. To secure legal ownership over their property in case of death, parents own their farms jointly, but most everything else is owned and controlled by men. Women give even their egg money to male family members. Wives have the responsibility for maintaining the appearance of the lawn and the area surrounding the barn, and they must keep the house neat. They grow most of their food and are good cooks. Women make all of the clothes for the family and prepare lunches to be served during Sunday services, which are held in private homes.

The Amish often have ten children and more. They believe that their children belong to God and that they only take care of them. Most of these children are delivered at home, and babies are breast-fed if possible. Newborns may sleep with their parents for the first few months, which is convenient for breast-feeding. Toilet training, carried out without fuss or compulsion, usually begins when children reach two years of age. Most

Amish children speak only German during the first four or five years of their lives and are only taught English when they start school. The Amish believe that children should be trained for heaven first and then for adult life. The children do not receive allowances. Until they are twenty-one years old or are married, the money they earn for working for other people must be turned over to their fathers.

Silent prayers are said before and after each meal and table conversation is only for expressing likes and dislikes, discussing work to be done, decisions to be made, or family values. Because the Amish believe that their actions are more important than their reflections or thoughts, they do not teach their children common courtesies. For example, a loud belch after dinner is more acceptable for telling the cook that her food was enjoyed than a "thank you." —*Mitzie L. Bryant*

BIBLIOGRAPHY

Bender, Sue. *Plain and Simple: A Woman's Journey to the Amish.* New York: Harper & Row, 1989.

Juhnke, James C. *Vision, Doctrine, War: Mennonite Identity and Organization in America, 1890-1930.* Scottdale, Pa.: Herald Press, 1989.

Langin, Bernd G. *Plain and Amish.* Scottsdale, Pa.: Herald Press, 1994.

Nolt, Steven M. *A History of the Amish.* Intercourse, Pa.: Good Books, 1992.

Schlabach, Theron F. *Peace, Faith, Nation: Mennonites and Amish in Nineteenth-Century America.* Scottdale, Pa.: Herald Press, 1988.

Swander, Mary. *Out of This World: A Woman's Life Among the Amish.* New York: Viking Press, 1995.

See also Aging and elderly care; Bundling; Courting rituals; Home schooling; Hutterites; Marriage; Patriarchs; Religion; *Wisconsin v. Yoder.*

Menopause

RELEVANT ISSUES: Aging; Health and medicine; Parenting and family relationships

SIGNIFICANCE: The menopause is a rite of passage that not only affects women physically and emotionally but also affects their families

For centuries, the menopause was shrouded in either myth or utter silence. In many women's minds, the menopause was inextricably linked to infirmities and physiologic changes that heralded the beginning of the end of their lives as women and mothers. Due to the lack of scientific research into women's health issues, both men and women believed that the menopause was a disease for which there was no cure.

Medical Overview. The menopause is usually defined as the cessation of menstruation for a period of at least one year. As early as their midthirties, women's hormonal cycle may begin to change and their fertility begin to diminish. At this time, the store of eggs has been severely depleted, and the remaining follicles are less sensitive to hormonal stimulation from the follicle stimulating hormone (FSH) and luteinizing hormone (LH), which are secreted by the hypothalamus and the pituitary gland. During some months, a follicle may ripen and release an egg; during other months, no ovulation occurs. This stage of women's reproductive life, when the ovaries gradually decrease their function and menses become irregular, is known as perimenopause. The more general term "climacteric" is used to describe the years immediately preceding and following the menopause.

Without the release of an egg during ovulation, progesterone, which depends on the empty follicle (corpeus luteum) for production, is no longer secreted at all. Although estrogen levels also drop, the ovaries, adrenal glands, and fat cells still produce some estrogen. The uterine lining, then, is stimulated exclusively by estrogen and continues to grow until it lacks a sufficient blood supply, which can take several months. At this time women may experience some of the symptoms of this decrease in estrogen and progesterone, such as hot flashes or vaginal dryness. However, the original triggers of the cycle, the hypothalamus and pituitary gland, continue to release FSH and LH in an attempt to stimulate ovarian activity. In fact, the level of FSH can reach thirteen times its normal level, and LH levels triple during this time—a sign that women have entered the climacteric. Eventually, the ovarian follicles no longer respond to hormonal prodding and the menopause is complete.

After the menopause, the ovaries and adrenal glands continue to produce some estrogen, but the androgens—the male sex hormones—that have been produced by the ovaries and adrenals as

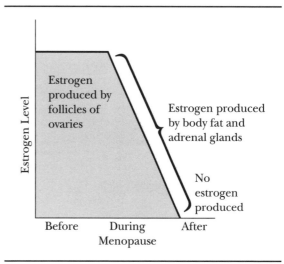

During the menopause, which may last for several years, estrogen production diminishes; after the menopause, estrogen is no longer produced by the body.

well, begin to play a larger role in maintaining women's hormonal health. Once estrogen reaches a low level, certain fat cells are stimulated to take up the androgens circulating in the blood and convert them to estrone, a weak form of estrogen. Although the amount of this type of estrogen is insufficient to induce fertility, it may be sufficient to alleviate some of the symptoms of the menopause.

Historical Perspective. The word "menopause" was coined in France, where it had been used in the medical literature of the 1880's. It did not appear in an English dictionary until 1887. The early work of the Austrian psychoanalyst Sigmund Freud, which described the menopause as a crisis period during which women mourned the end of their attractiveness and childbearing potential, lent some degree of credibility to the notion of the menopause as a mental illness. To some psychiatrists, the menopause was viewed as the end of a meaningful period in women's lives. Terms such as "midlife crisis" were used to explain the emotions women purportedly suffered during this time in their lives.

The introduction of synthetic estrogen in the early 1960's altered the notion that the menopause could be ignored by medical science, since it was a condition about which nothing could be done. Hormone replacement therapy became a

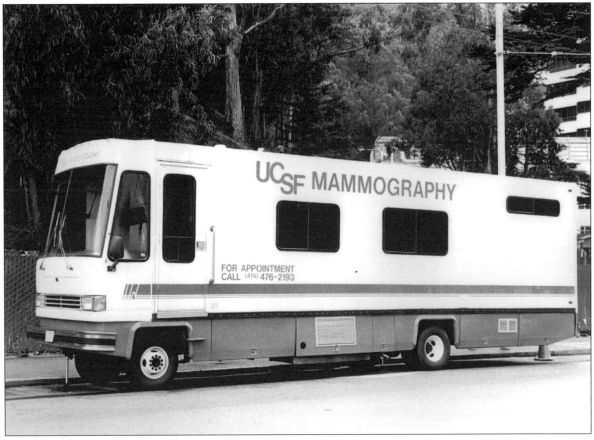

After women enter the menopause, their increased risk of breast cancer makes regular breast examinations (mammograms) advisable. (Ben Klaffke)

widely touted treatment for the menopause, and physicians began prescribing estrogen widely. However, questions about the safety and efficacy of estrogen replacement therapy arose in the late 1970's, when several studies showed a distinct relationship between endometrial cancer and the use of estrogen alone in postmenopausal women. As the menopause no longer was viewed as a disease and was being taken seriously by the mainstream medical establishment, drug companies sought to cash in on the menopause business.

The drug progesterone, which had been used to treat pregnancy disorders for many years, was added to estrogen treatment in order to prevent endometrial cancer. However, due to the possible increased risk of breast cancer, researchers continued to debate the issue of hormone replacement therapy. Alternatives to synthetic hormones—such as plant sources of estrogen and progester-

one—began to be investigated and used in combination with diet and exercise in an attempt to avoid the adverse side effects of pharmaceuticals.

Female Perspective. Before the late 1960's the end of women's reproductive capacity coincided with their declining worth to their families. As their children grew older and left the home, there was less for them to do, and, as they perceived it, their lives were less valuable. However, with the women's movement in the early 1970's, women began to view themselves differently, and gradually cultural stereotypes regarding women of all ages came into question. Careers became much more available and important to women. Women had more opportunities to lead fuller lives outside the home. These changes had a significant impact on family life in that women's roles began to move from that of housewives and mothers to that of working professionals. The menopause no longer meant the end of life but the beginning of a new life—a time when unfulfilled ambitions could be realized and new freedom enjoyed.

The menopause was once viewed as the beginning of inevitable sexual and emotional decline in women's lives. However, as women began living longer and staying healthier, researchers began to believe that the opposite could be true. That the menopause always leads to depression and decreased sexual desire was found to be a longstanding misconception. Many postmenopausal women enjoy active and fulfilling sex lives, and studies have shown that they are less likely than premenopausal women to suffer from major depression.

Male Menopause. While men in midlife experience many of the same symptoms as menopausal women, such as depression, anxiety, skin changes, a decrease in sexuality, and other signs of aging, there is no single event akin to the last period around which to focus these events. Thus, the tendency is for the menopause to be associated with and blamed for all the normal changes of midlife. The menopause focuses attention on the fact that women are getting older; it is the official confirmation of their passage into another stage of life.

Because Western culture places such a high value on youthful femininity, physical aging in women becomes linked to self-esteem and sexuality in a way that it does not in men. Reproductive ability is often confused with sexual ability. Men, on the other hand, do not have this marker of the end of their reproductive capabilities, and they also continue reproducing longer than women.

Many men make major career changes at this time in an attempt to actualize their lives or fulfill a secret ambition. Both men and women often evaluate their marriages during this "menopause" period. While some couples are able to attain a new level of intimacy and connection and are able to adapt to the changing needs of one or both individuals, so-called midlife crises may break up families and even destroy lives. *—Genevieve Slomski*

BIBLIOGRAPHY

Barbach, Lonnie. *The Pause.* New York: Dutton, 1993.

Callahan, Joan C., ed. *Menopause: A Midlife Passage.* Bloomington: Indiana University Press, 1993.

Cherry, Sheldon H., and Carolyn D. Runowicz. *The Menopause Book.* New York: Macmillan, 1994.

Jovanovic, Lois. *A Woman Doctor's Guide to Menopause.* New York: Hyperion, 1993.

McCain, Marian Van Eyk. *Transformation Through Menopause.* New York: Bergin & Garvey, 1991.

Minkin, Mary Ann, and Carol W. Wright. *What Every Woman Needs to Know About Menopause.* New Haven, Conn.: Yale University Press, 1996.

Rako, Susan. *The Hormone of Desire.* New York: Harmony Books, 1996.

See also Childlessness; Couples; Cult of True Womanhood; Empty nest syndrome; Fertility and infertility; Men's roles; Midlife crises; Mother-daughter relationships; Sheehy, Gail; Women's roles.

Men's roles

RELEVANT ISSUES: Economics and work; Parenting and family relationships; Sociology

SIGNIFICANCE: Men's roles in families are multifaceted, diverse, and in a state of flux, creating ambiguous and contradictory cultural visions concerning the place and legitimacy of "traditional" masculinity in family contexts

The traditional view of men as providers, protectors, patriarchs, and rugged individualists has given way to a new scrutiny of the diversity and complexity in men's work and family roles. Another ideal of manhood and masculinity has emerged, which emphasizes emotional openness and relational interdependence in place of dispassionate independence. These perspectives reject the idea that manhood is the opposite of womanhood or that masculine individuals lack feminine characteristics.

While men's roles in families are not monolithically determined by those of women, they are interdependent. As such, changes in women's roles, primarily characterized by greater involvement in paid employment, have created the conditions for corresponding changes in men's family involvements. The feminist movement has sharpened society's awareness of the interface between work and family roles by promoting economic equity between men and women. While female labor-force participation has increased significantly, there has not been a corresponding reduction in women's responsibility for home and family, because a majority of men have not fully embraced the equal sharing of domestic roles. Even among college-educated men, there is greater willingness to accept women in the workplace than to internalize the need for increased involvement in domestic roles.

Multidimensionality of Men's Roles. Men simultaneously fulfill multiple roles in the family. For instance, husbands and fathers in the nuclear family may also be sons, brothers, uncles, sons-in-law, brothers-in-law, fathers-in-law, cousins, grandsons, and grandfathers in the extended family. Likewise, they may also be father figures to fictive kin. Given modern patterns of marriage, divorce, and remarriage, a significant percentage of men also fulfill stepfather, stepson, and stepbrother roles overlaid on their other roles. While fulfilling these positional roles, men may function as providers, protectors, caregivers, mentors, counselors, role models, and active community members as well.

Clearly, men's roles in families are multifaceted and multidimensional. They are also multiply determined. The size, geographic closeness, and emotional closeness of families and fictive kin are important components in influencing men's roles in families. These factors synergistically or antagonistically interact with other roles that men fulfill as workers, friends, and citizens. Cultural and subcultural norms, personality traits, family histories, and immediate circumstances also exert significant influences on the enactment of men's roles in families. Given the richness and interrelatedness of these factors, it is no wonder that there is significant individual variability in the range of family roles that men fulfill and in the quality of their role enactments.

Men's roles in families do not merely change across historical time as cultural prescriptions and prohibitions evolve; rather, they change throughout the development of the life course. The goals, aspirations, and role prescriptions men set as boys or youths become altered as they progress through different developmental stages in their maturation and as they experience different circumstances in their education, work, and relationships across time. As a result, individual men experience satisfaction in some realms (role fulfillment) and frustrations or disappointments in others. This leads to the recurrent evaluation of ideal versus realized roles in individuals that is associated with developmental change in the context of a changing society.

Men, Work, and Family Roles. Men's family roles are closely tied to the world of work because of the prevalence of the provider role in traditional constructions of masculinity and men's roles in the American family. With the rise of industrial capitalism, but not before, it became popular to cast men in the role of primary breadwinner. Since the end of World War II, when traditional male roles were embraced and emphasis was placed on men working in positions that would provide their families with an income, the trend has been away from traditionalism toward men being more nurturing, emotionally open, androgynous, and involved in domestic relationships and housework. Traditional views consider men to be family providers and women nurturers. From the 1960's to the 1990's such characterizations came to be portrayed as narrow and inadequate. Increasingly, however, there has been tension between men's efforts to fulfill their role as economic providers and their sufficient engagement in family life. In the context of gender roles in flux, job-induced absences can be viewed as an excuse for familial escapism.

While the breakdown of traditional roles is frequently associated with increases in self-fulfillment and personal freedom, the contradictory messages of manhood in flux have created ambivalence, uncertainty, challenges, and stress for men in families. Because the core of men's identity is not as firmly grounded as previously in their role as economic providers, serious questions have arisen concerning the very meaning of manhood and masculinity. By the 1990's it was less common for men to adopt the traditional role of breadwinning husbands, as more and more of them opted either to remain single or to become involved, if not equal, partners in the raising of children. While involved fatherhood has become a popular construct, data show that men in the United States are less likely to be fathers, that they are more likely to have fewer children, to delay becoming fathers, to spend less time living in households with children, and to have less leisure time to spend with families than in the past fifty years. In the 1990's divorce; single-parent, female-headed households; fathers' absence; defaults on court-ordered alimony and child-support payments; and domestic violence were at or near all-time highs. Consequently, while some men are investing more in direct involvement in family relationships, child care, and domestic work, others are fleeing family involvement at unprecedented rates. The question arises as to the economic and cultural conditions that underlie this development.

Changing Economy of Work and Gender. Since the turn of the twentieth century, there has been an expansion of women's employment and career opportunities, women's legal rights, and corresponding cultural support for equity in opportunity and reward structures. These changes have been accompanied by an increase in committed employment among women and an increase in the proportion of women who would work for personal satisfaction rather than out of economic necessity. The entry of significant numbers of women into the paid labor force has led society to seriously question the balance of roles between home and workplace and the equity of men's and women's roles both at work and in the family.

Corresponding with the increased and committed entry of women into the world of paid employ-

Whether they choose to be or not, men are role models to their children and are especially likely to be imitated by their sons. (James L. Shaffer)

A traditional role of fathers is to pass along their skills to their sons. (James L. Shaffer)

ment, men have experienced a decline in their economic status because of their decreasing ability to earn incomes. In comparison to women as a group, men receive higher average wages and are more likely to hold higher-paying and more prestigious jobs. However, since the 1970's men in the United States have lost earning power because of changes in the economy. Those men with the least education have been most affected, but even highly educated men have experienced falling average earnings. Between 1976 and 1984 the median inflation-adjusted income for men who were their families' sole providers fell 22 percent. Because workplace advantages have been seen as affording men economic and social power that have permitted them to be less involved in domestic relationships and household labor, the erosion of economic power has led many to question the level of men's involvement in the family. Conversely, as role diversification has led many men to be more involved in home life, which means that they spend more time and energy away from the workplace, employers have come to question men's commitment to work. Involved family men may be viewed by employers as being less committed to their jobs, resulting in their being denied promotions. In more severe cases, men have been reprimanded or fired because of conflicting role commitments to their families.

Corresponding to the reduction in men's earning power is a shift in occupational structure. Statistics have shown that between the 1950's and 1990's there has been a 17 percent drop in manufacturing positions and a 4 percent drop in public utilities and transportation jobs. During the same period there has been a 16 percent increase in service jobs, a 4 percent increase in wholesale and retail-trade jobs, and a 2 percent increase in insurance, real estate, and finance positions. Because positions in manufacturing, public utilities, and transportation generally pay higher wages than those in the retail, wholesale, finance, and service sectors, these shifts have contributed to the economic decline of families, increasing the need for dual-income and multiple-job families. Changes in occupational structure are also linked to increases in men's self-employment. Self-employment does not guarantee the same degree of income security or benefits as does working for employers.

As men's wages have fallen, women's earnings have provided dual-earner families with a measure of stability. However, because of wage inequity, women must work longer hours to earn incomes that are comparable to those of men. This has raised the issue of equity within the family and at the workplace. While men's wages fell during the 1980's, those of women rose an average of nearly 7 percent. Although wage inequity is illegal and declining, it is still pervasive. The wage gap between men and women remained at 28 percent during the 1990's. This alone has made it more efficient for men to work longer hours than women, since the same investment in hours yields 28 percent greater compensation for men than for women.

The combination of these trends has eroded men's ability to consistently or securely earn a family wage, undermining their traditional role as providers and calling into question their roles in families relative to those of women. Women's economic contributions to families have had a double-edged effect. While they have provided families with incomes that allow a consistent standard of living, they have also diminished women's economic dependence on men, which may facilitate emotional or relational independence as well. Some observers think that women's growing economic achievements are a factor contributing to high divorce rates.

Changing Families. Men's roles in families have changed over time partly because families have changed. The most prevalent family form of the 1950's, the nuclear family—with husbands and wives who had been married only once, a few children, a breadwinning father, and a stay-at-home mother—represented less than 7 percent of the American population by the late 1990's. This does not imply that the modal family of the 1950's should be heralded as the ideal from which U.S. society has fallen; rather, it simply serves as a benchmark from which to assess the pervasiveness of social change and the resulting turbulence in manhood and men's roles in families.

An increase in alternative family forms has gone hand in hand with a decrease in the permanence of marriage. These trends can be traced demographically and include lower marriage rates, increased cohabitation rates, delays in marriage age, delayed parenthood, smaller families, higher divorce rates, and higher rates of remarriage—patterns that have combined to create what is known as "serial monogamy." These changes, coupled with an increase in the prevalence of out-of-wedlock births, have increased the prevalence of noncustodial fatherhood.

Furthermore, parenting has come to be divorced from marriage. In recent years, changing legislation, public policy, and trends in living arrangements have increasingly distinguished fathering roles from marital status. Biological fatherhood does not guarantee that men will have access to their children. A full 30 percent of all divorces involve families with young children. The net result has been a dramatic increase in the proportion of single-parent families. Approximately 17 percent of white and 7 percent of African American single-parent families are headed by men. The remaining single-parent families are headed by never-married, separated, divorced, or widowed women. The prevalence of these families has resulted in an increased awareness of and appreciation for the contributions of men to child development and family functioning. It has also highlighted the importance of paternal visitation and involvement of father figures in family life.

Because men's roles in families are multidimensional and multiply determined, in the crosscurrent climate of rapid and massive transformation of workplace and families men's roles in families have undergone unprecedented change. Because the cultural climate is ambiguous, paradoxical, and multidirectional and because men's exposure to institutional change varies from individual to individual, there is great diversity in the construction and enactment of men's roles in families. While some men are absent, others are abusive or neglectful; while some are traditional providers, others are androgynous coparents; and some men are primary caregiving fathers.

Family scholars and counselors have come to recognize that the Zeitgeist of greater involvement of men in families is not a panacea. While men make positive contributions to the development and well-being of their families through committed involvement, there is increasing awareness that the quest to "have it all" both in careers and in families can lead to role overload. Men's involvement in families is most beneficial to all parties when it is intrinsically motivated and balanced with the developmental resources and needs of all other family members. —*Rob Palkovitz*

BIBLIOGRAPHY

Gerson, Kathleen. *No Man's Land: Men's Changing Commitments to Family and Work.* New York: Basic Books, 1993. Compelling analysis of diversity in men's negotiations in balancing commitments between breadwinning and involvement in family life in a changing society.

Hawkins, Alan J., and David C. Dollahite, eds. *Generative Fathering: Beyond Deficit Perspectives.* Thousand Oaks, Calif.: Sage Publications, 1997. In contrast to scholarship that focuses on men's inadequacies as parents, this collection of empirical papers and essays focuses on the work that fathers do in caring for and contributing to the life of the next generation.

Hood, Jane C., ed. *Men, Work and Family.* Newbury Park, Calif.: Sage Publications, 1993. Standard work cited in intellectual and policy discussions of the balancing act between men's work and family involvements, focusing on fathering and providing, men's role allocation and role change, and workplace organization and policy.

Lamb, M. E., ed. *The Role of the Father in Child Development.* 3d ed. New York: John Wiley & Sons, 1997. Third edition of the book that ushered in the importance and legitimacy of research on fathers.

Mackey, Wade C. *The American Father: Biocultural and Developmental Aspects.* New York: Plenum Press, 1996. Thought-provoking evaluation of a vast empirical data base that documents fatherhood as an important, unique, and central component of children's and men's development.

Rotundo, E. Anthony. *American Manhood: Transformations in Masculinity from the Revolution to the Modern Era.* New York: Basic Books, 1993. Historical treatment of gender as a social, cultural, and political force that shapes the lives of individual men and men's engagements with their families and communities.

Stearns, Peter N. *Be a Man! Males in Modern Society.* 2d ed. New York: Holmes & Meier, 1990. Review of historical periods and changes in manhood in Western society from the seventeenth century to the present.

See also Cultural influences; Family economics; Father figures; Father-son relationships; Fatherhood; Feminist sociology; Gender inequality; Grandparents; Patriarchs; Unwed fathers; Women's roles; Work.